LAW AND POLITICAL ECONOMY IN CHINA

The Role of Law in Corporate Governance and Market Growth

Applying a novel theoretical approach, Tamar Groswald Ozery combines law and political economy to deconstruct the role of law in China's market development since 1978. The book examines how economic and administrative powers within China's Party-state system have been legally and politically configured throughout China's growth process. Using a vast range of primary sources, Ozery illuminates how the law acts as a mediating institution that translates and gives shape to the relations between politics and economics. Using the evolution of public firms and corporate governance as a case study, the book illustrates the complex relationships between law, politics, and economic development, and sheds new light on the possible varieties of growth-supporting governance institutions in firms. By studying China's distinct market experience through the lens of law and political economy, the book offers a significant contribution to development studies, comparative corporate governance, and interdisciplinary discussions about China as a growth model.

Tamar Groswald Ozery is an assistant professor at the Hebrew University of Jerusalem. Previously, she was a Grotius Fellow (Michigan Law), a Research & Teaching Fellow (Harvard Law), and the editor of the Harvard Law School Forum on Corporate Governance. Her published scholarly works focus on Chinese corporate governance, cross-border investments, and party-state market relations. She is a frequent commentator on China's legal system, political economy, and global economic integration, and has testified before the US-China Economic and Security Review Commission. Prior to academia, she spearheaded the China department of a leading Israeli law firm.

ASCL Studies in Comparative Law

ASCL Studies in Comparative Law publishes monographs and collections that broaden theoretical and practical knowledge of the world's many legal systems. Published under the direction of the American Society of Comparative Law, the *ASCL Studies* examine legal problems in a comparative light to advance legal science, develop technical insights, and promote greater cooperation across jurisdictional and cultural boundaries. This book series serves legal practitioners and those seeking to improve law and justice by publishing in-depth comparative studies of specific legal problems in every area of law.

The series has two general editors. David Gerber is Distinguished Professor of Law and Co-Director of the Program in International and Comparative Law at Chicago-Kent College of Law, Illinois Institute of Technology. He is past President of the American Society of Comparative Law. Mortimer Sellers is Regents Professor of the University System of Maryland and Director of the Baltimore Center for International and Comparative Law. He is past President of the Internationale Vereinigung für Rechts-und Sozialphilosophie.

Law and Political Economy in China

THE ROLE OF LAW IN CORPORATE GOVERNANCE AND MARKET GROWTH

TAMAR GROSWALD OZERY
Hebrew University of Jerusalem

CAMBRIDGE
UNIVERSITY PRESS

CAMBRIDGE
UNIVERSITY PRESS

Shaftesbury Road, Cambridge CB2 8EA, United Kingdom

One Liberty Plaza, 20th Floor, New York, NY 10006, USA

477 Williamstown Road, Port Melbourne, VIC 3207, Australia

314–321, 3rd Floor, Plot 3, Splendor Forum, Jasola District Centre, New Delhi – 110025, India

103 Penang Road, #05–06/07, Visioncrest Commercial, Singapore 238467

Cambridge University Press is part of Cambridge University Press & Assessment, a department of the University of Cambridge.

We share the University's mission to contribute to society through the pursuit of education, learning and research at the highest international levels of excellence.

www.cambridge.org
Information on this title: www.cambridge.org/9781009158244

DOI: 10.1017/9781009158251

First published 2023

A catalogue record for this publication is available from the British Library.

A Cataloging-in-Publication data record for this book is available from the Library of Congress

ISBN 978-1-009-15824-4 Hardback

In memory of my grandmother, Raya (Raisa) Barhovik Skutel (1915–2011), who had seen many types of regimes in her lifetime and survived them all.

Contents

Figures

Tables

Preface

August 2009, a young foreign lawyer steps out of the gates of the Shanghai Hongqiao International Airport. Although she has been a student of China and of Mandarin Chinese for several years, it is her first visit to China as an adult, not to mention an adult on duty. She is nervous.

For the past three months, the lawyer and her team have worked tirelessly on a share purchase agreement (SPA) for the acquisition of shares in a Joint Venture (JV) that went awry. She was sent by her client, an American developer and supplier of AgroTech equipment, to make sure that the finalized deal actually goes through and that the JV's CEO, who is also the owner of the domestic Chinese partner in the JV and the JV's sole distributor in China, steps down. Luckily, she is accompanied by a mediator, a native of her country who joined the trip to help in the share purchase negotiations. The two locate their prearranged taxi among the bustling crowd of drivers angling for passengers.

On their way to the hotel, the lawyer cannot take her eyes from the windows. For six years she has been studying China from afar, yet nothing prepared her for the spectacular modern highways and skyscrapers she is now seeing. The trip is more than just a work visit for her; she is relocating to Shanghai for the next few years. Eager to catch every sight and code in her memory the name of every road in the place she will now be calling home, she is mesmerized with admiration and excitement. The mediator, amused, spits out "don't let that fool you." The banter falls on deaf ears.

Late afternoon, the lawyer and the mediator are set to meet with the Chinese partner at the firm's offices. The lawyer is only there to collect signatures on some ancillary documents and make sure the company chops are moved to the mediator's possession. Days and nights of remote negotiations and many rounds of revisions from both sides preceded this visit and the SPA has already been finalized and approved by both parties. "The meeting should be quick and smooth," she is reassured by the mediator.

But the Chinese partner, the CEO, is stalling. In fact, he completely ghosted them. For the next two weeks meetings are postponed repeatedly, and finalizing the deal is halted for no apparent reason. After some time, the lawyer and the mediator decide to show up unannounced at the firm's offices in an attempt to understand the situation. Surprisingly, they find the space half empty with occasional employees wandering about and no management on site. Even more alarming, the floor sign that used to greet clients and visitors with the JV's company name is nowhere to be seen. Instead, a name of a local distributor, the Chinese partner in the JV, decorates the building.

A few days later, the JV's head administrator (also its legal representative) agrees to meet with the lawyer and shed some light on the matter. The head administrator is seasoned in dealing with foreign investors. She was nominated by the American partner as his representative on that ground. Hopefully, the lawyer thinks to herself, she will be candid and have the client's best interests in mind. Reading between the lines (as the head administrator was not very generous with details), it seems that the Chinese partner was insulted by the SPA final draft. Apparently, a contingency provision in the SPA deliverables section stated that prior to his departure, the CEO should fulfill his duty and collect account receivables that were due to the JV under his management. Attesting her personal observation, the head administrator opined that in this moment of exchanging the final draft "the CEO lost his trust in his partners," and "his main objective changed to regain his honor."

Puzzled in disbelief that she now encountered what she always thought was an urban tale about Chinese "saving face" culture, the lawyer was alarmed. "The SPA has been finalized, the purchase price is already highly above value, an escrow account is standing to receive the sums!," she cried. The seasoned mediator, however, quickly responded "this means that he is now asking for more money."

After some days, when the lawyer was able to get ahold of the Chinese partner's legal team, she was told that the delay was due to "bureaucratic hurdles" as the CEO had received word that the purchase agreement would not be approved by the local authorities. Supposedly the escrow mechanism "is not looked upon favorably" when a foreign party acquires the shares of a Chinese partner. Once negotiations resumed, the CEO's legal team pushed for what they argued was a customary solution: In case the authorities would not approve the transaction, the sums will be released from escrow into the local partner's account, but he will be kept as a "passive nominee shareholder." This mechanism, per the legal team, was a common one designed to enable the execution of the SPA: a contractual arrangement that will de-facto transform the JV into a wholly foreign owned firm, while maintaining its current registration status. The local "partner" will forgo his voting rights, dividend rights, and any other rights in the company.

The foreign lawyer vehemently opposed such a deal. Her consultations with local counsels confirmed her understanding. Since the CEO will still be registered as a shareholder in a JV, he will be entitled to shareholders' governance rights under the PRC Company law. An attempt to enforce the proposed contractual arrangement in the future will de-facto require a court to ignore the provisions of the law. The chances for such a contract to be enforced are slim to none. Yet the client was eager to close one way or another. As a publicly listed company, enduring a conflict with a sole distributor in China would not be accepted well by the shareholders.

After several long months of further negotiations, the SPA finally went through, and the transaction was consummated with the appropriate authority approvals. In this process, the purchase price of the local partner's shares increased 30 percent above what has been agreed upon, and not due to any value increase in the firm. In fact, during that period, the company ceased operations almost entirely. The JV was practically held hostage and lost much of its distribution channels and clients to local competitors.

—

A serendipitous epilogue to the case came two years later. The foreign lawyer coincidently ran into the (former) head administrator of the JV and the full complexity of the episode was unveiled. Apparently, the CEO has befriended a local official in Shanghai and confided with him about selling his shares in the JV. The official (an administrator at either SAIC, local COFTEC, or SAFE), getting in the weeds of the negotiation process, told the CEO that the deliverables under the SPA requiring him to collect payments before his departure would embarrass the CEO with his local clients and sub-distributors. Instead, the official apparently offered, the transaction could be renegotiated on the basis of expected "bureaucratic hurdles" by the authorities. This would give the CEO more leverage to improve his departure terms and save face.

What the local official had gained from such friendly advice was left untold (and is likely unknown) to this day.

—

Today, the (former) Chinese partner works with several suppliers. He has since expanded his distribution network and supplies AgroTech equipment to former JV clients and others across China.

The (former) American partner continues its global operations, including the wholesale distribution of its products in China. It had since established a special advisory board for the Asian market.

[**The story is based on the author's personal experience. Identifying details have been altered.**]

Acknowledgments

I owe a great deal of gratitude to a long list of friends, family members, and mentors who provided guidance and support throughout the course of writing and producing this book.

First and foremost, my gratitude and admiration are due to my doctoral dissertation committee. My academic mentor, Nicholas Howson, whose wisdom and experience drew me to start my academic journey at the University of Michigan Law School. Nico read my work in and out. His sharp commentary and intellectual rigor pushed me forward to question existing boundaries and develop my own vision. My development as a legal sinologist would not have been the same without the knowledge I absorbed from Nico and his scholarship. I owe wholehearted thanks to Vic Khanna, whose teaching planted the seeds of my interest in bridging development theories with corporate law, and whose guidance helped me find my way in the labyrinth of academia. Curtis Milhaupt, of Stanford Law School, provided kind guidance in critical junctures. His scholarship had a profound impact on this book and on my development as a scholar.

I am also thankful to Theresa Kaiser-Jarvis, former Assistant Dean for International Affairs at the University of Michigan Law School, a friend and mentor, who supported every step of my research with undefeatable positivity. Also at Michigan, I extend my utmost thanks to the wonderful team at the Lieberthal-Rogel Center for Chinese Studies, particularly to Mary Gallagher and Yuen Yuen Ang, for welcoming me to the Center's intellectual life, providing me with an immensely collegial community of China scholars with whom to share my research. The interdisciplinary nature of this book benefited much from my discussions and exposures to the Center's activities and its scholars.

I am deeply indebted to mentors and colleagues at Harvard Law School, where I spent three years producing this book, particularly to the Harvard Law School Program on Corporate Governance and to the East Asian Legal Studies Program, which provided institutional support during my time there as a research and teaching Fellow. While at Harvard, I greatly benefited from thought-provoking discussions with foremost leaders and thinkers of corporate law in the United States and from esteemed China law experts. For sharing their time, observations, and insights with me, I extend my gratitude to Lucian Bebchuk, Jesse Fried, and Mark Roe. My deep gratitude to Mark extends also for giving me the opportunity to take part in joining him at teaching his Comparative Corporate Governance course. Mark's own work and his feedback had a great deal of influence on this book. I owe my utmost thanks to William Alford, the Director of the East Asian Legal Studies Program. I have been influenced and inspired by Bill's intellectual contributions to China studies for many years. I am humbled and fortunate to have benefited from his charitable spirit and keen interest in my work.

The final steps in writing this book were accomplished during the first year of my tenure as an Assistant Professor at the Hebrew University of Jerusalem. There, I thank the Department of Asian Studies department and particularly my colleagues at the China section for their support, feedback, and curiosity toward my work. I am grateful to Barak Medina at the Faculty of Law, Hebrew University of Jerusalem, and to Assaf Hamdani, at Buchman Faculty of Law, Tel Aviv University, for their continuous guidance and support on my path. I also thank the anonymous reviewers of this book and the ASCL Series editor who provided suggestions and constructive criticism that improved the manuscript.

Immeasurable appreciation is owed to my partner, Shamir Ozery, for his friendship, his love, and his endless support in the journey of writing and producing this book; my parents, Ida and Shlomo Groswald, for their counsel and unconditional love; and my children, Negev and Gefen, for giving me the opportunity to practice patience and forbearance, skills much needed in writing a book.

T.G.O
Jerusalem, Israel
July 2022

About the Book

This book examines the evolution in the role of formal law through four decades of market reforms in China. It employs two layers of analysis: the market development macro layer and the corporate governance and capital market micro layer. The macro layer, Part II, establishes the analytical framework of the book. It shows how the law translates and secures political-economic power dynamics within the Party-state system. By examining the evolving functions of law through the different eras of market reform, the analysis shows how formal law supports the Party-state's efforts to strike a delicate balance between its own needs for macro control, the interests of various hierarchies within the Party-state, and those of market participants, thereby configuring China's unique socialist market economy. The micro layer, Part III in the book, implements the framework. It digs deep into the development of corporate governance and the Chinese capital market and considers how law and political economic determinants entwine in shaping the business environment in which public firms operate.

Drawing from a chronological study of an extensive archive of laws, regulations, policies and normative opinions issued by organs of the Chinese Party-state since economic reforms began in 1978 until the present, the book sheds a new comparative light on a long-standing debate about the role of law in economic development and about the possible varieties of growth-supporting governance mechanisms.

Through its interdisciplinary approach, connecting deep knowledge about China's political economy, law and development theories, and corporate governance practices, the book aspires to produce novel insights about the relationship between law, economic development, and politics in contemporary China.

**A note about the cover: The front face of the coin portrays the mythical ancient creature Xiezhi (獬豸), a symbol of traditional Chinese law that represents righteousness. Xiezhi is believed to possess a divine ability to sense and fight corruption.

Abbreviations

AMC	Asset Management Companies
BRI	Belt and Road Initiative
CAC	Cyberspace Administration of China
CBIRC	China Banking and Insurance Regulatory Commission
CBRC	China Banking Regulatory Commission
CCDI	Central Commission of Discipline Inspection
CCP	Chinese Communist Party
COFTEC	Commission of Foreign Trade and Economic Cooperation
CRES	Commission for Restructuring the Economic System
CSRC	China Securities Regulatory Commission
JV	Joint Venture
M&A	Mergers and Acquisitions
MOF	Ministry of Finance
MOFCOM	Ministry of Commerce
NDRC	National Development and Reform Commission
NIE	New Institutional Economics
NPC	National People's Congress
NPCsc	National People's Congress Standing Committee
PBoC	People's Bank of China
PRC	People's Republic of China
RMB	Renminbi (the Chinese currency, also known as Yuan)
SAIC	State Administration for Industry and Commerce
SAFE	State Administration of Foreign Exchange
SAMR	State Administration for Market Regulation
SASAC	State Asset Supervision and Administration Commission
SERC	State Economic Reform Commission
SME	Small Medium Enterprise
SOE	State-Owned Enterprise
SPC	Supreme People's Court
TVE	Township and Village Enterprise
WFOE	Wholly Foreign-Owned Enterprise
WTO	World Trade Organization

Introduction

Over the past four decades, China has made impressive strides to establish a modern legal system. The Chinese Party-state[1] has devoted great attention and resources to the use of law in governing markets. The array and scope of economic law-making and institutions have been particularly astounding.

The conventional premise for embracing law in the context of economic reform calls for a modern legal system as a prerequisite for economic development. The premise suggests that economic exchange between unfamiliar parties requires reliable, uniformly applicable norms and institutions that provide credible commitments for growth. The widely accepted way to define norms in a predictable and uniform manner and to secure the expectations of rights recipients (i.e., market participants) is through a legal system. Without secured property rights, it is argued, market activity will be discouraged.

Yet as many critiques of this conventional "economic-rights-security → leading growth" premise show, China achieved substantial growth and developed markets irrespective of the quality of its legal institutions. Indeed, four decades of economic development in China are surrounded by this great puzzle.[2]

Within its broad growth puzzle, the development of China's financial markets, particularly its publicly listed firms and their corporate governance system, is especially intriguing.

Capital markets and the firms that populate them are important components in any growth-oriented economy. Firms are the primary vehicle through which large-scale production and commerce take place. Capital markets, in turn, facilitate external

[1] The term "Party-state" refers to a one-party system in which one political party directs both the political process and the administrative governance carried by the state.

[2] The puzzle is of course much broader. Throughout its economic trajectory, China has resisted many policy measures that have long been considered essential for economic growth, including rapid liberalization of monetary policy and trade, privatization, and a Western-style rule of law. China's distinct economic path spreads along a spectrum of governance dimensions, leaving foreign policymakers, practitioners, and academics across a variety of disciplines puzzled. The role of law in China's development is but one, prominent, aspect of China's growth puzzle.

finance beyond relational-based exchange, making capital accessible and less costly for firms. They enable large-scale trade of economic rights between unfamiliar parties while facilitating information flow between firms and investors. This informational function is expected to ensure the allocation of capital to the most deserving firms (commonly referred to as the "efficient allocation of capital"), thereby aiding good firms to grow and expand. Public firms and capital markets are thus considered important steps in financial development and in the overall advancement of the economy – the deeper the capital market, the greater the prospect for further economic growth in a given country.[3]

Here too, and not without controversies, the conventional wisdom has coalesced around certain prescriptions of what may propel capital market development, and by extension growth:

- Dispersed ownership is more conducive to capital market development than concentrated ownership.[4]
- Private ownership is a precondition for prosperous firms and for deep capital markets,[5] while state ownership and heavy statist or political intervention impede market development.[6]
- Law is eminent. Robust legal institutions, particularly those associated with investor protections, are essential.[7]

China, however, misses the mark on these well-established prescriptions.

Take, for example, China's leading spot in the desired Fortune Global 500 list,[8] to which it had ascended in 2020.[9] Close to 75 percent of the Chinese firms on this list are formally owned by the Chinese government (forty-eight firms are owned by the central government, thirty-two by the local level of SASAC, and twelve firms by state-owned financial institutions).[10] Many ostensibly private firms on the list have some state

[3] Note that this does not mean that capital markets are crucial for economic growth; the evidence for that is far from conclusive. Yet, scholars are largely in agreement that growth can be expanded when capital market activity increases.

[4] R. La Porta et al., "Corporate Ownership around the World," *Journal of Finance* 54(2) (1999) 471.

[5] M. Boycko et al., *Privatizing Russia* (MIT Press, 1997).

[6] Friedrich Hayek is known for developing a theory according to which legal systems with traditions that constrain government intervention (common law) are more compatible with a market economy than legal systems in which government power was more freely asserted (civil law). See P. Mahoney, "The Common Law and Economic Growth: Hayek Might Be Right," *Journal of Legal Studies* 30 (2001) 503.

[7] See Chapter 1 discussing the traditional framework, below.

[8] Note, the Fortune Global 500 list includes firms by total revenue size. Many firms in the list are not publicly listed.

[9] In 2020, China topped the list with the largest number of firms (124 including mainland China and Hong Kong, excluding Taiwan), exceeding Western leadership of the list for the first time in history. A. Murray & D. Meyer, "The Fortune Global 500 Is Now More Chinese than American," *Fortune* (Aug. 10, 2020), https://perma.cc/HA66-KSVN. Note, however, Chinese firms still lag behind US firms in terms of total revenue. See "Visualize the Global 500," *Fortune*, https://perma.cc/UC3E-2TBZ.

[10] 独家解读2020年(财富)世界五百强上榜国企名单 [Interpretation of the 2020 Fortune Global 500 List of State-Owned Enterprises, Report by the State-Owned Assets Supervision and Administration Commission of the State Council], Aug. 11, 2020, https://perma.cc/T2EW-EUFP.

FIGURE 0.1 Total market capitalization, compared

investments as well or are subject to the political clout of the Chinese Communist Party (CCP) even without any state ownership. Haier Group, Huawei, and even Alibaba and Tencent are among the Fortune Global 500 private firms that arguably have ties to the Party-state.[11] Clearly, concentrated state ownership and political influence did not stand in the way of these firms' expansion and their global prominence. Quite the contrary.

China's capital market has similarly avoided the conventional receipt for growth while sustaining one of the fastest capital market growth rates in economic history (Figure 0.1).

China's capital market has seen largely constant and significant growth, as measured by total market capitalization and by the number of firms listed. At the end of 2005, mainland China stock exchanges – the Shanghai Stock Exchange (SSE) and the Shenzhen Stock Exchange (SZSE) – had 1,377 public companies with a market capitalization of 401.8 billion USD. In 2010, the number of listed firms reached 2,063 with a total market capitalization of 4.028 trillion USD. By the end of 2019, China's capital market reached a striking 3,777 firms listed, with a total market capitalization of 8.5 trillion USD (Figure 0.2).[12]

As seen in Figures 0.1 and 0.2, the growth of China's capital market is telling in relative terms as well. In less than three decades, the market grew to be the second largest in the world, outgrowing veteran competing markets. It now represents 10.1 percent of global stock market capitalization.[13]

[11] C. Milhaupt & W. Zheng, "Beyond Ownership: State Capitalism and the Chinese firm," *The Georgetown Law Journal* 103(3) (2014) 665.

[12] Data drawn from the World Bank. World Bank capital market data on the United Kingdom extends only through 2014.

[13] China's total market capitalization is second only to the United States', whose market capitalization represents thirty-six percent of the global market capitalization.

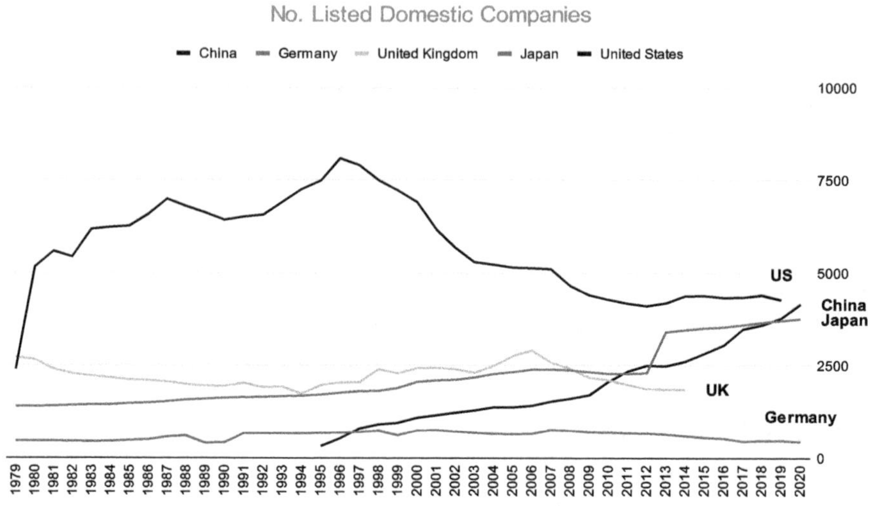

FIGURE 0.2 Number of listed companies, compared

Interestingly, notwithstanding the preference by some Chinese firms to list offshore (mainly high-growth tech companies), the number of IPOs (initial public offering) in China continues to rise, reaching 429 IPOs in 2017, 36 percent of global IPOs that year.[14] This occurred while the OECD reports that capital markets in other countries have been shrinking,[15] and despite China's known stringent IPO approval system (recently being gradually replaced), and the relatively high cost of capital for Chinese issuers.[16] Extreme levels of oversubscription to Chinese domestic IPOs suggests high demand on part of public investors.[17] The demand by foreign investors is perhaps even more striking.[18]

14 There was a sharp decline in 2018 and a rise thereafter with 197 IPOs in 2019. See "Global IPO Trends: Q4 2017," *EY Report*, at 15–18, https://perma.cc/4RMQ-2Q4M; *Cf.* "Global IPO Trends: Q4 2019," *EY Report*, at 16–19, https://perma.cc/4RNS-Y9UR. Note, these numbers represent mainland China only, excluding IPOs of "Chinese firms" in Hong Kong. The IPOs of Chinese firms comprise a substantial number of the Hong Kong IPO market. *See infra* note 33. After including IPO numbers in Hong Kong, greater China markets had 394 IPOs in 2020 (up until and including Q3), forty-five percent of global IPOs. See E. Cheng, "Chinese Companies Are Leading the IPO Rush Amid a 'Flight from Uncertainty'," CNBC (Oct. 27, 2020), https://perma.cc/WBZ3-MK2K.

15 "OECD Corporate Governance Factbook 2019," OECD 18–21 (2019), www.oecd.org/corporate/Corporate-Governance-Factbook.pdf.

16 Y. Qian et al., "Initial Public Offerings Chinese Style" (Jan. 13, 2021) (working paper), https://papers.ssrn.com/sol3/papers.cfm?abstract_id=3682089.

17 Of course, price restrictions may artificially boost demand.

18 T. Groswald Ozery, "Illiberal Governance and the Rise of China's Public Firms: An Oxymoron or China's Greatest Triumph?," *University of Pennsylvania Journal of International Law* 42(4) (2021) 921 (an effort to explain the puzzle of foreign investments in the Chinese capital market).

If a reliable, effective, and efficiency-oriented legal system was in place, the picture above would not have been so puzzling. Such a legal system would have presumably supported private ownership and other investors' rights, overcome a multitude of structural predicaments that characterize public share ownership in China, reduced the cost of doing business and raising capital, and thereby would have supported and explained growth. Having such a system in operation would have conformed to many prevailing views in both law and development and comparative corporate governance analyses.

The rise of firms in China and the growth of its capital market, however, had little to do with such a legal framework. Indeed, as this book and others have shown, the impressive development above has happened even while the Chinese Party-state maintains market control, state ownership, and weak legal institutions. State ownership and political governance mechanisms are deployed in many Chinese firms, and their presence is growing. Not only have these mechanisms not receded as the market grew strong, in fact they have only amplified, while many corporate laws and traditional governance institutions remain weak by design.

Many prior studies have explicated this puzzle, pointing to the ways in which China's growth diverges from the "economic-rights-security → leading growth" premise.[19] The problem lies in that most critiques of the premise rely on the same analytical framework that highlights the economic functions of law. Consequently, the studies inevitably undervalue the role of law in China's development process. Put differently, focusing on the economic functions of law, legal scholarship naturally pivots around the quality of rights-securing legal institutions, particularly private enforcement through the court system. As a result, many scholars across disciplines and popular thinking outside China assess the role of law in China as a mere political instrument, a marginal governing tool secondary to political edicts, or simply view it as window dressing with little contribution to the country's economic rise.[20] When one looks only to the economic-rights-securing promises of law, a disregard for the role of law in supporting China's growth becomes almost inevitable.

[19] Clarke has labeled this premise "The Rights Hypothesis." D. C. Clarke, "Economic Development and the Rights Hypothesis: The China Problem," *The American Journal of Comparative Law* 51(1) (2003) 89; see also X. C. Long, "Does the Rights Hypothesis Apply to China?," *The Journal of Law and Economics*, 53(4) (2010) 629; F. Upham, "From Demsetz to Deng: Speculations on the Implications of Chinese Growth for the Law and Development Theory," *New York University Journal of International Law & Politics*, 41(3) (2009) 551; J. K. M. Ohnesorge, "Developing Development Theory: Law and Development Orthodoxies and the Northeast Asian Experience, *University of Pennsylvania Journal of International Economic Law* 28(2) (2007) 219.

[20] Several studies share the position taken in this book and do not find a simplistic instrumentalist view about law in China satisfactory. Recent studies that offer a more intricate analysis of Chinese law instrumentalism include T. Zhang & T. Ginsburg, "China's Turn toward Law," *Virginia Journal of International Law* 59(2) (2019) 306; S. Liu, "Cage for the Birds: On the Social Transformation of Chinese Law, 1999–2019," *China Law and Society Review* 5(2) (2021) 66; S. Wang, *Law as an Instrument: Sources of Chinese Law for Authoritarian Legality* (Cambridge University Press, 2022), pp. 162–177.

In this book, I call to reevaluate that approach.[21] The framework that was used thus far, although valuable in questioning the "economic-rights-security → leading growth" premise itself, does not explain China's growth puzzle and creates a dissonance with the extent to which the Party-state has been advancing the use of law to govern markets over the reform eras.

We have been too quick to dismiss the role of law in China's economic development as we have neglected to fully evaluate and understand its political functions. The book offers an alternative framework through which to observe China's growth puzzle and to assess the role of law within it. The alternative framework studies the relationship between formal law and market development in China from the vantage point of political power dynamics. Analyzing the role of law through this framework allows us to appreciate the full functions of law in the development process. It suggests that the law supports China's market development in a multitude of ways, notwithstanding its slow-to-evolve, and at times limited, economic functions.

The book employs two layers of analysis: the market development macro layer and the corporate governance and capital market micro layer.

Part I delineates the conceptual and analytical frameworks underpinning the book. Chapter 1 explains the traditional framework that commonly guides thinking about the role of law in development and in financial markets specifically. Chapter 2 presents the difficulties with the traditional approach and offers law and political economy as an alternative analytical framework.

Part II establishes the new framework by tracking the evolving role of law in China's market reforms and identifying how the two functions of law – economic and political – have developed side by side, each supporting the other. I examine the legal configurations of political-power dynamics through a systematic investigation of the vast body of market-related primary and secondary sources of law and CCP documents that have been promulgated in China since early reforms until the present day. This part of the book offers a macro layer of analysis which outlines a three-stage shift in the allocation of market governance authorities within the Party-state system through legal evidence:

Chapter 3 looks at the role of law during the Early Reform Era (Dec. 1978–1991), when the Party-state vested economic decision-making authorities with its local governments, giving them a relatively free rein to experiment with and administer economic activity by limiting central government law-making. Chapter 4 moves on to examine the subsequent Legal Modernization Era (ca. 1992–2009) – a golden age for legal reformers in China. During this era, market governance authorities were reconfigured and recentralized with the central state through a massive project of national-level institutional and legal reforms. This reconfiguration of powers

[21] Yu Guanghua took a similar perspective combining law with politics to understand economic development in his book: G. Yu, *The Roles of Law and Politics in China's Development* (Springer, 2014).

via the legal system also set the foundation for what is known today as China's state capitalism. Chapter 5 examines the current era, which I label the Legalized Politicization Era (2010–present). During this era, the consequences of state capitalism brought a new reconfiguration through law in two directions, intensifying the presence of the regulatory state in the market on the one hand while shifting substantial market governance powers directly to the CCP itself on the other.

Relying on these findings, Part III then applies the suggested analytical framework of law & political economy at the micro level by delving deep into China's corporate and capital market development puzzle. Here, the book merges questions about the role of law in development with inquiries on the evolution of financial markets and corporate governance specifically. This Part uses the alternative analytical framework developed in Parts I and II to better understand the evolution of the public firm and the role of law in China's capital market growth. It demonstrates how the explanatory power of law and political economy can bring more clarity to China's evolving approach to corporate governance. Here, I analyze the evolution of the public firm in China and pay particular attention to the creation and efficacy of corporate governance institutions, both traditional and idiosyncratic, that operate in the market:

Chapter 6 focuses on the emergence of the public firm in China and looks at how the legal framework that governed firms in the early stages of market development was shaped by, and helped secure, the political-economy dynamics of that time. Chapter 7 moves on to examine the corporate governance institutions that developed during the legal modernization era. The chapter provides a thorough analysis of traditional corporate governance mechanisms, both internal and external to the firm, showing how China's facially convergent, investor-oriented corporate governance framework diverges in practice. It illuminates the political functions of law in this era, showing how the corporate governance framework supported the reconsolidation of powers and the shift toward state capitalism. The chapter also offers comparative insights drawn from additional systems of corporate governance and analyzes the implications of China's corporate governance framework for investors. Chapter 8 looks at the recent politicization of corporate governance in the current era. It explicates how the CCP has advanced its corporate governance capacities and its roles in governing markets more broadly, through the use of law. Chapter 9 considers the potential benefits and costs of using a politicized corporate governance system as a functional alternative in the Chinese market.

The analysis illuminates how political-power shifts at each era of development resulted in the reconfiguration of the legal framework that governs the market, and how such reconfiguration, in turn, helped secure a new political-economic equilibrium. These iterative dynamics also mobilized market participants (both economic and political) to develop and deploy various growth-promoting mechanisms within firms and in the market at large. Such mechanisms at times supported, at times impeded, and at times substituted for conventional corporate governance institutions.

When applied to China's capital market development puzzle, the law and political economy framework not only helps us to better understand the existing infirmities in the Chinese market but also may hold the key to understanding its unprecedented success. The framework, furthermore, provides new insights on the different functions that the law may hold in the development process.

PART I

Economic Development and the Role of Law

Scholars have long regarded certain attributes of corporate governance (i.e., a term that can be broadly defined as the legal and market mechanisms that govern the relationships between different constituents of a firm), particularly legal institutions that protect investors, as engines for financial development, capital market expansion, and growth. Yet, the development of China's market challenges many of the underlying assumptions in such theories and leaves its observers puzzled. Consequently, many have dismissed the role of law in China's economic rise. But they have neglected to consider the political functions of law and how these functions have bolstered the development of the Chinese market. Chapter 1 unpacks the traditional framework that shapes how scholars and policymakers think of corporate governance and its role in financial development and market growth. Chapter 2 offers law and political economy as an alternative analytical framework through which to address the puzzle and the role of law within it.

1

The Traditional Framework

The linkages between corporate governance, financial development, and economic growth more broadly have a long intellectual pedigree. Legal scholarship in the field, specifically, has drawn upon two main strands of literature, law and development studies and the new institutional economics (NIE) tradition. These strands of thought, both developed in the Western parts of the world, in many ways laid the foundation of the main building blocks of corporate governance scholarship – the theory of the firm, agency costs analysis, and eventually the law and finance approach.

Law and development took root as a distinct field of legal studies following World War II, when efforts to reform legal systems around the world became systematic.[22] Growing out of the "modernization movement" of broader social sciences,[23] law and development theorists supported the notion that the adoption of certain principles, said to characterize the "advanced" societies of the time, can accelerate stages of development in others. Particularly, it was argued, underdeveloped societies can march toward modernity and prosperity by the "diffusion of capital, institutions and values from the First World … involv[ing] the emergence of a free market system, rule of law, multi-party politics, … and protection [of] human rights and basic freedoms."[24] Having modern laws was thus perceived to be a prerequisite to development.

With the rise of neoclassical economics, however, the development discourse turned away from thinking about law to ideas of limited government as the basis

[22] The observation that law and economic development are related is of course much older, dating back at least to the nineteenth-century sociologists and political economy thinkers Max Weber and Karl Marx and their views on the rise of capitalism in Western Europe. For an intricate examination of Weber's thesis about the connection between capitalism and the existence of a "logically formal and rational legal system," see, A. H. Y. Chen, "Rational Law, Economic Development and the Case of China," *Social & Legal Studies* 8(1) (1999) 97.

[23] D. Trubek & A. Santos, "Introduction: The Third Moment in Law and Development Theory and the Emergence of a New Critical Practice." In D. Trubek & A. Santos (eds.), *The New Law and Economic Development: A Critical Appraisal* (Cambridge University Press, 2006).

[24] K. Davis & M. J. Trebilcock, "The Relationship between Law and Development: Optimists versus Skeptics," *The American Journal of Comparative Law* 56 (2008) 895, at 900.

of growth theories. Neoclassical economics highlighted market components, consequently shifting the focus away from more holistic ideas of development (e.g., redistributive justice, mortality rates, education levels, human rights, and individual freedoms) toward economic growth particularly. The impact is still felt today in scholarly and popular writing where economic growth and the concept of development are often treated as one. In scientific studies as well, a rise in the total size of the economy (the increase per capita in a country's gross national product [GNP] or gross domestic product [GDP]) serves as the prominent indicator of development across many disciplines of social science.

After the collapse of the Eastern Bloc, neoliberal ideas and aspirations for a globalized world spread with gusto, and the advanced economies became ever more invested in reforming the developing and transitional world through the Washington Consensus. The Washington Consensus framework highlighted market-based criteria as policy prescriptions for reforms. Rapid liberalization of trade and prices, wide-scale privatization, deregulation, and restrained state powers, among other components, were pushed forward by policymakers and international financial institutions (i.e., the IMF, World Bank, and regional development banks) as conditions for aid programs. Many of the recipient countries, however, incurred persistent, sometimes deeper, economic crises. Enduring debt crises and economic instability in Latin America; recessions and the failure of shock therapy big bang privatization reforms in East Europe and the former Soviet Union; and ultimately the Asian Financial Crisis, called for reconsideration of the Washington Consensus approach.[25] It became clear that treating market variables alone cannot produce growth. Much of the failure was attributed to the lack of appropriate legal, social, and economic institutions in the recipient countries. And thus, the thinking about rule of law and the role of law in development emerged again.[26]

A major contributor to this reemergence was the rise of NIE that gained attention and impact as a new branch in development economics. This approach brought the question of institutional structures, including law explicitly, back into economic analysis. As John Ohnesorge puts it, "it could be said that the NIE opened the door for economists to concern themselves with pretty much any aspect of the legal system."[27]

Ronald Coase and Douglass North, two of the most influential thinkers of the NIE, highlighted the need for securing property rights and an effective, impartial judicial system. Their works provided theoretical foundations upon which the discipline of corporate governance later developed.

North focused on the quality of institutions as the source of differences between rich and poor countries. The main role of institutions in society, per North, is to

[25] J. E. Stiglitz, "More Instruments and Broader Goals: Moving toward the Post-Washington Consensus." In A. B. Atkinson, K. Basu, J. N. Bhagwati, D. C. North, D. Rodrik, F. Stewart, J. E. Stiglitz & J. G. Williamson (eds.), *Wider Perspectives on Global Development* (Palgrave Macmillan, 2005), 16.

[26] Trubek and Santos discuss this as a "Third Moment in Law and Development Theory," note 23.

[27] Ohnesorge, *Developing Development Theory*, note 19, at 244–246.

provide stable structures for human interaction and reduce uncertainties. Rich countries have developed low-cost, credible institutions that reduce uncertainties, and prominent among them are prescribed property rights and an impartial judicial system to enforce contracts and support trade. Property rights and enforceable long-term contracts secure the expectations of market participants and thus create incentives to engage in socially productive economic activity.[28]

Coase, in two of his seminal pieces, *The Theory of the Firm* and *The Problem of Social Costs,* dealt with micro-economics and started to unpack how firms operate and what incentivizes their constituents. Coase explained that firms emerge and engage in long-term contracting to minimize costs and maximize value. His work set the foundation for a transaction costs theory.[29] Well-defined property rights (which he defined as the distribution of rights and obligations) minimize transaction costs, which then impact how firms operate and grow.[30] Building upon Coase's theories, property rights are now considered a basic component in the institutional structure of the business firm and in the economy more broadly.[31] These theoretical developments began to open up the black box of the firm for further theorizing, including path breaking theories about agency relationships within firms and their costs. In the context of the business firm, agency relationship is a form of contract under which a principal engages an agent to perform services on her behalf and delegates decision-making authority. The separation between ownership and control that stems from such a contract creates information asymmetries and gives rise to conflicting interests between the principal and her agent. Agency theory became one the main theoretical building blocks of corporate governance as it seeks to devise institutions that mitigate the costs of monitoring agents.[32]

Taken together, following the works of NIE, development studies across disciplines have been concerned with the institutions that propel economic activity and market growth. While the works of Coase and North view institutions as being both formal and informal,[33] improving the function of formal institutions, and of legal

[28] D. C. North, *Institutions, Institutional Change and Economic Performance* (Cambridge University Press, 1990), particularly at 54, 61–69, 92–104, 107–117.

[29] These seminal works were published may years before NIE has spread as a new branch of economics. The transaction cost theory and the term itself was further developed by O. E. Williamson, "The Economics of Organization: The Transaction Cost Approach," *American Journal of Sociology* 87(3) (1981) 548.

[30] H. R. Coase, "The Nature of the Firm," *Economica* 4(16) (1937) 386; H. R. Coase, "The Problem of Social Cost," *Journal of Law and Economics* 3 (1960) 1. (known as Coase Theorem).

[31] O. Hart & J. Moore, "Property Rights and the Nature of the Firm," *Journal of Political Economy* 98(6) (1990) 1119.

[32] M. Jensen & W. Meckling, "Theory of the Firm: Managerial Behavior, Agency Costs, and Ownership Structure," *Journal of Finance Economics* 3.4 (1976) 305; E. F. Fama, "Agency Problems and the Theory of the Firm," *Journal of Political Economy* 88(2) (1980) 288.

[33] Coase: Transaction costs (costs of exchange) "depend on the institutions of a country: its legal system, its political system, its social system, its educational system, its culture, and so on [...] a complex interrelated

institutions specifically, has become an essential element in economic development policies worldwide.[34]

Policymakers and law professionals have thus pushed for legal reforms designed according to the successful institutional settings of rich markets (mostly, the United States). Legal reforms, directed to enable and support economic activity while limiting interventionism by governments, focused on creating modern, clear, and predictable private economic laws (e.g., property, contracts, and enterprise laws) and professionalizing independent enforcement institutions to secure economic rights.[35] The role of the court system was viewed as protecting businesses not only from misconducts between private participants but also against government incursion; judicial independence was therefore emphasized. Similarly, administrative law was devised to constrain government powers and reduce rent-seeking.[36]

These developments and the focus on "economic-rights security" received special attention in the financial world, where the advancement of financial markets is widely seen useful, if not necessary, to propel economic growth and create wealth.[37] The primary constituents in financial markets are capital contributors, i.e. investors. Thus, the guiding idea suggests that clear and predictable property rights and enforceable protections against the abuse of investors function as the needed guarantees that secure investors, and are crucial for the growth of firms. Absent such conditions, investors will be disinclined to invest in firms. This will raise the cost of capital in the given market, thin financial markets will develop, and the economic growth prospect of the market will be negatively impacted.

These views were reinforced by the parallel development of modern finance that introduced empirical methodologies for testing such economic hypotheses. Financial economists applied cross-country statistical analysis to test whether and how specific attributes in a given system propel financial development more than others. These included, for example, the country's legal origin,[38] the ownership structure of firms in

structure." R. Coase, "The New Institutional Economics," *The American Economic Review* 88(2), Papers and Proceedings of the Hundred and Tenth Annual Meeting of the American Economic Association (May 1998), at 72–74. North, *Institutions and Economic Performance*, note 28, at 4: "Institutions include any form of constraint that human beings devise to shape human interaction. Are institutions formal or informal? They can be either, and I am interested both in formal constraints – such as rules that human beings devise – and in informal constraints – such as conventions and codes of behavior."

34 C. W. Gray, "Reforming Legal Systems in Developing and Transition Countries," *Finance & Development*, (Sep.) (1997), at 14–16.

35 K. Dam, *The Law-Growth Nexus: The Rule of Law and Economic Development* (Brookings Institution Press, 2006).

36 Trubek & Santos, *The Third Moment in Law and Development Theory*, note 23, at 9–12; Ohnesorge, *Developing Development Theory*, note 19, at 247–249.

37 R. King & R. Levine, "Finance and Growth: Schumpeter Might Be Right," *The Quarterly Journal of Economics* 108(3) (1993) 717; A. Demirgüç-Kunt & M. Vojislav, "Law, Finance, and Firm Growth," *The Journal of Finance* 53(6) (1998) 2107.

38 Among others: R. La Porta et al., "Law and Finance," *Journal of Political Economy* 106(6) (1998) 1113; R. La Porta, et al., "Legal Determinants of External Finance," *Journal of Finance* 52(3) (1997) 1131; S. Djankov

the market,[39] and a range of corporate governance variables held as indicators for the quality of investor protections.[40] While many have critiqued the studies (particularly the hypothesis of *legal origin* as a determining factor),[41] the notion that financial development requires high-quality institutions, particularly investor protection institutions, has become conventional wisdom. This fertile line of research had a meaningful impact on development policies worldwide. It induced international development organizations to produce detailed indices and codes of corporate governance as prescriptions for how a country may achieve deeper and more active financial markets to boost economic growth. Importantly, through these prescriptions, the American model of corporate capitalism with investors' interest at its center has become the focus of convergence.[42]

This approach flourished until the Global Financial Crisis (2008–09). The crisis exposed what many have criticized as the social and economic costs of globalization. Liberal capitalism started to lose its appeal. In the corporate governance context, the crisis illuminated the possible consequences of the wide adoption of one-set solutions modeled after American corporate capitalism principles and triggered thoughts about renewed divergence. Recipient countries started to look for alternative models to draw from.

Indeed, as Part III in this book will show, a reversal from an apparent convergence in corporate governance institutions has been at the core of the Chinese Party-state policies and laws over the past decade. But even prior to recent formal reversals, the Chinese market did not follow the prescriptions depicted by the conventional framework. This poses two questions which this book is set to explore: How markets, particularly the capital markets and the firms that populate them, develop in China; and what exactly is the role of law in that process.

et al., "The New Comparative Economics," *Journal of Comparative Economics* 31(4) (2003) 595; R. La Porta et al., "The Economic Consequences of Legal Origins," *Journal of Economic Literature* 46(2) (2008) 285.

39 Among others: S. A. Shleifer & R. W. Vishny, "A Survey of Corporate Governance," *Journal of Finance* 52 (1997) 737; La Porta et al., *Corporate Ownership around the World*, note 4; S. Claessens et al., "The Separation of Ownership and Control in East Asian Corporations," *Journal of Financial Economics* 58(1–2) (2000) 81.

40 Among others: R. La Porta et al., "Investor Protection and Corporate Governance," *Journal of Financial Economics* 58(1) (2000) 3; S. Djankov et al., "The Law and Economics of Self-Dealing," *Journal of Financial Economics* 88(3) (2008) 430.

41 The literature is voluminous. Examples include critiques based on offering an alternative political–economic explanation to finance: R. Rajan & L. Zingales, "The Great Reversal: The Politics of Financial Development in the Twentieth Century," *Journal of Financial Economics* 69 (2003) 5; E. Perotti & A. Schwienbacher, "The Political Origin of Pension Funding," *Journal of Financial Intermediation* 18(3) (2009) 384; M. J. Roe & J. I. Siegel, "Political Instability: Effects on Financial Development, Roots in the Severity of Economic Inequality," *Journal of Comparative Economics* 39(3) (2011) 279. Studies pointing to culture as an alternative determinant: for example, R. M. Stulz & R. Williamson, "Culture, Openness, and Finance, *Journal of Financial Economics* 70(3) (2003) 313. And critiques based on the empirical validity of the studies: for example, H. Spamann, "Law and Finance Revisited," Harvard Law School John M. Olin Center Discussion Paper No. 12, 2008; K. Pistor, "Rethinking the Law and Finance Paradigm," *BYU Law Review* 6 (2009) 1647.

42 H. Hansmann & R. Kraakman, "The End of History for Corporate Law," *The Georgetown Law Journal* 89(2) (2001) 439.

2

Law and Political Economy[43]

A New Paradigm

Chapter 1 delineated the traditional thinking about what propels market development and motivates the design of many modern corporate governance systems around the world to focus on investor protection institutions. Providing credible commitments to investors through clearly defined, strong, and predictable rights and reliable legal institutions that can enforce those rights (i.e., economic-rights security) is regarded as preconditions for financial market development and by extension impact the market growth potential of a given economy.

But as explained in the Introduction, China did not follow this paradigm and thus poses a puzzle. Investor protections and relevant legal institutions took time to establish, and yet the capital market emerged and even flourished. When relevant institutions were finally in place, they proved to be weak in practice despite their modern form, and yet the market continued to advance.

Puzzled by this reality, popular views often conclude that the law in China is but a political mirage.[44] Media commentaries positing a complete disregard for laws in China are easily found and are perhaps understandable as they often rely on one's own assumptions and experiences with how legal institutions *should* function in the economy and what form they *ought* to carry.[45]

Skepticism about the contribution of law to China's market growth is prevalent in scientific studies as well. Many legal experts of China question the impact of law

[43] Law and political economy is an evolving approach in legal studies that explores the intersection between law, politics, and the economy. Generally, the field can be said to investigate "how relations of power are legally and politically configured and reconfigured over time and in distinct periods, and how in turn this conditions the development of the economy." M. Wilkinson & H. Lokdam, "Law and Political Economy." In M. Sellers & S. Kirste (eds.), *Encyclopedia of the Philosophy of Law and Social Philosophy* (forthcoming) (Springer Nature, 2024).

[44] "The Party needs the law to give the appearance of objective impartiality … More bluntly, the Party wants the credibility of impartial and independent law without the political danger." R. T. P. Alcala et al., "China and the Rule of Law: A Cautionary Tale for the International Community," Just Security (June 28, 2018), www.justsecurity.org/58544/china-rule-law-cautionary-tale-international-community/.

[45] Examples exist throughout the different reform eras. See, e.g., S. WuDunn, "Shenzhen China's Lawless Boomtown," *The Ottawa Citizen* (1991), B7; "Survey: Behind the Mask," *The Economist* 370 (8367) (2004), 4–S4; "Realigning Justice; Rule of Law," *The Economist* 412 (8900) (2014), 35–36.

reform on economic outcomes in various stages of China's market development or express doubts about its future significance. Others, often scholars of comparative development economics, tend to disregard the role of legal rights and assurances in the Chinese market altogether.[46]

Alternatively, it could be the case that formal law suffices to propel growth, particularly where the potential economic gains are high. Perhaps the expectations of investors for a fair game, superficially assured by rights established on the books, are enough to motivate investments regardless of the quality of legal institutions and protections in practice. Or at least it could be the case that formal law suffices to sustain investors' confidence until they are finally burned by the system (i.e., appealing looking laws can delay investors' disillusionment from the system to a further point in the development horizon, perhaps not yet reached in China's case).

Having modern sophisticated laws is surely important for investors. Yet public outcries against shareholder abuses and internationally known accounting debacles in Chinese firms since the very early days of public share offerings make it unlikely that modern and familiar looking laws are enough to support investors' confidence in the system. Similarly, even a "high-risk high-gain" environment cannot sustain investments for long when investors see that local conditions make the expropriations of their (even superior) yields a high probability. While these replies to China's growth puzzle cannot be ruled out completely (particularly in a high-risk high-gain environment, as is seen in China's debt investment sector), the mere existence of formal laws as a growth driver is too simplistic explanation and cannot resolve the presence of sophisticated repeat-players such as high-value individuals and domestic and foreign institutional investors who are increasingly present in the Chinese market.[47]

A way to address and perhaps resolve part of the puzzle is the possibility that something else, other than law, is providing credible commitments that sustain growth and support continued market development. Personal reputation, trust relationships,[48] the fostering of political connections,[49] and the Chinese Communist Party's (CCP) involvement in firms[50] have been offered in corporate studies as partial

46 For the former view, see e.g., S. Lubman, "Looking for Law in China," *Columbia Journal of Asian Law* 20 (2006) 1; W. P. Alford, "The More Law, the More…?" In N. Hope et al. (eds.), *How Far across the River?: Chinese Policy Reform at the Millennium* (Stanford University Press, 2003) 122. For the latter, see e.g., D. Kennedy & J. E. Stiglitz (eds.), *Law and Economics with Chinese Characteristics: Institutions for Promoting Development in the Twenty-First Century* (Oxford University Press, 2013); Dam, *The Law-Growth Nexus*, note 35.

47 Discussed in Part III, Chapter 7, "Law and Political Economy Configurations of Conventional Corporate Governance Mechanisms" under Section 1, Internal Governance Mechanisms.

48 F. Allen et al., "Law, Finance, and Economic Growth in China," *Journal of Financial Economics* 77 (2005) 57, at 59: "corporate governance mechanisms, such as those based on reputation and relationships […] support the growth of the private sector."

49 W. Zhang & J. Li, "Weak Law v. Strong Ties: An Empirical Study of Business Investment, Law and Political Connections in China," *Review of Law & Economics* 13(1) (2017) 1.

50 T. Groswald Ozery, "The Politicization of Corporate Governance: A Viable Alternative?" *The American Journal of Comparative Law* 70 (2022); avac007, https://doi.org/10.1093/ajcl/avac007.

functional substitutes for quality legal institutions. I have taken this direction myself in previous works where I examined the part of political substitutions in explaining the allure of the Chinese market to foreign investors specifically.[51] The existence of local substitutions brings up interesting cost and benefit questions and possible implications for future development and convergence theories (some of which are discussed in Part III, Chapter 9).

The aforementioned possibilities are not absolute and are not mutually exclusive. But they all seem to imply that law is not a determinant and substantive factor in China's market growth trajectory and is perhaps even marginal.

But if law does not have a determining effect on how China's markets will develop and grow, why has there been an extraordinary rise in legalization and regulatory activism with respect to markets over the past several decades? Since the first era of economic reforms was launched in 1978, China has made massive strides to establish a modern legal system. Scholars view China's project of legal reform to be "an event of epic historic proportions."[52] The scope and array of economic rulemaking and institutions have been particularly impressive.

Many studies raise the question of the shifting general attitude toward law in present-day China.[53] Yet understanding the evolving utilization of law in governing China's financial markets, specifically, has not been addressed in a systematic fashion thus far.

To clarify, this book is largely a qualitative study drawing on a sheer number of market governance archival documents (see more on methodology and caveats in later sections of this chapter). It is mostly interested in illuminating the different functions of law in the market, rather than in proving causal effects between law and growth. Nonetheless, while compiling my data, I noticed occasional quantitative results at several junctions. I bring those forward as further (soft) illustrations of my arguments, or when they suggest observations with potential importance and interesting questions for future studies.

For example, Figure 2.1 shows the high volume of *market-related* rulemaking activity throughout the four decades of reform in relation to GDP growth. Figure 2.2 shows the same, in relation to capital market growth as measured by the rise in the number of publicly listed companies. When looking at the trends in market rulemaking activism and comparing them with China's growth trajectory (Figure 2.1), two main points are evident: There seem to be some alignment between shifts in market-related rulemaking (primary law and secondary regulations) and GDP growth, but such trend alignment dissipates in the recent decade (2011 onward). Additionally Figure 2.2 suggests that there might be some lagging connection between peaks in the number of listed firms and periods of high

51 Groswald Ozery, "Illiberal Governance," note 18.

52 W. P. Alford, "A Second Great Wall?" *Cultural Dynamics* 11(2) (1999) 193, at 193.

53 A. H. Y. Chen, "China's Long March towards Rule of Law or China's Turn against Law?" *The Chinese Journal of Comparative Law* 4(1) (2016) 1; C. F. Minzner, "China's Turn against Law," *The American Journal of Comparative Law* 59(4) (2011), 935; Zhang & Ginsburg, "China's Turn toward Law," note 20; Wang, *Law as an Instrument*, note 20. And more broadly, R. Peerenboom (ed.), *China's Long March toward Rule of Law* (Cambridge University Press, 2002).

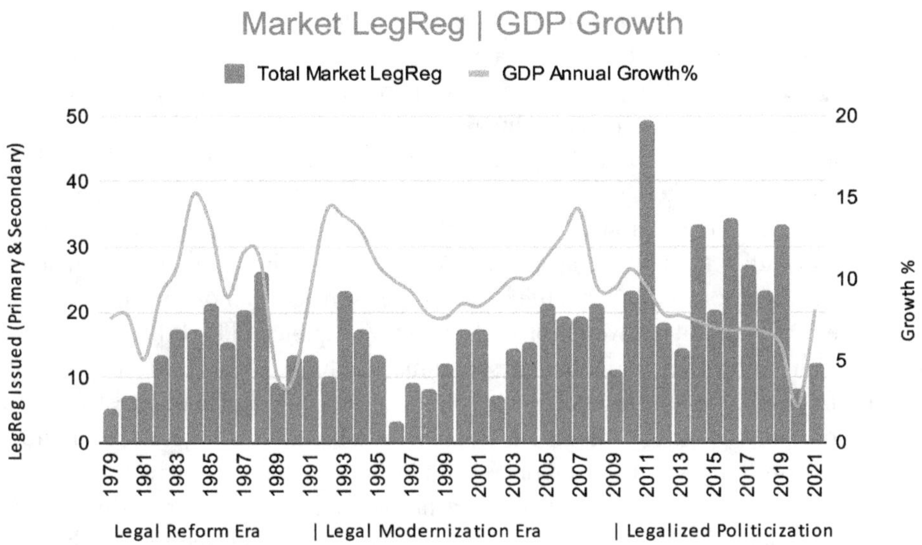

FIGURE 2.1 Market rulemaking activism vs. GDP growth

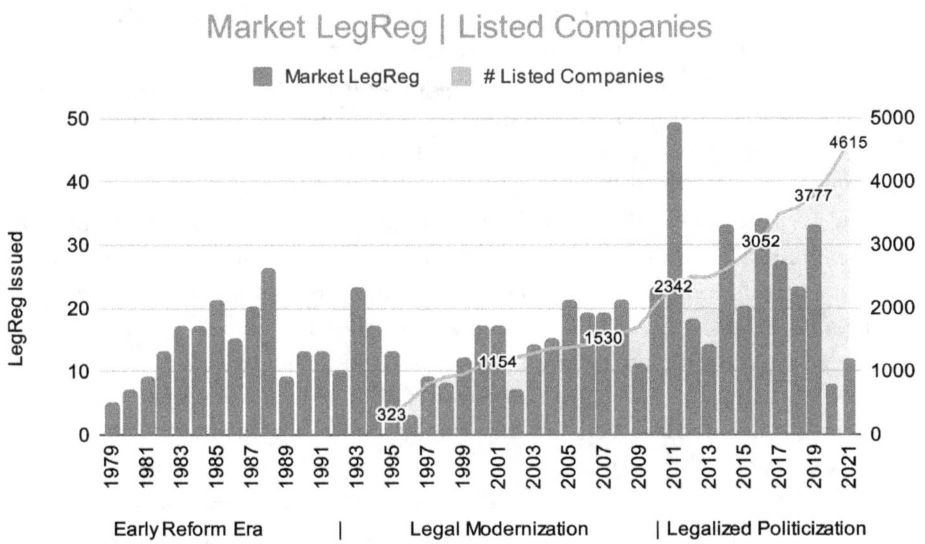

FIGURE 2.2 Market rulemaking activism vs. rise in public firms

levels of market-related rulemaking. The qualitative study of legal developments throughout the book provides possible explanation as it gives details on the legal framework that was established during periods of rulemaking activism throughout the eras, including significant laws that govern public firms. For example, the stock exchanges were opened formally in 1990 but the national company and securities laws were enacted in 1993 and 1998, respectively, and were revised at the end of 2005. The years between 2010 and 2012 and then 2015 saw activism in rulemaking that promoted public issuances through the mixed-ownership reform. The connection between the level of activism in market-related rulemaking and the peak in the number of listed firms for the more recent years, as seen in Figure 2.2, seems, however, more tenuous.

These figures cannot of course tell us much about the *nature* of relationship between law and market growth. They mostly validate that there is room for questions. After all, China's growth puzzle itself implies that the causation is missing. Numerous studies attest to the gap between black letter law in China and law in practice.[54] It has been established that the law, and the legal system more broadly, is weak from the vantage point of investor protections (see Chapter 7). This brings us back to the question: Why does the Party-state spend massive human resources and political capital (and real capital) to establish a voluminous number of sophisticated laws, regulations, and institutions to govern financial markets, if it can govern economic behavior by informal means and replace such institutions with various substitutions?

Since President Xi rose to power, there has been even a further push to "rule the country according to law" as well as to deepen economic reforms, including by more market-oriented regulatory activism. These legal advancements are quite intriguing given the broad consensus that legal rights, even economic ones, are not fully secured. Even more intriguing is the parallel move to institutionalize and legalize mechanisms of political governance.[55] Naturally, important questions arise: Why would an authoritarian single-party regime turn to a "law-based governance" (*yifa zhiguo*) given that it can easily subvert its own laws? Why resort to law? If formal law does not perform its economic functions, how can we explain its massive rise? What is the use of all this law in the market? Does the law advance the Party-state's plans for a "socialist market economy" in ways that its other governing mechanisms cannot? The coinciding trends of the use of law suggest that it is the form of law – not only its content – that generates adaptations of politics and practice.

Of course, a view that law is for appearance only does not conflict with, and perhaps is even bolstered by, the rise of formal law devices throughout China's market trajectory (i.e., law as a value-adding window dressing). But while the appearance of having modern regulated markets is certainly important for the Chinese Party-state, the analysis in this book suggests that the window-dressing explanation for the rising presence of law is too simplistic. Textual analysis of CCP policies, internal speeches, market laws and regulations, and their legislative histories indicates the use of a sophisticated, consistent rhetoric and sincere considerations for the development of the domestic market. The evidence does not fit well with a simplistic explanation for a rising legality in the market.

54 Examples include: K. Pistor & C. Xu, "Governing Stock Markets in Transition Economies: Lessons from China," *American Law and Economics Review* 7 (2005) 184; D. C. Clarke, "The Execution of Civil Judgments in China," *The China Quarterly* 141 (1995) 65.

55 J. DeLisle "The Rule of Law with Xi-Era Characteristics: Law for Economic Reform, Anti-Corruption, and Illiberal Politics," *Asia Policy* 20 (2015), 23; J. P. Horsley, "Party Leadership and Rule of Law in the Xi Jinping Era," Brookings Institution Publications: Global China Initiative (2019).

The data suggests that the increasing role of law in regulating the Chinese market should find explanation elsewhere. Perhaps the law offers something additional that justifies increasing its utilization with respect to markets. Is the law significant to market development in ways that are not contemplated by the traditional development and corporate governance thinking?

To examine these questions, this book unpacks China's development puzzle through an analysis of the political dynamics at play – a path seldom taken in the economic-law literature. In doing so, the book proposes a new theoretical framework through which to analyze the role of law in market development.

The framework involves looking at political–economic shifts and identifying how they impact the utility of law in governing markets. In turn, the analysis also illuminates how the law translates and secures political–economic changes, in an iterative process that shapes the incentives of political actors to support market economic activity.

In the process of collecting and analyzing the data for this book, the dual functionality of law was clearly revealed. This should not be surprising, as it is well accepted that the law in China is inextricably entwined with politics – the notion that the legal system is, in fact, a "political-legal system" (*zhengfa xitong*).[56] Thus far, this recognition has produced rich scholarship that gives deeper consideration to political components mostly in fields of public law.[57]

[56] S. Liu, "The Shape of Chinese Law," *Peking University Law Journal* 1(2) (2014) 415.

[57] Notable exceptions here are studies that examine the connection between law, politics, and economic results through analyzing informal relations, such as political connections, and their impact on granting and securing rights. This book, however, looks at a different angle of "politics" – mainly, institutional power dynamics.

For the studies, see X. Zhang, "The Role of Legal Institutions in Dealing with the Financial Crisis in China." In D. L. Yang (ed.), *The Global Recession and China's Political Economy* (Palgrave Macmillan, 2012); W. Zhang & J. Li, "Weak Law v. Strong Ties: An Empirical Study of Business Investment, Law and Political Connections in China," *Review of Law & Economics* 13(1) (2017), 1–45; W. Shen, "Risks of Chinese Shadow Banking and Choice of Regulatory Tools" [中国的影子银行风险及规制工具选择], *China Legal Science* 4 [中国法学4] (2014), 164–166.

The literature on law and politics connections in the public law sphere is quite voluminous. Few examples include W. P. Alford, "Of Lawyers Lost and Found: Searching for Legal Professionalism in the People's Republic of China." In W. P. Alford et al. (eds.), *Raising the Bar: The Emerging Legal Profession in East Asia* (Harvard University Press, 2007); H. Fu, "Autonomy, Courts, and the Politico-legal Order in Contemporary China." In L. Cao, I. Y. Sun & B. Hebenton (eds.), *The Routledge Handbook of Chinese Criminology* (Routledge, 2013), at 76–88; K. Hand, "Resolving Constitutional Disputes in Contemporary China," *East Asia Law Review* 7 (2012) 51; X. He, "Administrative Law as a Mechanism for Political Control in Contemporary China." In S. Balme & M. W. Dowdle (eds.), *Building Constitutionalism in China* (Palgrave Macmillan, 2009) 143; L. Li, "'Rule of Law' in a Party-state: A Conceptual Interpretive Framework of the Constitutional Reality of China," *Asian Journal of Law and Society* 2(1) (2015) 93; J. Li, "The Power Logic of Justice in China," *The American Journal of Comparative Law* 65(1) (2017) 95; Z. Liang (ed.), *Rule of Law in China: Institutions, Discourse, and Practice* [法治在中国：制度,话语与实践] (China University of Political Science and Law Press, 2002) [中国政法大学出版社, 2002]; R. Peerenboom, "What Have We Learned about Law and Development, Describing, Predicting, and Assessing Legal Reforms in China," *Michigan Journal of International Law* 27(3) (2006) 823; S. Zhu, "'Judicial Politics' as State-Building." In S. Balme & M. W. Dowdle (eds.), *Building Constitutionalism in China* (Palgrave Macmillan, 2009), 23.

The lesser attention to politics in China's economic law literature than in the areas of public law is perhaps to be expected. In the public law sphere, statist-Leninist influences are more pronounced, and scholars seem to agree that convergence is less likely, thus giving more room for discussions in the sociopolitical functions of law.[58] Moreover, the public law sphere is traditionally more prone to "antagonistic contradictions" (the Maoist notion of *duikangxing maodun*), where the potential for social and political frictions brings direct CCP intervention to the fore. The broad consensus in the public law sphere views Chinese politics as undermining the authority and independence of law and legal institutions, and as holding China back from getting closer to (a Western-style) rule of law.[59] While some scholars note mutually reinforcing aspects in the relation of law and politics (e.g., concerning regulatory pluralism in the environmental domain,[60] or concerning legal reforms more broadly).[61]

Issues regarded as within private law, however, and particularly private economic law (with the exception of state-owned enterprise [SOE] reform[62]) are focused on relationships between private parties and have been generally viewed as politically neutral, governed by what Fu Hualing refers to as a more "normal legal system, less politicized, (and) reform-oriented,"[63] where it was believed that the Party had shown more deference to the law and to state institutions.

The view that disconnects law from politics in the economic sphere has been bolstered by the global spread of ideas of liberal capitalism and the general appeal of Law and Economics theory, which direct laws around the world as politically detached, technocratic tools for increasing efficiencies and maximizing gains. Relatedly, the expectation for a future convergence with a Western-led rights-securing form of capitalism has been particularly widespread in writings about Chinese economic law.[64]

58 Liu, *Cage for the Birds*, note 20; Zhang & Ginsburg, "China's Turn toward Law," note 20.

59 B. Liebman, "A Return to Populist Legality? Historical Legacies and Legal Reform." In S. Heilmann & E. Perry (eds.), *Mao's Invisible Hand: The Political Foundations of Adaptive Governance in China* (Harvard University Press, 2011) 165; S. B. Lubman, *Bird in a Cage: Legal Reform in China after Mao* (Stanford University Press, 1999); C. Minzner, "Legal Reform in the Xi Jinping Era," *Asia Policy* 20 (2015) 4, at 4–9.

60 B. Van Rooij et al., "The Authoritarian Logic of Regulatory Pluralism: Understanding China's New Environmental Actors," *Regulation & Governance* 10(1) (2016) 3.

61 Zhang & Ginsburg, "China's Turn toward Law," note 20.

62 While SOE legal reforms can hardly be viewed part of private economic law, forms of mixed ownership complicates the distinction. For literature that highlights political determinants in relation to legal reforms in SOEs, see G. Wang, "The Political Function of Chinese State-Owned Enterprises: Problems, Challenges and Countermeasures" [中国国有企业的政治功能:问题,挑战与应对], *Review of Economic Research* 63 [经济研究参考63] (2012) 37, at 37–38; as well as J. Wang, "The Political Logic of Corporate Governance in China's State-Owned Enterprises," *Cornell International Law Journal* 47(3) (2014), 631.

63 H. Fu, "Duality and China's Struggle for Legal Autonomy," *China Perspectives* 1 (2019) 3.

64 C. Xi, "In Search of an Effective Monitoring Board Model: Board Reforms and the Political Economy of Corporate Law in China," *Connecticut Journal of International Law*, 22 (2006) 1, at 27; more generally, J. A. Cohen, "Was Helping China Build Its Post-1978 Legal System a Mistake?" *Virginia Journal of International Law Online*, 61 (June 2020) 1–30.

Thus, the normative economic functions of law, that is, the law's rights-securing functionalities that bring economic gains, have been the focus of discussion for the past decades,[65] while the *political functions* of economic law and their relation to development received scant attention.

As the political–economic fabric in China evolves and opens up for frictions, the neutrality presumption about economic laws requires closer scrutiny. The Party's direct return to the market over the past decade, constructed through and by the law, should leave no doubt that politics, law, and economic development are deeply intertwined under the CCP's rule. The challenge is to understand exactly how they interact, and through that to open a door for a continuous reevaluation of the functions and various contributions of law to China's market development. This book, through the analytical framework suggested here, hopes to open that door.

NOTES ON METHODOLOGY

This book draws mostly on qualitative textual legal analysis and time-series data visualizations of an extensive body of governance documents pertaining to market reforms that were issued throughout China's development trajectory (see "Classification of China's Development Trajectory" in Part II).

The term "law," as used throughout the book and unless stated otherwise, is treated broadly and encompasses both formal law and legal institutions. When black letter law is addressed, it includes formal norms issued by an authorized central level body, thus including legislation and regulation as detailed below.

The term "legal institutions" does not refer only to the organizations comprising the legal system (the People's Courts, the People's Procuratorate, the China lawyers association, etc.). Rather, it is used here more broadly to refer to social constraints that have been enshrined through the constitutive power of positive law. These include state laws and regulations, the regulatory capacity of political organizations, economic rights and their legal constructs (e.g., ownership and property rights), and legal forms of enterprise organization (e.g., companies). To clarify, a "firm" would not be considered a legal institution (rather, it is an organization), but its legal constructs – that is, legal personality, shares, the corporate form, etc. – would.

[65] M. Faure & G. Xu, *Economics and Regulation in China* (Routledge, 2014); W. Zhang, *The Rules of Capital* [资本的规则] (China Legal Publishing House, 2017).

In fact, the sheer portion of studies about Chinese corporate governance, including most of the ones I cite in Part III, follows a law and economics approach or is at least motivated by law and economics assumptions. Notable exceptions are discussed therein too.

1 *Dataset*

Formal Laws

The legal dataset was collected from Chinese language legal databases, namely PKUlaw.com (*Beida Fabao*) also known as "lawinfoChina," as well as "China Law & Reference." I examined documents that were issued by organs of the central Party-state only. I looked at PRC constitutional revisions throughout the period for their market-related aspects. I followed Keller's taxonomy,[66] with some expansions, when collecting the body of primary national laws (*falü*) by the NPC; secondary administrative regulations by the State Council (*xingzheng fagui*) including additional regulatory documents that are commonly treated as secondary regulations, that is, regulations, provisions, decisions, measures, implementation rules, and guiding opinions (*guiding, tiaoli, jueding, banfa, shishi xize, and zhidao yijian*, respectively); as well as tertiary administrative regulations, meaning departmental rules (*bumen guizhang*) issued by relevant organizations under the State Council, that is, national-level ministries and commissions, including their notices (*tongzhi*) and joint notices (*lianhe tongzhi*). To clarify, while opinions and guiding opinions (*zhidao yijian*) are not a source of authoritative formal law under the PRC Legislation Law, they are normative documents with a binding regulatory effect in practice and thus were included in my data and analyzed accordingly.[67] The entire data collected and analyzed included both effective and expired norms, as well as their interim provisional form.

Policy

The inspected dataset includes all PRC National Economic and Social Development Plans (China's "five-year plans") issued since reform and opening began; CCP Charter revisions; publicly available Communiques of the CCP Central Committee Plenary Sessions, Central Committee decisions, circulars, opinions, and joint guiding opinions collected from various formal websites of the CCP as well as from PKUlaw.com. These were complemented by media coverage about CCP interactions and speeches to the business community, including news and reports by designated CCP media outlets (primarily the CCP's Journal *Qiushi* and *People's Daily*).

Additional Sources

In constructing the theoretical framework in Part II, beyond analyzing the data, I additionally drew on secondary sources and particularly the works of political scientists

66 P. Keller, "Sources of Order in Chinese Law," *The American Journal of Comparative Law* 42(4) (1994) 711, at 724–729.

67 Jurisprudence discussions in China generally treat decisions and opinions by the State Council to have the same binding effect as administrative regulations. See J. Huang, "The Legal Definition and Effect of 'Normative Documents'"["规范性文件"的法律界定及其效力"], *Legal Studies* 7 [法学 7] (2014), available at Research Center for Constitutional and Administrative Law of Renmin University of China, https://archive.ph/tb4fo.

whose studies identify political power shifts within China's Party-state organization. These cover mostly the Early Development Era and the Legal Modernization Era. For the Legalized Politicization Era, at the time of writing this book, studies documenting political power shifts are scarce. I thus relied solely on textual legal analysis and market observations for identifying political power shifts during that era. In Part III, where the analytical framework is applied to observe changes with respect to corporate reforms and the capital market specifically, I complemented the textual analysis with occasional case observations based on public firms' disclosures (drawn from the SSE and SZSE disclosure platforms and from cninfo.com.cn), and media reports. Also in Part III, where I discussed the CCP's disciplinary functions in SOEs, beyond formal laws and policy, I relied on disciplinary enforcement cases that I collected from the online roster of the Central Commission for Disciplinary Inspection, and media reports.

Details about the data selection process are included in the Appendix. As can be seen from the Appendix, the dataset used for this book significantly expands the body of policy and laws surveyed in prior studies that were similarly interested in understanding the role of law in China's market development.[68]

2 *Analysis*

Data collection and time-series visualization methods were employed to identify shifts in the utilization of market-governance authorities and thereby establish the working hypothesis of the book – that there have been political–economic shifts across China's reform eras, and that such shifts can be observed through regulatory powers.

Next, textual analysis method was used to observe trends in the mobilization of law toward political and economic reforms in the following manner: In Part II, through textual analysis of the legal and political datasets, I observe how political-economy dynamics throughout China's market trajectory are communicated and translated into law. With parallel, I also track how changes in law are in turn designed to secure the power shifts intended by the polity. In Part III, I apply the macrolevel framework at the microlevel. I delve deep into the evolution of the public firm and into China's corporate governance to see whether and how the analytical framework fits. Additionally, I look to media reports, firms' disclosures, and secondary material to assess how market participants (both political and economic) responded to the legal institutions that have taken form following each political–economic shift.

In applying the above methodologies, examining the legal configurations of political power flows, the following observations became apparent:

(1) The Party-state uses the law as a medium through which internal power hierarchies are allocated, maintained, and contained. Put differently, the law

[68] Mainly the article by Clarke et al., which inspired this part of the book. D. C. Clarke, P. Murrell, & S. Whiting, "The Role of Law in China's Economic Development." In T. Brandt & L. Rawski (eds.), *China's Great Economic Transformation* (Cambridge University Press, 2008) 375.

functions as a mediating institution that translates and gives shape to the relations between politics and economics.

(2) These law and politics relations have implications on the ground. By facilitating political–economic regularity, the law pushes growth forward within the framework of a socialist market economy. This has meaningful effects on market participants, at times impeding, yet at times supporting economic activity, development, and growth.

Together, the macro and microlevels of analysis support the grand proposition of the book – an analytical narrative that puts the dynamics of law and political economy at the center of China's growth puzzle is sorely needed.

GOALS AND CAVEATS

Since this book is interdisciplinary at its core and draws upon a variety of literatures (law and development, corporate governance, China's political economy, development economics), it is important to clarify not only what this book *is* but also what *it is not*.

First, this book does not purport to solve China's growth puzzle. Rather, it highlights overall trends in the political mobilization of law, which impact market growth. Accordingly, the book explicates China's growth puzzle and builds upon it to better understand the evolving role of law in China's market development. One of the book's primary objectives is to illuminate how the law, political economy, and market development intertwine. Readers, therefore, should not expect to find a clear identification of China's recipe for growth. Relatedly, it is impossible to isolate law from politics, as this book argues by illuminating the dual functions of law in the market, and thus impossible to draw causal inferences about the contribution of each to China's market growth.

This also means that one should not take this book to endorse an alternative role for law in the development process. Rather, the complexity of intertwining components presented here, and the prominence of China's idiosyncratic political organization, suggest that China's growth model is not transferable to other systems around the world, whatever that "model" entails. (To clarify, nontransferability does not equate lack of influence.)

Second, it is important to clarify that the book does not provide an all-inclusive account of law and political economy in China. As explained above, the book relies on the vast body of official pronouncements and promulgations to draw on the relations between *formal* law (broadly defined) and political–economic change. Equally important for China's political economy and the space reserved for the law in the market are the intricate relations between private sector participants and the Party-state that often take a nonformal form. Informal modes of exchange between market participants continued throughout the reform alongside the developing formal legal system. This was in part a necessity (given the weaknesses of the formal system) and in part a conscious element of China's reform strategy (experiment first, law after[69]). Informal mechanisms have a considerable role in governing the Chinese market to this day. Their persistence has bearings on the status and efficacy of legal institutions. Such relations are considered through secondary materials, mainly in Part III, but are not at the book's core.

Third, the book does not analyze trends in enforcement, nor does it evaluate the quality of enforcing institutions. This is not a mistake in the research design. Private litigation and enforcement are certainly pivotal elements when assessing the efficacy of legal institutions. They are, however, not the only important factors. Indeed, this book calls for a reevaluation of the role of positive law in development. It thus offers only a limited discussion in the enforcement of rights, relying on secondary material, when discussing the efficacy of traditional corporate governance institutions (Part III, Chapter 7).

Finally, reliance mostly on formal pronouncements and promulgations raises another, more obvious, challenge – the existence of internal Party norms, unwritten conventions, and informal policies as confounding factors. This is an important point and a challenge for every China scholar, and perhaps particularly for legal sinologists as they wish to evaluate how the formal system of governance functions. Indeed, this book cannot possibly cover all junctions of political relations with formal law. From an empirical vantage point, this raises a concern that the data cannot reflect the full scope of integration of politics and law. The approach taken here is a realist and modest one, one which seeks to illuminate one path in which law and politics intertwine and mutually impact China's development process, a path that previous works tended to overlook, particularly with respect to economic law and financial markets.

69 S. Heilmann, "Policy Experimentation in China's Economic Rise," *Studies in Comparative International Development* 43(1) (2008) 1.

PART II

China's Development Trajectory and the Role(s) of Law

To unpack the dynamics between politics and law in China's market reforms, it is valuable to start with understanding the process involved in constructing and implementing China's socio-economic development plan, known as the Five-Year Plan(s).[1] Clarifying this process will help us better understand the intricate interplay of law and politics in constructing the blueprint for economic reform. This will be useful as we delve into the different eras of China's development trajectory in the following chapters of Part II.

THE MAKING OF A FIVE-YEAR PLAN

The allocation of authorities within the Party-state system concerning the economy was established in the early years of China's reform and opening.[2] The Chinese government – the State Council (under the Premier) and its agencies – are delegated the authority to design and execute economic policy, while the National People's Congress oversees the state council. The Chinese Communist Party (CCP) maintained macro-level control. One of the main tools that ensures macroeconomic control is the five-year plan.

1 In different periods, some elements of the process may have been different. The description below depicts the current state of affairs.

2 "On The Reform of the System of Party and State Leadership" [党和国家领导制度的改革], Deng Xiaoping (Aug. 18, 1980), *Selected Works of Deng Xiaoping* [邓小平文选] Vol. 2, at 322–342.

China's socio-economic development scheme is revisited every five years by the Central Committee of the CCP.[3] In this process, the progress achieved under the current ongoing five-year period is studied continuously, while a new policy blueprint for the subsequent period is being drafted. Media reports indicate that the drafting process from start to finish takes about three years. The review and drafting process is overseen by the top echelon of China's political leaders – the members of the Politburo and the Politburo Standing Committee[4] – through discussion and consultation meetings of relevant leading small groups (*zhongyang lingdao xiaozu*).[5] In recent years, aspects related to socio-economic development and reform have been coordinated by two main groups: the Central Finance and Economic Affairs Commission and the Central Commission for Comprehensively Deepening Reforms. Both were leading small groups that have been recently elevated to Party commissions and are headed by the CCP General Secretary, Xi Jinping.

The commissions receive reports and suggestions from various Party organs and state departments, prominent among them are the State Administration for Market Supervision (SAMR, which was recently established) and the National Development and Reform Commission (NDRC, discussed below), and work to consolidate and recommend development guidelines. Often, the process involves soliciting opinions from additional government agencies, various interest groups, grassroots organizations, entrepreneurs, and academics.[6] The results and draft guidelines are presented to the Central Committee plenum by the senior politician who is the second in command in the Politburo Standing Committee (and is also the state Premier), the "no. 2 hand" in the Party-state political hierarchy. The Central Committee seats are occupied by senior party members, most of whom hold parallel senior official roles in the government (such as provincial governors, ministers, military generals, and leaders

3 The CCP's Central Committee is the locus of political power in China and constitutes the Party's highest organ of authority. It has around 370 full and alternating members, who are nominally elected by the National Congress of the CCP (CCP National Congress) for a five-year term. The Central Committee convenes annually and functions in the interim through its standing committee.

4 At the apex of the Central Committee sits the Politburo (the twenty-five leading officials of the CCP) and its Standing Committee members the top leadership of the CCP (five to eleven members, historically). Currently, the CCP Politburo Standing Committee seats seven members.

5 "Leading Small Groups" [中央领导小组] (*Zhongyang lingdao xiaozu*) are CCP organs that operate as an interagency executive committee in major functional areas to increase political coordination between the relevant party, state, and military institutions, in several areas of responsibility. Not much is known about the exact operation of the leading small groups. They are regarded as an important feature of the CCP's decision-making apparatus, providing regular consultations in junctions of overlapping areas and authorities, thus supporting the Party Politburo member who is assigned to the specific functional area. S. Heilmann and L. Shih, "Central Leading Small Groups: Top-Level Decision Making under Xi Jinping." In S. Heilmann (ed.), *China's Political System* (Rowman & Littlefield, 2016), at 169–172.

6 See, for example, Xinhua News report, noting the collection and sorting of over 1 million comments in the process of drafting the fourteenth five-year plan (2021–25), which is the one in force currently: "China Focus – A Glance at Drafting Process of CPC Proposals for China's New Development Plan," XinHuaNet (Nov. 5, 2020), https://archive.ph/kMVqe.

of major state-owned enterprises). The plenum of the Central Committee is convened and chaired by the Party Secretary. The plenum discusses the results and the draft guidelines and eventually approves a draft of national economic and social development guidelines for the next five-year period. The approval of the draft is normally passed during the Fifth Plenum of an incumbent CCP Central Committee.[7] This normally happens two years before the turnover of leadership to a new CCP Central Committee composition. An incumbent CCP Central Committee thus prepares the socio-economic blueprint for the succeeding leadership to follow.

After the draft has been consolidated and approved at the Party level, it is presented by the Premier and stands for review and approval at the state level by the National People's Congress (NPC), China's national legislature and formally the highest organ of state power. There, a designated committee (in recent years, the Financial and Economic Committee of the NPC) reviews the draft guidelines. At this stage, some adjustments of the plan might be suggested. When the NPC convenes its annual meeting, the review results are presented, and the draft guidelines for a national economic and social development scheme are approved by the legislature.[8] Once passed, a formal resolution is publicized, thereby promulgating China's new "five-year planning outline," better known as China's "five-year plan."[9] The plan reflects the socio-economic development priorities to be followed at all levels of the state bureaucracy for the coming five years.

As will be shown in the chapters of Part II, the process at times results in a constitutional amendment, designed to reflect socio-economic adjustments to changes in China's development conditions and aspirations.[10] The constitutional provisions are of limited practical effect as China's constitution is not justiciable in and of itself. Therefore, a series of national level laws and regulations will often follow to translate the constitutional principles onto justiciable laws. Such national laws function to enshrine, refine, or overhaul earlier normative documents that had been issued on an interim basis before the socio-economic conditions for a unified national law "were ripe."

7 Some exceptions exist, usually when more than one meeting is held annually, such as during the 13th CCP Central Committee, which adopted the draft in its Seventh plenum (December 1990), as well as during the 12th CCP Central Committee, which adopted the draft in its Fourth plenum (September 1985).

8 Constitution of the People's Republic of China [中华人民共和国宪法], adopted by the Fifth Nat'l People's Cong. and promulgated on December 4, 1982 [The 1982 PRC Constitution, or the PRC Constitution]. The 1982 PRC Constitution, as amended, is the one still in force today. It had replaced the 1954 constitutions of the revolutionary era and the short-lived 1978 constitution. See ibid., art. 62(10).

9 See, for example, The Resolution of the Fourth Session of the 13th National People's Congress, on the 14th Five-Year Plan for National Economic and Social Development and an Outline Vision for 2035, adopted by the Nat'l People's Cong., Mar. 11, 2021 [第十三届全国人民代表大会第四次会议关于国民经济和社会发展第十四个五年规划和2035年远景目标纲要的决议], https://archive.ph/auM6V.

10 J. Chen, "The Revision of the Constitution in the PRC: A Great Leap Forward or a Symbolic Gesture?, *China Perspectives* 53 (2004).

In turn, at the local level, Local People's Congresses review and approve the economic and social development reports and their budgets and future development plans prepared by their respective Local People's Governments.[11] The NPC's supervision over the actions of government units is thus ensured through both horizontal and vertical authority lines.[12]

One of the most significant national government bodies involved in constructing and executing the five-year plan is the NDRC – a ministry-level department of the State Council (the central government) that oversees the consolidation and implementation of the five-year plan across the state apparatus.[13] The NDRC submits its annual work reports to the NPC for approval, yet its mission is defined on its formal website as "to implement the CCP's Central Committee policies and decisions on development and reform," and "to strengthen the party's centralized and unified leadership over development and reform."

Since the different organs and agencies of the government and the Party start their preparations to implement the plan before the guidelines are approved and without awaiting formal promulgation,[14] the NPC is often perceived in this process as a rubber stamp. Indeed, much has been written about the formalistic functions of the NPC.[15] The Party exercises supreme power over state institutions in many ways, and the NPC is no exception. The CCP nominates all the candidates of leading state official positions and decides on their future career trajectory. The chairman of the NPC Standing Committee concurrently serves on the CCP Politburo Standing Committee. Similarly, the great majority of NPC members are also party members (73 percent, at the time of writing). Moreover, the CCP also exercises its powers over the entire state apparatus, including the NPC, through its control of various Party organizations embedded within state institutions. At the top organs, the leading members of such Party organizations often concurrently hold leading official roles in other state institutions. The supremacy of the CCP over state bodies, including the NPC is indisputable. The constitution of the PRC is a formal testament to that fact.[16] Finally, the number 2 hand in the politburo is the Premier, not the chairman of the

[11] The 1982 PRC Constitution, art. 99.

[12] The 1982 PRC Constitution, arts. 100, 104, 107, 110.

[13] People's Republic of China, National Development and Reform Commission website "Main Functions of the NDRC," https://archive.ph/nrV7e. The NDRC was established in 2003 when the authorities of two separate state agencies – the State Planning Commission and the State Development Planning Commission – were merged under one ministry-level department.

[14] For example, the draft of the current five-year plan has been approved by the CCP Central Committee at its annual meeting, the Fifth Plenum in October 2020, then ratified by the NPC in its annual meeting in March 2021. The draft has been circulated and studied by party and state institutions in the interim.

[15] Reviewed in S. Jiang, "Written and Unwritten Constitutions: A New Approach to the Study of Constitutional Government in China," *Modern China* 36.1 (2010) 12, at 23–25.

[16] Amendment to the Constitution of the People's Republic of China [中华人民共和国宪法修正案 (2018)], promulgated by Announcement No.1 of the Thirteenth Nat'l People's Cong., Mar. 11, 2018, see preamble, arts. 1 & 5.

NPC, which means that the government's top executive holds the higher political authority. This indicates that the authority of the national legislative body is politically constrained even with respect to the executive government (State Council).

And yet, considering the entire process of designing, executing, and overseeing the five-year plan, the picture seems much more collaborative and mutually reinforcing than just robber stamping the CCP's decisions. The process described above combines contributions from all layers of the Party-state apparatus – the Party, the government, the national legislature, local People's Congresses, and certain interest groups in the society.[17] Jiang Shigong, a preeminent political theorist, has presented the view held by many conservative constitutional scholars in China that China's political sovereignty and the core of its constitutional regime are established on a model of interactive contributions and connections between the Party and the state.[18]

In a recent plenary meeting preparing the draft government work report for the fifth session of the 13th National People's Congress, Li Keqiang, the state Premier stated:

> [A]s an important constitutional duty, the State Council reports to the National People's Congress and accepts the people's supervision. It is important to draft a good government work report, listen to the views of the people and adopt good advice, and respond in a targeted manner to the concerns of the masses, market entities and society at large. These [actions] are conducive to building consensus, facilitating new ideas and practical measures, boosting confidence and further driving this year's government work.

It was reported that the Government Work Report (Consultation Draft) was also sent to all provinces, autonomous regions, municipalities directly under the Central Government, and relevant departments and work units of the central state organs for comments.[19]

The five-year plan is thus a high-level blueprint reflecting the leadership's priorities for the coming five-year period, but it is constructed and implemented in an iterative and collaborative process. State institutions, at the central and local levels, take regulatory and administrative action to translate the national five-year plan into

17 C. Young Nam. "From "Rubber Stamps" to "Iron Stamps": The Emergence of Chinese Local People's Congresses as Supervisory Powerhouses." *The China Quarterly* 171 (2002): 724–740 (arguing that Chinese legislators no longer function as mere rubber stamp, based on the conduct and influence of provincial-level local people's congresses).

18 Jiang, *Written and Unwritten Constitutions*, note 15, at 24:

> 'People's sovereignty' in China has its own two bodies, the CCP and the NPC. The former embodies the fundamental law that acts as the absolute constitution; the latter embodies the fundamental law codified in the written constitution.

In this model, the political importance of the NPC lies in that, through the constitution and the law, it "gradually transforms the Party from a 'revolutionary Party' to a 'ruling Party' and then to a 'constitutional Party'."

19 "Li Keqiang presided over a plenary meeting of the State Council to discuss the 'Government Work Report (Draft for Comment)' Han Zheng and others attended" [李克强主持召开国务院全体会议讨论《政府工作报告（征求意见稿）》韩正等出席] Xinhuanet (Jan. 20, 2022), https://archive.ph/bEar9.

action, each within its own vertical or horizontal authority lines. While it is the responsibility of central and local level institutions to design detailed plans within their respective fields, to craft the tools needed for implementation, and to oversee and assess progress year to year, the ultimate oversight authority for the execution of China's economic and social plan and approval of the national budget to carry the plan through lies formally with the NPC.[20] Work reports and the annual work plans of the government are presented and approved by the NPC annually. The NDRC functions as the main institutional bridge with respect to China's socio-economic development trajectory, connecting the CCP with the NPC, government organs, and the market. The governance powers exercised in the making of the five-year plan are thus both highly consolidated and at the same time decentralized.[21]

CLASSIFICATION OF CHINA'S DEVELOPMENT TRAJECTORY

The following chapters of Part II will analyze China's market reform process chronologically, examining mutual interactions between law and politics.

To put China's development trajectory into its chronological context, it is valuable to first identify its stages before diving deep into the legal configurations of each stage.

This book divides China's development trajectory into the following three primary stages.

The first and early stage of economic transition – the Early Reform Era (Dec. 1978–91).[22] The era began in December 1978 with the Third Plenum of the Eleventh Central Committee of the CCP, which set the stage for "Reform and Opening" as the economic agenda of the time.[23] The focus of this early transition stage was on experimenting with various methods of economic activity that would boost productivity levels in the state sector as well as attracting foreign direct investments to China's budding market. This era is widely researched by political scientists, economists, and legal scholars and is known as an era in which law played a relatively marginal role.

The second stage of economic transition, which this book refers to as the Legal Modernization Era (ca. 1992–2009), begins with the 14th Party Congress in which the CCP proclaimed its new goal to establish a "Socialist Market Economy."[24] This

[20] The 1982 PRC Constitution, art. 62(10).

[21] A contemporary expression of China's "Democratic Centralism".

[22] Political economist Barry Naughton termed the period "Growing Out of the Plan" representing the period in which China gradually stepped out of the planned economy, allowing "above plan production," while avoiding a grand political struggle. See B. Naughton, *Growing out of the Plan: Chinese Economic Reform*, 1978–1993 (Cambridge University Press, 1995).

[23] See Communiqué of the Third Plenary Session of the 11th Central Committee of the Communist Party of China [中国共产党第十一届中央委员会第三次全体会议公报], adopted and promulgated by the Third Plenary Session of the 11th Cong. of the Communist Party of China, Dec. 22, 1978.

[24] The Congress was held in October 1992; the economic-focused plenum was held a year later. See Decisions on Issues Concerning the Establishment of a Socialist Market Economy [中国共产党第十四届中央委员会第三次全体会议公报], promulgated by the Third Plenary Session of the 14th Central Comm. of the Communist Party of China, Nov. 14, 1993 [the 14th Party Congress Decisions].

era saw a robust enactment of economic laws and the building of central–state institutional capacities, which resulted in a market constructed around state capitalism. Much of China legal studies scholarship focuses on this era.

Finally, the third and current stage in China's economic transition (2010–present), in which the Party-state has advanced a "Mixed Ownership Economy," focuses on social stabilization while also calling for markets to play a more "decisive role" in the economy (even specifically addressing the financial markets). As readers will find in the book, this is also the stage during which certain market mechanisms actually seem to have been curtailed. The Party advances ever more directly and overtly into the market, with the aid, and under the guise of law. The book will refer to this still unfolding stage as the "Legalized Politicization Era."

The classification of the first and second eras initially relied on secondary studies, mainly from political science and development economics, that have identified political–economic power shifts within China's governing apparatus. The recognition of such shifts gains further support through the legal analysis offered in the book. Given that studies of the third (and current) reform era are still limited, the political economic contours of the era have been identified and delineated based on legal analysis alone. The data collection and textual analysis at the core of this book thus also serve to corroborate existing studies about China in development economics and political science literature through legal findings, confirming how political–economic shifts have been enshrined in law (see Methodology section in the Appendix).

Finally, a word of caution lest anyone is misled by this classification of transitioning stages: China is often referred to as a transitional economy but the fact that its economic trajectory goes through various stages of transition does not make it so. A "transitional economy" implies a process toward an end goal that is most commonly identified with ownership privatization and a liberal market economy. Some economists have perhaps optimistically viewed China's development trajectory as representing a "gradual privatization," as if an end result of complete privatization is inevitable.[25] Most China observers, however, agree that full privatization is not and never was the end goal of the Chinese Party-state under any CCP-led regime. Establishing a private market economy was far from the Party-state's goals, as has been quite clearly expressed in CCP proclamations, policies, and laws stating an aspiration to establish a "socialist market economy." While over several decades, there has been some reduction in the state's direct equity holdings in PRC firms, coupled with varying spurts of growth in small to medium enterprises often called "private," these reductions in formal equity shares do not amount to even a gradual reduction

[25] G. Roland, "Political Economy Issues of Ownership Transformation in Eastern Europe." In M. Aoki & H. K. Kim (eds.), *Corporate Governance in Transitional Economies* (The World Bank, 1995) 37, at 47–49.

in overarching control over the Party-state-operated assets, capital, people, and institutions.

Accordingly, the term "economic transition" in this book refers only to the gradual nature of constructing the institutions, laws, and policies discussed; it does not imply any traditional assumptions about the end goals of the reform. The transitional nature of reform in China has been paving a way for the establishment of a "socialist market economy with Chinese characteristics."

3

Early Reform Era (December 1978–1991)

The post-Mao development era was formally initiated with the Third Plenary Session of the 11th Central Committee of the Chinese Communist Party, held in December 1978. The plenary session (also known as a Central Committee Plenum) announced the era of "reform and opening" that marked a comprehensive shift in China's economic thinking toward modern reforms and opening. Development economists have viewed the period as initiating a shift from "plan to market," through which the PRC gradually and incrementally "grew out of the plan" (i.e., out of the planned economy).[26] The reforms materialized despite continuous ideological controversies within the CCP on the direction and breadth of economic opening. This was done thanks to Deng Xiaoping and other reformers' success in enlisting the support of local governments and establishing an ideological legitimation for the reforms. "Socialism with Chinese characteristics" became the new term of the era. It stretched the acceptable ideological contours of socialism, introducing a blurry rationalization for expanding markets within socialism.[27]

The reform was not only a change in economic thinking. Mao's era had left the country impoverished and its bureaucracy shattered. To facilitate economic development, the state bureaucracy had to be modernized, and institutions had to be rebuilt anew. This was an opportunity to rethink the relationship between the Party and the state and begin larger reforms of China's governance system.[28] The role of law and of legal institutions evolved accordingly.

—

[26] Naughton, *Growing out of the Plan*, note 22.

[27] The first use of the term is attributed to Deng Xiaoping in June 1984, and it was later enshrined in the CCP and PRC constitutions. See E. Vogel, *Deng Xiaoping and the Transformation of China*, Vol. 10. (Belknap Press of Harvard University Press, 2011), at 465.

[28] K. E. Brødsgaard, "Institutional Reform and the Bianzhi System in China," *The China Quarterly* 170 (2002) 361.

ERA OVERVIEW: THE TWO FUNCTIONS OF LAW ARE UNVEILED

One of the most meaningful aspects of economic reforms in China, which ultimately changed not only the Chinese economy but also its governance, was the devolution of administrative and economic powers from the central government to the localities. As is well documented by China-focused economists and political scientists, the decentralization of economic authority during the early reform years instigated China's economic growth, while providing necessary political impetus for market reforms. Through fiscal contracting between the central government and provincial governments, the leadership was able to push economic reforms while preventing political upheaval. Political scientist Susan Shirk highlights fiscal decentralization as "the cornerstone of the CCP leaders' political strategy to build support for economic reform."[29]

Fiscal contracting expanded the economic autonomy and responsibility of local governments. It introduced varying revenue-sharing arrangements tailored to each province (percentages of revenue remitted to the center) and shifted spending responsibility along with greater autonomy over expenditures to the provinces. Experimentation with this scheme started in 1977, even prior to the formal initiation of "reform and opening." It was expanded as a national trial plan and adopted by several State Council notices in the early 1980s.[30]

A major element of economic decentralization was the gradual delegation of meaningful governance powers over the means of production to local governments. During the Early Reform Era, economic activity was conducted predominantly by state-owned enterprises (SOEs), and increasingly by local collective enterprises (a new form of ownership that was later referred to as Township and Village Enterprises [TVEs]).[31] China's economic system thus became largely dependent

[29] S. L. Shirk, *The Political Logic of Economic Reform in China* (University of California Press [California Series on Social Choice and Political Economy], 1993), at 149.

[30] "State Council Notice on Carrying Out the Financial Management System of Apportioning Revenues and Expenditures while Contracting Responsibility According to Levels," 1981, cited in Shirk, *The Political Logic of Economic Reform*, note 29, at 165.

[31] The similarly termed *collectives* of Mao's era were organized around China's *danwei* ("working units") and were subject to direct administrative control of local governments and party committees. Their members did not enjoy any ownership rights. The reform era collectives were gradually released from their local working units. While TVEs presented various types of ownership and governance rights, they were "collectively owned" and thus formally considered part of China's public sector even while many operated in practice as private enterprises. Their members enjoyed "use rights" which gave them real interests in the profits and assets of the enterprise. Some members enjoyed participation in management, even though the enterprise was often sponsored and informally directed by local officials. See H. Chao & X. Yang, "Private Enterprise in China: The Developing Law of Collective Enterprises," *International Lawyer* 19(4) (1986) 1215, at 1219; C. P. W. Wong, "Interpreting Rural Industrial Growth in the Post-Mao Period," *Modern China* 14(1) (1988) 3; Y. Huang, *Capitalism with Chinese Characteristics: Entrepreneurship and the State* (Cambridge University Press, 2008); and M. E. Rithmire, *Land Bargains and Chinese Capitalism: The Politics of Property Rights under Reform* (Cambridge University Press, 2015).

on whoever held governance authority over SOEs and TVEs that operated the country's main means of production.

In connection with their revenue sharing arrangements, local governments were delegated rights over a great number of state assets. For most provinces, sharing revenue arrangements calculated the profits of local SOEs as part of local revenue. Apart from several industries whose management, profits, and taxes were kept solely under the central government as national enterprises, the profits and taxes from local SOEs were shared. It is estimated that by 1985, SOEs controlled by the central government accounted for only 20 percent of total industrial output (of all enterprises at or above the township level).[32]

In this environment, local governments had to rely more on their own revenues and less on centrally allocated resources. They became dependent on local enterprises and foreign investments for revenue. A dual-track pricing mechanism emerged between the enterprises and local governments to encourage further production. Under dual-track pricing, enterprises were permitted to sell excess products beyond the state's planned quota at newly emerging market prices, remit part of the profits to the local government, and retain the rest. Fiscal contracting and the dual-track pricing mechanism thus incentivized local governments to develop innovative schemes to promote local industries and push for greater productivity in their regions.[33] As described by Lieberthal, the "decentralization of budgetary authority enabled many locales and bureaucratic units to acquire funds outside of those allocated through the central budget, which they could use to pursue their own policy preferences."[34]

The decentralization scheme was promoted through State Council notices and designated contracting with local governments, outside the nascent formal legal system. Yet, interestingly, as it built momentum, the new political–economic equilibrium found its way into the Party and the state constitutions and from there to lower-level legal norms.

Toward the end of the term of the 11th Party Congress, the leadership pushed forward an amendment to the Party Charter (sometimes referred to as the CCP Constitution).[35] Among other issues, the amendment addressed the allocation of

[32] S. Li & P. Lian, "Decentralization and Coordination: China's Credible Commitment to Preserve the Market under Authoritarianism," *China Economic Review* 10(2) (1999) 161, at 176–178.

[33] One such scheme was the experimentation with different forms of collaborative investment projects with foreign investors. Another was the "management contract responsibility" system, which incentivized managers to increase production. These schemes are discussed in Chapter 6 under the "Rise of the Large (Public) Firm."

[34] K. G. Lieberthal, "Introduction: The 'Fragmented Authoritarianism Model' and Its Limitations." In K. G. Lieberthal & D. M. Lampton (eds.), *Bureaucracy, Politics, and Decision Making in Post-Mao China*, Vol. 8 (University of California Press, 2018), at 8.

[35] Charter of the Communist Party of China [中国共产党章程], proposed by the 11th Central Comm. and adopted by the Resolution of the 12th Nat'l Cong. of the Communist Party of China on September 6, 1982 [The CCP Charter, or the Party Charter].

authorities within Party hierarchies. The Charter established the local-level Party cadres' responsibility to balance dependence and autonomy as one of the principles of the long-held communist notion of "Democratic Centralism."[36] The Charter now determined the responsibility of low-level party organizations to "not only ask for instructions from higher-level organizations but also independently act to solve problems that arise within their own jurisdictional responsibilities."[37]

The revised CCP Charter was quickly followed by the enactment of the 1982 Constitution of the PRC by the National People's Congress.[38] In detailing the principles of democratic centralism, the PRC Constitution stated explicitly: "The division of functions and powers between the central and local state agencies follows the principle of giving full play to the initiative and enthusiasm of the local governments under the unified leadership of the central government."[39]

The new political–economic equilibrium was thus enshrined as a constitutional principle, to be pursued by both the Party and the state.

In addition, both constitutional documents clarified that the basis and focus of China's economic system in the reform era was still the public sector. The CCP Charter stated that the main contradiction that should be occupying the party was the "contradiction between the growing material and cultural needs of the people and the backwardness of its social production." The focus of the CCP was to lead the people toward a socialist modern economy by "vigorously develop[ing] the social productive forces." The 1982 PRC constitution gave the rhetoric a more concrete tone, declaring that the foundation of China's economic system was its socialist public ownership: "ownership by the whole people and collective ownership by the working people." Public property was declared sacred and inviolable, while private economic activity was set as supplementary.[40]

Accordingly, in this period economic activity by the private sector remained limited to individual households of urban and rural working people. The socio-economic

[36] A Leninist concept highlighting "freedom of discussion, unity of action" within the revolutionary Communist party. The concept was adopted as a main component of Mao Zedong's thought as follows:

> Some comrades see only the interests of the part and not the whole; … they forget the system of democratic centralism, in which the minority is subordinated to the majority, the lower level to the higher level, the part to the whole, and the entire membership to the Central Committee …

Mao Zedong, "Rectify the Party's Style of Work," speech at the opening of the Party School of the Central Committee of the Communist Party of China, Feb. 1, 1942. In *Selected Works of Mao Tse-Tung*, Vol. III (English trans.) (Foreign Languages Press, 1965), at 35.

[37] The CCP Charter, arts. 10(3)–10(5).

[38] Constitution of the People's Republic of China [中华人民共和国宪法], adopted by the Fifth Nat'l People's Cong., promulgated on December 4, 1982 [The 1982 PRC Constitution, or the PRC Constitution].

[39] The 1982 PRC Constitution, art. 3. While the principle of democratic centralism was noted in the earlier 1978, 1975, and 1954 constitutions, there was no provision that explicated the division of powers in a similar fashion.

[40] The 1982 PRC Constitution, arts. 6–8, 11–12.

political agenda to focus on the public sector was clearly translated into laws and regulations of that time. Other forms of private economic activity, such as private enterprises (i.e., eight or more employees), were acknowledged in law only toward the end of the Early Reform Era.[41]

But if the economic reliance on the public sector was to be preserved even under reform and opening, the Party-state had to find ways to increase the sector's productivity. One such way was to focus attention on urban enterprises (as they carried most of China's industrial production capacity) and provide them with greater operational autonomy. Rethinking the relationship between the state and SOEs became the focus of the 12th CCP Central Committee (1982–87).[42] Production units started to separate from government bodies and to form into business enterprises. Dual-track pricing was a major step in advancing this separation; it provided enterprises with the necessary means to start operating on their own, re-invest in production innovation, and expand.[43]

As experimentation was taken to the next level as a national practice, state capacities were called into action and the wheels of the legal machinery moved into a higher gear. Legal institutions were established to support and govern the economic activity of public sector participants. Intermediate municipal-level People's courts were instructed to establish economic units to adjudicate economic disputes.[44] The Economic Contract Law established the rights and obligations of "legal persons,"[45] governing economic relations between SOEs and collective enterprises and organizations,[46] and was administered by the newly formed State Administration for Industry and Commerce (SAIC). Tax regulations were put forward to formalize the mechanism of profit retention following the dual-track pricing practice.[47]

41 See note 60 and the related text. D. C. Clarke et al., "The Role of Law in China's Economic Development." In T. Brandt & L. Rawski (eds.), *China's Great Economic Transformation* (Cambridge University Press, 2008) 375, at 388–389, note that the only legal way for larger private enterprises to exist at that time was by formally registering as collective enterprises while operating as private ones for a fee paid to local governments. This arrangement was called a "red-hat" enterprise.

42 The shift is noticeable in the Decision on Reforming the Economic Structure [中共中央关于经济体制改革的决定], promulgated by the Central Comm. of the Communist Party of China, at the Third Plenary Session of the 12th Central Comm., Oct. 20, 1984.

43 See Chapter 6, "The Emergence of Firms and the Capital Market", Section 1.

44 The Organic Law of the People's Courts of the People's Republic of China [中华人民共和国人民法院组织法], adopted by the Fifth Nat'l People's Cong., July 1, 1979, [released in Order No. 3 of the Standing Comm. of the NPC, July 5, 1979], effective Jan. 1, 1980, art. 24.

45 The Economic Contract Law of the People's Republic of China [中华人民共和国经济合同法], adopted by the Fifth Nat'l People's Cong., Dec. 13, 1981, effective July 1, 1982.

46 At that time, only public sector enterprises and organizations were treated as legal persons. The law was amended in 1993 to include all domestic registered and licensed business entities (still, not individuals) and was finally replaced by the 1999 Contract Law which regulated a broader set of economic relations, note 89.

47 Trial Measures for Converting State-Owned Enterprise Profits into Tax [关于国营企业利改税试行办法][国发(1983) 75 号]. approved by the St. Council, Apr. 24, 1983, release no. 75; Temporary Regulations on Levying Ownership Tax on State-Owned Enterprises [财政部关于对国营企业征收所得税的暂行规定], promulgated by the Ministry of Finance, Apr. 29, 1983, effective June 1, 1983.

State Council regulations promoted increased autonomy by establishing dual-track production and pricing in SOEs as a nation-wide practice.[48]

The expanded autonomy of enterprises was further enshrined between 1986 and 1988 in the enactment of the General Principles of Civil Law, which acknowledged enterprises as legal persons that can independently conduct business and assume civil rights and liabilities;[49] the Industrial Enterprises Law, which provided the legal framework for the establishment, organization, operation, and legal liability of SOEs and gave some direction on how government and enterprise relations should adjust;[50] and the Enterprise Bankruptcy Law, which governed the bankruptcy and winding-up of SOEs.[51]

Since SOEs already operated prior to these formal national-level legal recognitions, Clarke, Murrell, and Whiting note that the main contribution of this new regulatory framework was in introducing the principle that SOEs *should be* governed by formal national legislation.[52] Indeed, enacting these laws was perceived as an element of socialist modernization, whereby social economic activity is regulated by defined legal institutions of a sovereign modern socialist state.

Using formal national-level laws also had a meaningful political–economic function – the legal system was called upon to mobilize different Party-state organs to follow the reform plans.

These laws were enacted while China's economy was still mostly a planned economy. The Party-state strove to keep production and industrial capacities within macro state plans, even while allowing greater operational autonomy at the local level to boost growth. The idea was to gradually move away from mandatory state

[48] Interim Provisions of the State Council on Further Expanding the Autonomy of State-Owned Enterprises [国务院关于进一步扩大国营工业企业自主权的暂行规定] Guo Fa. [1984] No. 67, issued by the St. Council, May 10, 1984. (Regulating the dual-track production and pricing mechanism. Excess products were allowed to be sold at a price that is as much as 20 percent above the state price.)

[49] See Chapter III, Section 2, of the General Principles of The Civil Law of the People's Republic of China [中华人民共和国民法通则], passed by the Sixth Nat'l People's Cong. and promulgated by Order No. 37 of the President of the People's Republic of China on Apr. 12, 1986, effective Jan. 1987. This recognition in China's Civil Law in business enterprises as a "legal person" will be the legal basis for the later 1993 Company law recognition in the principles of separate legal personality of companies and shareholders' limited liability under the "modern enterprise system." See Chapter 6.

[50] Law on Industrial Enterprises Owned by the Whole People [中华人民共和国全民所有制工业企业法], adopted by the Seventh Nat'l People's Cong., promulgated in Order No. 3 of the President of the People's Republic of China, Apr. 13, 1988, effective Aug. 1, 1988.

[51] Law of the People's Republic of China on Enterprise Bankruptcy [中华人民共和国企业破产法 (试行)], adopted by the Standing Comm. of the Sixth Nat'l People's Cong., promulgated by Order No. 45 of the President of the People's Republic of China on December 2, 1986 (for Trial Implementation). The law was meant to improve asset management in SOEs through the threat of closing and the imposition of civil liability. However, as noted by Clarke et al., *The Role of Law in China's Economic Development*, note 41, at 382, it did not have an actual effect. The government largely avoided using its power to wind-up firms. [As discussed in Part III, the continued operation of non-performing and inefficient (now corporatized) SOEs remains one of China's main challenges, to this day.]

[52] Clarke et al., *The Role of Law in China's Economic Development*, note 41, at 390, stated with respect to the Industrial Enterprises Law.

plans toward state guidance aided by regulation.[53] Thus, to govern state-owned assets, which were by then mostly managed by local governments, the Party-state saw a need to use laws and regulations alongside plan directives.

While looking back and urging an update of the legal framework later in the 1990s, Yang Jingyu, the then Director of the Legislative Affairs Bureau of the State Council, explained:

> Regulation had an auxiliary role at that time… It was not only needed in order to concretize state plans and ensure thorough implementation in important situations, but also as an important basis and necessary supplement to formulate plans.
>
> […]
>
> The understanding at the time was that the [economic contract law] *regulates vertical and horizontal linkages* in the economy.[54] (emphasis added)

In Chinese political parlance, vertical linkages commonly refer to the hierarchical linkages between China's vertical administrative division from the central government down to the basic social-economic unit (through provincial governments, prefectures, counties, townships, and villages), while horizontal linkages commonly refer to the linkages between organs of equal status (e.g., between different government agencies, cities, industries, organizations, and enterprises). This suggests that the Party-state had chosen the legal system as means to separate the operations of state-owned assets from the government units that had spawned them, confine government economic activity, and signal to increasingly autonomous and powerful local governments and their officials that they are not without reins.

Apparently, the past practice of political and administrative directives did not suffice once economic units had to develop a degree of autonomy. The Party-state envisioned legal institutions as suitable means with which to reconfigure economic and administrative authorities within the state apparatus.

At this stage, the law was not called upon to attract private economic activity. In that sense, a recognition in its economic function was minimal at best. As Clarke, Murrell, and Whiting observed: "Early reform policy did not contemplate a major role for the private sector. It was about running the state sector better and therefore was not concerned with what might encourage entrepreneurship."[55] Scholars note

53 Resolution of the Fifth Session of the Sixth National People's Congress on the 1987 National Economic and Social Development Plan [第六届全国人民代表大会第五次会议关于1987年国民经济和社会发展计划的决议], adopted at the Fifth Session of the Sixth Nat'l People's Cong., Apr. 11, 1987.

54 Said in the context of deliberations on the amendment of the Economic Contract Law: Explanation of the draft "Amendment of the Economic Contract Law," by Yang Jingyu, Director of the Legislative Affairs Bureau of the State Council, at the second meeting of the Standing Comm. of the Eighth Nat'l People's Cong., June 22, 1993, *Gazette* of the Standing Committee of the Nat'l People's Cong., No. 5, 1993 [杨景宇(1993),关于中华人民共和国经济合同法修正案（草案）的说明，全国人大常委会公报，1993年第5号,页24].

55 Clarke et al., *The Role of Law in China's Economic Development*, note 41, at 377.

one important exception to this observation: private economic activity by foreign investors.

Here, the economic function of law was recognized and economic rights were addressed in law already from the very early days of reform. It was apparently acknowledged that foreign investors expect "modern" laws and these are thus necessary to attract foreign capital to Chinese Joint Venture projects. These projects partnered foreign companies with SOEs in designated special economic zones. Legal modernization of *private* economic activity thus began in China with the introduction of laws allowing foreign investments.[56] These laws established a separate and more attractive legal regime for foreigners but still with the public sector in mind; first and foremost, this legal framework was designed to induce the flow of necessary capital and know-how to China's SOEs.

Almost a decade into the reforms, the Party-state continued rethinking and reshaping its approach toward private economic activity and, in the process, redefined its use of the legal system and its perception towards the functions of law.

On the one hand, the legitimacy of the private economy was still highly contested within the CCP. Moreover, by that time, provincial governments had virtually complete responsibility for urban infrastructure development, housing, social care, etc., and were able to carry their responsibilities mostly through revenue generated by SOEs. A wave of private businesses in urban areas would have shifted labor and resources away from their assigned SOEs and could create unwelcomed competition. It also had the potential to bring urban unrest in an already overheating economy. Local governments, therefore, had reasons to confine the growth of the private sector.

One the other hand, those within the leadership that had pushed for reforms were nonetheless able to expand the space for the private economy by formally keeping it auxiliary, narrow, and gradual, while at the same time de facto allowing informal economic activity to continue developing by a lax approach toward local governments' mandates. This approach was translated into a relatively limited number of

56 In order of enactment: Central Committee Document No. 50, July 15 1979 (which granted Guangdong and Fujian special policy with flexible measures to attract foreign investments) as cited in Vogel, *Deng Xiaoping and the Transformation of China*, note 27, at 399. Law of the People's Republic of China on Chinese-Foreign Equity Joint Ventures [中华人民共和国中外合资经营企业法], adopted at the Fifth Nat'l People's Cong., July 1, 1979, by Order No. 7 of the Chairman of the Stand. Comm., Nat'. People's Con'., effective July 1, 1979; The Law of the People's Republic of China on Economic Contracts Involving Foreign Interest [中华人民共和国主席令], adopted by the Standing Comm. of the Sixth Nat'l People's Cong., promulgated by Order No. 22 of the PRC President, Mar. 21, 1985, effective July 1, 1985; Law of the People's Republic of China on Foreign-Capital Enterprises [中华人民共和国主席令], adopted by the Sixth Nat'l People's Cong., promulgated and effective by Order No. 39 of the PRC President, Apr. 12, 1986 (following successful attraction of foreign capital through joint ventures between the state sector and foreign investors in the Special Economic Regions, this law took a step further to allow for the first time a legal business entity wholly owned by foreigners); The Law of the People's Republic of China on Chinese-Foreign Contractual Joint Ventures [中华人民共和国中外合作经营企业法], adopted by the Seventh Nat'l People's Cong., promulgated and effective by Order No. 4 of the PRC President, Apr. 13, 1988 (setting more flexible terms for joint ventures and enabling other forms of foreign investment beside equity capital contribution).

national laws, and mostly provisional national administrative regulations. In doing so, the reformers were able to assuage objections from more conservative voices within the Party as well as to avoid antagonism from local leaders.[57]

On October 1987, at the CCP's 13th National Congress (1987–1992), Zhao Ziyang, then the General Secretary of the CCP and the state Premier, stated:

> In the primary stage [of socialism], it is necessary to develop a variety of economic sectors under the premise of public ownership as the main component....

The CCP's National Congress recognized the private economy as a *necessary* and *beneficial supplement* to a dominant public sector. This new state-and-market relations called for a shift in the role of law and a more extensive use of law:

> The new economic operational mechanism should generally be that the state regulates the market and the market guides enterprises. The state applies economic measures, legal measures, and necessary administrative measures to regulate the relationship between supply and demand in the market and create a suitable economic and social environment, so as to guide enterprises to make correct business decisions. Realizing this goal is a gradual process, and conditions must be actively created to this end.[58]

Party and state institutions were directed to formulate policies and laws in order to "guide and supervise" private economic participants and protect their legitimate interests.

This call was quickly answered. The PRC Constitution was amended to acknowledge the private economy as "complementary" to the socialist public economy. The amendment stated that the legitimate rights and interests of private economy participants are to be protected by the state as well as to be "guided, supervised, and administered by the state." The amendment also emphasized that the private sector economy may "exist and develop within the limits prescribed by law and regulation."[59]

These developments point to a new function of formal legal institutions, introducing both regularity and economic rights consciousness into a narrowly confined yet growing and now politically acknowledged private sector. The economic functions of the legal system thus started to evolve.

Accordingly, a series of laws and regulations were promulgated to formally recognize new private ownership forms while adhering to the political accords stated above. Still, the newly created legal right to establish private enterprises (defined

57 For the various voices and political struggles surrounding the reform era, see Vogel, *Deng Xiaoping and the Transformation of China*, note 27, particularly at 447–449.

58 "Advance along the Road of Socialism with Chinese Characteristics," Report by Zhao Ziyang at the 13th Nat'l Cong. of the Communist Party of China, Oct. 25, 1987, https://archive.ph/kpdKC, see Part IV, "About the Reform of the Economic System."

59 Amendment to the Constitution of the People's Republic of China [中华人民共和国宪法修正案 (1988)], promulgated by Announcement No. 8 of the Seventh Nat'l People's Cong., Apr. 12, 1988. See art. 11.

as "a privately funded economic entity which employs eight or more employees," including sole-proprietorships, partnerships, and limited liability companies)[60] was granted only to certain groups in the society, largely those not posing a threat to the SOE-base of the urban economy – that is, villagers, the unemployed, and retired state sector workers.[61]

Since private economic activity was growing under the radar of formal law and regulatory supervision, much was left to the discretion of local officials.

Toward the end of the early reform period, as economic interactions between government institutions, SOEs, and private participants increased, the potential for frictions arose and led to discussions about the need to have formal restrictions on state powers. Here too, the legal system was called upon to create safeguards against arbitrary government action (with mainly local government officials in mind) in the enactment of the Administrative Litigation law. The law gave Chinese citizens *limited* standing to contest against government actions in court.[62]

Clarke, Murrell, and Whiting, analogizing the process of legal reform to Barry Naughton's economic reform coinage "growing out of the plan," note how "the process of legal reform [can] be described as growing out of the system of administrative directives." They explain that decentralization and the increasing autonomy of enterprises reinforced the need for generally applicable laws as alternatives to solving disputes by specific commands under the planned economy. They add, "decentralization, the market, and a private sector do not make these changes inevitable, but they do create demands that can be addressed by legal reforms."[63] Their analysis well demonstrates the idea that legal reform and the space for law in the economy constitute an evolving process of supply adjusting to demand.

[60] The Provisional Regulations on the Administration of Individual Household Industrial and Commercial Activity in Urban and Rural Areas [城乡个体工商户管理暂行条例], promulgated by the St. Council, Aug. 5, 1987 (recognized individual and household economic activity through registered sole proprietorships, and granted them with some protections); Opinions on the Establishment and Development of Business Groups [关于组建和发展企业集团的几点意见], promulgated by the Nat'l Econ. Sys. Reform Comm'n & the Nat'l Econ. Comm'n, Dec. 16, 1987 [Business Groups Opinions] (recognized Business Groups as a "multi-level organizational structure" with separate legal personality); Provisional Regulations on Private Enterprises [中华人民共和国私营企业暂行条例], promulgated by the St. Council on June 25, 1988, article 2.

[61] Provisional Regulations on Private Enterprises, ibid., arts. 3, 11.

[62] Administrative Litigation Law of the People's Republic of China [中华人民共和国行政诉讼法], adopted by the Nat'l People's Cong., promulgated Apr. 4, 1989, effective Oct. 1, 1990. At the time, the law was considered by many as an important step toward "rule of law." The law determined that actions by government agencies (note – state, but not party organs) need to have justification in formal laws and regulations and provided a basis for citizens to sue government officials. For the development of administrative law in China, see R. Peerenboom (ed.), *China's Long March toward Rule of Law* (Cambridge University Press, 2002), at 398–449; H. Ma & X. Kong, "40 Years of the Rule of Administrative Law: Enhancements, Experience, and Expectations," *Frontiers of Law in China* 13(4) (2018) 497.

[63] Clarke et al., *The Role of Law in China's Economic Development*, note 41, at 378–379.

Notwithstanding, that analysis does not capture in full the evolving political–economic utilization of law beyond market demands. The chronology depicted above reflects that during the Early Reform Era, laws and regulations were utilized by the Party-state to configure and allocate political-economic powers.

Legal reforms, that is, the narrowing and expanding scope of utilizing legal institutions, not only followed bottom-up demands of a sprouting market but were also politically initiated, tailored by China's reformers to enlist political leaders and mobilize vertical and horizontal institutions behind China's new socio-economic plan.

SUMMARY REFLECTIONS

From the very early stages of market reforms in China, legal institutions were utilized for their political function, mainly to reconfigure economic authorities within the Party-state organization. Even limiting the use of legal institutions had a political function. Economic decentralization reshaped China's political economy. A new political–economic equilibrium was created, one in which an economic power shift from the center to the localities was negotiated and eventually consented to. This allocation of economic authority had to be delineated in a unified manner, particularly after the decade of institutional and political upheavals that preceded "reform and opening", and also had to allow sufficient plasticity to encourage experimentation. The Party-state thus resorted to a limited utilization of uniform laws in the early 1980s (Figure 3.1).

As the era progressed, the need to use laws to allocate and confine the economic power of local officials started to surface in the late 1980s, as decentralization created innovative, business-oriented, and increasingly autonomous and competitive local

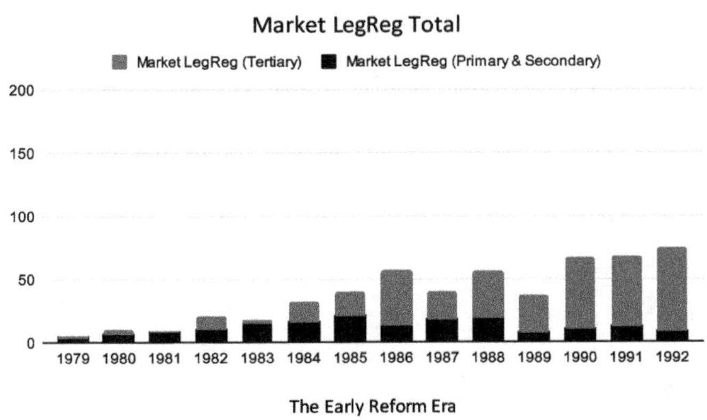

FIGURE 3.1 Newly issued and rev'sd market LegReg during the Early Reform Era

governments.[64] In parallel, as the economy grew and market demand arose, legal institutions were advanced with a mission to regulate the budding markets, including recognizing lawful rights and responsibilities. In this process, law was used to carve out and legitimize politically palatable forms of market activity, including by limited designated groups of private participants. Other forms of economic activity that were less politically palatable were not acknowledged in law and were thus permitted to continue under informal and more autonomous local experimentation and provisional administrative regulations.

Tailoring the use of legal institutions this way increased political acquiescence with the reform. It paved out a limited but growing space for the market without destabilizing the political–economic equilibrium. In this process, the two functions of law in the market were formed and unveiled.

[64] Jean Oi has dubbed this "local state corporatism." J. Oi, "Fiscal Reform and the Economic Foundations of Local State Corporatism in China," *World Politics* 45(1) (1992) 99, at 100.

4

Legal Modernization Era (1992–2009)

While the early reform era instigated China's economic growth and development, decentralizing authority to local governments also resulted in social and economic instabilities.[65] Depletion of central resources, overheated local investments, growing inequality, rapid inflation, local protectionism and bureaucratic battles, as well as rising concerns by public-sector workers who faced, for the first time, competitive forces and a risk of unemployment – all of these outcomes generated governance and social instabilities that eventually resulted in the violent suppression at Tiananmen square, on June 4th, 1989. Following June 4th, a period of retrenchment halted economic reforms.[66]

When economic reforms began again in late 1992, China's second development stage ensued.

The next two decades are known as China's modern reform period. Across disciplines, the period is described as one in which there was a growing embrace of modern governance and market institutions. This was also the period during which China's integration with the world economy grew significantly, as China gradually became an export-led economy and opened an increasing number of industries to foreign investors.[67] From the perspective of legal scholarship, the literature covering this period tends to focus on the adoption of modern laws and of market-supporting legal institutions (hence the term used here, Legal Modernization Era).[68]

Indeed, legal reforms were part of the impetus of this new development era. However, in this book, I offer an additional vantage point. Instead of looking at legal

[65] Shirk, *The Political Logic of Economic Reform*, note 29, at 181–190. For a discussion of local protectionism, rent seeking, and corruption as a consequence of decentralization in the context of the evolution of firms, see Part III.

[66] B. Naughton, "Inflation and Economic Reform in China," *Current History* 88(539) (1989) 269.

[67] S. Husted & S. Nishioka, "China's Fare Share? The Growth of Chinese Exports in World Trade," *Review of World Economics* 149(3) (2013) 565; Y. Huang, *Selling China: Foreign Direct Investment during the Reform Era* (Cambridge University Press, 2003).

[68] The literature documenting China's legal reforms in this period is voluminous. One of the seminal works is Randall Peerenboom's book, Peerenboom, *China's Long March toward Rule of Law*, note 62.

construction through the prism of market supporting changes alone, which naturally draw attention to the economic functions of law, I highlight both the economic and the political functions of law and examine how both supported China's market development during this era of reform. The analysis shows that the approach to law during the era was not unified. Two waves are observed: In the 1990s, law was used mainly in its political function, reconfiguring economic authorities toward recentralization. In the first decade of the 2000s, the economic function of law seemed to increase, but not without political determinants.

ERA OVERVIEW: A "SOCIALIST MARKET ECONOMY" IS CONFIGURED THROUGH LAW

From the early 1990s onward, Chinese law and legal institutions have seen tremendous progress.[69] William Alford astutely referred to China's broad project of legal development in this period as an "event of epic historic proportions," noting that "no other major modern society has endeavored in such short a time to reconstruct its legal system in so extensive and novel a fashion."[70]

The greater use of laws and legal institutions in governing markets specifically soared as well (Figure 4.1), with some of the most fundamental national economic laws being established at both turns of the era. Tertiary regulations by central state bodies were particularly prominent. The years just prior and following the CCP's 15th Central Party Congress (1997), in which the Party proclaimed a turn toward "Rul[ing] the country according to law and building a socialist ruled-by-law country,"[71] saw much activism in market-related rulemaking, but mostly by organizations of the state council. By the early 2000s, an increasing body of national-level economic laws and regulations gradually replaced many of the fragmented and probationary rules used earlier.[72] A set of new laws were also used to build state capacity,

[69] B. L. Liebman, "Assessing China's Legal Reforms," *Columbia Journal of Asian Law* 23(1) (2009) 17, at 18.

[70] W. P. Alford, "A Second Great Wall? China's Post-Cultural Revolution Project of Legal Construction," *Cultural Dynamics* 11 (1999) 193.

[71] See Jiang Zemin Report at the 15th Nat'l Congress of the Communist Party of China [江泽民在中国共产党第十五次全国代表大会上的报告], Sept. 12, 1997, https://archive.ph/alV1C [Report at the 15th Party Congress]. Ch. VI ("Reforming the Political Structure and Strengthening Democracy and the Legal System").

There is an active debate on the translation of the terms used, *yifa zhiguo* [依法治国] and *shihuizhuyi fazhi guojia* [社会主义法治国家], as they have been translated at times as "rule of law" by commentators both in and outside China as well as in Chinese Party-state addresses. I touch upon this further below.

[72] It should be noted, however, that an "experimentation first" strategy is still used to introduce new economic measures into the market.

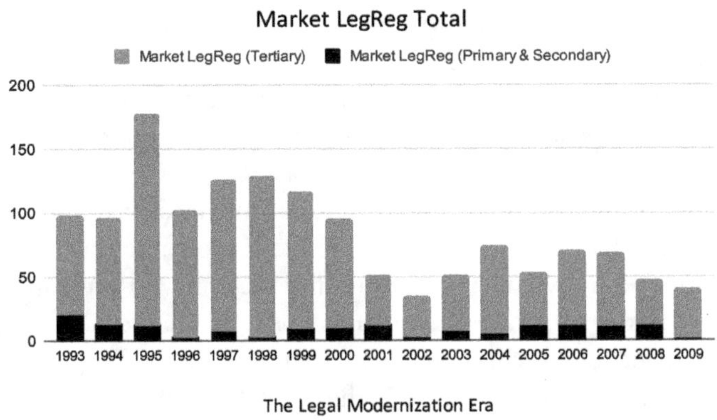

FIGURE 4.1 Newly issued and rev'sd market LegReg during the Legal Modernization Era

instituting many of China's most significant market regulators and prescribing their vast regulatory authority over different segments of the rising markets.

Where did the turn toward law in this era come from?[73] Many within and outside China advocated the idea that economic progress requires a predictable and accountable government.[74] Party-state proclamations reflect the CCP's adoption of this approach. Legal modernization seemed necessary to support the growing market and establish the global legitimacy of the regime, particularly following the Tiananmen suppression.

To be sure, a top-down more economically conscious reform agenda was not the sole contributor to the rising role of law and legal institutions in this era. Bottom-up market demand had an important impact on the speed and scope of legal development as well. As economic changes took hold throughout the era, demand for more predictable and uniform standards of economic conduct arose. Faced with the upsurge of commercial disputes between unfamiliar parties (as a result of market growth), modern laws and legal institutions had fertile grounds to take root.

Indeed according to law and development prescriptions, the turn toward law in this era was to be expected due to the promises of the economic function of law – the notion that having a modern legal system that secures economic rights supports

73 But see the arguments for a reversal and a turn *against* law in the midst of the era, from the mid-2000s onward: C. Minzner, "China's Turn against Law," *The American Journal of Comparative Law* 59(4) (2011) 935 (assessing a return from the operation of formal law and legal institutions in dispute resolution, in favor of informal means including mediation and Party political work as the preferred means to resolve citizen grievances); B. Liebman, "A Return to Populist Legality? Historical Legacies and Legal Reform." In Heilmann, S. & Perry, E. (eds.) *Mao's Invisible Hand: The Political Foundations of Adaptive Governance in China* (Harvard University Asia Center, 2011) 165 (depicting a shift away, during the 2000s, from legal procedures toward populist forms of dispute resolution in resemblance of Mao's era approach toward law).

74 A. HY. Chen, "The Developing Theory of Law and Market Economy in Contemporary China." In G. Wang & Z. Wei (eds.), *Legal Developments in China: Market Economy and Law* (Sweet & Maxwell, 1996).

growth in the market. Yet, as shown below, advances made in the use of law in the market were not clean from significant political determinants. A strong internal need arose to re-consolidate macro economic controls with the central Party-state. This political-economic factor is strongly evident in laws supporting the rise of state capitalism in this era.

Next, I turn to analyze legal and policy documents issued during the Legal Modernization Era. The analysis shows that the use of economic law in this period was consciously tunneled in two main directions: the use of law to structure and support the creation of markets (i.e., the economic function) and the use of law to reconfigure governance capacities and boost more centralized regularity within the Party-state system (i.e., the political function). Of course, these functions entwine to a degree – while utilizing law for its economic function, political determinants may be present, and vice versa. Nonetheless, the review suggests that the Party-state acknowledged these two functions of law, and utilized the law in this fashion systematically from this point onwards.

It could be argued that the use of law to advance regularity within the Party-state system is natural given that the role of law in all other aspects of social life was on the rise during the same period. But there were also specific political determinants that brought about the need to establish the use of law for its political functions. This was not just a process of social modernization.

When considering the political outcomes of the Early Reform Era, the political determinants for the rising role of law in allocating economic authorities within the Party-state system itself become clear. The instabilities of the 1980s and the retrenchment period that followed highlighted the fact that the central–state-led (mainly urban) economy was lagging behind the growing public and private sectors of localized markets. Certain local governments grew economically powerful while the central government was exposed in its weaknesses, having depleted its resources and being unable to control local overinvestments and an overheating economy. This political–economic reality caused China's policymakers to take a step back from decentralization and reassert control over growing chunks of the market.[75] As China's economy developed and grew, so did its aspirations for a global economic position, further reinforcing the Party-state's need for centralized means of control. As will be seen below, laws and regulations were utilized to aid this political–economic shift towards state capitalism.

Despite the Party-state's effort to rein in the market and pave its direction, as markets grew strong and open so did opportunities for accumulating individual and local economic and political power continue to grow. State capitalism backfired. Toward the end of the era, concerns for political instability intensified and resulted in the Party-state's decision to shift powers in a completely different direction, adjusting

[75] B. Naughton & D. Yang (eds.), *Holding China Together: Diversity and National Integration in the Post-Deng Era* (Cambridge University Press, 2004), at 8.

the use of law accordingly during the last and current Legalized Politicization Era (Chapter 5).

1 *The Use of Law to Structure the Market*

From (Re)instating Economic Reforms through Facilitating Macro-control

The Legal Modernization Era itself can be divided into two stages. Political motivations permeated much of the purportedly market-oriented legal reforms of the early 1990s. The process produced a combination of laws that preempted markets and governed what had not yet existed in practice, alongside laws that responded to markets after significant delays. The result was a surge in a bizarre mix of laws and regulations that often were not suited to market conditions. As a consequence, during the first decade of legal modernization, while the use of law increased, the economic functions of law were still weak or altogether missing.

To support market growth and prepare for China's accession to the WTO, many of the laws had to be revised shortly after their enactment. Following the accession, the legislation wave in the mid-2000s produced modern laws and legal institutions that were much more apt for the task of governing a form of a market economy. Still, this was not the sole motivation behind the wave of new laws as well. The Party-state's growing desire to reconsolidate macro control is strongly evident in laws supporting the rise of state capitalism in this era.

First Decade of Legal Modernization

After the retrenchment period, China's leaders had to find ways to re-establish reforms. The central Party-state defined a new vision for the evolving relationship between central economic planning and market forces (which at the time still mainly involved local improvisation and limited private initiatives).

In his 1992 tour of southern China, Deng Xiaoping explained his new vision:

> [P]lanning and market forces are not the essential difference between socialism and capitalism. A planned economy is not the definition of socialism, because there is planning under capitalism; market economy happens under socialism, too. Planning and market forces are both ways of controlling economic activity.[76]

As described by Sebastian Heilmann, this reflected a shift from "[p]lanning … as a substitute for markets … [to] planning with and for markets."[77] Thinking about economic planning had shifted from specific interventions to a more macro, strategic,

[76] Deng's Southern tour is said to be the factor that gave a decisive political push to renew and enhance economic reforms. Quoted at the People's Daily (en), "Market Fundamentalism is Unpractical" (Feb. 3, 2012), https://web.archive.org/web/20151003084506/http://en.people.cn/90780/7719657.html

[77] See S. Heilmann, "Economic Governance – Authoritarian Upgrading and Innovative Potential." In J. Fewsmith (ed.), *China Today, China Tomorrow: Domestic Politics, Economy, and Society* (Rowman & Littlefield Publishers, 2010) 109, at 114–116.

policy planning that would support and be supported by market forces. In defining the relationship between planning and market forces in this way, the Party was able to reinstate the reforms without forgoing control.

The renewed impetus for reform was presented by Jiang Zemin (then the General Secretary of the CCP and the soon-to-be appointed President) in his October 1992 speech at the 14th Party Congress (1992–97). The speech supported returning to and accelerating the pace of reform and opening. Jiang introduced a new unifying message of creating a "*socialist market economy*" as the national agenda. Under the new scheme, public ownership would remain the backbone of the economy, but markets would be expanded and efforts to turn state enterprises into market participants (i.e., independent from government and efficient) would intensify.

The 14th Central Committee declared that the market should become "a fundamental factor in the allocation of resources under state macro-control."[78] This meant that state control was not to be abandoned but rather improved *through* the market. The Party Charter was amended accordingly. It stated that China had entered the "primary stage of socialism," a stage that "will take over a hundred years to surpass," during which the country's main task was to advance economically so as to gradually achieve socialist modernization. To do so, as declared in the amended Charter, the country should unleash its productive forces and create a "socialist market economy" that would maintain public ownership as the mainstay alongside multiple coexisting forms of economic activity. The Charter noted the need for openness and for learning management methods and laws that support modern production from the West.[79]

The following statement from Jiang's speech at the Third Plenum of the 14th Central Committee reflects the complex relationship that the Party sought in balancing economic planning with market forces as the basis of its new political–economic vision. The quote also highlights that this was set to be achieved through a trinity of mechanisms combining legal institutions, market forces, and policy measures:

> This year, one of the important features of consolidating and improving macro-control is to solve emerging conflicts and problems … deepening the reform mainly through the adoption of economic and legal means, supplemented by necessary administrative measures. Such practice was proved to be successful. … We all see that market mechanisms exert an increasing economic effect on our economic lives, but the stagnation in certain areas of reform has a [negative] influence on the establishment of new institutions and on the healthy development of the

78 See Decision on Issues Concerning the Establishment of a Socialist Market Economy [the 14th Central Committee Decisions], in the Communiqué adopted and promulgated by the Third Plenary Session of the 14th Central Comm. of the Communist Party of China [中国共产党第十四届中央委员会第三次全体会议公报], Nov. 14, 1993.

79 Charter of the Communist Party of China (1992 revision) [中国共产党章程(1992修改)], revs'd by the 14th Nat'l Cong. of the Communist Party of China, Oct. 18, 1992.

national economy. … This will require continuous overall design [in which] we need to emphasize the standardization of institutions and policy.[80]

The importance of the 14th Party Congress cannot be overstated. While the mechanisms for reform were to evolve and refine over time, the goal was set and the path forward was clear: establishing a socialist market economy in which the market and the state are mutually reinforcing.

It is also important to note that this vision was somewhat of a retreat from the approach towards the private sector as expressed only six years earlier by Zhao Ziyang in the 13th Party Congress during the Early Reform era: "a *necessary* and *beneficial supplement*."[81] This was likely a result of the Tiananmen events that gave the Party-state a taste of what more liberal tones of reform might entail for its future political, social, and economic stability. A more conservative tone within the Party took the lead after Tiananmen, and while it still acknowledged the need for reform it certainly corrected its course.

Following the new reform agenda, the relationship between the plan and the market had to be realigned. The legal machinery was called into action as a key agent. The law was thus advanced as part of the Party-state's effort to configure the new balance between planning and markets.

First to be adapted to the new political momentum for reform was the PRC Constitution. The amendments articulated the new national goal of "building socialism with Chinese characteristics."[82] References to economic central planning were replaced by references to the new pursuit of a "socialist market economy." The reference to the state sector changed from "state-operated" (*guoying jingji*) to "state-owned" economy (*guoyou jingji*), reflecting new legal consciousness of the importance of ownership. Mentions of the market having only a supplementary role were omitted.[83]

Within a year, charged with the new impetus and backed by a more centralized reform agenda, various departments of the state council promoted at least thirty-eight national-level regulations and normative documents, asserting their authority over chunks of the budding markets.[84] Earlier interim provisions and probationary

80 Translated quote from President Jiang Zemin's November 14th, 1993 speech at the Third Plenum of the Fourteenth Central Committee of the Chinese Communist Party [江泽民在中国共产党第十四届中央委员会第三次全体会议上的讲话]. Full version available here [in Chinese]: https://archive.md/s3x96.

81 Note 58 and the related text.

82 Amendment to the Constitution of the People's Republic of China [中华人民共和国宪法修正案(1993)], adopted by the Eighth Nat'l People's Cong., promulgated Mar. 29, 1993 [the 1993 Constitutional Amendment].

83 1993 Constitutional Amendment, amendments in the preamble & articles 7, 15, 16, 33, as well as article 17 for the management of collectives. The change also reflect an acknowledgement of the state's ownership rights and the move to professional management, discussed in Part III.

84 See Relevant Regulations on Strengthening Macro-control [关于加强宏观调控的有关规定], collected by the General Office of the St. Council and issued in State Council Notice No. 52 [1993], Aug. 16, 1993, https://archive.ph/NQe6u.

local schemes were replaced by national laws and regulations, adjusting to the Party's call to establish a "socialist market economy."

One of the primary indications that the center was reasserting authority over the economy through the use of law was the overhaul of the tax system. In 1994, policy-makers moved away from the localized sharing arrangements under the fiscal contracting system and toward a unified, more market-based, and centrally controlled tax sharing system.[85] While the new system continued to delegate expenditure responsibilities to local governments, it also established a uniform and an expanded basis for the various taxes levied. The new system clearly delineated which taxes should be transmitted to the central government, which should be kept by the local government, and which should be shared.[86] The reform of the tax system had a meaningful role in enhancing the governance capacities of the central government.

Another interesting example of a central-level scheme to assert authority over the burgeoning market through law can be seen in the process of amending the 1981 Economic Contract Law. This example reflects an effort to amend a meaningful economic law in ways that would serve the political purpose of power consolidation but also ended up being responsive to the needs of the market as the two motivations aligned in this case:

The amendment of the economic contract law was pushed forward by SAIC and the State Economic Reform Commission (SERC). It was explained that the previous law was "unable to meet the requirement of a socialist market economy and of transforming government functions."[87] The amendment pushed by the central agencies was aimed to expand the regulatory authority of SAIC over a broader scope of economic activities. Interestingly, bottom-up voices seemed to approve. Before presenting the draft amendment to the NPC, the Legal Affairs Bureau of the State Council sent it for comments to more than eighty central departments, professional head offices, banks, courts, and local governments, as well as dozens of legal experts in civil and economic law. The results indicated that the market desired further adjustments to the draft to encompass *additional* forms of economic organization under SAIC authority. Apparently, there were active participants in the market that were not considered "legal persons" under the former law and the amendment draft, and thus were not covered, meaning not protected, by the suggested draft

85 Y. Zhang & L. Gong, "The Fenshuizhi Reform, Fiscal Decentralization, and Economic Growth in China," *China Economic Quarterly*, 4 (2005) 75.

86 Law on the Administration of Tax Collection [中华人民共和国税收征收管理法], adopted by the Standing Comm. of the Seventh Nat'l People's Cong., Sep. 4, 1992, effective Jan. 1, 1993, emended last Apr. 24, 2015; Decision on Implementing the Tax-Sharing Fiscal Management System [国务院关于实行分税制财政管理体制的决定,国发(1993)85号], issued by the St. Council, Dec. 15, 1993, effective Jan. 1, 1994; as well as the Circular on the Approval and Transmission of the Application Program for Industrial and Commercial Tax System Reform of State Administration of Taxation [国务院批转国家税务总局工商税制改革实施方案的通知, 国发(１９９３)９０号], issued by the St. Council, Dec. 25, 1993, effective Jan. 1, 1994.

87 See note 54 and the related text.

amendment. The market desired a broader regulatory certainty of SAIC supervision to be enshrined by the amended law, as it would reduce arbitrary treatment by local officials. The political and economic interests aligned. The draft was revised and approved by the NPC, acknowledging and thus regulating a broader scope of private economic activity under SAIC's authority.[88]

Additional meaningful national-level efforts toward governing the market through legal institutions included: the 1992 Normative Opinions, China's first national-level rules for business organization that were released by the State Commission for Restructuring the Economic Systems (CRES)[89] and replaced a year later by a national Company Law.[90] These laws have advanced a broad enterprise-organization scheme that consolidated authority over SOEs through corporatization and business group formation (discussed in Part III). Additionally, the Interim Provisions for the Administration of Share Issuance and Trade were issued by the State Council as China's first national-level rules on securities and replaced by a national Securities Law a few years later.[91] Issuing the interim provisions in 1993 was a fundamental step in the establishment of a national securities market shortly after (further discussed in Part III).[92] The Negotiable Instruments Law established unified modern payment methods;[93] a national Budget Law aimed to centralize financial management including determining central supervision powers over budget allocations;[94] and a national Price Law attempted to

[88] The Economic Contract Law, note 45, was amended in September 1993, and was eventually replaced by the PRC Contract Law [中华人民共和国合同法], adopted by the Ninth Nat'l People's Cong., Mar. 15, 1999 (currently ineffective, absorbed by the new PRC Civil code on May 28, 2020).

[89] Normative Opinions on Standards for Limited Liability Companies [有限责任公司规范意见], promulgated by the State Comm'n for Restructuring the Economic Systems, May 15, 1992; Normative Opinions on Standards for Companies Limited by Shares [股份有限公司规范意见], promulgated by the State Comm'n for Restructuring the Economic Systems, May 15, 1992 [together, the 1992 Normative Opinions]. Not having a formal status of law nor regulations but merely an "opinion" issued by an administrative special commission, the status of the 1992 Normative Opinions was subject to debate. However, the State Council confirmed in retrospect that they had the effect of a ministry-level regulation. See N. C. Howson, "China's Company Law: One Step Forward, Two Steps Back? A Modest Complaint," *Columbia Journal of Asian Law* 11 (1997) 127, at 137.

[90] The Company Law of the People's Republic of China, [中华人民共和国公司法], promulgated by the Standing Comm. of the Eighth Nat'l People's Cong., Dec. 29, 1993, effective July 1994 [the 1993 Company Law].

[91] Securities Law of the People's Republic of China [中华人民共和国证券法], promulgated by the Standing Comm. of the Ninth Nat'l People's Cong., Dec. 29, 1998, effective July 1, 1999.

[92] Interim Provisions on the Administration of Issuance and Trading of Stocks [股票发行与交易管理暂行条例], promulgated by Decree No. 112 of the St. Council, Apr. 22, 1993.

[93] Negotiable Instruments Law [中华人民共和国票据法], adopted by the Standing Comm. of the Eight Nat'l People's Cong., May 10, 1995, amended and effective, Aug. 18, 2004.

[94] The PRC Budget Law [中华人民共和国预算法], adopted by the Eighth Nat'l People's Cong., Mar. 22, 1994, effective Jan. 1, 1995, amended by the Standing Comm. of the Twelfth Nat'l People's Cong., Aug. 31, 2014, and amended for the second time by the Standing Comm. of the Thirteenth Nat'l People's Cong., Dec. 29, 2018.

balance planning and market forces in pricing, to create a uniform process of setting prices for products.[95]

Importantly, most of the new legal framework still focused on public sector participants. But toward the end of the 1990s, a shift began, and in 1997, the 15th Party Congress (1997–2002) recognized the private sector as "*an important part* of the socialist economy," having "great importance for the diverse needs of the people … and for promoting the development of the national economy."[96]

This, of course, did not mean that public ownership was to be overlooked. Public ownership maintained its dominance as the foundation of the socialist market economy. State ownership, it was clarified, was still the pillar of the economy while other forms of ownership were to be developed side by side.

Reforming the public sector to increase its efficiency and quality was still the focus of reform under the socialist market economy framework. One of the primary schemes to do so was to curb bureaucratic interference in all but the largest, most strategic firms – the concept of "grasping the big, releasing the small" *zhua da fang xiao* strategy. Small and medium enterprises were to be released to private hands or combine state and private ownership. This scheme required pushing the modernization of SOEs forward through their incorporation, a shift to a share-based system,[97] and a shift in perception toward private capital.

The Party Charter and the PRC Constitution were amended to reflect the new nuanced approach toward the private sector.[98] The amendment to the PRC Constitution in 1999 stated that private property was an *important component* within the socialist market economy. Diverse forms of ownership were acknowledged and "a variety of modes of distribution" were legitimized.[99] These acknowledgments signaled a more welcoming approach toward the private sector and an important ideological shift away from a pure social-Marxist theory that only accepted distribution of economic resources according to work. In these changes, the Constitution declared that various forms of earnings, such as revenue from capital (i.e., interest earnings), are legitimate.[100] (This received a more practical affirmation with the PRC Securities Law entering into effect soon after.) The amendments also legitimized income outside of work even for Party and state officials in their personal

[95] The PRC Price Law [中华人民共和国价格法], adopted by the Standing Comm. of the Eighth Nat'l People's Cong., Dec. 29, 1997, effective May 1, 1998. The law determined that the majority of prices will be set by market forces yet set up mechanisms to contain excessively high or low market prices. D. C. Clarke, "Legislating for a Market Economy in China," *The China Quarterly* 191 (2007) 567, at 574.

[96] Report at the 15th Party Congress, note 71. See Chapter V ("Reform of the Economic System and Economic Development Strategy").

[97] See SOE reform process in Part III.

[98] CCP Charter, revs'd by the 15th Nat'l Cong. of the Communist Party of China, Sep. 18, 1997. The amendment of the PRC Constitution [中华人民共和国宪法修正案(1999)], was adopted by the Ninth Nat'l People's Cong. on Mar. 15, 1999 [the 1999 Constitutional Amendment].

[99] The 1999 Constitution Amendment, arts. 5, 6, 11.

[100] Chen, *The Revision of the Constitution in the PRC*, note 10.

capacity. CCP and State Council regulations were issued to substantiate these constitutional changes.[101] And in his 2001 speech commemorating eighty years since the establishment of the CCP, Jiang Zemin indicated that private entrepreneurs could become party members.[102]

Through these steps, the CCP signaled that it represents not only the three revolutionary classes (workers, peasants, and soldiers, the historical–ideological bases of the CCP's legitimacy) but also the new social and economic elites. Political scientist Bruce Dickinson suggested that the CCP encouraged its members to show others how to "take the lead on getting rich," to generate political support for market reforms.[103]

The 15th Party Congress, and consequently the CCP Charter and subsequent PRC constitutional amendment, also specifically highlighted the need for improving the legal system to support the new approach. Areas such as property rights, fair competition, pricing, and trade were specifically brought to attention.[104] These developments certainly seem to indicate a recognition in the economic functions of legal institutions. The breadth of laws regulating private economic activity indeed grew thereafter.[105] The Party-state seems to have recognized that more room for markets required more room for a unified set of legal norms and institutions to provide predictability and secure the expectations of participants in a growing market.

At the same time, the same Party Congress also noted the use of law to improve political–economic coordination, highlighting the macro-control political functions of outwardly economic legal instruments:

> The socialist market economy should be improved so as to allow markets to play a fundamental role in resource allocation under the state's macro-control. […]

101 Provisions on Personal Investment Activity in Securities by Personnel of the Party and Government Organs [关于党政机关工作人员个人证券投资行为若干规定], Circular No. 10 [2001] issued by the General Office of the Central Comm. of the CCP and the General Office of the St. Council, Apr. 3, 2001. While the trading of stocks by Party and state officials took place throughout the 80s–90s, the income from such activity was considered illegal until the 1999 Constitutional amendment and subsequent regulations. Z. Chen, "Capital Markets and Legal Development: The China Case," *China Economic Review* 14 (2003) 451, at 456.

102 Speech at the Meeting Celebration of the 80th Anniversary of the Founding of the CCP, Jiang Zemin, July 1, 2001, https://archive.ph/JN4Rl.

103 B. Dickinson, *Wealth into Power: The Communist Party's Embrace of China's Private Sector* (Cambridge University Press, 2008), at 19.

104 See Report at the 15th Party Congress, note 71, at Chapters V and VI.

105 For example, Partnership Enterprises Law [中华人民共和国合伙企业法], adopted by the Standing Comm. of the Eight Nat'l People's Cong., Feb. 23, 1997, effective Aug. 1, 1997, amended by the Tenth Nat'l People's Cong. on Aug. 27, 2006; the Law on Individual Proprietorship Enterprises [中华人民共和国个人独资企业法], adopted by the Standing Comm. of the Ninth Nat'l People's Cong., Aug. 30, 1999, effective Jan. 1, 2000, these have expanded and legalized organizational forms for private business activity.

> Macro-control mainly uses economic and legal means. It is necessary to deepen the reform of the financial, fiscal and planning systems, and improve their macro-control means and coordination mechanism …

Political considerations were inherent in other fronts as well, and they too reinforced the need for consolidating control through law: During the same period, the Party-state had to deal with the implications of the Asian Financial Crisis (1997–99) and began to consolidate financial control as a precaution. The use of law facilitated this process.[106] This addressed the issues of the financial crisis and mitigated the mounting wariness of the centeral government about the illegal transfer of state assets to private hands, by narrowing the space for local government activism through market regulation. Furthermore, at that time, China's WTO accession was approaching; the market and the legal framework had to at least appear hospitable.

In concluding the first decade of the Legal Modernization Era, the period saw an increasing use of laws and regulations that, while contemplating the needs of market participants, were mostly tailored to address political necessities. Consequently, many of the laws did not align with market realities and necessities. They were perceived to be too rigid, prescribing mandatory rules without leaving sufficient room for business flexibility. The laws often did not prescribe any consequences for violations and thus did not provide guarantees or real protections.[107] The competitiveness of the market, both domestically and internationally, was weak. Instead of fostering economic activity, the legal framework has largely limited it.

The CCP recognized this, and the challenge was evident. The Party-state had to find ways to boost markets and increase international competitiveness, while not losing its control in doing so.

Second Decade of Legal Modernization

The chosen path forward was elaborated in the works of the 16th Party Congress (2002–07), which coincided with a leadership transition to the Hu–Wen administration (Hu Jintao as the new CCP General Secretary and President, and Wen Jiabao as the new Premier).

The 16th Party Congress outlined a path that was largely maintained throughout the tenure of the subsequent 17th Party Congress (2007–12) as well. In his report at the 16th Party Congress, sealing his tenure as the Party-state's top leader, Jiang Zemin had noted the need to establish a modern market system through competition and corporate governance, yet with a strong macro-control.[108] The report,

106 See discussion in reforming the banking sector below.

107 Clarke et al., *The Role of Law in China's Economic Development*, note 41, at 399.

108 "Build a Well-Off Society in an All-Round Way and Initiate a New Situation for the Undertaking of Socialism with Chinese Characteristics," Report by General Secretary Jiang Zemin at the 16th Nat'l Cong. of the Communist Party of China [全面建设小康社会，开创中国特色社会主义事业新局面-在中国共产党第十六次全国代表大会上的报告], Nov. 8, 2002. Part III discuss SOE reforms extensively.

titled *"Build a well-off society in an all-round way, and initiate a new situation for the undertaking of socialism with Chinese characteristics,"* specifically highlighted that SOE ownership reforms should find innovative solutions to improve SOEs' contribution to the economy, such as by promoting joint stocks and diversifying ownership, with the exception of enterprises that must remain wholly state-owned. The idea was to narrow direct state ownership through diversification and thereby reduce government intervention in the micro-economy (hoping to make the market more competitive), while not foregoing and even enhancing the central Party-state's macro control and intensifying its overall steerage of the economy.

The 16th Central Committee explicated the detailed goals in its Third Plenum:

> [I]mproving the economic system with public ownership as the main component, with diversified forms of ownership developing jointly as the basis of the economic system; to form and promote a mechanism that coordinates the development of the regional economy; build a unified, open, competitive and orderly modern market system; improve the macro-control of the system, the administrative management system and the economic legal system. …[109]
>
> [S]peed up the adjustment, layout and structure of the state-owned economy. It is necessary to adapt to the continuous development of economic marketization, further enhance the vitality of the public-owned economy, vigorously develop a mixed-ownership economy in which state-owned capital, collective capital, and non-public-owned capital participate in shares, achieve diversification of investment bases, and make the share-holding system the main form of public ownership.[110]

Additionally, it was also resolved to "develop large companies and conglomerates with international competitiveness."[111]

Per the Plenum, in order to achieve these overarching goals, several simultaneous schemes were to be pursued:

(i) a macro-plan that would segment the market according to varying desired degrees of ownership diversification;
(ii) reform state-assets' management and supervision;
(iii) reform the state's administrative management system (i.e., institutional reforms); and
(iv) strengthen Party leadership over the socialist market economic system.

109 Decision of the Central Committee of the CCP on Several Issues Concerning the Improvement of a Socialist Market Economy [中共中央关于完善社会主义市场经济体制若干问题的决定], adopted at the Third Plenary Session of the 16th Central Comm., Oct. 14, 2003, art 1(2).

110 Ibid., art. 2(4).

111 Ibid. Lin and Milhaupt identify the roots of this CCP scheme to appear even earlier, in the NPC's approval of the Ninth Five-Year Plan, passed by the Eight Nat'l People's Cong., Mar. 17, 1996. See L-W. Lin & C. Milhaupt, "We Are the (National) Champions: Understanding the Mechanisms of State Capitalism in China," *Stanford Law Review* 65 (2013) 697, at 714, note 51.

These meant that while the individual, private, and other non-public economies were recognized as important forces, the Party-state had something more particular in mind. The new development plan to segment the market with varying degrees of ownership diversification meant that the central Party-state would determine in which industries competitive market forces were to be encouraged, and which would remain exclusively or dominantly publicly owned.[112] Thus, within the public sector, SOEs would be categorized as those requiring absolute or relative control. In the former, central-state control would be enhanced and consolidated. In the latter, the capital base of the enterprise would be diversified (infusing SOEs with private capital), and various forms of asset management would be advanced to try to improve efficiency and competitiveness. In industries designated as "competitive," the Party-state would not only provide recognition of the private sector but would also actively remove obstacles for its growth.

The notion of constructing the whole industrial system based on mixed ownership of private and public capital began to take form. Legal tools and institutions were to be utilized across all relevant schemes to make sure of this.

The infusion of private capital into SOEs as a component of SOE reforms was of course not new, but it accelerated in this period via a more structured and comprehensive implementation of the *zhua da fang xiao* strategy in the designated industries.[113] This involved grasping the largest and the most strategic enterprises, which tended to be controlled by the central government, and releasing the small ones either to local government restructuring plans, private market participants, or in some cases dissolving such firms and taking them apart. (The implementation of the strategy took place at a high volume during the years of the 17th Congress [2007–2012] through waves of mergers and acquisitions, when it aligned with yet another reform strategy called "mixed ownership" [discussed in Chapter 5]).

This component in the Party-state market development scheme was a strong motivation for the Party-state to advance a more market-supporting legal framework. This was the beginning of what economist Barry Naughton recently termed "grand steerage" as China's approach to market development.[114]

And thus, the 16th Central Committee expressed a new commitment to

> [E]ncourage, support and actively guide the development of the non-public economy … to clean up or revise laws, regulations and policies, and remove institutional obstacles that limit the development of the sector.[115]

[112] On sectoral variations in market governance as a development policy in China, see R. Hsueh, "State Capitalism, Chinese-Style: Strategic Value of Sectors, Sectoral Characteristics, and Globalization," *Governance* 29(1) (2016) 85.

[113] As mentioned, the phrase, attributed to Zhu Rongji, was noted as early as in the 1997 government work report at the 15th Party Congress. But while the strategy started being implemented already as part of the Ninth Five Year Plan (1996–2000), it entered a deeper and broader implementation phase only after 2007 when the idea of a mixed ownership gained political focus.

[114] B. Naughton, "Grand Steerage." In T Fingar & J. C. Oi. (eds.) *Fateful Decisions: Choices that Will Shape China's Future* (Stanford University Press, 2020) 51.

[115] Decision on Several Issues Concerning the Improvement of a Socialist Market Economy, note 110.

One of the main obstacles, which was specifically addressed by the CCP, was the lack of a modern property rights system. While an increasing number of laws throughout the 1990s recognized several *organizational forms* for private economic activity, private ownership and other private rights to property were not acknowledged in law and thus received no formal protection. Informal governance continued to function as substitutes. Local protectionism, political incentives, network relations, and trust systems provided non-legal guarantees, de facto shielding against state expropriation of property, arbitrary state action, and violations of obligations between market participants. The operation of these substitutes had an important role in supporting economic activity when legal recognition and protections of property (and contract) rights were absent.[116]

Yet, such informal governance had its costs. It generated arbitrariness, resulted in contradicting norms that often violated norms of a higher administrative hierarchy, and amplified the dependence of market participants on local officials. Protectionism also generated capture, which, under China's administrative organization, created courts that are beholden to their local governments. Informal governance substitutes thus empowered the economic and administrative capacities of local governments at the expense of the center. In addition, throughout the 1990s and early 2000s, market demand for greater protection of private property rights intensified. The demand was particularly strong with respect to land ownership and land use. Land takings without compensation (mainly by local governments) became an acute problem that triggered a prolonged (and still ongoing) political and social debate. Taken together, as the Party-state began to actively support private markets and encourage their growth, it turned to formal laws and legal institutions to regulate rights of property.

Following the CCP's newly expressed commitment to the private sector, a constitutional amendment was passed to address the issue. The amendment reflected that the "non-publicly owned economic sector is now *encouraged and supported*" by the state (rather than simply acknowledged). Private property rights received a constitutional status for the first time and were declared inviolable. It was further determined that the administration and supervision of the non-public sector should be conducted in accordance with the law, and private and public property should be equally protected.[117] However, as scholars have noted, since it took several years until a formal national Property Law was adopted (2007), the practical implication of this constitutional recognition was limited.[118]

116 Clarke et al., *The Role of Law in China's Economic Development*, note 41, at. 399–403 and 406–408; L. Putterman, "The Role of Ownership and Property Rights in China's Economic Transition," *The China Quarterly* 144 (1995) 1047.

117 The 2004 amendment of the PRC Constitution [中华人民共和国宪法修正案(2004)], promulgated by the Tenth Nat'l People's Cong., Mar. 14, 2004 [the 2004 Constitutional Amendment], arts. 11, 13.

118 T. Xu, "The Right to Private Property and Its Enforcement: The Changing Public-Private Divide in the PRC," *Journal of Comparative Law* 4 (2009) 96. Ideological controversies within the Party and the public hauled the drafting process for several years. Mainly, the drafts of the property law were

The eventual legal recognition of property rights during the 17th Party Congress, toward the end of the era,[119] joined a series of important revisions to several business organization laws, including the Partnership Enterprise Law, the Company Law, and the Securities Law.[120] Absent these revisions, the constitutional proclamations would have had no efficacy.[121] These laws translated the constitutional support for private market activity into a more practical and justiciable legal framework. The updated legal framework expanded the market access of private market participants to industries that were previously restricted. It granted them, at least formally, equal access to financing and replaced mandatory market rigidity with more enabling, macro-level default rules with the central government's overarching supervision. These steps, along with a parallel institutional organization, to which I turn below, were as the apex of China's Legal Modernization Era.

The new CCP plan for industrial reorganization was followed by a government notice that operationalized the plan and clarified the appropriate industrial

criticized for violating the constitutional characteristics of the PRC as a socialist country. See J. Chen, *Chinese Law: Context and Transformation* (Martinus Nijhoff Publishers, 2008), at 374–389; S. Sui, "New Property Law Shakes Up China," *BBC News* (Mar. 8, 2007), http://news.bbc.co.uk/2/hi/asia-pacific/6429977.stm.

119 Property Law of the People's Republic of China [中华人民共和国物权法], adopted by the Tenth Nat'l People's Cong., Mar. 16, 2007 (currently ineffective, was absorbed by the new PRC Civil code on May 28, 2020).

120 Including but not limited to: Several Opinions of the State Council on Encouraging, Supporting and Guiding the Development of Individual, Private and Other Non-Public Economic Sectors of the Economy [国务院关于鼓励支持和引导个体私营等非公有制经济发展的若干意见], issued by the St. Council, Feb. 19, 2005 (these have expanded market access to previously restricted industries, such as financing, infrastructure, national defense, public utilities, and social services). The revision of The Partnership Enterprise law (revs'd by the Tenth Nat'l People's Cong., Aug. 27, 2006, effective June 1, 2007), added "Limited Liability Partnership" to the menu of enterprise organization choices. This enabled enterprises ("legal person") to become partners, setting a more internationally "acceptable" tax regime for partnerships (taxing income directly from partners), and establishing bankruptcy process for partnerships. A long and controversial drafting process to revise the 1986 Enterprise Bankruptcy Law was finally concluded in August 2006, The Law of the People's Republic of China on Enterprise Bankruptcy [中华人民共和国企业破产法], adopted by the Standing Comm. of the Tenth Nat'l People's Cong., Aug. 27, 2006, effective June 1, 2007 (creating a more comprehensive bankruptcy regime and unifying the previously bifurcated bankruptcy treatment over SOEs with that of other legal person enterprises). The 1993 Company law was revised, wholesale, in 2005 (most recently amended Oct. 26, 2018), along with a revision to the PRC Securities Law. The Company Law of the Peoples Republic of China [中华人民共和国公司法], promulgated by the Standing Comm. Nat'l People's Cong., Dec. 29, 1993, revs'd Oct. 27, 2005; The Securities Law of the People's Republic of China [中华人民共和国证券法], promulgated by the Standing Comm. of the 9th Nat'l People's Cong., Dec. 29, 1998, revs'd Oct. 27, 2005 (the revision of these laws changed mandatory treatment of companies and listed companies into default set of rules, enabling more discretion to market participants), see discussion in these revisions in Part III.

121 As mentioned earlier, the PRC Constitution is not justiciable in and of itself. Constitutional provisions cannot be applied directly when deciding concrete cases and thus need to be enshrined in a lower-level legal norm to be examined by the court and have practical implications. K. Shen, "Is It the Beginning of the Era of the Rule of the Constitution-Reinterpreting China's First Constitutional Case," *Pacific Rim Law & Policy Journal* 12 (2003) 199.

segmentation.[122] Many secondary and tertiary administrative rules were promulgated by various central-government regulators to facilitate the aspired plan.

The time alignment between the enactment of the Property Law and the acceleration of market segmentation through mixed capital was important and likely not coincidental. The text of Hu Jintao's report at the 17th Party Congress suggests that the concessions that were made to the private sector were needed for the success of a mixed ownership reform that was then in the pipeline.[123] Here too, the law was mobilized to translate the Party-state's vision of the economy and its priorities as to who should hold economic powers. This was another indication that the legal developments in support of private economic activity throughout the Legal Modernization Era were part of a broad political–economic plan that determined how markets should function and how they should be organized. In developing legal recognition of property rights, reforming enterprise organization laws in support of small and medium enterprises, pushing a regulatory framework for capital market investments and the financial systems, the interests of market participants and the interests of the Party-state merged.

The analysis above shows how during the Legal Modernization Era the law was advanced to structure the market. The law translated the desired balance between planning and market forces into operational goals. These political functions of law aligned with the growing needs of the market, thus advancing the interests of market participants even while the economic functions of law remained weak.

Next, I turn to observe how the law was utilized to establish state capacities in the market during the same period.

2 *The Use of Law to Build Party-State Capacity*

Efforts to configure the institutional capacities of the central government took place throughout China's market development process. The Legal Modernization Era saw several major conceptual and institutional reforms that involved an extensive use of legal mechanisms across the Party-state organization for this purpose.

Party and state documents already from early on in the period highlight the role of law in rehabilitating the governance capacities of the Party-state. A 1993 document released by the Central Committee of the CCP and the State Council stated that to solve China's

122 Notice of the General Office of the State Council on Forwarding the Guiding Opinions of SASAC about Promoting the Adjustment of State-Owned Capital and the Reorganization of State-Owned Enterprises [国务院办公厅转发国资委关于推进国有资本调整和国有企业重组指导意见的通知(国办发[2006]97号)], issued by Notice No. 97 [2006] of the General Office of the St. Council, Dec. 5, 2006.

123 Hu Jintao's Report at the 17th Nat'l Congress of the Communist Party of China [胡锦涛在中国共产党第十七次全国代表大会上的报告], Oct. 25, 2007, https://archive.ph/awEYR [Report at the 17th Party Congress]. See Chapter V. "Promoting Sound and Fast Economic Development," in which Hu addressed the urgency of establishing a modern property rights system as the basis to the development of a "*mixed ownership sector*" and provided details as to related steps such as the encouragement of small and medium enterprises and certain improvements in the capital market, investment, and financial system.

problems, it must first "unify its thinking," expressing the need to "coordinate the pace of action" and "handle well the relationship between the parts and the whole," noting that:

> [T]he implementation of macro-control measures is affected due to inconsistent opinions [about the pace of reforms]… These are issues that are not easy to understand when observed from a local perspective.

The document called on party and state organs to improve and strengthen macro control over the development process as part of China's building of a "socialist market economy" and included the use of central laws and regulations among the relevant measures.[124]

Jiang Zemin's report at the 15th Party Congress (1997) brought up the need for more extensive legal reform not only in relation to market governance but also with regard to governance at large.[125] The subsequent 1999 amendment of the Constitution declared that "the People's Republic of China shall practice ruling the country according to law and building a socialist country governed by law."[126] A significant step following the amendment was a five-year plan for judicial reform. Its stated intent was to increase the impartiality of the People's court system and strengthen public trust.[127] Some translators and scholars consider these steps as the introduction of a Chinese-type "rule of law." Others see them as linguistic invocations absent a substantive change of views concerning the role of law in society.[128] Putting the contentions around the meaning of rule of law in China aside for the moment, these changes reflected that the space for legal institutions was set to expand with respect to both governing markets and governance capacities at large.

Party Level

Interestingly, Party documents during the same time reflect increasing concerns about instability. Reform and opening, from the decentralization process through

[124] Opinions of the Central Committee of the CCP and the State Council on the Current Economic Situation and Strengthening Macroeconomic Control [中共中央 国务院关于当前经济情况和加强宏观调控的意见], issued June 24, 1993 (Zhongfa 1993, No.6), https://archive.ph/hVa9S.

[125] Report at the 15th Party Congress, note 71.

[126] See 1999 Constitutional Amendment, article 5.

[127] Five-Year Reform Outline of the People's Court, 1999 [人民法院五年改革纲要, 1999], issued by the Supreme People's Court, legal release No. 28 [1999], Oct. 20, 1999. Five reform plans were initiated since (1999–2003, 2004–08, 2009–13, 2014–18, and 2019–23).

[128] A footnote will not do justice with the scope and depth of articles discussing this issue. See, for example, L. Cata Backer, "The Rule of Law: The Chinese Communist Party, and Ideological Campaigns: Sange Daibiao (The "Three Represents"), Socialist Rule of Law, and Modern Chinese Constitutionalism," *Journal of Transitional Law and Contemporary Problems* 16(1) (2006) 101; A. HY. Chen, "Toward a Legal Enlightenment: Discussions in Contemporary China on the Rule of Law," *UCLA Pacific Basin Law Journal* 17 (1999) 125; Chen, *Chinese Law: Context and Transformation*, note 119, at 63 (and the references therein); Peerenboom, *China's Long March toward Rule of Law*, note 62; C. Wang, "From the Rule of Man to the Rule of Law." In D. Cai & C. Wang (eds.), *China's Journey towards the Rule of Law: Legal Reform 1978–2008* (Brill, 2010), at 4–5 (describing a debate among Chinese legal scholars on the correct terminology).

the rising presence of foreign and private market participants, amplified opportunities for personal gain and abuse of power. Thus, aside from concerns about potential moral and ideological pollution, the development of the market also introduced serious challenges to the governing capacities of the Party-state. This not only challenged the power dynamics between the center and the local governments but also gradually took a toll on the Party's own cohesion and authority.

This was particularly evident in the second decade of the Legal Modernization Era. Calls to reunite behind the central Party-state intensified. The 2002 amendment to the CCP Charter included specific calls to improve Party leadership and governance and to strengthen the ability of the Party to fight corruption and endure rising risks.[129] To tighten its grip, the Party set a series of internal procedures to reform its own governance capacities.[130]

Legal institutions and notions of the rule of law (*yifa zhiguo*, literally "a law-based governance" or "ruling/administering the country according to law") as a tool for consolidating control and improving internal governance within the Party-state started to appear more frequently in both Party and state documents. These included the 2002 amendment to the CCP Charter:

> Persist in expanding socialist democracy, improve the socialist legal system, rule the country according to law (*yifa zhiguo*), and build a socialist rule of law country (*shihuizhuyi fazhi guojia*) and consolidate the people's democratic dictatorship. Adhere to the system of people's congresses … Strengthen national legislation and the work of law enforcement, so that the country's work will gradually advance on the track of legalization.[131]

And in subsequent internal Party rules:

> [We should] improve the system, mechanisms, and methods for the Party to lead economic work in accordance with the requirements of developing the socialist market economy…. The Party Committee should support the government in fulfilling its duties according to law, push government administration according to law (*yifa xingzheng*)… deepen the reform of the administrative system…use mainly economic and legal means to manage economic activity.

129 Charter of the Communist Party of China (2002 revision)[中国共产党章程(2002修改)], revs'd by the Sixteenth Nat'l Cong. of the Communist Party of China, Nov. 14, 2002, see preamble and Chapter VIII.

130 Decision of the Central Committee of the CCP on Strengthening the Party's Governance Capabilities [中共中央关于加强党的执政能力建设的决定], adopted at the Fourth Plenary Session of the 16th Central Comm., Sep 19, 2004, https://archive.ph/AMr1X [Decisions on Strengthening Party Governance].

The urgency of party building reforms was further highlighted and the Party building plan elaborated later in the Decision of the Central Committee of the CCP on Several Significant Issues Concerning Strengthening and Improving Party Building under New Circumstances [中共中央关于加强和改进新形势下党的建设若干重大问题的决定], adopted at the Fourth Plenary Session of the 17th Central Comm. of the CCP on September 18, 2009, [CCP Decision on Strengthening Party Building], https://archive.ph/XcqJD.

131 Charter of the Communist Party of China (2002 revision).

> Carry out the basic plan of rule of law (*yifa zhiguo*) and raising the level of legality among those in office. Governing according to law is the basic way of Party governance under the new historic conditions. Party leadership is the fundamental safeguard of rule of law.[132]

More practical plans to reform the governance capacities of the CCP included changes to the cadre and personnel appointment and evaluation system, enhancing the role of leading groups, introducing changes to Party grass-root organizations, improving coordination within democratic centralism, strengthening ties between the Party and the society at large, and finding mechanisms to address mounting corruption.[133] As will be seen in Chapter 5, these aspects and the use of legal tools to advance them have been amplified in the current era.

State Level

At the state level, capacity building through law included the legal establishment of central-government institutions with vast regulatory authority over market development. The aim was to centralize previously fragmented economic decision-making powers (fragmented as in spread and duplicated across multiple central state bodies, with broad leeway and too little supervision over local authorities) with fewer and stronger central government agencies. The goal was:

> [To] abolish 'secondary dealers' between the state and enterprises, and to eliminate the organizational stronghold of un-separated government and enterprises.

In early 1998, the NPC approved the State Council Institutional Reform Plan, which followed the 15th CCP Central Committee plan to restructure the "government administrative management system." The plan detailed a series of institutional reforms to establish a leaner and better coordinated governance and streamline control over the economic system.[134] The Institutional Reform Plan noted the aim to strengthen the role of law in constructing the institutional reorganization scheme.[135]

[132] Decisions on Strengthening Party Governance, note 131, arts. 4(5), 5(2), respectively.

[133] Decisions on Strengthening Party Governance, note 131, art. 9, as well as CCP Decision on Strengthening Party Building, note 131.

[134] The plan was approved by the NPC on Mar. 10, 1998. See State Council Institutional Reform Plan [国务院机构改革方案], State Council Gazette, Issue No. 9 (901), Apr. 22, 1998 [Institutional Reform Plan].

[135] This was further promoted by the Decision of the State Council on Comprehensively Promoting Administration by Law [国务院关于全面推进依法行政的决定], issued by the St. Council (Guo Fa [1999] No. 23), Nov. 8, 1999. The decision called governments at all levels and their working departments to strengthen the construction of their governance system, and comprehensively promote law-based administration and build a law-based government to "rectify problems that hinder the development of the economy and society." Separating government from enterprises and governance affairs is elaborated as one of the methods.

In the following year, 77 national-level economic laws and regulations were declared null and void, 131 remained in force, and 40 were revised. The number of state council institutions shrank from 40 to 29, most of which were economic department and industrial ministries. Provincial governments followed suit with a similar institutional reform shortly after.[136]

The steps to consolidate regulatory authorities through central institution building accelerated in the second decade of legal modernization, during the 16th and 17th Party Congresses (2002–12)[137] and particularly after the Second Plenum of the 17th Central Committee. The Plenum decided to highlight law-based governance reforms:[138]

> [U]nder the unified central leadership, encourage local integration of real reform and innovation… fundamentally transform government organization and personnel to a more scientific, standardized, and legalized … government. In the next five years, it is necessary to accelerate the transformation of government functions, deepen the reform of government institutions, strengthen administration according to law and institutional building….
>
> The central government should strengthen the macro-management of economic and social affairs, further reduce and delegate specific management matters, and devote more energy to formulating strategic plans, policies, regulations, and standards, and maintaining the unity of the national legal system, decrees, and markets. Local governments should ensure the effective implementation of the central policies and national laws and regulations, strengthen the overall coordination of economic and social affairs in the region, strengthen enforcement and law enforcement supervision responsibilities….[139]

This was further operationalized throughout the decade by several State Council regulations in which lower-level government hierarchies were instructed on how to strengthen "administration according to law" in all aspects of social and economic management.[140]

Administrating by law and the efforts to consolidate governance authorities included clear steps in the market.

[136] See details on the implementation of the 1998 Institutional Reform of the State Council [１９９８年国务院机构改革], as published on the Central Government Portal (Jan. 16, 2009), https://archive.ph/jvLm5.

[137] Notice of the State Council on Distributing an Implementation Outline for Comprehensively Promoting Administration by Law [国务院关于印发全面推进依法行政实施纲要的通知], issued by the St. Council (Guo Fa [2004] No. 10), Mar. 22, 2004.

[138] Opinions on Deepening the Reform of the Administrative Management System [关于深化行政管理体制改革的意见], adopted at the Second Plenary Session of the 17th Central Comm. of the Communist Party of China, Feb. 27, 2008.

[139] CCP Opinions on Deepening the Reform of the Administrative Management System, ibid.

[140] Notice of the State Council on an Implementation Outline, note 138, as well as Decision of the State Council on Strengthening the Administration of Municipal and County Governments [国务院关于加强市县政府依法行政的决定], issued by the St. Council (Guo Fa [2008] No. 17), May. 12, 2008; Opinions of the State Council on Strengthening the Building of a Government Ruled by Law [国务院关于加强法治政府建设的意见], issued by the St. Council (Guo Fa [2010] No. 33), Oct. 10, 2010 (expired).

Prominent among the many schemes for central government institution building were the reorganizations of the state-assets management system, the economic-reform administration system, and the financial system.

The establishment of the State Asset Supervision and Administration Commission ("SASAC") in 2003 was the hallmark of state-asset management reform. In creating a national state assets agency, the Party-state aimed to consolidate the ownership interests of the state under one central ministry-level state body.[141] Before this consolidation, the ownership function over state assets, on behalf of the people, was carried out by various state enterprise groups, holding companies, and state asset management entities at multiple levels (e.g., various lines of bureaus and ministries in different sectors in both the central and local government levels).[142] As put by Donald Clarke, the establishment of SASAC "represented the furthest step yet taken in bringing under a single administrative umbrella the state's activities as enterprise owner (as opposed to an economic regulator)."[143] The hope was that a centralized body that assumed the rights and responsibilities on behalf of the state would better represent and protect the state's interests as an owner.[144] Also, fraud and asset tunneling cases that were revealed in many SOEs and a wave of corporate scandals in 2001 merited a consolidation of control over state assets. Through a more centralized system for supervision and management of state assets, SASAC was meant to facilitate better monitoring of the management of state assets and to ultimately increase the profitability of SOEs.[145]

Both the financial system and the central institutions for administering economic reforms went through similar organizational overhauls during the same period. As part of the 1998 Institutional Reform of the State Council, the State Planning Commission was restructured into the State Development Planning Commission. This solidified a shift from a planned economy to macro-development planning. The commission was responsible for formulating macro-development plans and for macro-economic management. In 2003, with the second wave of authority consolidation, it merged with several other agencies to form the present-day National Development and Reform Commission (NDRC).[146]

141 More specifically, SASAC's authority oversees central SOEs and local SOEs are overseen by local branches of SASAC, which are under the professional supervision of central SASAC yet subject to the patronage of local governments. The Interim Regulations on the Supervision and Management of State-Owned Assets Enterprises [企业国有资产监督管理暂行条例], adopted by the St. Council, May 13, 2003, and promulgated by Decree No. 378, May 27, 2003.

142 See "SASAC'S Responsibilities and Targets," People's Daily (en) (May 22, 2003), https://archive.ph/vCf6w.

143 Clarke, *Legislating for a Market Economy*, note 96, at 576.

144 The formal capacity of SASAC to act as the shareholder on behalf of the state was established in law only six years after the agency was created. Law of the People's Republic of China on State-Owned Assets of Enterprises [中华人民共和国企业国有资产法], promulgated by the Standing Comm. Nat'l People's Cong., Oct. 28, 2008, effective May 1, 2009.

145 The creation of SASAC and its functions as a shareholder as discussed extensively in Part III.

146 For a contemporary analysis on the structure and powers of the NDRC, see M. Wu, "The China, Inc. Challenge to Global Trade Governance," *Harvard International Law Journal* 57 (2016) 261, at 275–277, 292–293. For details on the institutional restructuring in the space of merger control and

In the budding securities market at the end of the 1990s, the State Commission for the Reform of the Economic System (CRES), was promoted to a high-level policymaking commission directly under the State Council (the highest organ of the Chinese government) with the state premier as its top official.[147] The CRES was tasked with bringing forth plans related to enterprise reform and stock issuance in SOEs and had broad authority to translate policy into rules through its guiding opinions. The fragmented regulatory authority over the securities market was also consolidated under one national body, the China Securities Regulatory Commission (CSRC). The idea was to consolidate regulation and oversight authorities in the emerging securities market from the hands of various local branches of the People's Bank of China (PBoC). The CSRC thus moved up the administrative ladder and took a position as a ministry-level agency directly under the State Council with broad authority to regulate the securities market.[148] The CSRC's administrative status and powers were established in the (then) newly enacted Securities Law.[149]

In the rest of the financial industry, China's Banking Regulatory Commission (CBRC) was formed as the national regulator of the banking sector, and its operations were established under the Banking Supervision Law.[150] The Law on the People's Bank of China (known as the Central Bank law) and the Law on Commercial Banks were amended[151] to transfer regulatory authority that had been vested with the PBoC to the CBRC.[152] At

antitrust supervision during the same years, see A. H. Zhang, *Chinese Antitrust Exceptionalism: How the Rise of China Challenges Global Regulation* (Oxford University Press, 2021), at 35–41.

147 1998 Institutional Reform Plan, note 135.

148 The institutional changes in China's securities market are discussed further in Part III.

149 See article 7, 1998 Securities Law, note 92: "the securities regulatory authority under the State Council shall implement a centralized and unified regulation of the nationwide securities market in order to ensure their lawful operation."

150 Banking Supervision Law of the People's Republic of China [中华人民共和国银行业监督管理法], adopted by the Standing Comm. of the Tenth Nat'l People's Cong., December 27, 2003, revs'd by the Standing Comm. of the Tenth Nat'l People's Cong., Oct. 31, 2006.

151 Law of the People's Republic of China on Commercial Banks [商业银行法], adopted by the Standing Comm. of the Eighth Nat'l People's Cong., May 10, 1995, amended by the Standing Comm. of the Tenth Nat'l People's Cong., Dec. 27, 2003. Decision of the Standing Committee of the National People's Congress on Revising the Law of the People's Republic of China on the People's Bank of China [中华人民共和国中国人民银行法] adopted by the Standing Comm. of the Tenth Nat'l People's Cong., Dec. 27, 2003.

152 Four specialized national state-owned banks in China (known as "the Big Four") provide credit for businesses (their scope of services increased gradually): The Agricultural Bank of China, The Bank of China, The Construction Bank of China, and the Industrial and Commercial Bank of China. In 1983, the PBoC was designated as China's Central Bank separate from these specialized banks. The Central Bank and the Specialized Banks have regional branches. The banking system was decentralized as local bank branches were subordinated to both the banking hierarchy and to the local government where they operated. Consequently, financial decentralization contributed to local government power accumulation and to overall governance decentralization since local levels had great influence over the credit decisions of the local branches of the Central Bank and Specialized Banks. The regulatory authority over the commercial banking system was first consolidated and vested with the PBoC during the first consolidation wave in mid-late 1990s (during the first decade of the legal modernization era) when the Party-state advanced with fiscal reforms. Shifting the regulatory authority to a new

the same time, Central Huijin Investment Ltd. was created as a shareholding investment entity, organized under the PBoC but as a separate legal entity, to direct state investments and execute government policies with respect to China's financial institutions.[153]

SUMMARY REFLECTIONS

During the Legal Modernization Era, the use of law was advanced in pursuit of two main policy directions: to structure the market through industrial segmentation with varying degrees of central–state control, and to reconfigure the centralized governance capacity of both the Party and the state. Advancing these two priorities, the law paved the channels for consolidating macro control in the market. Notably, in these processes, while the political functions of law had an overriding effect, the use of law seemed to be responsive to market demands as well. A growing private sector, both encouraged and steered by law to strengthen macro control, is ultimately a sector that can break loose from local protectionism, thus limiting dependence on local powers. Similarly, the same private sector can infuse capital to industrial segments destined for greater competition alongside the state. The law, therefore, advanced market considerations as well, when they aligned with political–economic purposes. It was used for fine-tuning a balance between macro-control and market forces as political–economic determinants dictated.

Building institutional capacity and fostering industrial segmentation took place at a time when the geopolitical climate opened opportunities for outbound expansion. The law thus helped fulfill yet another newly stated goal of the Party-state: developing international presence and prowess. Together, these paths of the use of law aided designated firms to amass power. As will be further demonstrated in Chapter 7, the law thus became a backbone in the construction of China's state capitalism.

In these respects, the law in China is a means of engineering social and economic outcomes. As is often the case in many other systems, it is shaped and designed by the priorities of those in power. In the case of China, the goal was to translate and operationalize the Party-state's vision of a "socialist market economy" in which the central Party-state has overarching macroeconomic control while still fostering market development and growth.

commission under a new law was an additional effort to consolidate administrative control over the banking system.

See Y. Qian & B. R. Weingast, "China's Transition to Markets: Market-Preserving Federalism, Chinese Style," *Journal of Policy Reform* 1 (1999) 149.

It is interesting to point out that commercial banks are separated from the so-called "policy banks" – The Agricultural Development Bank of China, the China Development Bank, and the Export-Import Bank of China. These banks were created in the 1990s to handle all "policy-based" lending, that is, lending not based on market criteria (in practice, however, Chinese banks of every level (local/central) are subject to political influence, making market-based lending limited for commercial banks as well).

153 Wu, *China Inc.*, note 147, at 273–275. In 2007, Central Huijin was further reorganized as a wholly owned subsidiary of China's newly established sovereign wealth fund – China Investment Corporation – which operates directly under the state council.

5

Legalized Politicization Era (from 2010 to Present)

As the relationship between the state and the market has continued to evolve throughout the current era, the utilization of law and of legal institutions in governing markets continued to develop as well.

In this era, the law has been assigned a meaningful and more explicit role in directing capital flows and paving the direction in which markets should evolve. The use of law in building Party and state capacities has grown more prominent during this era as well. Legal rhetoric received new emphasis under the banner of a "socialist rule of law country" (*shihuizhuyi fazhi guojia*). This impetus pushes the political functions of law in two main directions: enhancing the market-related capacities of the state and elevating the Chinese Communist Party (CCP)'s own direct agency in the market.

Taking notice of the two functions of law has become ever more relevant. Legal institutions are being used to secure a new political–economic equilibrium within the Party-state system. I will first look at why and how this came to be and then move to examine the legal instruments that solidify this shift.

It should be noted, the past decade has been full of political–economic commotion not least due to a swift deterioration in China's global image. Consequently, when one searches for trends and patterns in the use of law, it is impossible to isolate domestic causes from the effects of such global circumstances. Nonetheless, there are observable aspects in China's approach to governing markets that began before the geopolitical climate deteriorated. It is on these domestically driven determinants that the discussion will focus.

—

ERA OVERVIEW: POLITICAL–ECONOMIC EQUILIBRIUM SHIFTS FOCUS – THE PARTY STEPS IN

Notwithstanding China's great achievements in thirty years of reforms, numerous economic and political challenges have arisen. The challenges reached a boiling point at the turn of the era (ca. 2010) and demanded solutions. The answer came from an unexpected direction, resulting in yet another political–economic equilibrium shift. This time around, economic powers are moving from the state to the Party. Here too, the law is a vital facilitator of such shift.

Economic Determinants

At the end of the prior development era, the Chinese market had concluded three decades of unprecedented development and growth. The central Party-state was able to promote domestic financial market growth and global economic integration, while orchestrating multitude market capacities for itself – regulator, enforcer, financier, and direct owner. The system that emerged featured behemoth internationally competitive corporate groups, often state-controlled, that have amassed political and economic power, aided by subsidies and government mandates to fulfill industrial policy priorities. This situation was dubbed by many as China's "state capitalism" (the rise of state capitalism is discussed in detail in Chapter 7).

At the same time, China's state capitalism brought many economic challenges. The accumulation of debt is primary among them. In the years following the world financial crisis, when the central government was called upon to provide local governments with hefty stimulus packages, the scope of China's local government and corporate debt emerged as a major source for potential financial and social instability.[154] It became clear that the future of China's economic progress was imperiled by a deep debt problem.

At around the same period, indications appeared that China was entering the middle-income trap. China's demographic balance – its aging population and declining workforce – created an impending shortage of labor; its economy was still heavily reliant on exports but was gradually losing its competitive global advantage as wages were rising; and its annual GDP growth started decreasing year after year.[155] Commentators within and outside China opined that China was reaching a turning point that will hinder its ability to sustain economic growth.[156]

To deal with the consequences of the prior decades and address the approaching economic turning point, the leadership came up with a new socio-economic development plan. This scheme, still in force today, has several lead components:

[154] A. Y. Liu et al., "China's Local Government Debt: The Grand Bargain," *The China Journal* 87(1) (2022) 40.

[155] World Bank indicators show an annual decrease of GDP growth since 2010, the last year of two-figure growth rate (10.63 percent). Until that year, China's average annual growth rate was 10 percent. In 2020, China's annual GDP growth rate stood at 2.34 percent, the lowest it was since Mao's era in China.

[156] Y. Yao, "The Relationship between China's Export-Led Growth and Its Double Transition of Demographic Change and Industrialization, *Asian Economic Papers* 10(2) (2011) 52; X. Zhang et al., "China Has Reached the Lewis Turning Point," *China Economic Review* 22(4) (2011) 542; 'A. Singh et al., "Chronicle of a Decline Foretold: Has China Reached the Lewis Turning Point?," In *China's Economy in Transition: From External to Internal Rebalancing* (International Monetary Fund, 2013).

Starting with the twelfth five-year plan (2011–15) and throughout the current era, the broad development agenda turned to focus on building China's technological prowess. Creating an innovation-based economy also became China's new avenue for increasing its global competitiveness in lieu of exports.[157]

With parallel, looking for new avenues for growth, the Party-state initiated the Belt and Road Initiative (BRI), a plan that paved the way for Chinese firms to enter new markets in Euro-Asia-Africa through infrastructure construction and investment projects.[158]

In addition, one of the main economic goals set by China's policymakers was to improve industrial self-sufficiency and raise productivity gains. Here there was a dire need to correct industrial overcapacity, industries in which supply and demand were greatly misaligned, including finding answers to China's mounting debt problem (i.e., deleveraging China's financial market). Policymakers' attention gradually turned away from exports to economic measures that would induce production for the domestic market, boost consumption, and cut off access capacity. In other words, China's economic policy has turned inward.[159] While clearly this inward-facing turn addressed China's own economic trajectory, it has accelerated in recent years due to the growing negative world views toward China and suspicions about cross-border Chinese trade and investments. The legal system has been instrumental in advancing these new industrial schemes.

In terms of its political function, the use of law has been essential in ensuring that both the state and the Party apparatuses have enough political capital to advance the complex set of goals detailed above. In terms of its economic function, the legal system in this era has been mobilized in at least one main direction – to direct

[157] Few of the hallmark industrial policies designed to advance China's technological prowess include: (1) "Made in China 2025," an industrial strategic plan to upgrade China's manufacturing sector within ten years by shifting from a low-cost industrialized country to a technology-based powerhouse. See Made in China 2025 [中国制造2025], issues by a Notice of the St. Council (Guofa [2015] No. 28), May 19, 2015; (2) "China Standards 2035" [中国标准2035], a national research project that was initiated in 2018 to research and develop a strategic layout for setting up world leading standards in the fields of engineering, science, and technology. The research project was concluded in 2020 and implementation plans are currently being constructed by SAMR, the newly formed state council agency for market regulation [国家市场监督管理总局] and its National Standardization Administration Committee [国家标准化管理委员会]; (3) China's Military-Civil Fusion (*junmin ronghe*) [军民融合], is yet another important technological industrial policy. The scheme is designed to harness the innovative power of the private sector to develop, produce, and export technology that has dual-use capabilities in order to speed up the modernization of the PLA and enhance China's military-industrial base.

[158] Several Opinions of the CPC Central Committee and the State Council on Developing a New System of Open Economy [中共中央、国务院关于构建开放型经济新体制的若干意见], issued by the Central Comm. of the Communist Party of China and the St. Council, May 5, 2015.

[159] "The Standing Committee of the Politburo of the CCP Held a Meeting" [中共中央政治局常务委员会召开会议], People's Daily Online [人民网] (May 15, 2020), https://archive.ph/3hMfo; J. Blanchette & A. Polk, "Dual Circulation and China's New Hedged Integration Strategy," CSIS (Aug. 24, 2020), www.csis.org/analysis/dual-circulation-and-chinas-new-hedged-integration-strategy; J. Boulter, "China's Supply-Side Structural Reform" (Reserve Bank of Australia, Dec. 2018).

capital flows. Just as legal instruments were utilized to effectuate market segmentation in the prior era (and in that "structured the market"); in the current era, they are used to make sure that capital is being allocated according to the new socioeconomic priorities. Black letter law as well as additional legal institutions, such as the shareholding-position of the state and its regulatory capacity, have been elevated and mobilized in such a manner.

Not all of the new macro industrial schemes were necessarily translated into black letter law in national statutes or state council regulations. Some of these schemes are operationalized only through normative documents and tertiary administrative regulations (such as internal departmental rules).[160] As in earlier decades, this enables the flexibility required to adjust and respond to changing domestic and geopolitical circumstances and fine-tune the measures. Nonetheless, legal institutions have been instrumental.

The new economic policy that calls for increasing productivity gains, for example, while itself not enshrined in formal law, translated into a regulatory drive that cut down industries identified as underproductive. In this context, we witness new legal impetus to block the growth of industries that are assessed to be speculative, untamed, or wasteful (such as certain offshore mergers and acquisitions (M&A) activity, monopoly industries, the gaming industry, or online education businesses). This utilization of the legal machinery consequently tunnels resources to areas identified as more productive (e.g., vocational training, big data, and AI). Similarly, expanding the reach of state ownership into the private sector through minimal ownership positions, as has been pursued in fervor in recent years, is a use of the ownership capacity of the state – a legal institution – to produce the same capital steering effect.

In these developments we again witness the use of legal institutions to direct the market in lieu of market forces. The law here is used to advance a desired economic outcome and in this sense fulfills an economic function, albeit one set by the polity and *not necessarily* directed to secure the economic rights of market participants.

[160] For example, a search at pkulaw.com and China Law & Reference produced three non-regulatory documents by the State Council, twenty-three central-level departmental rules, and one SPC judicial interpretation discussing supply-side structural reform since 2016. The state council documents were non-regulatory reports, but they make clear that the plan applies at the national level: see, for example, The State Council Report on Promoting Supply-Side Structural Reform and Accelerating the Transformation and Upgrading of the Manufacturing Industry [国务院关于推进供给侧结构性改革加快制造业转型升级工作情况的报告], issued by the St. Council, Apr. 24, 2017. On the Belt and Road Initiative, there have been eighty-nine central-level departmental rules, twenty-six inner rules by industry organizations (e.g., chamber of commerce, stock exchanges), and six SPC judicial interpretations and opinions. The highest-level norm being two shared "opinions" by the CCP Central Committee and the State Council. The first, establishing the scheme, are the Opinions on Developing a New System of Open Economy, note 159. The second are the Opinions on Establishing the "Belt and Road" International Commercial Dispute Settlement Mechanism and Institution [关于建立"一带一路"国际商事争端解决机制和机构的意见], issued by the General Office of the Central Comm. of the CCP and the General Office of the St. Council, June 27, 2018.

Political Determinants

The economic determinants noted above and their impact on how the Party-state has recently advanced the use of law in governing markets are well recognized and receive attention recently. Much less recognized, however, particularly outside the China-research community, is how China's economic development impelled a shift within the Party-state system itself and how the legal system has been operationalized to secure such shift.

As China's economy grew larger and markets expanded and deepened, governing the markets became more complex and the levers exerting controls weakened. Domestically, the combination of a slowing economy, rising socio-economic gaps, corruption, and the rise of state capitalism that bred capture and conflicts, met with public discontent. Public discourse and intellectuals within China voiced criticisms against corruption and the weakening of institutions and of governance.[161] Specific concerns raised include for example: the weak functions of the NPC in supervising government organs; local people's congresses being deeply involved in administrative and economic affairs while neglecting public opinion and legislative work; governance reforms at the local level lagging behind the center's plans; lack of law enforcement unity; general disrespect for the organs of the central state among officials and Party members; judicial bodies captured by local constraints; and local leaders (mainly heads of party committees) with concentrated powers "parading" their status.[162] The critics conveyed that the central state was "not firm enough to stop such phenomena."[163]

On top of the above, as markets grew open while growth was slowing, the Party itself started confronting a serious legitimacy crisis. Many observers of China believe that the legitimacy of the Communist Party hangs on its ability to sustain economic growth and is thus threatened by the slowing economy.[164] Growth and market opening created serious socio-economic gaps and generated a class of wealthy crony capitalists,

[161] These open critiques might have been encouraged by Wen Jiabao's work report calling to "create conditions for the people to criticize and supervise the government." Wen Jiabao, *Government Work Report*, delivered at the Third Session of the Eleventh Nat'l People's Cong., Mar. 5, 2010.

[162] For example, G. Zhu, "Lagging and Overstepping: An Overview of Local Political Development" [滞后与超越:中国地方政治发展总体观], *Wuhan University Journal of Social Philosophy Science* [武汉大学学报（哲学社会科学版）] 3 (2010) 328; J. Shao, "Can the National People's Congress Ask the Government to Serve the People?" [人大可以向政府为民请命吗?], Aisixiang (Mar. 3, 2010), https://archive.ph/mXREW; R. Zhou, "Correct the Relationship between Yourself and the People" [摆正自己和人民的关系], Aisixiang (Mar. 11, 2010), https://archive.ph/hjlJu (the author is the former deputy editor in chief of the People's Daily);

[163] Zhu, *Lagging and Overstepping*, ibid.

[164] Z. Keck, "Chinese Elites: The Real Threat to the Communist Party," Diplomat (Jan. 28, 2014), https://thediplomat.com/2014/01/chinese-elites-the-real-threat-to-the-communist-party/ (emphasizing the challenge in rebalancing the economy while maintaining benefits for the political elite); D. Shambaugh, "The Coming Chinese Crackup," *Wall Street Journal* (Mar. 6, 2015), www.wsj.com/articles/the-coming-chinese-crack-up-1425659198 (pointing to China's economic "systemic traps" and Xi's reform efforts as one of the indicators to the regimes vulnerability and instability); J. Stowell, "An Economic Downturn in China Is the Greatest Threat to Chinese Domestic Security – How Long Can

many of whom are Party members. A number of them have been linked to corruption and have received broad social criticism. The link between Party members, cronyism, and corruption reduces the cohesion around the communist ideology as an instrument of control and thus deepens the threat to the legitimacy of the regime. Finally, in addition to general legitimacy concerns, the ability of the CCP to exert control over the state's administrative system and the individuals operating it has weakened as individuals' economic incentives to defy unitary discipline increased.[165] Indeed, the consequences of the prior decades of devolution of administrative and economic authority in the service of economic development loom large and have destabilized the central Party-state organization. And so, toward 2010, at the turn of the era, economic growth has become the main basis for the Party's legitimacy, on the one hand, and one of the main threats to its political unity and hold on power, on the other.

These realities suggested that the Party-state was losing its political capital. The earlier attempts to resolve the spillover effects of market development did not suffice. Consolidating powers at the central government level did not bring optimal results and perhaps even backfired. Many economic and governance challenges remained, and now new ones, consequences of state capitalism, were adding up. The severity of the situation was explicitly recognized by China's leaders. Party-state documents from the current era reflect a sense of urgency to step in and find solutions.[166]

the Social Contract in China Endure?," *Global Security Review* (May 28, 2018), https://globalsecurityreview.com/degree-chinas-internal-stability-depend-economic-growth/; https://globalsecurityreview.com/threats-legitimacy-power-chinese-communist-party/ (viewing "sustained economic growth" as a new mandate of heaven).

[165] A. G. Walder, "The Quiet Revolution from within: Economic Reform as a Source of Political Decline." In *The Waning of the Communist State: Economic Origins of Political Decline in China and Hungary* (University of California Press, 1995).

[166] The challenges are emphasized routinely in CCP rhetoric and are wrapped within Xi Jinping's "New Era" rhetoric of national rejuvenation. For representative examples, check:

Xi Jinping, "Understanding the New Development Stage, Applying the New Development Philosophy, and Creating the New Development Dynamic," Speech at a seminar for provincial and ministerial-level officials on studying and implementing the guiding principles of the Fifth Plenary Session of the 19th CPC Central Committee, January 11, 2021, published in *Qiushi Journal* (English edition), No. 9, 2021, https://archive.ph/fqved.

Xi Jinping's report at the 19th Nat'l Congress of the Communist Party of China, "Secure a Decisive Victory in Building a Moderately Prosperous Society in All Respects and Strive for the Great Success of Socialism with Chinese Characteristics for a New Era," Oct. 18, 2017. Translation available here: https://archive.md/u6y7q:

> Both China and the world are in the midst of profound and complex changes. China is still in an important period of strategic opportunity for development; the prospects are bright but the challenges are severe. All comrades must aim high and look far, be alert to dangers even in times of calm, have the courage to pursue reform and break new ground… Achieving national rejuvenation will be no walk in the park; it will take more than drum beating and gong clanging to get there. Every one of us in the Party must be prepared to work even harder toward this goal … Realizing our great dream demands a great struggle. It is in the movement of contradictions that a society advances; where there is contradiction there is struggle. If our Party is to unite and lead the people to effectively respond to major challenges, withstand major risks, overcome major obstacles, and address major conflicts, it must undertake a great struggle with many new contemporary features…

And so, in the new era, beyond economic determinants that have pushed the need for devising a new economic development plan, political determinants have made it clear that governance capacities within the Party-state system had to be reinforced as well. The legalized politicization era therefore reveals a political-economic change. The effort to construct "a socialist rule of law" is a prominent tool in securing such a change. It operates to enhance macro controls in the market, reinforcing the capacities of central state institutions, on the one hand, while opening up pathways for direct CCP agency in the market, on the other. This equilibrium shift, secured with the aid of the legal system, bears significant implications for the Chinese market and the participants therein (discussed in Chapters 8, 9).

—

1 *Reinforcing State Capacities in the Market*

Throughout China's economic trajectory, the Party-state has been testing the tradeoffs between market control and economic growth in search of the right balance that would suit its vision of a socialist market economy. Preserving overall *macroeconomic* control is largely accepted to be a primary component of the Chinese Party-state authoritarian system and thus remained a persistent feature of economic governance throughout the reform eras. Identifying a desirable level of *micro* economic control and maintaining it within desired confines, however, has been much more contentious and is constantly in flux.

As seen earlier, Party rhetoric offers a good reflection of the evolving approach toward the desired balance. The early years of the current era, particularly following the Third Plenum of the 18th Central Committee (2013), reflected an unprecedented market-oriented rhetoric. The Plenum Communiqué reiterated that public ownership is the main component in China's economic system, but it also noted:

> A core issue is to properly handle the relationship between the government and the market, *to allow the market to play a decisive role in resource allocation* and the government to play its role better.
>
> …
>
> [B]oth the public ownership economy and the non-public ownership economy are important components of the socialist market economy, and *both are an important foundation* in the country's economic-social development.[167] (emphasis added)

The CCP Central Committee's Decisions on Comprehensive Deepening the Reforms, issued following the Plenum, specifically promoted the notion of mixed ownership and acknowledged the need to expand the financial market. It explicitly

[167] Communiqué of the Third Plenary Session of the 18th Central Committee of the Communist Party of China [中国共产党第十八届中央委员会第三次全体会议公报], adopted and promulgated by the Third Plenary Session of the 18th Central Comm. Communist Party of China, Nov. 12, 2013.

addressed the capital market, calling for a reduction of entry barriers by simplifying and accelerating the process of issuing shares to the public.[168]

The legal framework adjusted to such calls. Particularly noteworthy in this context is the 2018 establishment of the Science & Technology Innovation Board of the Shanghai Stock Exchange, a step that Xi himself reportedly pushed for,[169] and the 2019 amendment of the PRC Securities law. These steps were designed to shift away from heavy screening of firms that seek to issue their shares to the public for the first time (IPO) toward a registration system with lesser entry barriers.[170] Also noteworthy is an overhaul of the securities investment fund industry, which went through complete revisions of its legal and institutional framework to accommodate new investment fund structures,[171] and the revision of the Small and Medium-Sized Enterprises Law (SME Law), which, for the first time, legally defined the development of small and medium enterprises as part of China's long-term development strategy.[172] In November 2021, a designated stock exchange for SMEs commenced operations in Beijing to facilitate raising external finance, thus infusing capital to support these firms.

At the time, many commentators within and outside of China applauded the decisions of the 18th Central Committee and the subsequent legal changes, reading them as an official shift away from the superiority of the public sector.[173] Some even saw these developments as a further step toward what many predicted would ultimately be an embrace of full-fledged open markets. These interpretations led to much surprise and dismay when the Party-state started exercising a more heavy-handed regulatory approach toward certain market industries in recent years (reviewed below). The steps caught many by surprise and seemed contradictory.[174]

[168] Decision on Certain Major Issues Concerning the Comprehensive Deepening of Reform [中共中央关于全面深化改革若干重大问题的决定], promulgated by the Central Comm. Communist Party China, Nov. 15, 2013 [Decisions on Comprehensive Deepening the Reforms].

[169] "Xi Jinping: The Science and Technology Innovation Board Will Be Established on the Shanghai Stock Exchange and the Registration System Will Be a Pilot" [习近平：将在上海证券交易所设立科创板并试点注册制], Xinhua, Nov. 5, 2018, https://archive.ph/2EyDA.

[170] The PRC Securities Law, last amended and effective by the Standing Comm. of the Thirteenth Nat'l People's Cong. Dec. 28, 2019, effective Mar. 1, 2020.

[171] Securities Investment Funds Law of the People's Republic of China [中华人民共和国证券投资基金法], adopted by the Standing Comm. of the Tenth Nat'l People's Cong., Oct. 28, 2003, revs'd by the Standing Comm. of the Eleventh Nat'l People's Cong., Dec. 28, 2012; then amended by the Twelfth Nat'l People's Cong., Apr. 24, 2015.

[172] The Law of the People's Republic of China on the Promotion of Small and Medium-Sized Enterprises [中华人民共和国中小企业促进法], first enacted by the Standing Comm. of the Ninth Nat'l People's Cong., Jun. 29, 2002, revs'd by the Standing Comm. of the Twelfth Nat'l People's Cong., Sep. 1, 2017, effective Jan. 1, 2018. [The SME Law] *Ibid.* arts. 33, 34.

[173] See sources cited in J. Wang, & C-H. Tan, "Mixed Ownership Reform and Corporate Governance in China's State-Owned Enterprises, *Vanderbilt Journal of Transnational Law* 53 (2020)1055, at 1065.

[174] L. Wei, "China's Xi Approaches a New Term with a Souring Taste for Markets," *The Wall Street Journal* (Oct. 16, 2017); N. R. Lardy, *The State Strikes Back: The End of Economic Reform in China?* (Peterson Institute for International Economics, 2019); M. Schuman, *"The Undoing of China's Economic Miracle,"* The Atlantic (Jan. 11, 2021).

A more careful analysis of the CCP's proclamations and laws that followed the Third Plenum, however, reveals once more the dual functions of law. For example, the new legal framework that established the legal operations, rights, and responsibilities of new investment fund structures came to fruition due to the new impetus to broaden the state's ownership capacity in the market, which was to take form through new state investment vehicles (discussed below). Similarly, the revision to the SME Law was needed to pave the way for state support in SMEs that engage in certain economic activities that are prioritized in the new era, including developing applications for certain technologies (e.g., Internet, cloud computing, big data, and AI), national defense research and production, and military–civil integration.

The dual functionality of law is clear: the economic interests in expanding and supporting markets aligned with the political priorities of the era, rendering the circumstances "ripe enough" for the use of national laws and regulations that pursue both interests in tandem. Viewed through this analytical framework, the law in these developments is again directing capital to where the Party-state thinks it is needed the most. In doing so, the law is translating and giving shape to the desired balance between macro control and market growth, and fostering both.

Mixed Ownership: Casting the State's Net Wide

An important legal institution that is used in order to promote the desired balance between macro and micro control is state ownership. State ownership in industrial and commercial enterprises is a significant tool through which both macro and micro controls can be flexibly exercised. This explains why state ownership has been a constant feature of market reforms and experimentation throughout China's development trajectory. Various schemes to reform Chinese SOEs were devised in this process, including the SOE modern enterprise reform (corporatization), the creation of pyramid holding groups, the *Zhua da fang xiao* (grasping the big and releasing the small) approach discussed earlier, and the more recent mixed ownership program. Through these reforms, the ownership basis of SOEs diversified and the direct ownership of the state in industrial firms has declined. The stated goal was to limit micro interventions by the government and make SOEs more productive. But this also created externalities on the Party-state's ability to exert *macro* market controls. The levers of coordination and oversight through which macro control is maintained weakened and conflicting interests abound.

And thus, with decreasing levels of direct state ownership, a pressing need arose to relieve the externalities and secure macro-level controls by other means. This is where we see the current era's reinforcement of the Party-state capacities vis à vis the market and the law's contribution to this process. Currently, two main legal instruments are mobilized at the state level for that purpose: state ownership and regulatory capacities.

In terms of the ownership capacity of the state in the market, the current era is characterized by an expansion of the reach of the state as a minority investor in the private sector. The policy underpinning this process is known as the "mixed ownership reform" *(hunhe suoyouzhi)*. Mixed ownership is the Party-state's broad blueprint to blend public and private ownership in industrial firms. Under this scheme, the state is casting its ownership net wider in the private sector, even while generally diluting its direct holdings in individual firms. In this manner, the state gains access to information and potentially the ability to affect important corporate decisions in the private sector, thus expanding its pathways for macro control.

Diversifying the capital base of enterprises has taken place since the early 1990s. The term mixed-ownership itself was used randomly to refer to the diversification of ownership in SOEs. A change in the utilization of mixed-ownership started with the 17th National Party Congress. There, Hu Jintao's report at the Central Committee (2007) mentioned a "mixed ownership economy" in the context of the urgent need to establish a modern property rights system.[175] (As noted earlier, this was likely the turning point that put an end to the political controversy around the enactment of the Property Law the same year.) In the speech, the reference to a mixed ownership *economy* was made as if to point to a distinct sector that was to be developed alongside the public and private sectors. Three years later, in 2010, the State Council issued guiding opinions that somewhat clarified what the mixed-ownership sector would entail, and which industries were targeted for implementation.[176] The guiding opinions even encouraged mixed ownership businesses to "go global" through operational support from the government. Two years later, State-Owned Assets Supervision and Administration Commission (SASAC) issued its own regulations with more specific details, instructing its lower divisions not only on how to expand private capital injection into SOEs but also on how to advance mixed ownership in the opposite direction, creating joint state and private funds (and funds of funds) that were to invest jointly in private businesses in emerging industries domestically and overseas.[177] This signaled a whole new horizon for the mixed ownership reform.

One of the main tools to push for mixed ownership in the market has been through directing M&As. The regulatory machinery has been particularly active during the Legalized Politicization Era in that avenue.

As seen in Figure 5.1, in the past decade, the mixed ownership policy has been promoted in high gear.[178] A different breakdown of the data revealed that since the

[175] "Taking modern property system as the basis, [for] developing a mixed-ownership economy," Report at the 17th Party Congress, note 124, Chapter V(6).

[176] Several Opinions of the State Council on Encouraging and Guiding the Healthy Development of Private Investment [国务院关于鼓励和引导民间投资健康发展的若干意见], issued by Order No. 13 of the St. Council, July 5, 2010.

[177] Guiding Opinions on Actively Introducing Private Investment in the Restructuring and Reorganization of State-Owned Enterprises [关于国有企业改制重组中积极引入民间投资的指导意见 (国资发产权[2012]80号)], released by Notice No. 80 [2012] of the State-Owned Assets Supervision and Administration Comm'n of the St. Council, May 23, 2012. See at art. 8.

[178] On the various rounds of the mixed-ownership reform, see Wang & Tan, *Mixed Ownership Reform and Corporate Governance in China*, note 174.

Out of a total number of administrative regulations governing M&A activity, close to 88 percent (87.8) were issued from 2007 onward, after the CCP emphasized its goal to diversify the capital base of SOEs (491 items).

The following chart presents trends in the regulatory framework over M&A (including also tertiary administrative regulations, i.e., central level industry specific rules), out of a total of 559 regulations, grouped into the different development eras.

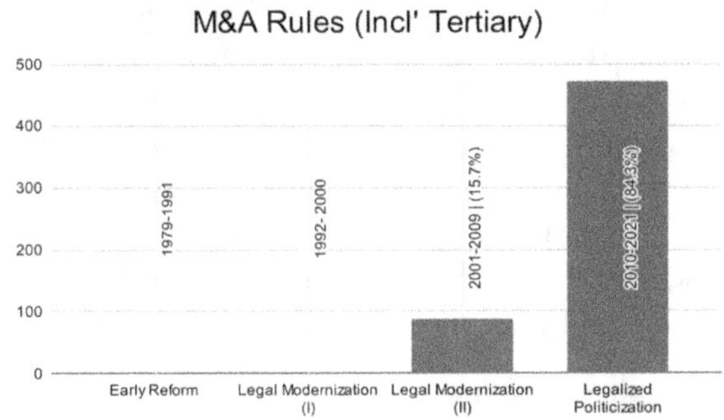

FIGURE 5.1 M&A rules by era classification

embrace of the socialist market economy framework (1993),[179] the number of central-level regulations and departmental rules that mention the term "mixed-ownership" rose from an average of 3.5 documents per year (during 1993–2013) to an average of 34.25 documents per year (2014–21). The upsurge clearly follows the Third Plenum of the 18th Central Committee. The Third Plenum of the 18th Central Committee (2013) made official the mixed ownership economy as a component of the "current stage" in China's economic development. The Decisions on Comprehensive Deepening the Reforms that followed guided central and local state organs (including the NPC and the State Council on its various ministries) to advance the mixed ownership goal. It also clarified that mixed ownership entails "cross-shareholdings by, and mutual blends of, state-owned capital, collective capital, and non-public capital."[180]

A set of important guiding documents issued by the CCP and State Council followed.[181] Indeed, in the following years, the state expanded its ownership reach into the private sector by utilizing a variety of complex market and legal instruments. These include open market share purchases, M&As, direct investment contracts, and ownership structures that are being carried out by newly created state capital investment

[179] At the 14th Central Committee Decisions, note 78.

[180] Decisions on Comprehensive Deepening the Reforms, note 169, art. 2(6).

[181] CCP Central Committee and State Council Opinion on Deepening the Guidance of State-Owned Enterprise Reform [中共中央、国务院关于深化国有企业改革的指导意见], issued by the CCP Central Comm. and the St. Council, Aug. 24, 2015. [SOE Reform Guiding Opinions]; Opinions of the State Council on the Development of Mixed-Ownership Economy by State-Owned Enterprises [国务院关于国有企业发展混合所有制经济的意见(国发(2015)54号)], issued by release No. 54 of the St. Council, Sep. 24, 2015.

vehicles, including, most recently, a form of "golden shares" in certain private firms that provide preferred rights for state investors.[182] An interesting state investment structure has been a joint form of "private" equity funds that feature cooperation between a state fund alongside a private professional fund manager. Reports indicate that such joint "fund of funds" arrangements have reached 2.14 trillion yuan since 2015.[183] Typically, the government fund plays the role of a limited partner in the lower-level funds, delegating investment decisions to a general partner – often a local state-controlled company with industry expertise or a private fund – as the professional manager.

These developments are designed to support, yet control, the shift toward a technology-based growth model. Many of the private firms that receive state investments through the legal instruments devised under this scheme belong to innovative knowledge-rich sectors.[184] These methods of metastasizing the ownership capacity of the state thus utilizes legal instruments and market forces, in tandem, to direct capital flows in pursuit of the political–economic priorities of the Party-state.

Intensifying the Presence of the Regulatory State

As seen above, China was approaching an economic turning point and a legitimacy crisis at the same time (ca. 2010). Intensifying the role of the regulatory state was a response to both growing concerns. From an economic perspective, an enhanced regulatory capacity could help steer markets to new economic avenues prioritized by the Party-state and thereby compensate for weakening macro-controls. From a political perspective, a stronger regulatory state would centralize and unify governance not only with respect to market participants but also vis à vis internal power conflicts within the Party-state apparatus. It could thereby (re)solidify the governing powers of the central Party-state over the economy.

Indeed, an intensifying presence of the regulatory state in the market, compared to the prior decade, has become noticeable. By the "regulatory state," I refer to the state's capacities as a rule maker and a rule enforcer, including its legislative, regulatory, oversight, and administrative enforcement functions.

The high level of activism in market related formal rulemaking is noticeable during the current legalized politicization era at all layers of the central hierarchy of legal norms; primary law (NPC), secondary administrative regulations (State Council), and tertiary administrative regulations (departments of the State Council).

[182] I discussed the possibility of introducing a "Golden Share" mechanism in China in: T. Groswald Ozery, "Minority Public Shareholders in China's Concentrated Capital Markets – A New Paradigm?," *Columbia Journal of Asian Law* 30(1) (2016), 1.

[183] See the Hefei Model, discussed in T. Hancock, "How China's Communist Officials Became Venture Capitalists," Bloomberg (Feb. 6, 2022). More broadly, L. Lin, *Venture Capital Law in China* (Cambridge University Press, 2021).

[184] H. Chen & M. Rithmire, "The Rise of the Investor State: State Capital in the Chinese Economy," *Studies in Comparative International Development* 55(3) (2020) 257.

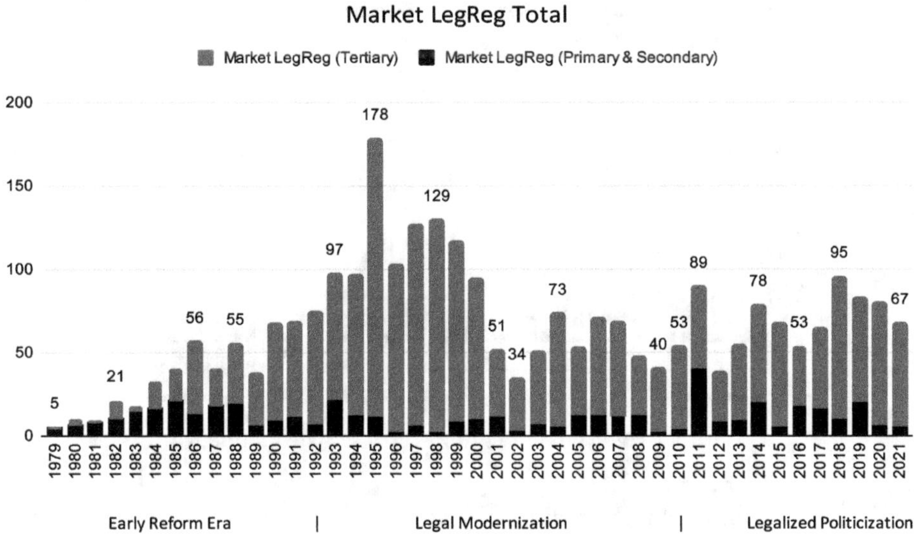

FIGURE 5.2 Newly issued and rev'sd market LegReg (annual) per era

Market-related rulemaking has seen an upward surge specifically in 2011. Much of the rise is attributed to primary and secondary rulemaking. As seen in figure 5.3, the number of administrative regulations issued by the State Council particularly surged. Looking at market-related rulemaking activism throughout the current era reflects a slight increase in exercising the legislative capacity of the NPC as well (annual average, per era: 1.15, 3.16, 4 accordingly).

Together, Figures 5.2 and 5.3 reflect an intensifying rule-making capacity of the regulatory state in the market during the current era relative to prior years and eras.[185]

Textual analysis of important Party decisions corroborates the quantitative data, supporting that there was indeed an effort to intensify the regulatory presence of the state in the market throughout the era. The core of this is reflected in the growing prominence of rule of law rhetoric in the new era. As seen earlier, already in the late 1990s and throughout the Legal Modernization Era, notions of the rule of law (*yifa zhiguo*) started surfacing in official Party and state promulgations. During the Third Plenum of the 18th Central Committee of the CCP, building a socialist rule of law country (*shihuizhuyi fazhi guojia*) became one of the regime's stated priorities.[186]

185 As the figures also reflect, during the first wave of power consolidation, that is, the first decade of the Legal Modernization Era (1993–2001), the level of rulemaking activism at the tertiary level, that is, by departments of the State Council, was even higher. Yet. activism by the NPC and the State Council itself was lower than in the current era.

186 Communiqué of the Third Plenary Session of the 18th Central Committee of the Communist Party of China [中国共产党第十八届中央委员会第三次全体会议公报], adopted and promulgated by the Third Plenary Session of the 18th Central Comm. Communist Party of China, Nov. 12, 2013.

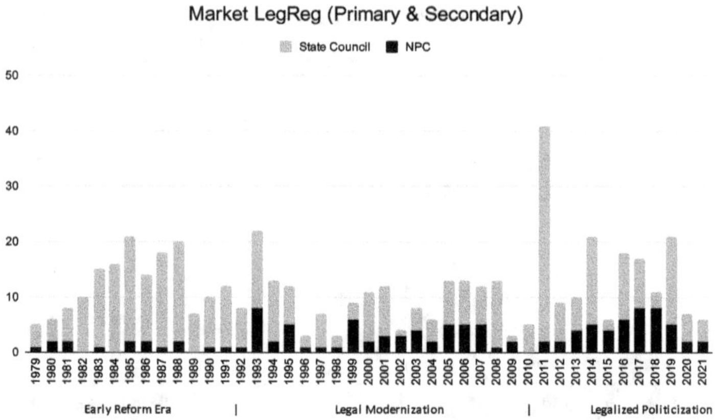

FIGURE 5.3 Market LegReg NPC vs. State Council

The new reform blueprint discussed above – the 18th Central Committee Decision on Comprehensive Deepening the Reforms (2013) – addressed the matter of a law-based governance 75 times and included a chapter dedicated to the construction of the rule of law.[187] Within this chapter, a special emphasis was given to centralizing governance capacities:

> [R]elatively centralized law enforcement powers … focus on solving the problem of overlapping powers and responsibilities … establish an administrative law enforcement system with unified powers and responsibilities … strengthen supervision over administrative law enforcement … perfect the system of normative documents and the mechanism of legality review over major policy decisions.

A year later, for the first time in history, an entire CCP Central Committee plenum – the Fourth Plenum of the 18th Central Committee of the CCP – was dedicated to the issue of "building a rule of law system of socialism with Chinese characteristics."[188] Following the Plenum, in 2014, the CCP Central Committee issued the Decisions on Rule of Law.[189] This was a "rule of law blueprint" that dealt with the need to refine and boost the powers of Party-state institutions that were entrusted with governance capacities and to advanced internal checks and balances that conformed with China's vision of a socialist rule of law, that is, with Party leadership as its core.

The Decisions included over 180 items for reform across six major aspects on which the rule of law construction efforts should focus:

[187] Chapter 9 in the Decisions on Comprehensive Deepening the Reforms, note 169.

[188] Communiqué of the Fourth Plenary Session of the 18th Central Committee of the Communist Party of China [中国共产党第十八届中央委员会第四次全体会议公报], adopted and promulgated by the Fourth Plenary Session 18th Central Comm. Communist Party of China, Oct. 23, 2014.

[189] Decision on Certain Major Issues Concerning Comprehensively Advancing the Rule of Law [中共中央关于全面推进依法治国若干重大问题的决定], promulgated by the Fourth Plenary Session of the 18th Central Comm. Communist Party China, Oct. 28, 2014, [Decisions on Advancing the Rule of Law]

(1) Strengthen the implementation of the Constitution and the legislative system as a whole (including enhancing legislative efforts in key areas with specific economic and financial areas noted for further legislative work); (2) reform the administrative government to better align with a law-based administration (including, e.g., the legalization of administrative institutions, powers, procedures, responsibilities, and accountability); (3) centralize oversight over the judiciary and the People's Courts system to enhance fairness and credibility; (4) popularize the law through social awareness and education to rule of law compliance; (5) build a legal service apparatus that would support and promote the ideas of a socialist rule of law with Chinese characteristics; and (6) strengthen internal rule-based governance within the Party and solidify the Party's leadership over the entire project of rule of law governance.

Article 1 in the Decisions on Advancing the Rule of Law explained the necessity of the rule of law project:

> Rule of law [*yifazhiguo*, governing the country according to law] is a necessary requirement for implementing the country's governance system and for modernizing its governance capabilities … and to deepen comprehensive reforms. … It is related to the long-time stability of the Party and the country. … To enhance the Party's governing power abilities and its governance level, we must comprehensively advance the rule of law.[190] (brackets added)

The Decisions also connected the emphasis on the rule of law directly to Xi Jinping's "national rejuvenation" agenda. The leadership believed that the reform had entered a "critical period" in which China was facing "complex challenges and volatile situations both domestically and internationally."

The 19th Party Congress continued along the same line, stating in 2021 that "comprehensively advancing law-based governance is … a profound revolution in China's governance."[191] The law is seen as a required tool that can promote regularity within the Party-state system itself. It can help coordinate and mitigate internal conflicts, local protectionism, rent seeking, shirking, and abuse of power.

Clearly, the importance of law has risen. The political utilities of law have been elevated. This is a recognition of the benefits that law-based governance has to offer in rebuilding the political capital of the Party-state. Resorting to law is needed not only for economic development but also to purify politics (*zhengzhi qingming*, i.e., integrity of the political system). This recognition has led to an overall legalized politicization in China, with considerable implications for governance,[192] and for governing the economy specifically.

190 Decisions on Advancing the Rule of Law, note 189, art. 1.

191 Resolution of the Central Committee of the CCP on the Major Achievements and Historical Experience of the Party's Century-long Struggle [中共中央关于党的百年奋斗重大成就和历史经验的决议], adopted by the Sixth Plenary Session of the 19th CPC Central Comm., Nov. 11, 2021.

192 For an initial discussion, see J. P. Horsley, "Party Leadership and Rule of Law in the Xi Jinping Era," *Brookings Institution Publications: Global China Initiative* (2019).

In the years following the two Decisions of the Third and the Fourth Plenums of the 18th Central Committee, a series of reforms ensued in the areas that were designated for rule of law construction, including reforms in the court system,[193] the administrative system,[194] the legal education system,[195] the rulemaking system,[196] and the Party's own governance system.[197] Certain laws relating to the allocation of governance powers were amended in an effort to refine the regulatory powers and procedures of state institutions. Primary among these were a much-needed effort to standardize legislative activity with the amendment of the Legislation Law,[198] a long-delayed amendment to the Administrative Litigation Law,[199] several revisions to the Administrative Penalty Law,[200] and a newly enacted Supervision Law.[201] In early 2018, a constitutional amendment was approved by the NPC, which sealed the notion of a socialist rule of law country as a constitutional principle, with Party leadership at its core.[202]

193 For judicial reforms, see, for example, R. E., Stern et al., "Automating Fairness? Artificial Intelligence in the Chinese Courts," *Columbia Journal of Transnational Law* 59 (2020) 515 (analyzing automation court reforms that are meant to enhance oversight through information transparency); Y. Wang, ""Detaching" Courts from Local Politics? Assessing the Judicial Centralization Reforms in China," *The China Quarterly* 246 (2021) 545 (discussing the centralization of budgetary control and the efforts to increase judicial independence from local politics); for a broader overview on judicial reforms, see K. H. Ng & X. He, *Embedded Courts: Judicial Decision-making in China* (Cambridge University Press, 2017).

194 W. Tong, "Progress and Compromise: A Review of the Amendment to the Administrative Litigation Law" [进步与妥协:行政诉讼法修改回顾], *Administrative Law Research* [行政法学研究] 4 2015 22.

195 O. Naftali, "Law Does Not Come Down from Heaven: Youth Legal Socialization Approaches in Chinese Textbooks of the Xi Jinping Era," *Journal of Current Chinese Affairs* (forthcoming, 2022) (discussing legal socialization through legal education in the Chinese school system).

196 For example, J. Horsley, "China Implements More Participatory Rulemaking under Communist Party," *The Regulatory Review*, Mar. 15, 2018, www.theregreview.org/2018/03/15/horsley-china-implements-participatory-rulemaking/ (discussing procedural revisions that are designed to enhance public participation in the rulemaking process); J. Horsley, "China's Central Government Seeks to Rein in Regulatory Documents," *The Regulatory Review*, May 7, 2019, www.theregreview.org/2019/05/07/horsley-china-central-government-rein-regulatory-documents/ (discussing recent steps to curb the abusive aspects of regulatory guidance documents).

197 Changes in the Party governance system following the rule of law agenda are discussed below.

198 The Legislation Law of the People's Republic of China [中华人民共和国立法法], adopted by the Ninth Nat'l People's Cong., Mar. 15, 2000, amended by the Twelfth Nat'l People's Cong., Mar. 15, 2015.

199 The Administrative Litigation Law of the People's Republic of China [中华人民共和国行政诉讼法], adopted by the Seventh Nat'l People's Cong., Apr. 4, 1989, as amended for the first time by the Standing Comm. of the Twelfth Nat'l People's Cong., on Nov. 1, 2014, and for the second time by the Standing Comm. of the Twelfth Nat'l People's Cong., June 27, 2017, effective July 1, 2017.

The 2017 amendment allowed the People's Procuratorate to advance public interest lawsuits following certain actions or inactions by an administrative organ, ibid., art. 25.

200 The Administrative Penalty Law of the People's Republic of China [中华人民共和国行政处罚法], adopted by the Eighth Nat'l People's Cong., Mar. 17, 1996, amended by the Standing Comm. of the Eleventh Nat'l People's Cong., Aug. 27, 2009, amended by the Standing Comm. of the Twelfth Nat'l People's Cong., Sep. 1, 2017, and last revs'd by the Standing Comm. of the Thirteenth Nat'l People's Cong., Jan. 22, 2021, effective Jul. 15, 2021.

201 The Supervision Law of the People's Republic of China [中华人民共和国监察法], promulgated by the Standing Comm. of the Thirteenth Nat'l People's Cong., Mar. 20, 2018.

202 Amendment to the Constitution of the People's Republic of China [中华人民共和国宪法修正案 (2018)] Promulgated by Announcement No. 1 of the Thirteenth Nat'l People's Cong., Mar. 11, 2018. See preamble, arts. 1 & 5 [the 2018 Constitutional Amendment].

What did this mean for the market specifically? First, at a conceptual level, the political and the economic goals that have led to reinforcing the governance capacities of the state and paved the use of Chinese rule of law as the framework, entwine to a high degree.

In his explanation of the Decisions on Advancing the Rule of Law (2014), Xi Jinping noted that elevating the role of the law in governance through the rule of law framework was instrumental in nature and is highly needed to carry China's economic development trajectory forward:

> The Plenum Decision drafting process … reflecting the need of raising rule of law levels in order to move reform and development forward in all areas, it is not a matter of rule of law for the sake of rule of law.
>
> …
>
> Constructing a socialist rule of law system with Chinese characteristics … [is an] inevitable requirement for realizing the modernization of the State's governing system and governing capacity, and is an inevitable requirement for comprehensively deepening reform.…[203]

As was also noted by Xi, a government ruled by law is needed to curb rent-seeking behaviors, deal with operations outside the scope of authority, elevate the legitimacy of administrative decisions, and strengthen restraints and accountability on government powers. All of these were also mentioned in the context of utilizing public assets (e.g., "the allocation and use of financial funds, the supervision over state-owned assets, government investment, government procurement …").

At a more practical level, the framework that regulated market economic activity started adjusting to the new law-based governance approach. A wave of regulatory activism to repeal or amend economic laws engulfed the market. The edict to refine governance authorities within the Party-state system pushed forward long-awaited changes in economic laws, and a mountain of implementation regulations and adjusting rules across central government institutions and departments assigned to governing markets. A non-comprehensive list includes: amending the Law on Promoting the Transformation of Scientific and Technological Achievements,[204] long-awaited revisions of the Budget Law,[205] the

[203] Xi Jinping, Explanation on the "Decision of the Central Committee of the CCP on Several Major Issues Concerning Comprehensively Advancing the Rule of Law" [关于《中共中央关于全面推进依法治国若干重大问题的决定》的说明], *Qiushi Journal* [求是] 2014/21, https://archive.ph/me88o.

[204] Law of the People's Republic of China on Promoting the Transformation of Scientific and Technological Achievements [中华人民共和国促进科技成果转化法], first adopted by the Standing Comm. of the Eighth Nat'l People's Cong., May 15, 1996, amended by the Standing Comm. of the Twelfth Nat'l People's Cong., Aug. 29, 2015.

[205] The Budget Law of the People's Republic of China [中华人民共和国预算法], adopted by the Eight Nat'l People's Cong., on Mar. 22, 1994, revs'd by the Standing Comm. of the Twelfth Nat'l People's Cong., Aug. 31, 2014, later amended by the Standing Comm. of the Thirteenth Nat'l People's Cong., Dec. 29, 2018. The Budget law regulates Central and local governments' revenue and expenditures, it is aimed to "strengthen budget constraints, management and supervision, and establish a comprehensive, standardized, and transparent budget system."

Competition Law,[206] the SME Law mentioned earlier,[207] a series of amendments to the Criminal Law,[208] amendments to the Securities Investment Fund Law,[209] an amended Company Law[210] and Securities Law,[211] a complete set of revisions to China's intellectual property regime,[212] and a Civil Code that integrated previous stand-alone civil laws (including contracts) into a unified code.[213] In addition to the revisions updating old laws, new laws were enacted to fill in existing legislative gaps.

[206] The Anti-Unfair Competition Law [中华人民共和国反不正当竞争法], promulgated by the Standing Comm. of the Eight Nat'l People's Cong., Sep. 2, 1993, revs'd for the first time by the Standing Comm. of the Twelfth Nat'l People's Cong. Nov. 14, 2017, revs'd last by the Standing Comm. of the Thirteenth Nat'l People's Cong., effective Apr. 23, 2019. For a comprehensive discussion on the political economy behind the law, see Zhang, *Chinese Antitrust Exceptionalism*, note 147.

[207] The SME Law, note 173.

[208] There were eleven amendments to the Criminal law [中华人民共和国刑法修正案] in total and three after the new reform agenda. These include the ninth amendment promulgated by the Standing Comm. of the Twelfth Nat'l People's Cong., on Aug. 29, 2015; the tenth amendment promulgated by the Standing Comm. of the Twelfth Nat'l People's Cong., on Nov. 4, 2017; and the eleventh amendment promulgated by the Thirteenth Nat'l People's Cong., Dec. 26, 2020. These amendments include revisions that expanded and refined corruption and bribery crimes.

[209] Securities Investment Funds Law of the People's Republic of China [中华人民共和国证券投资基金法], adopted by the Standing Comm. of the Tenth Nat'l People's Cong., Oct. 28, 2003, revs'd by the Standing Comm. of the Eleventh Nat'l People's Cong., Dec. 28, 2012; last amended and effective by the Twelfth Nat'l People's Cong., Apr. 24, 2015.

[210] The Company Law of the People's Republic of China [中华人民共和国公司法], promulgated by the Standing Comm. of the Eight Nat'l People's Cong., Dec. 29, 1993, revs'd Oct. 27, 2005, amended by the Standing Comm. of the Twelfth Nat'l People's Cong., Dec. 28, 2013, last amended and effective by the Standing Comm. of the Thirteenth Nat'l People's Cong., Oct. 26, 2018, Oct. 26, 2018.

[211] The Securities Law of the People's Republic of China [中华人民共和国证券法], promulgated by the Standing Comm. of the Ninth Nat'l People's Cong., on Dec. 29, 1998, revs'd Oct. 27, 2005, amended Aug. 31, 2014, amended and effective by the Standing Comm. of the Thirteenth Nat'l People's Cong. Dec. 28, 2019.

[212] Including the following decisions to establish designated intellectual property courts: Decision of the Standing Committee of the National People's Congress on the Establishment of Intellectual Property Courts in Beijing, Shanghai, and Guangzhou [全国人民代表大会常务委员会关于在北京、上海、广州设立知识产权法院的决定], adopted by the Standing Comm. of the Twelfth Nat'l People's Cong., Aug 31, 2014; Several Decision of the State Council on Accelerating the Construction of an Intellectual Property Great Power Under New Conditions, issued by the St. Council release No. 71 [国发(2015)71号], Dec. 18, 2015; Trademark Law of the People's Republic of China [中华人民共和国商标法], adopted by the Standing Comm. of the Fifth Nat'l People's Cong., Aug. 30, 1982, amended Feb. 22, 1993, amended, Oct. 27, 2001, amended for the third time, Aug. 30, 2013, amended and effective by the Standing Comm. of the Thirteenth Nat'l People's Cong., Apr. 23, 2019; Patent Law of the People's Republic of China [中华人民共和国专利法], adopted by the Standing Comm. of the Sixth Nat'l People's Cong., Mar. 12, 1984; amended for the first time on Sep. 4, 1992, amended Aug. 25, 2000, amended Dec. 27, 2008, amended and effective by the Standing Comm. of the Thirteenth Nat'l People's Cong., Oct.17, 2020; Copyright Law of the People's Republic of China [中华人民共和国著作权法], adopted by the Standing Comm. of the Seventh Nat'l People's Cong., Sep. 7, 1990, amended first on Oct. 27, 2001, amended on Feb. 26, 2010, amended and effective by the Standing Comm. of the Nat'l People's Cong., Nov. 11, 2020; Provision on the Implementation of Copyright Treaties [实施国际著作权条约的规定], issued by Order No. 105 of the St. Council, Sep. 25, 1992; revs'd Nov. 29, 2020.

[213] The Civil Code of the People's Republic of China [中华人民共和国民法典], adopted by the Thirteenth Nat'l People's Cong., May 28, 2020, effective Jan. 1, 2021.

Particularly relevant here are the newly enacted E-Commerce Law,[214] a framework (currently in process) to regulate overseas listing of domestic issuers,[215] and a series of laws related to national security and information protection with implications for market participants, including the National Security law,[216] the Archives Law,[217] the Cybersecurity law,[218] Data Security Law,[219] and the Personal Information Protection Law.[220]

Alongside lawmaking, the stronger role of the regulatory state in the market is also felt in more stringent enforcement by the central government's administrative authorities. Administrative enforcement has risen in recent years, particularly against economic activities that are tagged as socially harmful, too speculative, or underproductive. This rising trend, described by popular media as "regulatory crackdowns," include a wave of limitations and enforcement actions against outbound investments and M&A to limit the flow of capital to certain industries such as foreign media outlets, entertainment, and real estate,[221] intense market surveillance of securities trading targeting market fraud and insider trading,[222] strict enforcement of new financial, antitrust, and data regulations in the platform economy space,[223] shutting down China's burgeoning virtual currency mining industry for its speculative

[214] The Electronic Commerce Law of the People's Republic of China [中华人民共和国电子商务法], adopted by the Standing Comm. of the Thirteenth Nat'l People's Cong., Aug. 31, 2018, effective Jan. 1, 2019.

[215] Provisions of the State Council on the Administration of the Overseas Issuance and Listing of Securities by Domestic Enterprises (draft for comments) [国务院关于境内企业境外发行证券和上市的管理规定(草案征求意见稿)], released for public comments by notice of China Sec. Reg. Comm'n, Dec. 24, 2021.

[216] The National Security Law of the People's Republic of China [中华人民共和国国家安全法], adopted by the Standing Comm. of the Twelfth Nat'l People's Cong., July 1, 2015.

[217] The Archives law of the People's Republic of China [中华人民共和国档案法], first adopted by the Standing Comm. of Sixth Nat'l People's Cong., Sep. 5, 1987, amended July 5, 1996, amended for the second time on Nov. 7, 2016, and revis'd by the Standing Comm. of the Thirteenth Nat'l People's Cong., June 20, 2020, effective Jan. 1, 2021.

[218] The Cybersecurity Law of the People's Republic of China [中华人民共和国网络安全法], adopted by the Standing Comm. of the Twelfth Nat'l People's Cong., Nov. 7, 2016, effective June 1, 2017. (Enacted to "safeguard cyberspace sovereignty and national security, and social and public interests… promote the healthy development of economic and social informatization"). Ibid., art. 1.

[219] The Data Security Law of the People's Republic of China [中华人民共和国数据安全法], adopted by the Standing Comm. of the Thirteenth Nat'l People's Cong., Jun. 10, 2021, effective Sep. 1, 2021.

[220] The Personal Information Protection Law of the People's Republic of China [中华人民共和国个人信息保护法], adopted by the Standing Comm. of the Thirteenth Nat'l People's Cong., Aug, 20, 2021.

[221] Guiding Opinions on Further Guiding and Regulating the Direction of Overseas Investments [关于进一步引导和规范境外投资方向的指导意见], jointly issued by the National Development and Reform Comm'n, The Ministry of Commerce, People's Bank of China, and the Ministry of Foreign Affairs, and approved and promulgated by the St. Council, Aug. 4, 2017.

[222] H. Huang, "Enforcement of Chinese Insider Trading Law: An Empirical and Comparative Perspective," *The American Journal of Comparative Law* 68(3) (2020) 517.

[223] A. H. Zhang, "Agility over Stability: China's Great Reversal in Regulating the Platform Economy," *Harvard International Law Journal* 63(2) (forthcoming 2022).

and energy consuming nature,[224] limiting China's entertainment industry (including gaming and media influencers) due to "spiritual pollution" and underproductivity,[225] limiting China's ed-tech industry for its financial and social toll on household income (presumably also a way to shift resources to more favored vocational schools)[226], and more.

As noted earlier, to many observers this seemed like a pendulum shift from what was taken as a pro-market approach in the 18th Party Congress. In response, leading government officials released several notices attempting to assuage market participants about the Party-state's intent to continue its support of private economic activity. From the Chinese leadership's vantage point, boosting the regulatory capacities of the state is meant to close regulatory loopholes, protect consumers, reduce fraud, add stability, and regain macro control that will assist in steering market forces toward China's new macro development priorities.

In summary, the use of legal institutions (including state ownership and its regulatory capacities) helps reinforcing the presence of the central state in the market, in order to achieve a range of economic and political goals:

(1) enhance the oversight capacity of the state to compensate for the loss of macro-controls due to the shrinking of direct state ownership and the opening of markets;
(2) narrow the ability of the state as shareholder and local officials to intervene directly in the daily affairs of industrial enterprises, and thus let market forces allocate resources on a routine basis;
(3) actively support the growth of private firms in designated industries;
(4) gain better access to information about strategic industries with potential economic benefits (e.g., innovative, technology-rich, strategic industries), and thereby improve the pathways for mobilizing economic participants for social and national security purposes.[227]

These may seem contradictory under a liberal or a neoliberal capitalist approach, but under a socialist market economy, such economic and political usages of law complement each other and often even align.

[224] Notice by the National Development and Reform Commission and other Departments on Correcting Virtual Currency "Mining" Activities [国家发展改革委等部门关于整治虚拟货币"挖矿"活动的通知], issued Sep. 3, 2021.

[225] L.-H. Liang, "The Truth behind China's Online Gaming Crackdown," *The Wired* (Sep. 4, 2021), www.wired.co.uk/article/gaming-china-crackdown.

[226] Opinions on Further Reducing the Burden of Students' Homework and Off-Campus Training in Compulsory Education [中共中央办公厅 国务院办公厅印发，关于进一步减轻义务教育阶段学生作业负担和校外培训负担的意见], issued by the General Office of the Central Comm. of the CCP and the General Office of the St. Council, July 24, 2021. "State Council Encourages Vocational Education Reform," Press Release: The State Council (Feb. 13, 2019), https://archive.ph/KK4a4.

[227] On the various usages of the state's shareholding capacity, even while holding a minority position, as a way to advance policy goals, see Tamar Groswald Ozery, Testimony before the U.S.-China Economic and Security Review Commission, Hearing on "U.S. Investment in China's Capital Markets and Military-Industrial Complex," Mar. 19, 2021, www.uscc.gov/hearings/us-investment-chinas-capital-markets-and-military-industrial-complex.

2 *Pathways for Party Agency in the Market*

Side by side with reinforcing state capacities vis à vis the market, the legalized politicization era has also seen the growing presence of the CCP in the market. While the CCP has always stood behind economic policymaking,[228] and even steered the conduct of important market participants, it is only in the current decade (at least since reform and opening ensued) that the CCP has done so overtly. The Party is increasingly and openly encroaching on the powers of state institutions, blurring the lines of Party and state separation as they were delineated under Deng Xiaoping's 1980s reforms. At that time, the State Council and its agencies were delegated with the authority to design and execute policy related to markets while the Party maintained overall control mostly in the shadows.

The rising presence of the Party in the Chinese market is gaining the attention of scholars. Some commentators started replacing the term "state-capitalism" with "Party-state capitalism"[229] to reflect the open encroachment of the Party over the long-established dominance of the state in the economy. Most intriguing is the use of law and legal instruments to facilitate and secure this shift. This is a further indication that the political functions of law are intensifying and with them also the importance of law to the Party-state system.

The Party as a Market Regulator

Intensifying the regulatory state and refining its ownership capacity as an investor, as described above, do not mean enhancing the independence of state institutions. To the contrary, China's rule of law project also includes strengthening Party leadership, including its power over the law-making and regulatory processes. In recent years, the Party's direct involvement in legislation and regulation has been enhanced.[230] Recent Party guidelines require that the drafting of laws and regulations on politics, and on major areas of the economy and of society, will be deliberated by the Central Committee, or by the Party committee or its leadership group at the relevant administrative level.[231]

As several scholars have observed, there has indeed been a more open involvement by the CCP in the law-making process during the years of the 18th and 19th

[228] See explanation on the design and approval process of the Five-Year Plans in the preamble of Part II, "The Making of a Five-Year Plan."

[229] M. Pearson et al., "Party-State Capitalism in China," *Current History* 120(827) (2021) 207.

[230] See Decisions Concerning Some Major Issues in Comprehensively Moving Forward Ruling the Country According to Law [中共中央关于全面推进依法治国若干重大问题的决定], adopted at the Fourth Plenary Session of the 18th Central Comm. of the CCP. Oct. 29, 2014.

[231] Ibid. See also Y. Feng & J. Zhou, "Strengthening Party's Leadership in Legislative Work" [加强党对立法工作的领导], *Qiushi.com: Hongqi Wengao* [求是网:红旗文稿] (Jan. 11, 2022), https://archive.ph/40Qge, citing the 2016 "Opinions of the Central Committee of the Communist Party of China on Strengthening the Party Leadership over Legislative Work" [中共中央关于加强党领导立法工作的意见] (the opinions could not be found in the public domain).

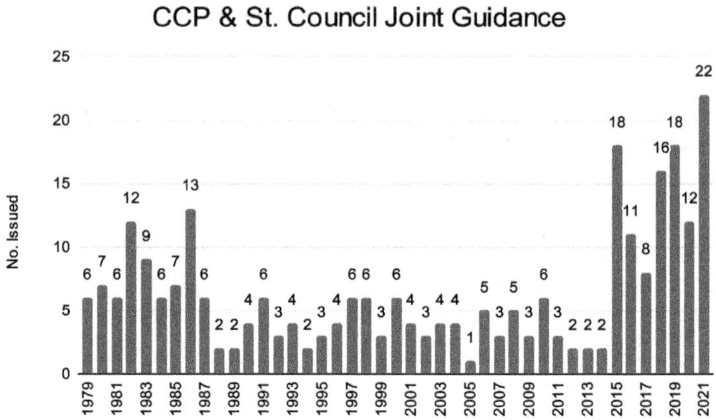

FIGURE 5.4 Number of issued CCP and St. Council joint guidance per year

Party Congresses.[232] One sign of that is the sharp rise in the number of normative documents that were jointly issued by the State Council and the Party's Central Committee (Figure 5.4).

To note, while opinions and guiding opinions are not a source of authoritative formal law under the PRC Legislation Law, they are normative documents with a binding regulatory effect in practice.[233] As Jamie Horsley notes, "such documents often provide the policy basis for subsequent legislation and are sometimes cited as the direct basis – rather than a law – for government rules."[234]

When observed based on era classification, Figure 5.5, a rise in the average number of joint guidance opinions issued annually clearly confirms the intensifying presence of the Party as a market regulator during the current era of legalized politicization.

Here too, content analysis provides further support. The rising presence of the Party in rulemaking has manifested specifically in the context of market governance, whereby an increasing number of opinions (*yijian*) and guiding opinions

[232] The broader trend was observed in J. Chen, "Out of the Shadows and Back to the Future: CPC and Law in China," *Asia Pacific Law Review* 24(2) (2016) 176. See also Horsley, *China's Participatory Rulemaking*, note 196 (noting how recent rulemaking procedures by the State Council require CCP consultation and approval during the rulemaking process).

[233] Particularly since issued alongside the State Council. Jurisprudence discussions in China generally treat decisions and opinions by the State Council to have the same binding effect as administrative regulations. See J. Huang, "The Legal Definition and Effect of 'Normative Documents'" ["规范性文件"的法律界定及其效力], *Legal Studies* 7 [法学 7] (2014), Research Center for Constitutional and Administrative Law of Renmin University of China, available here: https://archive.ph/tb4fo.

[234] Horsley, *Party Leadership and Rule of Law in Xi's Era*, note 192.

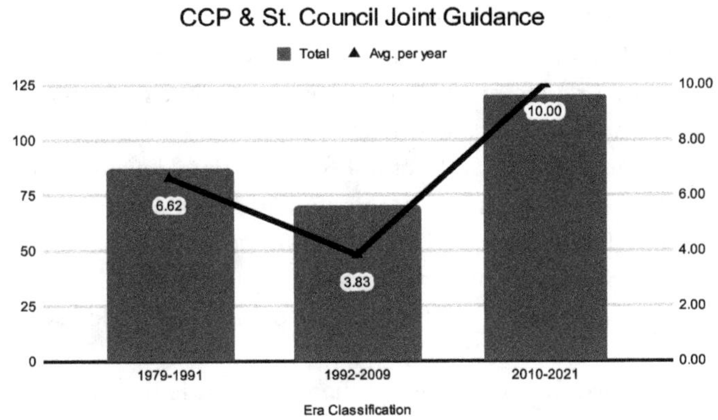

FIGURE 5.5 CCP and St. Council joint guidance annual avg. by era

(*zhidao yijian*), issued by the CCP alongside the State Council, now "regulate" economic activity. The growing number and substance of such opinions indicates that the CCP is expanding its direct governing capacity over public and private market participants.[235]

[235] Noteworthy here are:

The SOE Reform Guiding Opinions, note 182;

Opinions of the CPC Central Committee and the State Council on Creating a Sound Entrepreneur Growth Environment, Advocating Excellent Entrepreneurship and Better Using Entrepreneurs' Role [中共中央、国务院关于营造企业家健康成长环境弘扬优秀企业家精神更好发挥企业家作用的意见], issued by the Central Comm. of the CCP and the St. Council, Sep. 8, 2017;

Opinions of the CCP Central Committee and the State Council on Creating a Better Development Environment and Supporting the Reform and Development of Private Enterprises [中共中央、国务院关于营造更好发展环境支持民营企业改革发展的意见], issued by the CCP Central Comm. and the St. Council, Dec. 4, 2019;

The CCP Opinions on Strengthening the United Front Work of the Private Economy in a New Era [中共中央办公厅印发、关于加强新时代民营经济统战工作的意见], issued by the General Office of the Central Comm. of the CCP, Sep. 15, 2020;

Several Opinions of the CCP Central Committee and the State Council on Strengthening Financial Services for Private Enterprises [中共中央办公厅国务院办公厅印发,关于加强金融服务民营企业的若干意见], issued by the General Offices of CCP Central Comm. and the St. Council, Xinhua News, February 14, 2019;

Opinions of the CCP Central Committee and the State Council on Accelerating the Establishment of Credit Supervision, Warning and Punishment Mechanism for Dishonest Persons Subject to Enforcement [中共中央办公厅国务院办公厅印发、关于加快推进失信被执行人信用监督、警示和惩戒机制建设的意见], issued by the General Offices of CCP Central Comm. and the St. Council, Sep. 25, 2016;

Opinions of the CCP Central Committee and the State Council on Strengthening the Protection of Intellectual Property Rights [中共中央办公厅、国务院办公厅印发、关于强化知识产权保护的意见], issued by the General Offices of CCP Central Comm. and the St. Council, Nov. 24, 2019.

The Party as a Direct Market Participant

In recent years, the Party has stepped directly into the governance of industrial firms, bolstering and at times replacing many traditional corporate governance institutions that operate both inside and outside firms.[236]

The Charter of the CCP, as well as the PRC Company Law, prescribe a role for a Party organization (for simplicity, "corporate Party committee") in any company established and registered in the PRC territory with at least three Party members.[237] The CCP is thus recognized as a distinct corporate stakeholder with a reserved capacity within Chinese firms, whether private or state-controlled with or without foreign investment.

The CCP itself, beyond any traditional shareholder role the state may have, thus became a legal corporate constituent with unique interests and a distinct capacity to convey, direct, and monitor the ways these interests are pursued. Unlike the state's shareholding capacity, the internal operations of this CCP capacity in firms is not regulated and is not subject to any transparent corporate procedures (or other) checks and balances established in law.

As Chapter 8 in this book will detail, the CCP's presence in firms is not a new feature. The option to establish a Party committee has been included in law at least since the first modern company law was enacted in 1993. But the corporate governance capacities of the Party committee were previously opaque. Moreover, it was not deployed systematically outside several meaningful state-controlled firms. There has been a change in both respects in recent years. The corporate governance roles of the corporate Party committee have been clarified and expanded. They include direct provisions for corporate oversight and disciplinary functions, as well as a more overt participation in decision making. Perhaps most interesting is the role that corporate Party committees are expected to take in the process of legal compliance. Corporate Party committees have been given explicit roles to monitor not only violations of Party rules within the firm but also to address violations of the law (broadly defined).

Institutionalized Market-Related Party Organizations

Prominent in the CCP's effort to amplify its direct involvement in governance, including in governing markets specifically, are recent institutional changes within the Party. Such changes involve the recent rise in number and the formalization of several central Leading Small Groups (*lingdao xiaozu*) sometimes referred to as the "nerve

[236] Tamar Groswald Ozery, The Politicization of Corporate Governance: A Viable Alternative?, *The American Journal of Comparative Law* 70 (2022); avac007, https://doi.org/10.1093/ajcl/avac007.

[237] Charter of The Communist Party of China (2017 revision) [中国共产党章程 (2017修改)], rev'sd by the Nat'l Cong. of the Communist Party of China, Oct. 24, 2017; The PRC Company Law, note 210, art. 19 ("The Chinese Communist Party may, according to the Constitution of the Chinese Communist Party, establish its organizations in companies to carry out activities of the Chinese Communist Party. The company shall provide necessary conditions to facilitate the activities of the Party.").

center" of Party's decision-making system. The leading small groups are informal Party bodies, bridges between the party and state, that collect information, coordinate, and produce guidelines on important policy areas. Thousands of such small groups exist across the different levels of the Party-state organization. They may be established ad hoc as a special task force assigned to handle an emerging issue or be a more fixed feature in certain policy areas. A leading small group is chaired by a senior Party member and includes representatives from Party and state bodies. Due to this structure, they have a higher political authority within the Party-state system than the administrative bodies that handle the given issue. They can override conflicts between relevant administrative units over policy responsibilities and budgets. The number and scope of the CCP's leading small groups have risen in recent years.[238] Several central level leading small groups have now been elevated to semi-institutionalized Party Commissions "operating as political supra-ministries coordinating policies" with Xi Jinping at their helm.[239]

One such commission with particular relevance to the market is the Commission for Comprehensively Deepening Reforms, which holds vast decision-making authority over China's reform trajectory.[240] The body was established as a leading small group in 2013 before being elevated to a commission in 2018. Similarly, the Central Leading Group for Cybersecurity and Informatization, established in 2013 and elevated as the Central Cyberspace Affairs Commission in 2018, and the National Security Commission that was established as a commission in 2013, both have direct governance impact on market activity since national security and economic security issues increasingly align. Finally, the Audit Commission and the Commission for Comprehensive Law-based Governance, both established in 2018, also exert influence on how markets are regulated and supervised.

The precise differences between a leading small group status and a commission status are unclear. Some have opined that a commission bears a higher-ranking status, with the highest approval and coordination authority for the Party and state leadership on the selected issues. It is also a more formalized body within the Party organization, which is likely to give it more formal power to direct policy in the given field.

In addition to these changes, some Party mechanisms have been formally *institutionalized within the organizations of the state* as super-ministries. Such super-ministries function as structural bridges between the state and the Party, clearing up procedural pathways of coordination directly to the newly established semi-institutionalized Party Commissions under the Central Committee. This structural reorganization in the current era utilizes legal

[238] C. Johnson et al., "Xi's Signature Governance Innovation: The Rise of Leading Small Groups," CSIS (Oct. 17, 2017), www.csis.org/analysis/xis-signature-governance-innovation-rise-leading-small-groups.

[239] N. Grünberg, "The CCP's Nerve Center," MERICS (July 1, 2021), https://merics.org/en/short-analysis/ccps-nerve-center-0.

[240] S. Heilmann (ed.), *China's Political System* (Rowman & Littlefield, 2017), at 169–172.

instruments – formal institutional capacity building through the law and in certain cases the constitution – to tighten Party oversight and direct involvement in regulating markets.

For example, the Cyberspace Administration of China (CAC, established in 2014) is a state institution but reports directly to the relevant Party Commission (Central Cyberspace Affairs Commission) and functions as its executive arm in the state organization. Similarly, the recent reorganization of China's supervision apparatus incorporated the Party's anti-corruption body – the Central Commission for Disciplinary Inspection (CCDI) – into a newly created National Supervision Commission, a state organ.[241] Here the organizational method followed the principle of "one body two names" [一套人马，两块牌子] (*yi tao renma, liang kuai paizi*).[242] Institutionalizing the CCDI, a Party body, as part of the state organization, granted the CCDI wide formal authority to monitor, investigate, and sanction misconduct by Party *and* state agents.

It is too early to ascertain the result of these institutional changes.[243] It is possible that the recent enhancement of the Party's involvement in the market will come at the expense of state institutions and diminish whatever autonomy they had developed through the Legal Modernization Era. The prominence of the Party's Commission for Comprehensively Deepening Reforms, for example, likely confines the leeway of the NDRC in devising the specific contours of economic and social reform plans. Similarly, the Party's involvement in the monitoring of SOEs through the CCDI's presence within the National Supervision Commission was meant to bolster existing monitoring mechanisms but could result in weakening the authority of supervision bodies within SASAC (I expand on this in Chapter 8). Generally, the more that Party bodies (e.g., corporate Party committees within firms) utilize their newly expanded mandate to oversee legal compliance by market participants, the weaker administrative enforcement bodies and other traditional monitoring institutions might become.

SUMMARY REFLECTIONS

Throughout China's market development trajectory, the Party-state has sought to come up with the right balance that would combine macro planning with the ability

[241] The 2018 Constitutional Amendment, note 202, added Chapter III, Sector 7, arts. 123–127; PRC Supervision Law, note 201.

[242] See The Central Editorial Office Explanation on the Meaning of "One Institution, Two Brands" for Public Institutions [中央编办对事业单位"一个机构两块牌子"含义做出政策解释], *Anxian Human Resources and Social Security Bureau* [安县人力资源和社会保障局], Apr. 11, 2008 (archived Nov. 8, 2014, https://web.archive.org/web/20141108100030/; http:/axsyglj.my.gov.cn/ax/218735752308064256/20080411/180515.html; on Wikipedia page: https://archive.ph/oZsE4).

[243] Some scholars suggest that it is not authoritarian institutional building that we see under Xi Jinping, but rather the erosion of the "authoritarian rules of the game" for the greater exercise of personal power at the hands of President Xi.

C. F. Minzner, "China after the Reform Era," *Journal of Democracy* 26(3) (2015) 129.

to have micro interventions when needed, alongside advanced market forces. This has resulted in continuous reallocation of powers to govern markets within and between various Party-state authorities and hierarchies. The struggle to reach an ideal political–economic equilibrium that would fit China's socialist market economy intensified as the economic and political externalities of the first three decades of reform peaked.

This raised the need to reinforce Party-state capacities in the market, a shift that has taken form through the use of law and legal institutions in various substantive ways discussed above. The data reflects, moreover, that during the current Legalized Politicization Era (2010–present), the average number of newly issued market related rules issued by the three pillars of governance in the Party-state system (i.e., CCP, NPC, State Council) has risen to 24.5 promulgations per year, compared with 14.2 promulgations per year during the Legal Modernization Era (ca. 1992–2009), as well as during the Early Reform Era (Dec. 1978–91).

Beyond the rise in the average number of market related rules, a shift is apparent in the powers therein (see Figure 5.6). Consolidating state powers was always bound with stronger, unified, powers for the CCP, but the current era features a specific focus on constructing the CCP's direct agency in the market. This process reflects the heightened importance of the political functions of the law.

Politicizing the market is a clear element of China's economic development plan in the new era. In combining the two aspects, boosting the regulatory state and legalizing politicization, the current era could result in an increased level of regularity but a decreased level of normative law. At least according to the Party-state's vision, however, this element is designed to support economic development and growth. It has been pursued to remedy the perils of the past and cope with the expected challenges of the future.

Concluding Part II

The preceding chapters in Part II provide a chronological description and analysis of market-related legal constructs that were established throughout China's development trajectory. The description delineated three chronologically separate transition periods: the Early Reform Era (Dec. 1978–91), the Legal Modernization Era (ca. 1992–2009), and the Legalized Politicization Era (2010–present).

Incentives matter for the behavior of market participants. As is well established in the literature, in the early decades of China's market development, local governments had strong incentives to push economic development forward. Local governments and their officials became politically and economically invested in the economic growth of their jurisdictions. They were, therefore, also strongly incentivized to exercise and guarantee economic "rights" (in loose form), even when no such rights were acknowledged formally in law. The relative absence of stringent national-level legal constructs enabled such flexibility.

In the later decades of economic reforms, the *central* government and its officials developed direct interests, both economic and political, in market reforms and thus were incentivized to construct a range of legal institutions that performed both functions – support growth and at the same time secure a new, recentralized, political–economic equilibrium.

Economically, the central government developed direct economic interests in many of China's industrial segments and in its emerging national champions. Making more efficient, stronger, and internationally competitive state-controlled firms, by fostering state capitalism, served the economic interests of the central government both directly (gains from ownership and taxes) and indirectly (gains from market growth and international prowess). In this process, the incentives to guarantee economic rights and boost economic performance shifted as well. The state thus became heavily invested in supplying laws and developing the legal system in ways that suit the Party-state goals and its vision of a socialist market economy.

Politically, reducing local autonomy and consolidating macro-control has become a primary goal. Constructing central level legal institutions to regulate

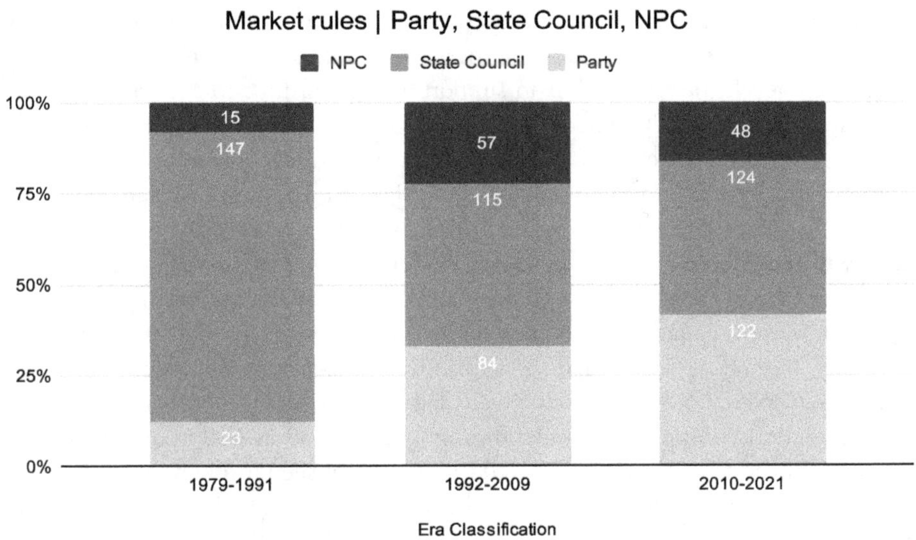

FIGURE 5.6 Market rules (% and No.) issued by the CCP, St. Council, NPC, per era

markets, including institutions with economic functions (i.e., prescribing economic rights to private market participants), served this goal well.

During the current era, there has been an additional shift in the political–economic equilibrium, driven in part by the CCP's intensified legitimacy crisis, the perils of under-controlled industries and corporate groups under state capitalism, and China's economic turning point. These realities coalesced the various interests of the Party, resulting in its turn to assert control over governing markets more directly and overtly.

Indeed, as Figure 5.6 shows, throughout the three eras of reform classified in this book, there have been shifts in the exercise of market regulatory authority between the three pillars of governance within the central Party-state system, as measured by activism in market-related rulemaking.

Clearly, in the Early Reform Era (Dec. 1978–1991), the State Council was dominant while the Party had taken the back seat and market-related national law making was relatively dormant. This corroborates the textual analysis in Chapter 3 and the understanding that early years of reform required provisional solutions that will enable more leeway to local governments. During the Legal Modernization Era (1992–2009), the Party and the NPC had gradually taken more prominent role in market-related rulemaking at the expense of the government. This dovetails Figures 4.1 and 5.2 that show a decline also in newly issued market-related tertiary administrative regulations, in the second decade of that era. These data points align well with the textual analysis in Chapter 4. that pointed to the efforts to restructure both Party and state capacities in the market during the Legal Modernization Era, in which the law was utilized to structure the market as well as to establish central government market institutions. As discussed there, these steps were designed to support the economic functions of the market and aid its development (make market governance leaner) as well as to support a political function (consolidate the governing powers over the market). Finally, Figure 5.6 also clearly reflects how the CCP has increased its activism in market rulemaking during the current Legalized Politicization Era at the expense of both the NPC (mostly) and the State Council. The CCP's share of total market-related rulemaking increased to 41.5 percent, compared with 32.8 percent during the Legal Modernization Era, and 12.4 percent during the era reform era. The data corroborates the analysis brought in Chapter 5 discussing various capacities through which Party presence in the market has risen.

To conclude, the power dynamics within the Party-state system depicted in this Part of the book are observed qualitatively, based on an analysis of the substance of laws, regulations, and policies issued throughout the eras, as well as quantitatively, measured by the scope of market-related rulemaking as seen throughout the figures. Together, the analysis shows that the law has been instrumental in constructing and securing the Party-state's desired political economic shifts throughout the various eras of economic reform and development.

Analytically, the chronological review and textual analysis of market-related rulemaking devised in this book, and corroborated in the data visualizations, illuminate the heavy weight of political determinants in China. Yet, it also shows the various ways in which economic development and political dynamics are mutually reinforcing and highlights the dependencies between political economy and the law in China. Observing China's market development trajectory through a law and political economy framework suggests that the law supports China's market development in a multitude of ways, notwithstanding its evolving and at times limited economic functions. The law is a medium through which internal power hierarchies are allocated, maintained, and contained. It functions as a mediating institution that translates and gives shape to the relations between politics and economics.

Law and politics interact in a reciprocal relationship, creating an interdependent and course-correcting development process. As I move to show next through micro-level analysis (Part III), these dynamics mobilize economic participants, political actors, and institutions in ways that impact China's market growth. Such interdependency between law, politics, and economics illuminates the importance of law for the process of forming markets in China.

* * *

PART III

Law and Political Economy in Corporate China

Interlinkages between the business sector and the polity can be found, to varying degrees, in all regime types. Businesses impact governments through lobbying and other forms of political participation.[1] In the opposite direction, geopolitical affairs, domestic politics, and the political views of market participants exert influence on the internal governance of firms and at times even on firm performance.[2]

Notwithstanding these established notions, somewhat ironically, the prevailing approach that guides legal scholarship in the sphere of (economic) law and development often disregards political–economic determinants. Disconnecting law from

[1] I. Mathur & M. Singh, "Corporate Political Strategies," *Accounting & Finance* 51 (2011), 252; R. Morck et al., "Corporate Governance, Economic Entrenchment, and Growth," *Journal of Economic Literature* 43 (2005) 655; P.-Y. Néron, "Business and the Polis: What Does It Mean to See Corporations as Political Actors?," *Journal of Business Ethics* 94 (2010), 333.

[2] M. K. Chin et al., "Political Ideologies of CEOs: The Influence of Executives' Values on Corporate Social Responsibility," *Administrative Science Quarterly* 58(2) (2013), 197; J. P. Kalt & L. A. Turki, "Political, Social, and Environmental Shareholder Resolutions: Do They Create or Destroy Shareholder Value?," *Harvard Law School Forum on Corporate Governance* (June 17, 2018), https://corpgov.law.harvard.edu/2018/06/17/political-social-and-environmental-shareholder-resolutions-do-they-create-or-destroy-shareholder-value/; D. Gounopoulos et al., "The Consequences of Political Donations for IPO Premium and Performance" (Nov. 19, 2018) (unpublished manuscript). https://ssrn.com/abstract=3181171.

Specifically in the Chinese context: J. P. H. Fan et al., "Politically Connected CEOs, Corporate Governance, and Post-IPO Performance of China's Newly Partially Privatized Firms," *Journal of Financial Economics* 84 (2007), 330; J. D. Piotroski & T. Zhang, "Politicians and the IPO Decision: The Impact of Impending Political Promotions on IPO Activity in China," *Journal of Financial Economics* 111(1) (2014), 111.

politics is prevalent in financial markets and corporate law analysis specifically as well.[3] The paradigm approach looks at the relationship between economic factors – such as, rise in demand; economies of scale; technological progress (affecting productivity gains) – and legal institutions, mainly the existence of clearly defined property rights and effective enforcement of contracts, to explain changes in organizational structures and market growth. As observed by Milhaupt and Pistor, the legal system is viewed in these endeavors as "a fixed and politically neutral institutional endowment."[4] Throughout modern history, this conceptual and analytical divide between law, markets, and politics have guided legal harmonization efforts around the world. The drive for convergence has been particularly prevalent in economic laws and institutions, corporate governance institutions among them.

When confronted with the Chinese context, however, this approach is especially perplexing. The rise of Chinese firms and the growth of its capital market does not find explanations in economics or legal constructs alone. Rather, observing China's corporate and capital market development removes any doubt about the interconnectedness between politics, law, and economic outcomes.

Several studies have begun to address these complex relationships.[5] The focus of most of these studies has been on bureaucratic incentives or the fostering of institutional and personal connections to the Party-state as forces that either support, override or substitute the law. For example, Wang Yuhua has observed the impact of foreign investments on local governments' support of legal reforms suggesting that the regime's relationship with organized interests groups impacts the approach toward law;[6] Zhang Xianchu considered the interplay between law and politics

3 Few notable exceptions include: M. Pagano & P. Volpin, "The Political Economy of Corporate Governance," *American Economic Review* 95 (2005), 1005; M. J. Roe, "Political Preconditions to Separating Ownership from Corporate Control," *Stanford Law Review* 53 (2000), 539; M. J. Roe & M. Vatiero, "Corporate Governance and Its Political Economy." In J. N. Gordon & W.-G. Ringe (eds.), *The Oxford Handbook of Corporate Law and Governance* (Oxford University Press, 2018), 56; B. R. Schneider, "A Comparative Political Economy of Diversified Business Groups, or How States Organize Big Business," *Review of International Political Economy* 16 (2009), 178–201.

4 C. J. Milhaupt & K. Pistor, *Law & Capitalism* (University of Chicago Press, 2008), at 1–14.

5 In development economics literature the relations are explored more frequently but commonly lead researchers to discount the role of law. For example, F. Allen et al., "Law, Finance, and Economic Growth in China," *Journal of Financial Economics* 77 (2005) 57. For the analytical process that lead to such result and additional studies, see Part I, Chapter 1.

A number of studies consider political determinants in broader areas of economic law, including: L. Brandt et al., "Changing Property-Rights Regimes: A Study of Rural Land Tenure in China," *The China Quarterly* 232 (2017), 1026–1049 (formal and informal guarantees of property rights in land allocations); M. E. Gallagher, *Authoritarian Legality in China: Law, Workers and the State* (Cambridge University Press, 2017) (bureaucratic and political bargaining in the labor market and their impact on legal consciousness); A. H. Zhang, *Chinese Antitrust Exceptionalism: How the Rise of China Challenges Global Regulation* (Oxford University Press, 2021) (bureaucratic and political motivations behind China's competition law).

6 Y. Wang, *Tying the Autocrat's Hands: The Rise of the Rule of Law in China*, Cambridge Studies in Comparative Politics (Cambridge University Press, 2014).

in the handling of the 2008–09 financial crisis;[7] Zhang Wei and Li Ji highlighted the impact of legal and political institutions on R&D investments;[8] and Shen Wei pointed to political economic factors behind China's regulatory approach toward shadow banking.[9] There are also several important contributions specifically in the corporate governance literature that touch upon the interplay of law and politics in the governance of firms.[10] And few studies even ventured into looking at politics through the capacities of the Communist Party itself (as opposed to the state).[11]

The studies above offer profound insights on the formal and informal institutions at play in the Chinese market. Yet, no study thus far offered an analytical political economic framework that can explain changes in organizational structures and corporate governance overtime.

In the remainder of the book, I delve deep into China's corporate and capital market development. I use the explanatory power of law and political economy as developed in Parts I and II of this book, to bring more clarity to China's evolving approach to corporate governance. The purpose is to better understand the role played by formal law in governing Chinese public firms and ultimately in China's capital market growth, as well as to unpack the political–economic determinants that drove its evolution.

To reiterate a point made earlier in the introductory chapters, this book calls for a reevaluation of the role of positive law in development through its relations with politics. Accordingly, in Part III as well, I use political economy as an analytical

7 X. Zhang, "The Role of Legal Institutions in Dealing with the Financial Crisis in China." In D. L. Yang (ed.) *The Global Recession and China's Political Economy* (Palgrave Macmillan, 2012).

8 W. Zhang, & J. Li, "Weak Law v. Strong Ties: An Empirical Study of Business Investment, Law and Political Connections in China," *Review of Law & Economics* 13(1) (2017).

9 W. Shen, "Risks of Chinese Shadow Banking and Choice of Regulatory Tools" [中国的影子银行风险及规制工具选择] *China legal Science* 4 [中国法学4] (2014), 164–166.

10 D. C. Clarke, "Law without Order in Chinese Corporate Governance Institutions," *Northwestern Journal of International Law & Business* 30 (2010), 131; N. C. Howson, "'Quack Corporate Governance' as Traditional Chinese Medicine: The Securities Regulation Cannibalization of China's Corporate Law and a State Regulator's Battle against Party State Political Economic Power," *Seattle University Law Review* 37 (2014), 667; J. Leng, *Corporate Governance and Financial Reform in China's Transition Economy* (Hong Kong University Press, 2009); C. Milhaupt & W. Zheng, "Beyond Ownership: State Capitalism and the Chinese Firm," *The Georgetown Law Journal* 103(3) (2014) 665; G. Yu, *Comparative Corporate Governance in China: Political Economy and Legal Infrastructure* (Routledge, 2007); C. Xi, *Corporate Governance and Legal Reform in China* (Wildy, Simmonds & Hill Publishing, 2009).

11 T. Groswald Ozery, "The Politicization of Corporate Governance: A Viable Alternative?," *The American Journal of Comparative Law* 70 (2022); avac007, https://doi.org/10.1093/ajcl/avac007; T. Groswald Ozery, "Minority Public Shareholders in China's Concentrated Capital Markets – A New Paradigm?," *Columbia Journal of Asian Law* 30(1) (2016), 1; N. C. Howson, "China's Restructured Commercial Banks – The Old Nomenklatura System Serving New Corporate Governance Structures? In A. Martha, M. Zhu, & J. Cai, (eds.), *China's Emerging Financial Markets: Challenges and Global Impact* (Wiley & Sons Inc., 2009), 123; L. Y-H. Lin & C. J. Milhaupt, "Party Building or Noisy Signaling? The Contours of Political Conformity in Chinese Corporate Governance, *The Journal of Legal Studies* 50(1) (2021), 187; J. Wang, "The Political Logic of Corporate Governance in China's State-Owned Enterprises," *Cornell International Law Journal* 47(3) (2014), 631.

framework through which to explain changes in the legal framework that governs firms and configures ownership organization in the market. This is to say, I do not intend to provide an all-inclusive account of law and political economy determinants in Chinese firms and the capital market. For example, informal modes of exchange between economic and political market participants have a considerable role in governing the Chinese market to this day. Their persistence has significant bearing on the status and efficacy of legal institutions and impact the quality of enforcement by the People's Courts system. Still, such relations are not at the core of my analysis, and are considered through secondary materials. Rather, my contribution in this Part of the book lies in observing how power dynamics within China's Party-state organization throughout the eras of reform modify the political and economic interests of market participants; how this process drives changes in positive law, ownership structures, and other legal institutions that govern firms; and how such changes eventually affect capital market developments.

Like the chronological framework in Part II above, the analysis here looks at each reform era separately, yet the discussion at times expands beyond the particular era to make relevant connections to subsequent tightly related events.

The study reveals that the reconfiguration of political–economic powers at each stage of development mobilized policymakers and market participants to design and employ different governance mechanisms (both orthodox and idiosyncratic) with respect to firms. These mechanisms triggered changes in ownership organization in the market. They also triggered, supported, boosted, and often times substituted for more conventional corporate governance institutions, thereby reflecting the evolving space for the law in China's marketization process and its interwoven relations with politics. Corporate governance emerged for both of its functions – economic and political. The result today is a capital market that continues to grow, even though it is governed in unusual ways and often promotes unconventional goals. The law and political economy framework, therefore, not only explains the ailments in the Chinese market but also holds the key to understanding its unprecedented success. Such framework might even provide indications about the possible prospect for the market.

6

Corporate Governance under Market Experimentation

THE EMERGENCE OF FIRMS AND THE CAPITAL MARKET

To fully understand China's law and capital market development conundrum one must first consider how modern firms and the capital market came to form and how their early emergence fit within the Party-state's overall economic development plans.

The following account focuses on two key elements: (1) the rise of the large (public) firm and (2) the creation of the capital market as a platform for the offering and exchange of securities. The review reflects how during the first two decades of economic transition, China's public firms emerged and were able to expand by raising external capital while preserving high levels of ownership concentration. Moreover, the capital market developed while relying mainly on transitional, often informal, experimental mechanisms. Only halfway into the development of firms and capital markets did a policy-guided embrace of corporate governance institutions seen in other successful economies began in China. In these respects, China did not diverge much from the ways in which many other capital markets evolved. Indeed, in many other capital markets, law and market institutions followed, rather than led, economic development. The main point of divergence featured at that stage was mainly the fact that the capital market was designed first and foremost for state-owned firms. Ultimate state ownership remained prominent even while external finance was flowing into corporatized, listed, state-owned enterprises (SOEs). State ownership and political control are mutually reinforcing. And thus, when institutions started to adjust and resemble their counterparts in more advanced economies, political functions were still at their core. This feature of the Chinese capital market has remained even at later development stages when direct state ownership gradually narrowed down, and still today.

1 *The Rise of the Large (Public) Firm*

The rise of public firms in China, like much of China's market growth, owes its origins to China's economic and administrative decentralization of the 1980s. Partial autonomy released to local level governments in the first decade of reforms expanded their discretion to take economic initiative in the newly emerging business sector. One such initiative was a Party-sanctioned local effort to experiment with various forms of organizational ownership within state enterprises. The initiative that started in the mid-1980s was later expanded to the national level and became known as the SOE corporatization scheme. These experiments supplanted the nascent market forces; they were meant to incentivize economic activity in SOEs and to induce firms and their managers to develop more efficient measures of operations and thereby to increase the productivity of the public sector. The corporatization experiment also took the place of the abrupt privatization approach that was common in other transitional economies.[12]

The emergence of the public firm in China was thus strongly directed by political economy considerations. Legal mechanisms, such as the corporate form, share ownership, and rights listing, were devised to fulfill both economic and political functions with the latter being the dominant at this stage. The result was local state control over a great number of China's most significant listed firms, one of the main attributes of China's socialist market economy still today. The following sections provide an overview of how public firms emerged, business groups were created, and the Chinese Party-state became a dominant, often controlling, corporate shareholder, while illuminating the dual function (economic and political) of the newly formed market and legal institutions.

Political–Economic Decentralization and SOEs

Under Mao Zedong's command economic system (1949–76), SOEs and urban and rural collective enterprises carried out most economic activity in China.[13] The basic unit for economic and social life, in both the collectives and SOEs, was the *danwei* – the working unit – which was a political as well as an administrative social-economic institution. Bound to the *danwei* for life, workers relied on it to provide their entire social welfare needs, including everything from housing and food to entertainment. The *danwei* exercised economic, social, administrative, and political control on behalf of the Party and state, extending the Party-state's presence and control to China's grassroots.

Above the working units, plant-level enterprises were organized into sectoral or geographical divisions, which were in turn assigned to various industrial bureaus.[14] Under administrative control and central planning, economic resource allocation was

[12] B. Black et al., "Russian Privatization and Corporate Governance: What Went Wrong," *Stanford Law Review* 52 (2000), 1731 (discussing mass privatization of large firms in Russia and its consequences).

[13] Under Mao, limited private economic activity was allowed from time to time to the peasantry. Private agriculture activity made up a very small portion of rural labor input. A. C. Mertha, "From 'Rustless Screws' to 'Nail Houses': the Evolution of Property Rights in China", *Orbis* 53(2) (2009), 233–249.

[14] T. Groves et al., "China's Evolving Managerial Labor Market," *Journal of Political Economy* 103 (1995) 873, 876.

executed by fiats that were driven by political and social needs rather than by supply and demand. The *danwei* itself had no economic independence; instead, it was assigned production quotas and was funded through the state budget to reach such quotas. Demand for the products was guaranteed through fixed outlets, which were transferred by command to the other *danwei* units within a given state-owned or collective enterprise. All "profits" were remitted to the state, and there was therefore no need for a modern taxation system.[15] Under this economic and social reality, production units had no need for external capital. They had no incentive to seek new business opportunities, expand their production capacity beyond orders, or operate efficiently.

Part II, Chapter 3, discussed the political process of decentralization during the early reform era (1978–91) and noted the broad effects on the allocation of economic decision-making authority within the Party-state system. The same decentralization process also directly impacted how ownership was organized and the market was formed. It shaped how firms were structured, business groups emerged, and how the capital market started evolving. Salient among these, economic decentralization directly informed how industrial enterprises were governed:

As seen in Part II, starting in the early 1980s and continuing throughout China's long process of economic transition, many aspects of the reform first took place in a trial-and-error experimental fashion before taking a broader national scope, and eventually being enshrined in law.[16] A similar process took place for reforming the governance system in enterprises. The primary goal was to boost productivity in SOEs and thereby to increase the revenue share of local governments (as per their mandate under the fiscal contracting scheme, the local governments' fiscal revenue sharing arrangement with the center). One of the first experiments was the introduction of "share units" into enterprises.

Although the term "corporatization" formally refers to the ownership organization reform taken in SOEs in the 1990s, the process of allocating share units had started already in the 1980s within collective enterprises in the countryside, before it had spilled over into SOEs.[17] Share units were issued and given primarily to enterprise

[15] S. Tenev et al., *Corporate Governance and Enterprise Reform in China: Building the Institutions of Modern Markets* (World Bank Publications, 2002), 10–11.

[16] Sebastian Heilmann refers to "experimentation under hierarchy" as a "process of policy generation that legitimizes local initiative while maintaining ultimate hierarchical control." S. Heilmann, "Experience First, Laws Later: Experimentation and Breakthroughs in the Restructuring of China's State Sector." In J. C. Oi (ed.), *Going Private in China: The Politics of Corporate Restructuring and System Reform* (Shorenstein Asia-Pacific Research Center, 2011), 95.

[17] The first local experiments with share issuance happened in the countryside before there was a formal acknowledgment of broad policy experimentation. For a detailed chronology of local initiatives and experiments with stock issuance and trading platforms, see C. E. Walter & F. J. T. Howie, *Privatizing China: Inside China's Stock Markets* (Wiley, 2006), at 21–22 (mentioning Provisional Management Measures that were released locally by the Shanghai Branch of the People's Bank of China in July 1984 as the first formal rules promulgated by a local government body to address the issuance of shares). The rules, known as the "Eight Articles" (*batiao*) limited the issuance of shares to newly

employees. In 1986, the State Council released regulations permitting local governments to select a few large and medium-sized SOEs in their jurisdiction, as formal pilots for shareholding experiments.[18] Still, the issued shares at the time provided a fixed and guaranteed dividend cash payment, much like a bank deposit, and therefore failed to create incentives to enhance productivity.

Local governments thus explored additional schemes to increase production in the SOEs under their jurisdiction. Within local governments' jurisdiction, officials were assigned to manage the state assets organized in SOEs. These appointed managers entered into "Management Contract Responsibility" arrangements with their local government units. Many of these new arrangements involved performance targets, compensation plans, and control rights,[19] including, for example, (1) contract-based arrangements between SOEs and their supervising government agency in which SOEs bargained for profit remittance targets, allowing the SOE to keep the surplus (in many cases, profits above target were distributed to workers and managers); (2) giving greater control to SOE managers over sales, pricing, production, and finally even on investments and labor decisions, in return for achieving profit remittance targets; and (3) when the central government introduced a share issuance system, managers and other senior employees received shares in their SOEs as an additional incentive to increase firm profitability.[20]

Such arrangements allowed the officials *quo* managers to have growing discretion over the use of the enterprise's generated profits. The goal was to incentivize managers to perform better. Local government officials who were assigned to manage the SOEs were then able to use the retained profits and their broadened managerial discretion to expand the assets under their management.

To further their authority, many opted to create SOE subsidiaries such as collective enterprises and joint ventures. To these affiliated businesses, they often provided local government sponsorship and personal patronage. This new form of asset diversification helped local government officials to gain more autonomy from supervising central government agencies. Consequently, local government

established "collective enterprises," excluding SOEs from the initial experiment. Yet, shares of collective enterprises could be held by SOEs or other collectives, as well as by specific types of individuals, excluding party officials. Peasants were permitted to invest in shares, and employees could (and were often encouraged to) purchase shares of the enterprises employing them. As Walter and Howie state, starting the experiments with the collectives and determining exclusions were meant to protect SOEs and party officials from the new, politically charged, capitalist initiative.

18 Prior to the formalized pilot, there was the approval of share issuance to Liaoning Fushun No. 1 Brick Factory in January 1980 as the pioneering share issuance; followed by share issuance by Chengdu Shudu Office Building Co. Ltd. the same year; share issuance by Shenzhen Baoan County United Investment Co. Ltd. in 1983; and share issuance by Beijing Tianqiao Department Store Co. Ltd. in 1984. Ibid, Walter & Howie, *Privatizing China*.

19 D. C. Clarke, P. Murrell, & S. Whiting, "The Role of Law in China's Economic Development." In T. Brandt & L. Rawski (eds.), *China's Great Economic Transformation* (Cambridge University Press, 2008) 375, at 415–416.

20 Groves et al., *China's Evolving Managerial Labor Market*, note 14.

officials assigned to manage or supervise SOEs accumulated power and emerged as dominant business players and powerful decision makers in their jurisdictions.

The process of economic decentralization and the mechanisms developed through local experiments, therefore, did not follow global strategies for stimulating market development which advocate for privatizing SOEs and developing reliable mechanisms that secure property rights and contract enforcement. Nonetheless, local experiments created underlying conditions that triggered growth. Local experiments, discussed below, also took part in the emergence of Chinese public firms. At the same time, decentralization fostered the accumulation of local powers at the expense of the central government. This had several negative effects on the governance of firms, particularly.

First, rent-seeking behavior and strong local protectionism arose, guiding economic and administrative decision-making, with respect to firms. Known aspects of economic protectionism include the approval of risky investment schemes often without solid feasibility checks and the influence of local government officials on the supply of bank credit and loans to SOEs. Another notable effect was on legal enforcement, which was tainted by selective enforcement in favor of local parties.[21] Protectionism also led to informal internal trade barriers that different provinces created against each other and which influenced the operation of firms by limiting cross-provincial business cooperation, expansion, and harmed the creation of market competition.

Second, economic decentralization created the potential for conflicts of interest at various levels, between the administrative role of individual officials and their role as SOE managers, as well as between the central and local governments.[22] In addition, multiple overlapping government agencies had a say in monitoring various aspects of the operations of SOEs in their jurisdiction, including labor, production, and resource allocation. This led to burdensome multilevel bureaucratic interference with SOE management by various state agencies and Party agents with conflicting interests.[23] These lines of conflict brought the concern that local officials (and SOE managers among them) are turning less attuned to central government goals and made coordination between central and local government organs more challenging.

21 This influenced a spectrum of legal procedures including debt collections, bankruptcy, prosecution, and adjudication. Protectionism also tainted other administrative processes, such as licensing, the allocation of labor, credit financing, taxation, and profit retention privileges. Protectionism in the People's Court system emanated from additional related factors; economic decentralization and local self-funding also meant that local governments were the ones to fund the operation of the judicial system in their locales. See R. Peerenboom, "The Judiciary: Search of Independence, Authority and Competence." In R. Peerenboom, *China's Long March toward Rule of Law* (Cambridge University Press, 2002), 280, at 311.

22 J. Oi, "The Role of the Local State in China's Transitional Economy," *China Quarterly* 144 (1995), 1132, at 1144–1145.

23 D. C. Clarke, "Corporate Governance in China: An Overview," *China Economic Review* 4 (2003) 494, at 497–498.

The central government was not blind to these concerns and tried to curb the developing ties between local officials and the budding market.[24] It pushed for the separation between the government role and the commercial management of SOEs.[25] Under this approach, government and party officials were not allowed, at least not formally, to manage enterprises directly while also serving in other public posts. (This is not to be equated with the Anglo-American "separation between ownership and control," which was introduced later through corporatization.)

Over time, however, the effort to separate government from enterprises proved ineffective. The separation was artificial and only added to existing operational difficulties. With little or no business or managerial knowledge, management appointees, now *former* government and military officials (members of the nomenklatura), were still conduits of the government unit that appointed them. Moreover, the appointing units continued to supervise the managers, a pattern that led to local corruption and capture. Being ordered to allow autonomy, the supervising state agencies were caught unprepared to the new business reality, lacking the capacity to monitor their appointed agents.[26] The concern for conflicts of interest materialized. New economic opportunities along with broader managerial freedom brought wealth extraction and asset stripping in SOEs. Managers freely partook in value and asset transfers and were not held accountable for losses by local governments.[27]

By late 1980s, the relative inefficiencies of SOEs became a point of growing concern, especially in light of increasing competition from an emerging private sector (still mainly rural) and the limited penetration of foreign businesses.[28] By the mid-1990s, forty-one percent of China's SOEs suffered losses.[29] While a new social layer of crony-capitalists began to emerge.[30] The former state officials and party members, in their capacity as managers, started to form a powerful interest group

[24] Decision on Reforming the Economic Structure [中共中央关于经济体制改革的决定], promulgated by the Central Comm. of the Communist Party of China, Third Plenary Session of the Twelfth Central Comm., Oct. 20, 1984, art. 6 (showing noticeable beginnings of this shift).

[25] H. Chao & X. Yang, "Private Enterprise in China: The Developing Law of Collective Enterprises," *International Lawyer* 19(4) (1986) 1215, at 1220 (citing several decisions that instructed Party and government officials to resign either from their company posts or from their public one).

[26] X. L. Ding, "The Illicit Asset Stripping of Chinese State Firms," *The China Journal* 43 (2000) 1 (describing a "bleeding of the state sector" into the private hands of manager-appointees and officials assigned to supervise them).

[27] D. Ziegler, "The Honeycomb of Corruption – A Little Reform in the State Sector Has Proved A Dangerous Thing," *The Economist*, Vol. 355 (Apr. 8, 2000), at CS8–CS10, www.economist.com/node/299621 (addressing the reforms as "reforms that have brought great complexity to the state sector's relations … 'managers of Chinese state firms essentially have ended up capturing a sizable portion of the widely scattered public property'").

[28] G. Jefferson, "Are China's Rural Enterprises Outperforming State-Owned Enterprises?," *World Bank China Series*, Research Paper No. CH-RPS 24, 1993 (focusing on the rapid growth of Town-Village Enterprises as the critical element in China's economic transition success).

[29] "China Plans New Bankruptcy Law," *Wall Street Journal* (Dec. 30, 1994), at A4.

[30] K. E. Brødsgaard, "Politics and Business Group Formation in China: The Party in Control?," *The China Quarterly* 211 (2012) 624.

whose personal interests became directly invested in the SOEs, but with little or no supervision and with strong impact over economic policy design. This process soon became the source of many of China's long standing corporate governance and capital market challenges – asset stripping from SOEs, corruption, and capture.

National-Level Schemes

Economic decentralization and the resulting accumulation of local powers were thus a main driving force behind the national level efforts that came next. The corporate form as an organizational ownership structure of SOEs was introduced. Corporatization as a legal instrument was utilized as part of the central Party-state's efforts to reconsolidate power and authority with the central government domestically, as well as to advance China's place in the world economy.

Facing the institutional challenges discussed above, central government agencies started to develop schemes for structural reform in enterprise organization. The State Commission for the Reform of the Economic System (CRES), without any prior move by the national legislature or even the Party, introduced a national plan of legal reforms for business enterprises.[31] The two policy documents, known as the 1992 Normative Opinions, defined different legal forms of organization for equity share-based enterprises. The 1992 Normative Opinions also prescribed normative business standards in such companies, introducing for the first-time modern principles of corporate organization.[32] Despite being issued by an administrative sub-unit rather than by a national legislator (the NPC or the State Council) and carrying the "opinions" title, the 1992 Normative Opinions are widely considered as China's first *de-facto* modern national business organization law.[33]

A few months later, the central Party-state picked up these agency-led efforts through two important enterprise-organization schemes: (i) the "modern enterprise system" and (ii) a plan to accelerate the formation of business groups. These were meant to rebuild the troubled state sector while introducing more consolidated administrative authority and control over SOEs.

The "Modern Enterprise System" – Corporatization and Share Ownership

The corporate form is widely considered to be particularly suitable for encouraging economic activity and market growth. Most local experimentation schemes

[31] Normative Opinions on Standards for Limited Liability Companies [有限责任公司规范意见], promulgated by the State Comm'n for Restructuring the Economic Systems, May 15, 1992; Normative Opinions on Standards for Companies Limited by Shares [股份有限公司规范意见], promulgated by the State Comm'n for Restructuring the Economic Systems, May 15, 1992. Hereinafter together, 1992 Normative Opinions.

[32] For example, enterprise legal personhood, shareholders' limited liability, share ownership, transferability of shares, and formal separation between management and ownership. See Normative Opinion on LLCs, ibid., arts. 1, 22, 28, 30, 39, 41–42.

[33] Not having a formal status of law and being the "opinions" of an administrative commission, the status of these opinions was subject to debate. In retrospect, the State Council confirmed their effect as a ministry-level regulation. See N. C. Howson, "China's Company Law: One Step Forward, Two Steps Back? A Modest Complaint," *Columbia Journal of Asian Law* 11 (1997) 127, 137.

in China did not include many of the hallmark features of the corporate form, including separate legal personality, limited liability, full transferability of shares, delegated professional management, and ownership by external investors. In the early 1990s, this started to change.

The Decisions of the 14th Central Committee in 1993 announced a shift toward a "modern enterprise system."[34] In doing so, the decisions endorsed a national process for SOE corporatization, in which a modern corporate form was adopted (although still on a probationary basis). By adopting the features of the modern corporation, it was hoped that productivity would increase and that efficiency considerations would start guiding the management of SOEs.[35] In addition, the corporate form was not only thought to be better suited for efficient management but was also essential in order to make external equity financing possible. Interestingly, however, several elements from the 1992 Normative Opinions, most notably economic-rights securing functions, traditionally linked with attracting external financing such as standards for shareholder protections, were not included in the CCP decision and were accordingly withdrawn from in the enactment of the subsequent, and first, PRC Company law.[36]

Adopting the contours of a modern corporation in law reflected the formal acknowledgment in corporate legal personality, limited liability, transferability of rights, and separation of ownership from management (which was referred to as "scientific management").[37] Furthermore, it meant a (re)conceptualization of property rights ideas and specifically ownership interests through shares, even if this was still exercised mainly by the state on behalf of "all the people."[38] Indeed, as part of the corporatization initiative, share ownership rights in enterprises were formally recognized. The significance of this should not go unnoticed and is especially striking given that China's first Property Law was enacted only in 2007.[39] Ownership of financial assets and particularly the economic rights attached to it were still openly

34 Decision on Issues Concerning the Establishment of a Socialist Market Economic System [中共中央关于建立社会主义市场经济体制若干问题的决定] [Communique], promulgated by the Third Plenary Session of the Fourteenth Central Comm. of the Communist Party of China, Nov. 14, 1993 [the 14th Central Committee Decisions].

35 D. C. Clarke, "Blowback: How China's Effort to Bring Private-Sector Standards into the Public Sector Backfired." In B. L. Liebman & C. J. Milhaupt (eds.), *Regulating the Visible Hand?: The Institutional Implications of Chinese State Capitalism* (Oxford University Press, 2015), 35.

36 The Company Law of the People's Republic of China [中华人民共和国公司法], promulgated by the Standing Comm. of the Eighth Nat'l People's Cong., Dec. 29, 1993, effective July 1994 [the 1993 Company Law].

37 Ibid., arts. 3–7.

38 Although all assets were possessed by the state in the traditional SOEs system, the corporatization process and share ownership can be viewed as distinguishing between administrative possession and the recognition of the state (and state bodies) as a property share owner.

39 On the controversies surrounding the Property Law enactment process, see S. Sui, "New Property Law Shakes Up China," BBC News (Mar. 8, 2007), http://news.bbc.co.uk/2/hi/asia-pacific/6429977.stm.

frowned upon at that time.[40] This had a simple ideological basis, as earnings from capital assets ran counter to the basic Marxist view of labor-based income. Thus, a share system that was taken beyond local experimentations and acknowledged in a formal national law had to be motivated by a strong national level incentive.

It is well established among China scholars that the corporatization scheme was designed to attract public finance to recover the failing state sector.[41] Yet, the shifts in China's political–economic equilibrium at the same time suggests that it was also an effort to consolidate authority and control over the process of business organization by (i) having central-state defined and limited formats to the administration of business organization and (ii) taking control over the speed and scope of local governments' experimentation.

In the process of corporatization, SOEs as industrial-ministerial or provincial-line state agencies were converted from their former organization into one of the corporate forms recognized under the newly enacted Company Law, which distinguished between three main corporate forms of organization: (1) a Limited Liability Company (LLC) (*youxian zeren gongsi*) intended for a small and more closely held group of investors, similar to the close corporation form in the United States; (2) a Joint Stock Limited Company, also known as a "company limited by shares" (CLS) (*gufen youxian gongsi*), which may be a listed company or an unlisted company, although the assumption was that a company will be established with the intention to list in the future; and (3) a Wholly State-Owned LLC (*guoyou duzi gongsi*), a special type of LLC wholly owned by a state body.[42]

As part of its reorganization, a corporatized SOE had to shed its social welfare functions and maintain only its productive assets and human capital.[43] The newly created legal entities were then either grouped under (1) central and local-level state bodies (e.g., central, provincial, and municipal government organs with jurisdiction over a particular industrial sector or region), which were now reorganized as holding companies with subsidiary "legal person" holdings, or; (2) organized with other existing PRC enterprises (such as collectives and other companies that were also controlled by noncentral government bodies) and given a "legal person" status.

40 Only in 2002, following Jiang Zemin's 2001 speech and the official proclamations of the 16th Communist Party Congress, were party members officially welcome to pursue investment-sourced income.

41 To establish this conclusion, scholars present the percentage of listed firms that originated from SOEs. For example, Clarke brings sources to show how at the end of 2000, of the 1,088 listed companies on both exchanges, over 900 were originally traditional SOEs. At the end of 2001, out of 1,160 listed companies, approximately 1,103 were originally traditional SOEs. D. C. Clarke, "The Independent Director in Chinese Corporate Governance," *Delaware Journal of Corporate Law* 31 (2006) 125, 131.

42 For the LLC form, see 1993 Company Law, arts. 3, 9, 19, 20. For the CLS form, see 1993 Company Law arts. 3, 73, 74. For the wholly state-owned LLC form, see 1993 Company Law arts. 3, 64.

43 The social welfare functions were transferred to "social affairs units" (*shiye danwei*) under relevant ministries. See D. L. Yang, *Remaking the Chinese Leviathan: Market Transition and the Politics of Governance in China* (Stanford University Press, 2004).

The controlling shares of the corporation were issued to the industrial ministry or to other national and local government units from which the corporation was created. The structural outcome of this corporate organization process was the consolidation of the productive assets and human capital of traditional SOEs and their vesting in several now-corporatized SOEs in which the central or the local government now had shares. It was assumed that the new corporate shareholding capacity of the state would eliminate conflicts between the various state agencies involved in the firms' operations since they would have one vehicle, the shareholder vote, to promote their goals.[44]

The 1993 Company law thus formally initiated the corporatization scheme at the national level. In streamlining the process of business organization, local experiments have moved under the central government's radar in a scheme that was now nationally (and gradually) applied. The use of the modern corporate form thus initiated not only a process of market reorganization but also a process of reconsolidation in the market. This was thereafter pursued in full swing throughout the subsequent Legal Modernization Era. By the mid-1990s, the State Council selected 100 large and medium-sized SOEs for a pilot program. The SOEs that were corporatized as CLSs could now raise equity investments from domestic and foreign investors and assign them shares in return. From this point onward, while companies with dominant state ownership were still colloquially called SOEs, it is more accurate to refer to such enterprises as state-*controlled* companies.

A survey of 2,343 pilot enterprises conducted by the State Statistical Bureau in 1997 revealed that 85 percent of the enterprises had corporatized into one of the legal corporate forms. Among these, 39 percent adopted the wholly state-owned form, 23 percent adopted the LLC form, and another 23 percent adopted the CLS form.[45] By the end of 2000, over 80 percent of all SOEs surveyed were transformed into corporations, and over 1,200 large enterprises were restructured specifically as CLSs.[46]

While the restructuring effort was carried out successfully and the corporatized firms quickly attracted outside financing (see Section 2), in practice, the contribution of this process to management quality, accountability, and efficiency was limited. One of the main reasons was the cognizant design of share ownership in the corporatized SOEs. Strategically refraining from privatization, the newly corporatized SOEs that turned to equity financing were required to maintain a third of their shares as state shares. These shares were classified as common, but untradeable shares and could be owned only by state entities. Another third of the newly issued shares were reserved for *legal persons*. These were also common but

[44] For a critique, see Clarke, *Corporate Governance in China*, note 23, at 497–500.

[45] J. He, "An Empirical Study on the Governance Structure of Listed Companies" [上市公司治理结构的实证分析], *Economic Research Journal* 5(8) [经济研究5(8)] (1998) 50.

[46] Tenev et al., *Corporate Governance and Enterprise Reform*, note 15. The total number of firms surveyed is not mentioned, and therefore, the percentage of CLS corporatization in SOEs is unclear.

untradeable shares and were only transferable to other legal persons with appropriate approvals that included price determination.[47] During that time, China's economic laws determined that legal persons were domestic organizations with formal legal personality, which meant that the definition in practice excluded individuals.[48] Moreover, since purely private businesses were at that time few in number, legal persons de facto meant enterprises that were state owned or state affiliated. This diversification of different types of common shares practically meant that about two-thirds of a listed company's shares were directly and indirectly held by organs of the state. It also meant that only about a third of the company's shares – the public float – were transferable.[49] This system isolated state shares from market forces and had implications on the valuation of listed companies. Most important, the potential disciplinary role of the capital market on the insiders of the firms was curtailed from the start.

To note, the share composition started to change only after the split-share structure reform was announced in 2005,[50] in which state-owned shares and legal-persons' shares were, in principle, gradually subjected to market discipline. Today, legal person shares are held by entities such as industrial enterprises (mostly SOEs), holding companies, nonbank financial institutions, and research institutions. Many of these legal person shares are largely still indirectly controlled by the state.

Even today, making state and legal person shares tradable does not mean these shares are suddenly being traded. State ownership in significant cases is retained. Either state bodies do not trade their shares in practice or they trade their shares through a private placement to another state-owned or state-affiliated enterprise particularly in industries that are designated for mixed ownership. Alternatively, as will be shown in Chapter 7, in many instances and often following policy directives, state ownership is reduced but control is maintained through mergers and acquisitions, diversification through holding groups and subsidiaries, group formation, and mixed ownership.[51]

47 W. Hou & E. Lee, "Split Share Structure Reform, Corporate Governance, and the Foreign Share Discount Puzzle in China," *European Journal of Finance* 20 (2014) 703, 709.

48 The Economic Contract Law governed agreements between domestic "legal persons." Those at that time were legal entities restricted to the state sector, SOEs and/or collectives. The law was amended in 1993 to include all domestic registered and licensed business entities, but still, not individuals. See discussion in Part II, Chapter 4.

49 F. Jiang & K. A. Kim, "Corporate Governance in China: A Modern Perspective," *Journal of Corporate Finance* 32 (2015) 190.

50 A self-assessment study conducted by the CSRC and China's State Economic and Trade Commission before the share-structure reform was launched found that 77 percent of China's controlling shareholders in a study that included 1,175 listed firms could be considered state entities, while in about a third of the companies a single-state shareholders held more than half of the shares. Clarke, *Law without Order*, note 10, at 148, note 58.

51 Another business strategy to raise capital is to leverage the firm. Debt capital does not require the state to give up control nor dilute its ownership interests and has become an acute problem especially for local-level SOEs.

Business Group Formation

Another key effort that the central Party-state took to reconsolidate control over SOEs was the acceleration of business group formation. As early as 1987, the CRES encouraged SOEs to organize as "business groups" (*qiye jituan*). In its Opinions for the Establishment and Encouragement of Business Groups, the enterprise group was defined as a multilevel organizational structure, with various circles of enterprises tied together by a charter and by shared organizational features, yet each with corresponding autonomy.[52] This organizational structure expanded in the following years until it was recognized as a national goal during the Legal Modernization Era, eventually applying systematically along former ministerial or sectorial line bureaus.[53]

Entities within the group are tied to a parent "core" company, above which the state presides. The core company functions as the holding company in the group. The main production enterprise within the group is the "group company" – the unit to which most of the state assets as well as economic and production activities were funneled through the corporatization process. Among the group companies are the corporatized SOEs that issued shares and raised equity capital from the public – the business group's publicly listed firm. These, in many cases, became China's national champions. Other enterprises under the same core company within the group provide related services to support the main corporatized listed firm, such as research and development or education subsidiaries, the group's finance company, and other service entities (subsidiaries or affiliated firms) that expand the group's network through contractual arrangements. Today, the picture that has emerged is one of an intricate layered network of dozens of related companies within business groups in specific industrial sectors.[54] Enterprise groups must register as such, a status that grants their various entities opportunities for preferential taxes, stock listing, and government contracts.[55]

The policy of accelerating business group formation was meant to encourage competition, prevent monopoly, promote technological progress, and improve economic efficiency through, among other ways, economies of scale.[56] In many key

[52] The Opinions on the Establishment and Development of Business Groups, issued by the State Comm'n on Restructuring the Economy and the State Economic Comm'n, recognized Business Groups as a "multi-level organizational structure" with separate legal personality. See Opinions on the Establishment and Development of Business Groups [关于组建和发展企业集团的几点意见], promulgated by the Nat'l Econ. Sys. Reform Comm'n & the Nat'l Econ. Comm'n, Dec. 16, 1987 [Business Groups Opinions].

[53] Brødsgaard, *Politics and Business Group Formation*, note 30, at 627–628. See Outline Report on the Ninth Five-Year Plan of National Economy and Social Development and the Perspective and Goals of 2010[关于国民经济和社会发展"九五"计划和2010年远景目标纲要及关于《纲要》报告的决议], promulgated by the Nat'l People's Cong., Mar. 17, 1996.

[54] L-W. Lin & C. Milhaupt, "We Are the (National) Champions: Understanding the Mechanisms of State Capitalism in China," *Stanford Law Review* 65 (2013) 697, at 717–721.

[55] The Business Group Opinions were further developed with the issuance of Guiding Provisional Rules on Business Group Registration[企业集团登记管理暂行规定], promulgated by the St. Council, Sept. 1, 2006, effective Jan. 1, 1997.

[56] Business Groups Opinions, note 52, art. 5.

industries, however, and especially after state assets were restructured under the national State-owned Assets Supervision and Administration Commission (SASAC) and its local branches in the early 2000s (discussed below) – which hold controlling or full ownership interests at the core parent company – group formation actually led to monopolistic and oligopolistic group power.[57] Since the reorganization of state assets in groups meant carving corporations out of industrial sector ministries and agencies, groups from inception were de facto confined to certain geographical areas or to a certain step in the production chain within a given industry.[58] Thus, while they were theoretically competing with parallel groups, they were in fact designated to accumulate market dominance in their defined areas.

While the group structure may have limited the development of domestic competition, it contributed to China's competitive abilities in the global market. As noted by Lin and Milhaupt, the government encouraged business group formation to foster the growth of national champions as engines of development.[59] Finally, the national endorsement of business group formation had an additional important goal, to aid the Party-state in "streamline[ing] control over the economy." In theory, by reducing information and coordination costs, national-level vertically integrated groups are able to transmit and implement economic policy more easily, serving and amplifying central-level control.[60]

From the very beginning of this strategy in the late 1980s, policymakers acknowledged that group formation could be a double-edge sword. The Business Groups Opinions cautioned against potential conflicting interests not only between various levels of group member companies but also between different levels of the state. The Business Groups Opinions emphasized that groups should not operate in ways that would damage national interests.[61] However, concerns have materialized at

57 For example, in the energy, petroleum, telecommunications, and chemicals industries. Milhaupt & Zheng, *Beyond Ownership*, note 10, at 690–691, note 129.

58 This is the case particularly for central–state held groups in strategic industries. One of the commonly mentioned examples is the asset reorganization of the Ministry of Petroleum Industry and corporatization of the resulting three national oil giants, China National Petroleum Corporation (CNPC), China Petroleum and Chemical Corporation (Sinopec), and China National Offshore Oil Corporation (CNOOC).

59 L. W. Lin & Milhaupt, *National Champions*, note 54, at 699, and 712–714.

60 Ibid., at 714. There are, however, several articles that suggest the opposite view in terms of business groupism at the local level. See J. P. H. Fan et al., "Institutions and Organizational Structure: The Case of State-Owned Corporate Pyramids," *Journal of Law, Economics, and Organization* 29 (2013) 1217 (arguing that group companies at the local level are designed to minimize political costs of state interference, further suggesting that this was implemented by local governments in an effort to assign them more credibility to nonintervention vis-à-vis investors); K. Su et al., "Pyramidal Structure, Risk-Taking and Firm Value: Evidence from Chinese Local SOEs," *Economics of Transition* 26(3) (2018) 401 (viewing business group formation as a form of decentralization that was aimed to reduce political influence on firms by increasing intervention cost along the layers of the pyramid); M. Zhang et al., "Pyramidal Structure, Political Intervention and Firms' Tax Burden: Evidence from China's Local SOEs," *Journal of Corporate Finance* 36 (2016) 15 (looking at the influence of state pyramids on corporate tax burden, arguing that group pyramids formed to protect local SOEs from political intervention).

61 Business Groups Opinions, note 52, art. 13.

both levels: the group system furthered local-level networks and it concentrated economic and administrative power in the hands of a few national champions and their leaders.

During the first few years of the scheme, the national-level endorsement of business groups boosted empire-building by the localities and widened the divide between central-level and local-level economic power. Local governments had used the opportunity to create pyramid-layered business groups that dissociated them from central government control.[62] This form of economic disentanglement from central control through local-group organization is an aspect of the shifts in China's political economy that carries implications today. Also, with respect to national-level groups, since many of the most important national champion groups were converted from previous industrial ministries, there was a strong political pressure to maintain their rank within the bureaucratic hierarchy.[63] As a result, business groups (at the central level) and the general managers of many of their corporatized SOEs still enjoy a status equivalent to that of a minister or vice minister in the state's hierarchical bureaucracy. This makes supervision over them by state administrative bodies charged with tensions and battles over authority.

In sum, the policy endorsement of business group formation has been a significant contributor to China's rising economic power, particularly in the international front. However, while the purpose was to consolidate and streamline control, it also amplified the conflicts of interest between the various authorities of the state, both horizontally and vertically. Furthermore, business group formation intensified conflicts at the group level itself. Having to consider group-level implications, the core company and its controlling state owner became further alienated from the shareholders' interests in each firm within the group.[64] At least from a domestic perspective, it seems that the economic rational of endorsing business group formation was limited by the political function the scheme was designed to achieve and that the process perhaps even backfired.

2 *The Formation of the Capital Market*

Capital market institutions operate to reduce the costs of raising external finance. This is achieved primarily by facilitating transactions in a large number of securities simultaneously, making information easily available to potential and existing investors, and reducing the costs of monitoring. Importantly, capital markets promote efficiency by allocating capital to the most deserving firms. The capital market in China, however, evolved primarily to serve other functions. The following review examines how the capital market, in its technical, narrow sense, formed in China,

[62] See sources in note 60 (positing that this was also a form for the local governments to attract investors by committing through the pyramid structure to less government interference).

[63] Brødsgaard, *Politics and Business Group Formation*, note 30, at 612.

[64] See discussion in Chapter 7, "'Chinese-Style' State Capitalism and Its Consequences for Public Shareholders".

focusing on the primary mechanisms through which stocks were issued and traded and the institutions that were created to govern them.

Like the creation of corporations, capital market activity in China was initiated locally and informally on an experimental basis, which was later broadened by provisional national schemes before finally being formalized via legal mechanisms. Also similar to the making of the corporate form, the justification for institutionalizing the capital market lay primarily in their function as a financing tool for SOEs.[65] While the stock markets were formally active since 1990, starting from the second half of that decade and throughout the Legal Modernization Era, the state started to support the system of public share issuance explicitly when searching for alternatives to bank lending. Scholars attribute this to the pressing need to rescue the troubled state sector, which became deeply indebted at that time.[66] This shaped stock market development ever since as a platform to finance the restructuring of SOEs, rather than as a marketplace that promotes efficient allocation of capital. The implications extend to the present, as is clearly evident in frequent Party-state measures for keeping stock prices up in order to sustain the value of corporatized state-controlled firms.

Beyond this, and as with the emergence of the public firm, the levers of the capital market have been moved not only for their economic functions but also, and perhaps even mainly, due to their political functions. The formal institutionalization of the capital market supported the political processes that took hold during the Legal Modernization Era. The administration of a national capital market supported the shifts in power dynamics that formed as the central Party-state made efforts to regain control over the emerging market.

Institutions and Share-Offering Platforms

The first few instances of share offering in Chinese entities after the initiation of market reform were tested offshore on the Hong Kong exchange or conducted informally by local institutions. This occurred during the second half of the 1980s. The initiators were local financial institutions, mainly local bank branches, special economic zones, securities companies, and local OTC trading centers.[67] In early 1990, two national stock exchanges formed under separate regulations issued by local branches of the People's Bank of China (PBoC). The State Council approved the establishment of formal securities exchanges in Shanghai and Shenzhen on June 2, 1990. The new Shanghai Stock Exchange opened on December 19, 1990 and was followed by the opening of the Shenzhen Stock Exchange in July 1991. Even after the two stock exchanges began to operate, informal local trading continued in major

[65] S. Green, *China's Stockmarket: A Guide to Its Progress, Players and Prospects* (John Wiley & Sons, 2003), at 20–25.

[66] Clarke, *Law without Order*, note 10, at 151–152.

[67] For a detailed account on local experimentation with share offerings, Walter & Howie, *Privatizing China*, note 17.

cities for some time.[68] The governance of the two formal stock exchanges remained in the hands of their respective local governments through "municipal securities commissions" in cooperation with the local branches of the PBoC and thus varied significantly. Each stock exchange was therefore effectively an administrative unit, integrated into the operation of its local government. Local officials from the various municipal bureaus were involved in all aspects of the stock exchange's operations – from the selection of which enterprises would be corporatized, through the approval of share issuance, to the listing process itself.[69] Moreover, given the absence of unified guidance on how to operate the exchanges, the stock exchanges largely operated on a trial-and-error basis. This practice, naturally, allowed much room for local discretion and protectionism and facilitated fraud and abuse. Dissatisfaction spread on mass and prompted citizens riots in scale that some described as "the most serious public disturbance in China since the 1989 crackdown…"[70]

Thus, here too, the initial establishment of the two stock exchanges in the 1990s was primarily designed to serve the incorporation process of local SOEs by providing them a platform to reach external finance. Other more common economic functions of capital markets, such as to provide options for interest-bearing use of household savings; offering a transparent, quick, and efficient source of financing (for all economic sectors); monitoring listed corporations; and allocating capital to the most deserving firms, were not part of the agenda. With weak economic functions, investors felt exploited and were enraged.

During 1992–93, after Deng Xiaoping's call to boost the development of the securities market and along with the enactment of a law for corporations, the central Party-state started to centralize its control over the two stock exchanges.[71] These efforts included consolidating the regulatory and supervisory authority over the operation or the exchanges, as well as gaining control over the issuance process itself. The latter involved the design of a quota system, addressed below. The main motive, as described by Walter and Howie, was the fear from losing control over the development process to local officials, who promoted issuances in selected corporations and consequently accumulated substantial economic and administrative power through the emerging capital market. The authors describe a "share fever" in both exchanges and a specific incident of over-subscription in Shenzhen, which created great disappointment among potential investors and provoked public riots against local protectionism. This led to the establishment of two national securities market regulators, the State Council Securities Commission and China's Securities Supervision and

68 Ibid., at 27.

69 Ibid., at 29–30.

70 A. P. Vandevelde, "Realizing the Re-Emergence of the Chinese Stock Market: Fact or Fiction," *Vanderbilt Journal of Transnational Law* 30 (1997) 579, at 592–593, note 74.

71 Interestingly, after Deng Xiaoping called for bolder experiments with the securities market in January 1992, as part of the renewed momentum for reforms, one of the immediate subsequent steps was to issue shares designated to foreigners (i.e., "B-shares"). This bears similarities with the use of legal institutions to attract foreign capital to joint ventures during early reforms, more than a decade earlier.

Management Committee.[72] The State Council subsequently issued a provisional "law" on securities, which set temporary mechanisms for share listing.[73] This temporary, yet important, document set the procedures for share issuance, trading, and disclosure by CLSs, prohibited insider trading practices, and established civil and criminal liability for securities violations for the first time. Honing their new national authority, the security regulators issued a complementary set of temporary rules,[74] which prohibited securities fraud and specifically addressed insider trading and other misconduct in the budding stock markets.

The efforts to consolidate authority over the securities market culminated with the adoption of a national law for securities.[75] Substantively, the 1998 Securities Law only supplemented the prior 1993 Provisional Regulations on Share Issuance. Organizationally, however, it was extremely meaningful as it centralized the regulatory authority and control over the stock exchanges and over the development of the securities markets more broadly, under the authority of one ministry-level state agency – the China Securities and Regulatory Commission (CSRC).[76] The CSRC has been responsible for China's securities markets ever since.

The Quota System

An important element in the effort to reconsolidate central state control over the stock market was the implementation of a quota system, officially in place from 1993 until 2000. Similar to the business group formation, however, this effort backfired as well and ended-up amplifying rather than mitigating the accumulation of regional power.

The quota system was a national effort to administer the process of share issuance and control its scope. It was intended to ensure that the newly available external finance would be funneled to selected state-owned companies, while controlling supply and thereby keeping prices of newly offered shares high. Technically, this administrative governance mechanism was based on a defined preapproved national pool of shares to be issued. The size of the national pool was determined annually

[72] Both institutions were founded in October 1992 and consolidated under China Securities and Regulatory Commission (the CSRC) following the enactment of the Securities Law in 1998.

[73] Provisional Regulation on the Administration of Issuance and Trading of Stocks [股票发行与交易管理暂行条例], promulgated by the St. Council, Apr. 22, 1993 [The Provisional Regulations on Share Issuance].

[74] Interim Procedures on the Administration of Stock Exchanges [证券交易所管理暂行办法], promulgated by the Securities Comm'n of the St. Council, July 7, 1993, art. 4 ("Stock exchanges are subject to the management of the local people's governments and the supervision and control by the China Securities Supervision and Control Comm." (a body under the Securities Commission of the State Council [SCSC] which preceded the [CSRC]); Provisional Measures for the Prohibition of Securities Fraud [禁止证券欺诈行为暂行办法], approved by the St. Council, Aug. 15, 1993, promulgated by the SCSC, Sep. 2, 1993.

[75] Securities Law of the People's Republic of China [中华人民共和国证券法], promulgated by the Standing Comm. of the 9th Nat'l People's Cong., Dec. 29, 1998 [1998 Securities Law].

[76] H. Huang, "The Regulation of Insider Trading in China: A Critical Review and Proposals for Reform," *Australia Journal of Corporate Law* 17(3) (2005) 281, at 284.

by the central government through the PBoC. Provincial governments (in the case of local firms) or central ministries (in the case of firms owned by a central ministry) then negotiated with their respective branch of the securities regulator on their allocated quota. Similarly, they bargained about which firm they would eventually recommend to the center for share issuance. After reaching an agreement, a request was submitted to the central securities regulator, which decided how to allocate the national pool between the regions and ministries. The central authority also decided which of the recommended companies would then enter a formal review process toward their initial public offerings. Each such company had to go through an individual approval process, during which information about the company was considered as well as its rule-obedience record. In their account of the quota system, Pistor and Xu point out that the central authority approved the firms recommended to it in most cases. This, they suggest, indicates that from the outset, the real power was in the hands of the local governments and the ministries in selecting the firms to begin with.[77]

As a side note, while the term quota system refers only to the mechanism for the selection of IPO issuers, the pricing of IPOs also went through similar transitional administrative governance methods. Initially, the relevant government level directly determined the price for an IPO issuance. Toward 1995, pricing started to be based on consultation and bidding between the issuing company, its underwriters, and the relevant local authority. It was only toward 2005 that the price for IPO issuance started to rely on open market inquiry and evaluation.[78]

As for quality control, in the absence of market price mechanisms to evaluate companies, the quota system was also intended to provide quality-guided administrative selection. This was designed by including incentives at both regional and company levels that were supposed to ensure an effective evaluation of companies prior to their selection. Regions whose selected companies performed well after their shares were issued were awarded larger future quotas. Companies that performed badly were subject to potential delisting, which could reduce the region's future quota. The purpose was to incentivize firms and local government officials to pass their recommendations to the center based on collected and verified information, and thereby to identify "more [rather] than less viable firms" as the potential issuers.

Commentators note several positive results of this administrative system, concluding that it was an important transitional mechanism that facilitated share issuances in the absence of advanced capital market mechanisms.[79] The quota system induced a level of information exchange and disclosure in the newly emerging

77 For a detailed account, see K. Pistor & C. Xu, "Governing Stock Markets in Transition Economies: Lessons from China," *American Law and Economics Review* 7 (2005) 184, at 197–198.

78 On the various transitional methods for IPO price determination, see C. Su & J. Yu, "Market-Oriented Reform of China's IPO System and Information Disclosure Regulation." In S. Cheng & Z. Li (eds.), *The Chinese Stock Market Volume I: A Retrospect and Analysis from 2002* (Palgrave Macmillan, 2014), 39.

79 Pistor & Xu, *Governing Stock Markets*, note 77.

capital market, a valuable factor in the absence of mandatory information disclosure standards and enforcement. Intense bargaining between the center and local governments encouraged interregional competition. Furthermore, it also introduced capital market growth measures as a basis for administrative decision-making for future quotas, which presumably incentivized local officials to keep a watchful eye on firms in their region.

At the same time, however, the implementation of the selection process within the quota system quickly became crooked. Increasingly motivated by personal considerations and selection biases, the system intensified local protectionism. The incentives and accountability methods described above backfired. Since local officials personally benefited from the image of better-performing companies, they had little incentive to press for reliable disclosure. Instead, they were prone to turn a blind eye to inaccurate reports or even actively assist firms in committing fraud.[80] Moreover, the system did not address matters of information disclosure in the post-IPO stage. It became clear that this transitional mechanism should be replaced by a formal approval process for IPOs with more transparent, impartial listing standards and disclosure rules for secondary trade. In that sense, the enactment of the 1998 Securities Law was the beginning of a turn from a rather arbitrary administrative system of share issuances to a more centralized and formal governance. In 2001, the CSRC issued new measures for the administration of IPOs, which formally ended the quota system.[81]

***

The review in this Chapter reveals the process through which public firms emerged in China, including the use of transitional legal and market mechanisms that had a meaningful influence on how the capital market developed and the functions it performed. Absent any other institutional framework, public firms developed through a process of local experimentation designed to finance China's struggling state sector. During the early years of the Legal Modernization Era, this was followed by nationally administered schemes that were guided by political necessities to regain political–economic control. Political economy, then, rather than economies of scale or technological advancement, motivated the creation of the public corporation in China. The emergence of the public firm and the formation of the capital market therefore not only reflect the limited, marginally growing, economic function of law in the early stages of China's capital market development but also illuminate the strong presence of political determinants in the function of emerging legal and market mechanisms.

80 Ibid., at 199–200.

81 Measures for the Administration of New Share Issuance by Listed Companies [上市公司新股发行管理办法], promulgated by the China Sec. Reg. Comm'n, Mar. 28, 2001. Note, however, that the actual implementation of the Quota System persisted until 2003.

7

Corporate Governance under State Capitalism

As shown in Chapter 6, a shift in economic power relations from the center to local governments was a major driving force at the dawn of the public corporation in China. Transitional, informal, and often locally initiated government experiments – rather than formal legal institutions – directed the emergence of firms and the capital market.

The limited role for legal institutions at this stage might be explained by the early stage of market development. Many countries walked a similar path, in which they were able to initiate a capital market where firms raised capital from investors even in the absence of a supporting legal system by using functional substitutions. Entrepreneurs and investors in emerging markets seem to be less deterred than expected by low-quality legal institutions.[82] Even in the most advanced markets, some scholars argue, the law followed rather than led capital market development which was ultimately instigated by bottom-up resourcefulness rather than by top-down legal mandates.[83]

Yet, the trajectories of developing and transitional economies also led to a common understanding that holds local alternatives as merely stepping stones, a transitional passage toward achieving a deeper and more advanced market. In other words, it is believed that while local substitutions can instigate markets, they can only go so far.[84] It is, therefore, widely understood that the importance of law for

82 A. Santos, "The World Bank's Uses of the "Rule of Law" Promise in Economic Development." In D. Trubek & A. Santos (eds.), *The New Law and Economic Development: A Critical Appraisal* (Cambridge University Press, 2006) 253, at 282–290. See also M. Pargendler et al., "In Strange Company: The Puzzle of Private Investment in State-Controlled Firms," *Cornell International Law Journal* 46 (2013) 569.

83 John Coffee, "The Rise of Dispersed Ownership: The Role of Law in the Separation of Ownership and Control," *Yale Law Journal* 111 (2001) 1 (arguing that private ordering by entrepreneurs and the stock exchanges in the United States triggered markets prior to regulatory action); P. G. Mahoney, "The Exchange as Regulator," *Virginia Law Review* 83 (1997) 1453, 1455 (preempting private regulatory action by the NYSE); Y. Miwa & M. J. Ramseyer, "The Value of Prominent Directors: Corporate Governance and Bank Access in Transitional Japan," *Journal of Legal Studies* 31 (2002) 273 (Firms in early twentieth century Japan created corporate governance arrangements by private ordering – they hired prominent industrialists to their board).

84 P. Murrell, "Institutions and Firms in Transition Economies." In C. Ménard & M. M. Shirley (eds.), *Handbook of New Institutional Economics* (Springer, 2008) 667, 688–690 (discussing "[T]he effect

development increases as markets develop. The rise in public finance is often treated as the turning point.[85] As the economy advances, financial assets take primacy over land as an important source of wealth.[86] Due to their intangibility, financial assets require a legal construct to exist.

Furthermore, it is held that during early stages of economic transition, the state is particularly vulnerable to rent-seeking behavior. Unregulated areas and nascent financial markets enable state capture more freely, allowing more opportunities for officials and their affiliates to capture the state for private benefit.[87] Alternative substitutions, especially informal ones, are often ambiguous and arbitrary and thus cannot fully overcome such problems.

Beyond early stages of market development and growth, therefore, the paradigm view expects local alternatives to give way to robust, market-oriented, legal institutions if further growth is to be achieved. Robust capital markets, particularly, are said to require high-quality, reliable, and internationally familiar investor protection mechanisms and disclosure standards that only particular legal institutions are said to provide.

The above understanding gets some support when one contrasts the limited presence of formal economic law in China in the Early Reform Era, and its rising presence thereafter, with China's GDP total growth seen in Figure 7.1, as well as with peaks in China's capital market growth measured by the number of listed firms, as seen in Figure 2.2 (Chapter 2).

Additionally, as this chapter will show, corporate governance took a more structured, investor-oriented turn toward centrally administered laws and legal institutions, particularly during the second decade of the Legal Modernization Era. In this process, China's policymakers formally embraced many of the legal instruments traditionally identified with corporate capitalism. This is also the period of a significant market growth.

And yet, at the same time, it is widely acknowledged that the causation in China is missing (in whichever causal direction one ascribes to), giving rise to China's growth puzzle. Many scholars observed how the law on the books does not necessarily reflect law in practice. From investors' economic perspective, the written law is an empty

of transitional institutions, [and the fact that they] eventually become outdated."). More generally see K. Davis & M. J. Trebilcock, "The Relationship Between Law and Development: Optimists versus Skeptics," *The American Journal of Comparative Law* 56 (2008) 895, 895–946 and note 162 (citing M. Trebilcock & J. Leng, "The Role of Formal Contract Law and Enforcement in Economic Development," *Virginia Law Review* 92 (2006) 1517, 1554–1565, and the references therein); R. Hausmann et al., Growth Accelerations, *Journal of Economic Growth* 10 (2005) 303.

85 K. Pistor, *The Code of Capital*, (Princeton University Press, 2019), at 8: "… especially financial capital, the intangible capital that exists only in law."

86 See generally T. Piketty, *Capital in the 21st Century* (The Belknap Press of Harvard University Press, 2014), Chapter 3.

87 K. Hoff & J. E. Stiglitz, *The Creation of the Rule of Law and the Legitimacy of Property Rights: The Political and Economic Consequences of a Corrupt Privatization* (Nat'l Bureau of Econ. Research, Paper No. 11772, 2005).

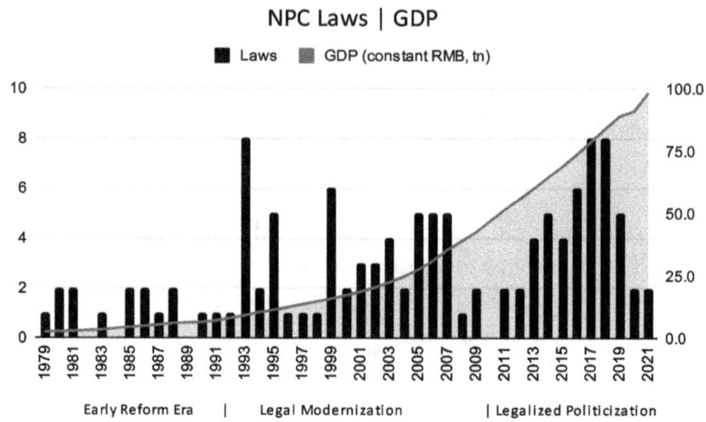

FIGURE 7.1 NPC economic laws to total GDP

vessel when rights are not secured in practice. And indeed, as the analysis below further shows, the economic functions of the adopted legal instruments remained low even while the use of law has risen. This suggests that the rise in formal law with respect to the capital market should find explanation elsewhere.

The growth of markets and the interests of market participants is thus only part of China's capital market law and development story. Here too, the rising space for law in the market finds explanation in the political functionality of law as well. Law and legal instruments have contributed to China's capital market development process in other ways that are overlooked when one only considers the perspective of investors in a growing market. But when thinking of the Legal Modernization Era as the period during which the Party-state fostered a form of state capitalism, the functionality of law in the market becomes clearer and so does its relationship with growth.

As productivity increased and firms expanded during the 1980s and 1990s, so did opportunities for abuse. Local economic power accumulated and introduced shifts in the delicate political equilibrium. To reconsolidate central–state control over capital market development, legal instruments were advanced, including, among others, the corporate form, share ownership, the public firm, and holding groups. Through the use of legal institutions, the market was reorganized around pyramid holding groups on top of which Party-state organs preside as dominant shareholders. As seen in Part II, during this period, the central state consolidated its powers also through control over capital financing, carried through a similar reorganization of the financial industry. This process culminated in the early 2000s, at a time when market group formation and a greater opening in the capital market aligned well with China's rising ambitions to take part in global competition. China's state capitalism was rapidly taking shape. Forming into a system in which the Party-state directly or indirectly functions as the controlling shareholder of most significant industrial groups and their domestic and globally listed companies; of the commercial and policy banks and financial industry firms; the overseer of all labor organizations; and at the same time acts as the market's regulator and the main enforcing power (through administrative enforcement).[88]

The following sections provide a systematic, comparative analysis of traditional corporate governance institutions and legal instruments that were embraced in China during the Legal Modernization Era, revealing a clear turn toward law, with some economic utility but with more significant political functions.

A TURN TOWARD LAW AND LEGAL INSTITUTIONS: CONVERGENCE WITH CORPORATE CAPITALISM?

As seen earlier, the opportunities and interests of a new variety of economic participants within the Party-state system started shifting when market economic activity was enabled. This echoed back into the system as the central Party-state, troubled by the shifts in internal political economy, turned to legal construction to reconsolidate its powers. A general turn toward a Chinese "rule of law" was announced as part of the 15th Central Party Congress [1997].[89] The increased attention to the legal system in governing firms and the capital market is a component fulfilling such broader turn to rule of law. The same Party Congress was also the first to use the term "corporate governance" as part of its economic reform plans.[90]

At the same time, market demand for law and the increasing openness to foreign investors were relevant factors as well, increasingly pushing for greater conformity with traditional legal institutions. In 2001, a wave of worldwide corporate scandals did not skip China. A number of large Chinese corporations were involved in accounting fraud and market manipulation, causing losses to investors and reflecting badly on China's state asset management system.[91] The troubles of the state sector,

[88] Commentators have taken different views as to the Party-state's involvement in the economy. Some have argued against the characterization of the Chinese economy as "state-capitalism," while others used the term more freely. *Cf.* N. R. Lardy, *Markets over Mao: The Rise of Private Business in China* (Columbia University Press, 2014) (considering the rapidly growing private business sector as a major driver of economic growth and employment in China today), with the various pieces in B. Liebman & C. Milhaupt (eds.), *Regulating the Visible Hand?: The Institutional Implications of Chinese State Capitalism* (Oxford University Press, 2015).

[89] Jiang Zemin Report at the 15th National Congress of the Communist Party of China [江泽民在中国共产党第十五次全国代表大会上的报告], Sept. 12, 1997. [Report to the 15th Party Congress]. Discussed in Part II.

[90] J. Fu, *Corporate Disclosure and Corporate Governance in China* (Kluwer Law International BV, 2010), 5, note 55 (referring to the CPC's Central Committee Resolution on Major Issues Regarding SOEs Reform and Development in the "Announcement of the fourth Plenary Session of the Fifteenth CCP National Congress").

[91] See Y. L. Duan, *Discussion on Large Shareholders' Equity Abuse and Cases* [论大股东股权滥用及实例] (Economic & Management Press, 2001) [经济管理出版社, 2001], summarizing various fraud cases, including the Yorkpoint Science & Technology stock scheme, the fall of Daqing Lianyi, Dong Fang Electronics, PT Hong Guang, Monkey King A, Lantian shares, Yi'an Technology, Yin Guangxia, and Zhengzhou Baiwen.

particularly, created urgency to adopt national corporate governance standards. As Zhiwu Chen noted: "These events provided the needed crash for legal change. Disappointed investors started to demonstrate in front of the CSRC building."[92] Together with the effect of the Asian financial crisis and the global competition China encountered following its 2001 WTO accession, these events led to extensive discussions about corporate governance and induced the formal embrace of many Western corporate governance institutions.[93]

And so, both economic and political considerations motivated the shift toward law during the Legal Modernization Era. Treating any one of these functions in isolation would be misleading. The *turn* toward law was grounded on its dual function.

By the early 2000s, an increasing body of national-level economic laws and regulations replaced many of the provisional governance mechanisms of the earlier era. Central–state agencies and institutions were created and given regulatory and supervision authority over the financial market.[94] The China Securities Regulatory Commission (CSRC) took a leading role in this turn. As part of the efforts to consolidate economic and administrative authority, the CSRC was given the administrative and political latitude to form national-level corporate governance schemes. One of its first steps was the 2001 Code of Corporate Governance for Listed Companies. The Code embodied the economic functions of law (i.e., a rights-securing law and finance approach to corporate governance). It was largely based on the OECD Principles of Corporate Governance and intended to improve the "modern enterprise system," standardize behavioral rules for directors, supervisors, and senior managers, and clarify shareholders rights. Among its provisions, it stipulated disclosure and voting standards for related-party transactions, specified duties that controlling shareholder owe to the company and other shareholders, required the disclosure of controlling shareholders' interests (including the ultimate controller), and emphasized the independent operation of the company from its controlling shareholders, including the introduction of a cumulative voting system

92 Z. Chen, "Capital Markets and Legal Development: The China Case," *China Economic Review* 14 (2003) 451, 464.

93 This is not to say that customary ideas and elements that are traditionally packaged within the term "corporate governance" were not considered earlier. To the contrary, some ideas, even some that are commonly tagged as "Anglo-American" (e.g., shareholder centrism and fiduciary duties) were contemplated before the establishment of the 1993 Company Law and long before their formal adoption in the 2005 Company Law. The penetration of these ideas, like many market developments in China, also happened on an experimental basis and lacked a primary law authority. See N. C. Howson, "The Doctrine That Dared Not Speak Its Name: Anglo-American Fiduciary Duties in China's 2005 Company Law and Case Law Intimations of Prior Convergence." In H. Kanda et al. (eds.), *Transforming Corporate Governance in East Asia* (Routledge, 2008) 193; N. C. Howson, "Corporate Law in the Shanghai People's Courts, 1992–2008: Judicial Autonomy in a Contemporary Authoritarian State," *East Asia Law Review* 5 (2010) 303 (2010).

94 See Part II, Chapter 4. A few examples include the CSRC (founded 1998), SASAC (founded 2003), China's Banking Regulatory Commission (CBRC, founded 2003), and the China National Development and Reform Commission (NDRC, founded 2003).

for the election of directors and an independent directors scheme.[95] Still, like many other corporate governance codes around the world, the Code presented guiding principles that were mostly broad and vague with no accountability measures for violators. It described best practices from which firms were left to choose.[96]

The highest state organs – the NPC and the State Council – also issued several proclamations and legal amendments that clearly reflects the formal acceptance of the economic functions of law:[97]

> The quality of listed companies must be upgraded. The quality of listed companies is the source of value for securities market investment…We should improve the structure of corporate governance of listed companies, and by following the requirements of the modern corporate system, form a check and balance mechanism among the power organ, the decision-making organ, the supervisory organ and corporate managers… We should regulate the acts of controlling shareholders and prosecute those committing acts to damage the interests of listed companies or those of small and medium-sized shareholders…

Accordingly, in 2005, the 1993 People's Republic of China (PRC) Company Law and the 1998 Securities Law were revised wholesale,[98] evidencing a shareholder empowering approach through more robust investors' governance rights. Formally, the revised statutes created various mechanisms for the protection of shareholders' rights and interests and strengthened other protections. These included enacting

95 Code of Corporate Governance for Listed Companies [上市公司治理准则], promulgated by the China Sec. Reg. Comm'n and the State Economic and Trade Comm'n, Jan. 7, 2001, rev'd Sep. 30, 2018.

96 For example, the first chapter of the code outlines shareholders' rights with neither explanations of these rights, nor of what would be a fair treatment of these rights and how a violation would be handled. Another example is the Code provision for independent directors in listed companies without granting them any designated voting powers. Ibid., arts. 49, 52.

97 Some Opinions of the State Council on Promoting the Reform, Opening and Steady Growth of Capital Markets [关于推进资本市场改革开放和稳定发展的若干意见], promulgated by the St. Council, Jan. 31, 2004. See also State Council Notice on Good Implementation of the Revised Corporate and Securities Law [关于做好贯彻实施修订后的公司法和证券法有关工作的通知], promulgated by the St. Council, Dec. 23, 2005. The Opinion emphasizes to various levels of the government the need to implement the revised Company and Securities laws, which established mechanisms for the protections of corporate constituents, in order to promote capital market development. Moreover, Chapter IV of China's 2008 White Paper on promotion of the "rule of law" deals specifically with "Legal Systems Regulating the Order of Market Economy," which points to the need for "safeguarding the lawful rights and interests of corporate investors and stakeholders." China's Efforts and Achievements in Promoting the Rule of Law[中国的法治建设], White Paper, promulgated by the Information Office of the St. Council, Feb. 28, 2008.

98 The prior 1993 Company Law was revised at the 18th meeting of the 10th National People's Congress of the People's Republic of China on October 27, 2005 and was last amended in 2018. PRC Company Law [中华人民共和国公司法], promulgated by the Standing Comm. Nat'l People's Cong., Dec. 29, 1993, rev'd Oct. 27, 2005, last amended Oct. 26, 2018, effective Oct. 26, 2018. [2005 Company Law for the 2005 version, and The Company Law when referring to the current version].
Securities Law of the People's Republic of China [中华人民共和国证券法], promulgated by the Standing Comm. of the 9th Nat'l People's Cong., Dec. 29, 1998, rev'd Oct. 27, 2005, last amended Dec. 28, 2019. [2005 Securities Law for the 2005 version, and 2020 Securities Law for the current version].

explicit fiduciary duties of corporate directors, supervisory board members, and officers; requiring nomination of independent directors in listed companies; enabling a derivative lawsuit for shareholders; and providing certain buy-back guarantees for shareholders.[99] Perhaps most striking, the 2005 Company Law also adopted something akin to fiduciary duties for controlling shareholders toward the company and other shareholders.[100] At the same time, the PRC Criminal Law was revised as well, and together the laws introduced much-needed formal recourse for injured shareholders as well as criminal liability based on securities law claims.[101] This framework provided a tailwind for the CSRC to take a stronger approach to investor protection. In the following years, the commission had issued a series of investor-supporting administrative regulations.[102]

These developments might be mistaken for convergence with Western corporate capitalism. If the governance of Chinese firms and the functions of the capital market indeed converged with corporate capitalism prescriptions for investor protections and capital market growth, then China's capital market growth and the domestic and rising global success of its firms during the same period could be explained on the basis of such belated legal convergence.

This conclusion, however, is based on merely facially similar investor-protecting laws and institutions and would be a mistake. The following examination of China's adoption of "shareholder primacy" – one of the flagships of corporate capitalism – will illustrate how seemingly convergent norms are in fact completely divergent, and how the economic function of seemingly convergent legal instruments is weak at best and perhaps completely absent.

1 *Shareholder Empowering Regulatory Action*

The 2005 Company Law defines the shareholders' assembly as the highest organ of authority in the company and grants it with an extensive list of powers.[103] It

[99] 2005 Company Law, arts. 22, 122, 142, 147–150, 151, 152.

[100] Ibid., arts. 20, 21.

[101] 6th Amendments to the Criminal Law of the People's Republic of China [中华人民共和国刑法修正案(六)], promulgated by the Standing Comm. Nat'l People's Cong., June 29, 2006, arts. 161–163, 169, 182: which set criminal liability in cases of (respectively) false reporting, and non-disclosure that leads to "serious damages to the interests of shareholders or any other person"; concealing or disposing of company property "so that serious damages are caused to the interests of the creditors or any other persons"; and the use of corporate position for personal gain, including accepting bribes and commissions in various forms (separate standard and procedure for criminal liability was set for public servants in state-owned corporations); violation of fiduciary duties by directors, supervisors, or senior managers of a listed company, or by a controlling shareholder or actual controller (as well as when the controller instigated other corporate officers to such violation) that have caused "serious loss to the interests of the company"; and manipulation of the securities or futures market.

[102] Some of which are elaborated below. For a fuller account, see Howson, "*Quack Corporate Governance*," note 10, at 698, 701–707.

[103] 2005 Company Law, arts. 37, 98, 99. This appeared even in the 1993 Company Law, art. 37 for LLCs and article 102 for CLSs.

goes beyond the mere protection of basic shareholder rights by enabling direct shareholders' governance participation through the shareholders meeting, with the following powers[104]: (1) to determine the company's operating guidelines and investment plans; (2) to elect and replace directors and supervisors (except for the representatives of the employees) and to decide their remuneration; (3) to approve reports of the board of directors; (4) to approve reports of the supervisory board; (5) to approve annual financial budget plans and accounts; (6) to approve plans for profit distribution and loss recovery; (7) to decide on changes to the registered capital; (8) to approve the issuance of corporate bonds; (9) to adopt resolutions on a corporate merger, division, change in the company's form, dissolution, or liquidation; (10) to amend the bylaws; and (11) to exercise other powers provided for in the bylaws. For certain fundamental transactions, a supermajority shareholder approval is required.[105]

A review of the remaining articles of the law further shows that the powers conferred on the shareholders' assembly even go much beyond these enumerated authorities. A resolution by the shareholders' general meeting is also required in other situations that are mentioned throughout the law. A shareholders' approval is required, for example, to execute the limited circumstances in which the company can purchase its own shares.[106] Their approval is required for the company to guarantee the debt of a shareholder or actual controller. Other "important matters" might also require a decision by the shareholders (e.g., "to transfer or accept any significant assets").[107] Moreover, even a decision on the issuance of new shares is not reserved to the board and can be decided by the general meeting.[108]

[104] 2005 Company Law, arts. 37(7)–(10). These rules apply to listed companies as well. Ibid., arts. 98–99. The articles also enable written consent in lieu of convening an actual shareholders' meeting, reducing the costs of shareholders' participation. See also arts. 104, 124, & 150.

[105] The general rule for a shareholder resolution is majority vote, 2005 Company Law, art. 103. Yet, some business decisions require approval by two-thirds of the voting rights of the shareholders present: bylaw amendments, changes in the registered capital of the company, resolutions concerning merger, split-up, dissolution, or change of the company form; as well as a decision to purchase or sell any important asset or to provide guarantees that exceed 30 percent of the company's total assets within a year. Ibid arts. 103, 121. Art. 16 is the only article in the law that addresses directly the concern about abusive related-party transactions, requires the approval of the majority of *disinterested shareholders* for guarantees given by the company to its controlling shareholder. 2005 Company Law, art. 16.

[106] Note the circumstances requiring the shareholders' assembly approval were narrowed down in the recent amendment by shifting approval in some of the circumstances to the board. Compare the 2005 Company Law before and after its 2018 amendment. 2005 Company Law, art. 142.

[107] 2005 Company Law, see art. 104; see also art. 124 (requiring a shareholders' meeting in situations where the number of disinterested board members are insufficient). Interestingly, the law even states the possible involvement of the shareholders' meeting in the hiring and dismissal of the company's accounting firm. 2005 Company Law. art. 169. The shareholders' meeting has the ability to demand the presence of a director, supervisor, and senior manager at its meeting, and such office holders have a duty to answer shareholders' inquiries presented there. 2005 Company Law, art. 150.

[108] 2005 Company Law, art. 133.

Individual shareholders are given an expansive right to information and document inspection,[109] as well as individual standing rights to approach the People's courts on procedural or substantive grounds.[110] Additionally, the 2005 PRC Company Law allows a group of shareholders with 10 percent or more equity interest in the firm to request a special shareholders' meeting and enables shareholders holding at least 3 percent of the firm's equity to submit shareholder proposals to the board.[111]

It clearly appears as though China's policymakers had opted for an empowering, shareholder-oriented corporate governance. The prescribed rights reflect an invitation for hands-on engagement in corporate decision-making that seems far beyond the powers conferred on shareholders in other systems, even those in US and UK corporate laws – the origins and foothold of shareholder-primacy notions.[112] Judged solely based on the provisions above, contemporary China offers one of the most robust shareholder-empowering corporate statutes in the world.

In practice, however, this facially shareholder-empowering regulatory framework does little to empower *public* shareholders (i.e., external investors) or restrict the behavior of corporate control parties against them. The formal participation rights granted under the Company Law apply generally to the "shareholder class" and do not operate to improve the position of *non-controlling* (thus *real* public or minority) public shareholders. While this arrangement may have worked in widely held markets, in a concentrated market, true commitment to outside investors should have carried mandatory provisions,[113] specifically tailored to minority public shareholders.[114] The shareholder-empowering approach taken in China serves in actuality only

[109] 2005 Company Law, art. 97.

[110] On procedural violation grounds, see 2005 Company Law, art. 22. For alleged violation of a shareholder's right for information, see art. 33. For a form of appraisal-related to specific circumstances in which the company buys back the shareholder's shares, see art. 74. For derivative suits, see art. 151. For individual lawsuits against directors or managers, see art. 152. See also art. 183 (requesting a dissolution in court).

[111] 2005 Company Law, arts. 101, 102.

[112] For example, in the United States, under the Model Business Corporation Act and Delaware General Corporation Law (DGCL), all corporate powers are vested with the board of directors, and the corporation is managed under their broad discretion, which has been expanded by the courts. According to the DGCL and the corporate laws of many other states, directors are nominated by the existing board and shareholders only have the right to vote on such nominees at the annual meeting. Generally, for shareholders to propose their own nominees, they need to initiate an expensive proxy contest. In addition, in staggered board firms, the ability of shareholders to remove directors without cause is limited. There are only a handful of matters that require shareholders' approval: amendments to the corporate charter (as opposed to bylaws, which can be amended by the board of directors), and mergers, consolidation, or a sale of all or substantially all assets. Shareholders may convene a special shareholders' meeting only if the company's bylaw permits them to do so, and a shareholder proposal is generally nonbinding. See Delaware General Corporation Law, Del. Code tit. 8 § 101–398. See generally Model Bus. Corp. Act (American Bar Association, 2002).

[113] Z. Goshen, "The Efficiency of Controlling Corporate Self-Dealing: Theory Meets Reality," *California Law Review* 91 (2003) 393.

[114] For examples of mandatory approaches in comparative concentrated markets, see notes 269–270 (discussing audit and compensation committees in Israel). On mandatory noncontrolling shareholders

to further the Party-state as the controlling shareholder in corporatized SOEs, the prevalent type of listed firms when such approach was embraced. The controlling shareholder will continue to govern the firm absolutely in a myriad of ways. For example, absent mandatory cumulative voting on board elections, the controlling shareholder will be the one to nominate and elect the company's directors, who in turn have singular power to appoint top management. The controlling shareholder's appointed board members will set the agenda for shareholder meetings and thereby be able to hinder any shareholder proposals from a 3-percent shareholder technically authorized under the Company Law. Similarly, since voting is not required and the law does not call for recusal of a controlling shareholder(s) vote, the controlling shareholder alone will usually satisfy any mandated supermajority requirement for the approval of certain transactions.[115] This is especially likely since no quorum is required to convene a shareholders meeting, and only the votes of those attending the meeting are counted.

In addition, the admittedly more "enabling" approach taken in the revision of the Company Law[116] enables the parties to contract around the default rules. This means that the 2005 amendment enables the controlling shareholder to contract into an even more robust control. Given the almost nonexistent bargaining power of minority shareholders, which is intensified by the pyramidal holding structure prevalent for many PRC issuers, any "opt-in" governance arrangement that is favorable to minority shareholders will not be adopted. Thus, as observed in a different context, "an interventionist state, concentrated ownership, and shareholder-friendly law may be mutually reinforcing, especially when the state holds large blocks of stock in its own right."[117]

Furthermore, lest anyone think that whatever minority shareholder governance rights are on offer can or will be enforced (whether mandatory or contracted-into), other structural impediments – grounded in China's political economy and reviewed below – cast a large shadow of doubt as to the ability of public shareholders to secure these rights.[118]

board representation in Italy, see note 236. On compelling institutional shareholders' vote on certain matters in Israel, see note 220.

For general data on countries that adopted minority veto rights, see OECD, *Related Party Transactions and Minority Shareholder Rights* (OECD Publishing, 2012). More generally on the use of disinterested shareholders' consent as a regulatory device in a dispersed market (Australia), see J. Hill, "Visions and Revisions of the Shareholder," *American Journal of Comparative Law* 48 (2009) 39, at 69–71.

115 For a list of matters that require supermajority consent, see note 105. A unique exception where the minority is *de facto* granted a negative veto is in article 16 of the 2005 Company Law, which requires the approval of a majority of *disinterested* shareholders for decisions to provide a guarantee to a shareholder of the company or to its actual controller. See 2005 Company Law, art. 16.

116 On the shift toward an enabling system in the 2005 Company Law amendment and the contrast with mandatory CSRC orientation, see Howson, "*Quack Corporate Governance*," note 10, at 698, 701–707.

117 L. Enriques et al., "The Basic Governance Structure: The Interests of Shareholders as a Class." In R.H. Kraakman et al. (eds.), *The Anatomy of Corporate Law: A Comparative and Functional Approach*, 2nd ed. (Oxford University Press, 2009) 55, at 85 (noting this with respect to France).

118 For a discussion on these institutional and structural predicaments, see Chapter 7, "'Chinese-Style' State Capitalism and Its Consequences for Public Shareholders".

Finally, at a conceptual level, there is also divergence in the notions of shareholder primacy itself. In the Chinese context, shareholder primacy stands for completely different ideas than those expressed under corporate capitalism. With the 1993 Company Law, when state-owned firms populated the market, the emphasis was on the authority of the shareholders' assembly as a collective, representing the interests of the public, rather than on the shareholders' interests as individuals. Some elements in the 2005 Company Law still resonate with this approach. In particular, the preamble and Article 5 state the company's obligation to social morality, mandate social responsibility, and point to the accountability of the company to the general public.[119] These articles reflect a much-criticized view of the company law as still speaking largely to state-owned firms.[120] Some commentators even suggested that China's shareholder primacy approach resembles its hierarchical political governance, in which the NPC is the source of authority for all lower governance levels.[121] Such a view overlooks the ultimate authority of the Party (in both the corporate and the governmental contexts), yet it certainly reflects the divergence from corporate capitalism notions. The consequences go beyond just theory. Such divergence carries real implications for decision-making and accountability. For instance, to whom are fiduciary duties owed?[122]

Relatedly, the widely accepted association of shareholder primacy with the notion of shareholder value (maximization of market share price) under corporate capitalism is not the norm in China. In the Chinese context, shareholder primacy, through the shareholders' assembly, instead reflects the primacy of the controlling shareholder's goals and interests, whatever they are in a given situation. This is another reminder that the Company law was enacted with SOEs in mind, where the controlling state shareholder, as the embodiment of the Chinese Party-state in firms, is seen to represent the *people*.

Thus, despite the formal recognition of shareholders' rights and the apparent borrowing of conventional corporate governance mechanisms, most of these institutions fail to perform their traditional economic functions. Investor protections remain weak in practice, and corporate governance has been deployed in ways that

119 2005 Company Law, art. 5 (When conducting business operations, a company shall comply with the laws and administrative regulations, social morality, and business morality. It shall act in good faith, accept the supervision of the government and general public, and bear social responsibilities.).

120 See generally Clarke, *Blowback*, note 35.

121 J. Liu, "Experience of Internationalization of Chinese Corporate Law and Corporate Governance: How to Make the Hybrid of Civil Law and Common Law Work?," *European Business Law Review* 26(1) (2015) 107, at 114 (interpreting the modern corporate law to mean that "the power of the corporations shall be from the shareholders, for the shareholders and by the shareholders.").

122 There are multiple options implied by the 2005 Company Law, art. 149 along with arts. 148, 150, and 151 with the derivative suit therein, posit the option of fiduciary duties owed to the company. Art. 151 suggests accountability to the shareholders' assembly. Art. 152, however, seems to be focused on the infringement of shareholders' interests (as individuals), raising a private right of action against directors and senior managers. Finally, the preamble and article 5 add the duties of the company, and by extension its representatives, to the general public. See 2005 Company Law, arts. 5, 148–152.

run counter to market efficiency. Notably, implementation is not hindered due to the lack of appropriate local adaptations as may have been the case for other transplants around the world.[123] Indeed, a number of commentators praise China's corporate governance framework as the product of a well-thought out, decades-long, intellectual sifting and cherry-picking process.[124] The mechanisms borrowed were not blindly transplanted but instead were carefully selected and tailored to the preexisting political infrastructure.

In short, traditional corporate governance institutions in China are weak by design. China's own political economy trumped the new laws and corporate governance mechanisms, just as it had created and then trumped the preceding provisional local arrangements. This time around, the source within China's political economy that is responsible for this consciously accepted weakness can be found in the regime's state capitalism attributes. China's state capitalism ascended during this transitional stage and has trapped a growing crowd of public shareholders in what I refer to as "structured predicament." As a result, instead of monitoring insiders and protecting investors, the market framework that evolved gave corporate control parties a license to expropriate with impunity. This, obviously, runs counter to the economic functions of any formally adopted and seemingly convergent legal instruments, as explained next.

"CHINESE-STYLE" STATE CAPITALISM AND ITS CONSEQUENCES FOR PUBLIC SHAREHOLDERS

1 *The State as an Ultimate Controller*

As seen earlier, the Party-state advanced legal instruments – the corporate form and the public firm – to reorganize the market and create corporatized nonprivatized

123 K. Pistor, "Patterns of Legal Change: Shareholder and Creditor Rights in Transition Economies," *European Business Organization Law Review* 1(1) (2000) 59; K. Pistor et al., "Law and Finance in Transition Economies," *Economics of Transition* 8 (2000) 325.

124 The adaptation to local conditions is reflected not only in the selection of various provisions from different legal systems but also through some uniquely Chinese characteristics adopted in the 1993 Company Law and maintained throughout its amendments. Examples include the "social-economic order" in the preamble and article 1 in both the 1993 and 2005 laws, the institution of legal representation, the dual board structure, and more. See R. C. Art & M. Gu, "China Incorporated: The First Corporation Law of the People's Republic of China," *Yale Journal of International Law* 20 (1995) 273, at 275 (on the idiosyncratic legal representative concept). Some Chinese commentators see this cherry picking from different systems as a unique Chinese model: S. Zhao, "The China Model: Can It Replace the Western Model of Modernization?," *Journal of Contemporary China* 19 (2010) 419, at 424 ("What Makes the Chinese Model Unique Is That the Communist Regime Has Safeguarded Its Own Policy Space as to When, Where and How to Adopt Western Ideas."). And others even track this model back to the Qing dynastic 1904 corporate law. Liu, *Experience of Internationalization*, note 121, at 112.

But see L. Fang, China's Corporatization Experiment, *Duke Journal of Comparative & International Law* 5 (1995) 149, at 260 (critiquing the 1993 Company Law for lack of its "contextualization to the lay of the land").

legal entities that are embedded within group structures that were meant to amplify the power of central state control while improving market productivity and efficiency. The use of the public firm had both an economic function to funnel capital into SOEs and improve their operations, and a political function, to push back against rising local autonomy (by having the central state fix the rules for enterprise organization and engineer how the market will be structured).

The result was the creation of pyramid holding groups, within which many of China's listed SOEs currently operate and on top of which Party-state organs preside as dominant, often-controlling, shareholders that operate through powerful human agents as corporate insiders – one of the main attributes of China's state capitalism.

The organizational structure that came with state capitalism presented insurmountable monitoring challenges and abundant opportunities for the abuse of public shareholders and affected both their governance and economic rights. Under the prevalent group structures and financial dependencies that were formed, firms could be easily harnessed in pursuit of national and political goals, as well as for the personal interests of their controlling parties (corporate insiders in SOEs and private firms and agents assigned to supervise on behalf of the state *quo* controlling shareholders in SOEs). The situation is also self-perpetuating, as China's state capitalism entrenched controlling parties and made future reforms particularly challenging.

Excess Opportunities for Self-Dealing by Agents

By turning in the early 1990s to the modern corporate form with its separation between ownership and control, China's policymakers sought to cure mushrooming self-dealing and asset stripping in SOEs, most of which by that time were locally run enterprises. As commentators note, however, this was an ill-fitting importation of a problem rather than a solution[125]: "[Yet] calls for government-owned enterprises to be independent of government 'interference' are calls for nothing short of utter non-accountability for management."[126] The separation of ownership and control during corporatization imported the paradigm vertical agency problem into a system with an already complex range of idiosyncratic institutional monitoring challenges.

Corporate theory suggests that when ownership is concentrated, the main beneficiary of any value increase in the firm is the controlling shareholder. With abundant inside information, controlling shareholders can also efficiently preempt market reactions by identifying managerial slack early and simply replacing badly performing managers. The controlling shareholder is therefore the corporate constituent that is most incentivized and best situated to monitor corporate insiders.

Under state corporate control, however, no ultimate *real* principal exists at the top of the state's holdings. This means that there is no principal who would personally benefit from monitoring and thus no one with the incentive to monitor the behavior

[125] T. Ruskola, *Legal Orientalism* (Harvard University Press, 2013), at 190, note 43.

[126] Clarke, *Corporate Governance in China*, note 23, at 498–499.

of corporate managers. This structural predicament became known as the "absentee principal" or the "absent owner" (*suoyouzhe quewei*).[127] This situation creates relative apathy toward corporate misconduct on the part of government officials, the representatives of the controlling-state shareholder. Consequently, firms in China became controlled by unmonitored powerful insiders (*neibu ren kongzhi*).[128] Vast self-dealing and looting of state assets took place not only by the insiders themselves but also by the agents assigned by the state to supervise them.[129] The modern corporate form, therefore, became conducive to corruption as well.

The absence of a real ultimate principal with enough incentives to monitor on behalf of the state was presented as one of the primary reasons that led to the establishment of SASAC in 2003.[130] SASAC was designed to replace various state-asset management enterprises with a unified national, ministry-level agency.[131] It was assigned to function on behalf of the State Council's role as a controlling corporate shareholder by exercising shareholder governance rights, its formal capacity established in law only almost six years later.[132] SASAC's shareholder governance rights are at least in principle more extensive than those granted to other shareholders by the Company Law.

The rights and interests of the state in its capacity as an investor are regulated outside the Company Law, in the SOE Assets Law. The law gives the state *quo* investor (SASAC, its local branches, and other bodies performing the state's capital contributor capacity) the power to *propose* candidates for directors and supervisors' positions, to the shareholders' meeting, in any "state invested enterprise" as well as to *propose* their removal.[133] These "boosted" governance rights are afforded to the state whether it has a controlling or noncontrolling stake in the enterprise. By

[127] Ibid., at 499.

[128] H. Huang & J. Chen, "The Rise of Hostile Takeovers and Defensive Measures in China: Comparative and Empirical Perspectives," *European Business Organization Law Review* 20(2) (2019) 363.

[129] Clarke, *The Independent Director*, note 41, at 148 ("a 2002 study of corporate governance by the CSRC and the SETC revealed, on the basis of self-reporting alone, that forty percent of listed companies engaged in related-party transactions with their top ten shareholders."). See also D. C. Clarke & N. C. Howson, "Pathway to Minority Shareholder Protection: Derivative Actions in the People's Republic of China." In D. W. Puchniak et al. (eds.), *The Derivative Action in Asia: A Comparative and Functional Approach* (Cambridge University Press, 2012), 243, at 248 and 254–257 ("'Tunneling' by individual insiders and controlling shareholders, both state and nonstate, by means of related-party transactions is notorious; in 2002 tunneling by controlling shareholders was estimated at 96.7 billion yuan, equivalent to the total amount of money raised in stock markets in the same year.").

[130] See *What We Do*, SASAC, https://archive.ph/pm56j.

[131] Several Asset Management Companies preceded the establishment of SASAC. The Asset Management Companies (AMC) was run by an Asset Management Agency under the supervision of the Ministry of Finance. They were assigned the task of recovering nonperforming loans owed to China's four state banks.

[132] Law of the People's Republic of China on the State-Owned Assets of Enterprises [中华人民共和国企业国有资产法], promulgated by the Standing Comm. Nat'l People's Cong., Oct. 28, 2008, effective May 1, 2009 [SOE Assets Law], arts. 1, 3.

[133] SOE Assets Law, arts. 22(3) & 23.

contrast, according to the Company law, only shareholders with 10 percent or more voting rights can request the company to convene a special shareholders' meeting in which shareholders holding 3 percent or more (separately or aggregately) can submit written proposals including on personnel-related issues and it is in discretion of the board chairperson whether or not to include such proposals in the special shareholders meeting.[134]

The state investor has the authority to establish an assessment system for managerial performance in state-invested enterprises and to determine standards for remuneration, authorities that otherwise lie with the board.[135] With respect to managers appointed by the state, the state shall be the one to determine remuneration standards, conduct their assessment, and decide on rewards and punishments according to such assessment results.[136]

In addition to these rights on personnel-related matters, the state *quo* investor has the power to decide on the transfer of state-owned assets (i.e., the rights and interests of the state) in any state-invested enterprise. This can be interpreted to give the state a de-facto veto right in certain transactions that otherwise would have been at the purview of the board, such as a merger of a subsidiary.[137]

The above provisions apply to any state invested enterprise. In "important" companies where the state holds a controlling stake, certain matters – such as mergers, split-up, dissolution, bankruptcy petition, any restructuring that will result in of the loss of state control "or any other meaningful matter…as prescribed by law and regulations" – should be first approved by the corresponding level of the people's government before the state representative casts a vote in the company's shareholders meeting.[138]

Beyond conventional company law fiduciary obligations that are owed to the company as a whole, the SOE Assets Law includes a form of fiduciary duty of directors, supervisors, and senior managers not only to the invested enterprise but also specifically to the interests of the state investor (regardless of its holding ratio),[139] as well as fiduciary responsibility of the invested enterprise itself to the state investor.[140] The law also determines liability for actions that caused losses of state-owned assets, specifically.[141]

Finally, in their account of SASAC's governance rights, Lin and Milhaupt note that the board of directors, the standard corporate governing body, seems

134 2005 Company Law, arts. 37(2), 39, 101, 102.

135 Compare SOE Assets Law, art. 27 with 2005 Company law, art. 46(9).

136 SOE Assets Law, ibid., ibid.

137 SOE Assets Law, Sec. 5 (Transfer of State-Owned Assets) (particularly arts. 51, 53). L-W. Lin & Milhaupt, *National Champions*, note 54, at 743, notes 135 & 136 (noting relevant court cases that invalidated contracts for the transfer of shares without prior SASAC approval).

138 SOE Assets Law, arts. 31–35, 39(3), 40, 53.

139 SOE Assets Law, art. 17.

140 SOE Assets Law, art. 26.

141 SOE Assets Law, art. 71.

entirely missing in some of the firms controlled by SASAC,[142] an absence that makes the state role in these firms even more determinative. This is of course in addition to SASAC's regulatory capacities. As it was formally granted vast authority to restructure, regulate, and supervise the companies under its control. These combined powers gave the agency strong influence on the reorganization of entire industries.

Still, it is important to note that notwithstanding the "boosted" rights of SASAC as a shareholder, the state's capacity as an investor is not without reins. Its shareholding capacity is exercised formally through the shareholders' assembly following defined corporate procedures and is therefore subject to potential scrutiny and corporate governance limitations. The SOE Assets Law makes clear that the state as an investor shall follow the Company law procedures for shareholder deliberation and voting even concerning major corporate decisions. The law also asserts to guarantee operating autonomy and limits intervention in day-to-day decision-making.[143]

Perhaps more importantly, despite its extensive formal governance rights SASAC faces strong resistance from various interested parties that de facto limits its ability to effectively monitor corporate insiders. SASAC shares its administrative powers with other national-level ministries with a say in relevant industries. It can also face strong resistance from the firms it supervises and facially controls, some of which are also ministry-level, economically powerful industry behemoths. Most importantly, SASAC exercises its governance powers, and particularly its control rights in management, in the shadow of an overall Party control.[144] This shadow control by the CCP is achieved through various means, including: (1) the closely followed recommendations of the CCP's Organization Department on the appointments of senior corporate managers in leading firms; (2) the training of most senior SOE managers through the Party school and training system; and (3) the Party personnel evaluation system. More recently, this control has been formalized and institutionalized into the governance of corporatized SOEs and firms more generally,[145] a change that is further undermining the corporate capacity and administrative authority formally reserved to SASAC.

Besides, even after the reorganization under SASAC, the Party-state regularly promotes multiple, often conflicting goals that its agents on the ground must balance. Despite the common perception that the Chinese Party-state operates as

[142] L-W. Lin & Milhaupt, *National Champions*, note 54, at 738, note 121 (noting that by the end of 2012, only 51 of the core parent companies of the 117 national business groups had established a board of directors).

[143] SOE Assets Law, arts. 13, 16, 30, 33, 35, 40, 46. But see matters for which prior government approval is needed in state-controlled companies, note 138 and related text.

[144] L-W. Lin & Milhaupt, *National Champions*, note 54, at 726–738 (referring to this relationship as "a highly institutionalized sharing arrangement between the Party and SASAC.").

[145] Discussed extensively in Chapter 8.

a unitary political organization, not only are there various interest groups at different levels of the state but also the interests of the Party itself might differ from those of state agencies and officials (at least when looking beyond senior levels of government positions in which the overlap of Party and state leadership roles is less common).

To conclude, despite SASAC's formal role in the organizational chain, it seems that its corporate capacity is an empty box, to be filled by whichever interested party (a ministry, Party-state organ, or individuals) is most invested in the situation and has the most political-economic power in each case. Assigning a central state agency as a controlling shareholder did not solve, and perhaps cannot solve, the problems that arise from the lack of an ultimate real principal. It only mirrors the institutional challenges that are already present within China's political economy.

In the crossroads of these competing forces are the corporate insiders and Party-state individuals who stand to gain from the disarray of conflicting institutional interests. Indeed, no matter how many layers are added to the institutional arrangement, as Donald Clarke notes, since the state (and the Party) is an abstract collective, it must necessarily operate through human agents.[146] State corporate control in China, therefore, features the same type of self-dealing concerns that the paradigm agency analysis envisages, yet it amplifies the problem by reproducing the links (agents) in the chain that can exploit the situation while weakening those with direct incentives to limit it. This is an exacerbated form of the well-known corporate monitoring predicament – "who monitors the monitors?,"[147] which is extended in China to multiple layers of agents inside and outside the firm.

Heightened Opportunities for Abuse by Controllers

As if these features of state-corporate control in China are not challenging enough, corporatized SOEs face further difficulties due to misaligned interests between their various shareholders. This includes conflicts within the horizontal (i.e. professional ministries and bureaus) and vertical (i.e., hierarchical) lines of the state itself, as well as conflicts between the state as the controlling shareholder and the "class" of public shareholders. To the extent that the state is able to incentivize its agents – both the officials assigned to monitor corporate insiders, and the professional managers appointed to operate corporatized SOEs – to pursue the state's goals rather than their own selfish interests, the benefits to the firm and its other shareholders might still be marginalized. Whichever goal ends up being prioritized, it will not necessarily align with the most efficient and productive business conduct.

146 Clarke, *Corporate Governance in China*, note 23, at 497–500. Clarke expressed this with respect to older forms of state asset management organization and before the reorganization under SASAC, but the substantive claim still stands.

147 R. J. Gilson, "A Structural Approach to Corporations: The Case against Defensive Tactics in Tender Offers," *Stanford Law Review* 33(5) (1981) 819, at 835–836 (discussing this question as part of the costs of the separation between ownership and control).

Thus, even under an assumption of benevolent, well-coordinated, state asset management that is able to monitor insiders effectively, the state as a controlling shareholder may direct the firm in pursuit of objectives that simply run counter to the interest of the firm as a profit-maximizing business. Examples of this in China include the use of state-controlled firms to advance geopolitical goals without sound expectations for economic return[148]; harnessing control over management to accelerate market reforms,[149] or to influence or even control market volatility;[150] and using state-controlled firms to advance broad social goals or to carry ad hoc social tasks, as seen recently when firms were mobilized to shift production lines to combat the spread of COVID-19.[151]

This phenomenon is not unique to the Chinese state's corporate control. There are many examples of governments using their corporate role to advance goals that a profit-oriented shareholder would probably avoid.[152] The reasons for this are not always clear since governments could presumably utilize other tools to reach the same results. And still, there are reported cases in which governments, in their shareholding

148 Examples include certain transactions as part of the One Belt One Road Initiative. Many of these projects are criticized for being economically senseless but nevertheless pass corporate governance approvals (even in private firms). See J. March, "The Rise and Fall of a Belt and Road Billionaire," CNN (Dec. 2018), https://perma.cc/U96S-EP9J; W. Wu, "How the Communist Party Controls China's State-Owned Industrial Titans," South China Morning Post (June 17, 2017), https://perma.cc/3L4P-MYPF.

149 M. Firth et al., "Friend or Foe? The Role of State and Mutual Fund Ownership in the Split Share Structure Reform in China," *Journal of Financial & Quantitative Analysis* 45 (2010) 685, at 692, 699–704 (managers of listed SOEs easily passed generous compensations to investors as part of a structural reform in the capital market, even when such decisions were against the economic interest of the firm, due to pressures to implement the reform quickly).

150 During the 2015–2016 market downturn, buy-sale orders of state-controlled insurance firms and financial institutions were directed by the Party-state to control market volatility. G. Wildau, "China's 'National Team' Owns 6 Percent of Stock Market," Financial Times (Nov. 25, 2015, https://perma.cc/2A9X-G6NA. Ad hoc trade suspensions to control supply and demand and stabilize the market where traders are called to heed "political consciousness" amidst important political events were reported as well. See H. Shen & S. Y. Xie, "That Calm Chinese Stock Market? It's Engineered by the State," *Wall Street Journal* (May 31, 2018), https://perma.cc/5CFL-LNU3.

151 Amidst COVID-19, companies were recruited to national mask-making effort regardless of their ordinary business lines. See, for example, the recruiting of the subsidiaries of Sinopec, an oil and gas giant. M. Borak, "Chinese Factory Live Streams Face Mask Material Production amid Coronavirus Shortages," *South China Morning Post* (Mar. 9, 2020), https://perma.cc/XB4Z-N7CH.
There are numerous additional instances whereby state-controlled firms were called upon to assist the government in a broad array of social tasks, from the Beijing Olympic Games and the Shanghai World Expo, to providing assistance following natural disasters. Wang, *The Political Logic of Corporate Governance*, note 11, at 663 ("According to a *Xinhua* report, twenty four hours after the Qinghai Yushu earthquake hit on April 14, 2010, China's big SOEs, including the state-owned airlines and airports, energy companies, telecoms, transportation firms, medical companies, and agricultural trading companies, were called upon by the CCP Central Committee and the State Council [*Dangzhongyang, Guowuyuan*] to participate in the rescue efforts by providing services and materials.").

152 See generally I. Bremmer, *The End of the Free Market: Who Wins the War between States and Corporations?* (Penguin Group, 2010); A. Musacchio & S. G. Lazzarini, *Reinventing State Capitalism: Leviathan in Business, Brazil and Beyond* (Harvard University Press,2014); C. Milhaupt

capacity, have harnessed their corporate control to maintain high employment levels in certain firms or industries.[153] In some cases, governments have directed corporate decision-making to uphold strategic control of specific industries (e.g., via strategic planning of M&A),[154] or fixed-sale prices through their corporate influence in order to curtail inflation,[155] or to ensure sufficient domestic availability of essential products.[156]

More broadly, it is well established that controlling shareholders can promote their interests more easily by enlarging their voting control relative to their cash flow rights.[157] This can be done through deploying legal structures, such as pyramidal ownership, dual-class shares, cross-shareholdings within business groups, voting agreements, and other business arrangements.[158] The result (and often the aim) of these ownership structures is the dissociation of public investors from governance, which allows the controller to extract private benefits of control more freely.[159]

& M. Pargendler, "Governance Challenges of Listed State-Owned Enterprises around the World: National Experiences and a Framework for Reform," *Cornell International Law Journal* 50 (2017) 473; C. Milhaupt & M. Pargendler, "RPTs in SOEs: Tunneling, Propping, and Policy Channeling." In L. Enriques & T. Tröger (eds.), *The Law and Finance of Related Party Transactions* (Cambridge University Press, 2019) (suggesting a distinction between tunneling, propping, and policy channeling). Following Milhaupt and Pargendler's analysis, most of the examples cited here would be considered policy channeling.

153 As was the case in Israel, where the state intended to execute its golden share veto right to block a merger of Israel Chemicals Ltd. with the Canadian Fertilizer Potash Corp., due to expected negative effects on the local workforce. See Yoram Gavison, "פוטאש-כיל עסקת" [Potash-ICL Deal], The Marker (Oct. 31, 2012), www.themarker.com/markets/1.1853965. Potash Corp. dropped its bid before the transaction was brought to approval. See "Canada's PotashCorp Drops Takeover Bid for Israel Chemicals," Haaretz (Apr. 25, 2013), www.haaretz.com/israel-news/business/potashcorp-drops-bid-for-icl-1.5239707). For an English source that emphasizes the political and social motives behind the position of the Israeli government, see P. Jordan, "Israel Wants Details on Potash Corp. Bid for Israel Chemicals Ltd.," Globe & Mail (Nov. 2, 2012), www.theglobeandmail.com/globe-investor/israel-wants-details-on-potash-corp-bid-for-israel-chemicals-ltd/article4893258/.

154 As in the Israel Chemicals Ltd. example. Ibid.

155 As in the case of fuel prices charged by Brazilian Petroleum company Petrobras. Milhaupt & Pargendler, *RPTs in SOEs*, note 152, at 6.

156 As in the case of Coal India price control policy below market prices and against public investor's objections. *See* Clarke, *Blowback*, note 35. On the Brazilian Petrobras and Brazilian Eletrobras, contractual overpayments to the government on various rights and services, see Milhaupt & Pargendler, *RPTs in SOEs*, note 152, at 3.

157 S. Claessens et al., "Disentangling the Incentive and Entrenchment Effects of Large Shareholding," *Journal of Finance* 57 (2002) 2741; S. Claessens et al., "The Separation of Ownership and Control in East Asian Corporations," *Journal of Financial Economics* 58(1–2) (2000) 81.

158 L. A. Bebchuk et al., "Stock Pyramids, Cross-Ownership, and Dual Class Equity: The Mechanisms and Agency Costs of Separating Control from Cash-flow Rights." In R. K. Morck (ed.), *Concentrated Corporate Ownership* (University of Chicago Press, 2000), 295.

159 R. J. Gilson, "Controlling Shareholders and Corporate Governance: Complicating the Comparative Taxonomy," *Harvard Law Review* 119 (2006) 1641, at 1645 ("increased productivity accrues to shareholders in proportion to their equity, while private benefits of control are allocated based on governance power."). But see Z. Goshen & A. Hamdani, "Corporate Control and Idiosyncratic Vision," *Yale Law Journal* 125 (2016) 560 (suggesting that entrepreneurs value corporate control because it allows them to pursue their vision the way they see fit, rather than necessarily to reap private benefits at the expense of public shareholders).

Increasing the state's voting control disproportionately to its cash flow rights was indeed actively pursued in China throughout its market transition to the present day. Legal instruments were main facilitators in this process. From the inception of the corporatization process with SOEs that raised passive equity capital while keeping state shares nontradable, through the reorganization of these firms into larger pyramid holding groups, and through more recent waves of M&A activity and the mixed-ownership reform that reduced the number of state-controlled businesses but enhanced the scope of state presence.[160] When it was completed, the Chinese Party-state – including central and local governments, ministries, and other state bodies – retained, and in fact leveraged, its ultimate control over the majority of the public firms.

One might argue that the state's pursuit of these tactics is no different than actions by private controlling shareholders, which are common around the world. In both cases, the controller uses the firm to facilitate private benefits of control (pecuniary or nonpecuniary).[161] When this is done at the expense of the firm and its other shareholders, such as through outright theft or by related-party transactions that are not at arms-length,[162] the extraction seems to be equally exploitative,[163] whether carried out by a state or by a private shareholder.

While this argument has conceptual merits, some practical differences should be pointed out. First, empirical research notes the prevalence of tunneling in Chinese state-controlled firms relative to other firms.[164] The use of intragroup transfers, such

With respect to China, see G. Jiang et al., "Tunneling through Inter-Corporate Loans: The China Experience," *Journal of Financial Economics* 98(1) (2010) 1 (finding that the use of intercorporate loans by controlling shareholders to siphon funds from publicly listed companies is most severe in firms where the controlling shareholders' controlling rights are larger than their ownership [cash flow] rights).

160 See the discussion on "Reinforcing State Capacities in the Market" in the current era, Part II, Chapter 5.

161 For the distinction between pecuniary and nonpecuniary benefits that controlling shareholders may extract at the expense of minority shareholders, see Gilson, *Complicating the Comparative Taxonomy*, note 159, at 1661–1667.

162 For the different aspects of related-party transactions, see L. Enriques, "Related-Party Transactions." In R.H. Kraakman et al. (eds.), *The Anatomy of Corporate Law: A Comparative and Functional Approach*, 2nd ed. (Oxford University Press, 2009).

163 The value extraction by corporate controlling shareholders received the name "Tunneling." For the seminal works on tunneling, see R. J. Gilson & J. N. Gordon, "Controlling Controlling Shareholders," *University of Pennsylvania Law Review* 152 (2003) 785; S. Johnson et al., "Tunneling," *American Economic Review* 90(2) (2000) 22.

164 M. Jian & T. J. Wong, "Propping through Related Party Transactions," *Review of Accounting Studies* 15(1) (2010) 70 (finding that abnormal related sales propping done for the benefit of the controller is more prevalent among state-owned firms and in regions with weaker economic institutions); Jiang et al., *Tunneling through Inter-Corporate Loans*, note 159 (discussing the scope of abuse by controlling shareholders through the use of inter corporate loans to siphon billions from hundreds of Chinese listed companies during the 1996–2006 period, and its significant economic consequences in firms); Q. Liu & Z. Lu, "Corporate Governance and Earnings Management in the Chinese Listed Companies: A Tunneling Perspective," *Journal of Corporate Finance* 13 (2007) 881 (suggesting

as through loan guarantees,[165] which allocate resources from publicly listed firms to private related parties, is particularly prevalent in China.[166] This suggests that there is something in the nature or the structure of state control in China that is different and more conductive to tunneling. Perhaps it is the multiple complex layers within the institutional structure that intensify conflicting interests as discussed above; perhaps the absentee principal; and perhaps it is the combination of these features that invites more opportunities for abuse from all directions.

Second, state controlling shareholders differ from private ones in the externalities of their actions on public shareholders. State controlling shareholders often have only an attenuated eye to profits. The persistent choice of the state to maintain control over various industrial firms rather than to diversify its investments as a passive equity investor raises at least a strong presumption that its reasons for maintaining control are not economic only.[167] Moreover, while the same might sometimes also be true for private controlling shareholders, a rational private investor will strive to maximize her own economic value (or that of her affiliates). Private investors that seek to use the corporation for other goals are quickly pushed by existing statutes (or case law) to pursue these goals through alternative forms of business organization.[168]

To maximize her private benefits, a private controller will deploy control either to self-deal or to monitor. In both scenarios, the controller first needs to make sure that the firm is sufficiently successful for value extraction. An increase in the general pie enlarges the delta that is then available for unequal distribution through, for example, connected transactions. When the controller has enough "skin in the

evidence that controlling shareholders use earnings management to tunnel); W. Q. Peng et al., "Tunneling or Propping: Evidence from Connected Transactions in China," *Journal of Corporate Finance* 17 (2011) 306; K. Su et al., "Ultimate Ownership, Risk-Taking and Firm Value: Evidence from China," *Asia Pacific Business Review* 23 (2017) 10 (examining risk taking and ownership structure in Chinese listed firms, showing that the presence of an ultimate controlling shareholder and the divergence between its control right and cash flow right, through pyramid structures, lead to lower corporate risk-taking and firm value); K. Wang & X. Xiao, "Controlling Shareholders' Tunneling and Executive Compensation: Evidence from China," *Journal of Accounting & Public Policy* 30 (2011) 89 (tunneling by controlling shareholders in China reduces the pay-performance sensitivity of executive compensation and suggesting that controlling shareholders have less interest to strengthen pay for performance measures due to their ability to extract value through private benefits of control).

165 N. Jia et al., "Coinsurance within Business Groups: Evidence from Related Party Transactions in an Emerging Market," *Management Science* 59(10) (2013) 2295.

166 H. Berkman et al., "Expropriation through Loan Guarantees to Related Parties: Evidence from China," *Journal of Banking & Finance* 3 (2009) 141.

167 At least by accepted theories of risk diversification through diversified portfolio investments.

168 The development of benefit corporations, nonprofit enterprises, and social purpose organizations reflects this. Especially in the United States, where SEC rules for shareholder proposals limit their substance and influence, and where case law developments around Dodge v. Ford precludes controlling shareholders from disregarding firm value maximization in pursuit of other, even socially value-maximizing, objectives. See J. R. Macey, "A Close Read of an Excellent Commentary on Dodge v. Ford," *Virginia Law & Business Review* 3 (2008) 177 (2008) (critiquing L. A. Stout, "Why We Should Stop Teaching Dodge v. Ford," *Virginia Law & Business Review* 3 (2008) 163.

game,"[169] even a rapacious controller will be interested in increasing value and thus in monitoring corporate insiders to some degree. The interests of a private controller, therefore, align with those of public shareholders at least to the point that enables self-enrichment.

When the state is the controlling shareholder, however, and aside from the self-dealing by its agents, the state often exerts its control for purposes that have only an attenuated link to economic value.[170] Recent evidence on corporate tax compliance in SOEs suggests that tax functions as a form of "dividend" to state controlling shareholders and as an excess cost to other shareholders.[171] Presumably, the state has low motivation to distribute dividends since it has other, perhaps more socially legitimate routes, such as taxes, to extract corporate value at the expense of public shareholders and the firm. Furthermore, as opposed to the portion that a private controller can extract, the expropriation by the state is not capped by the general corporate pie. The state can, and does, find ways to stream funds to its controlled firms when needed through cross-subsidizing firms[172] and from the deep pocket of its citizenry. The link between the financial strength of the invested firm and the scope of "private benefits" available for extraction by the state seems weak. One might argue that the state will be able to "take" more from a more profitable firm. It is also the case that for various reasons (not necessarily pecuniary) the Party-state is greatly committed to preventing a decline in the value of state assets. But as the evidence so far shows, this alone does not induce the state as shareholder to increase corporate *monitoring*.[173] Instead, so far, other methods to prevent the decline of value in state assets were applied more firmly.[174]

Finally, even when the Party-state as a controlling shareholder prioritizes economic value maximization in firms, it differs from private investors in its investment approach. The state as controlling shareholder is bound to aim at a pie that is far beyond that of a specific firm. The corporatization process and the subsequent group formation led to the state systematically holding ownership of stocks in competing

[169] A. H. Choi, "Concentrated Ownership and Long-Term Shareholder Value," *Harvard Business Law Review* 8 (2018) 53.

[170] For examples, see notes 148–151. There are of course examples in which a state controlling shareholder would act as a profit maximizing investor, increase the pie, and then take care of distribution. In these cases, such as in the Singaporean model of the State Holding Company Temasek or in various Sovereign Wealth Funds, the state is involved as a relatively passive investor, and its actions as a shareholder are largely economically oriented.

[171] Providing an agency cost analysis for tax compliance or avoidance in SOEs, the authors also found that their results are particularly pronounced for locally versus centrally owned SOEs and during the year of SOE term performance evaluations. See M. Bradshaw et al., "Agency Costs and Tax Planning When the Government Is a Major Shareholder," *Journal of Accounting & Economics* 67(2–3) (2019) 255.

[172] L-W. Lin & Milhaupt, *National Champions*, note 54, at 745.

[173] In Chapter 8, I discuss how while this commitment did not bring the state to monitor effectively, it is part of the reasons that recently induced the Party to fill-in the monitoring void within firms.

[174] For instance, by inducing state-controlled firms and financial institutions to rescue a declining stock market following the 2015–2016 market decline.

companies within the same industry. With its cross-industry ownership, the state adopts a broad view of profits that expands beyond a single firm across industries and the market at large.[175] Thus, even as a profit-oriented investor, when adopting an industry-level ("portfolio level") perspective, the Chinese state looks beyond the benefit of a specific firm. Some firms will be sacrificed for others, according to the state's relative ratio or following "portfolio-level" goals.[176]

If we were to view the state as a profit-oriented investor with holding positions in firms across industries, this should raise significant implications beyond firm-level governance as well. These include implications for market competition, an issue that recently caught attention in the West due to the phenomenon of common ownership.[177] The major difference here, of course, is that the Chinese Party-state, in contrast to ordinary institutional investors as common owners, has much larger stakes (or de facto control) and takes up an active position in its invested firms.[178] This reality makes both concerns – competition and the potential disregard for firm-level interests – more pressing.[179]

The analysis above does not imply any normative claim against state ownership in and of itself, nor against Chinese state's corporate control in China specifically.

[175] L-W. Lin & Milhaupt, *National Champions*, note 54, at 745 (referring to the organizational ownership structure under SASAC: "These realities suggest that the central-SOE sector as a whole, rather than individual firms, is of greatest concern to SASAC in carrying out its governance responsibilities… the practice of rotating top managers among firms in the same industry makes a good deal of sense if maximizing shareholder wealth at individual firms is less important to the controlling shareholder than building up a number of globally competitive firms in critical industries.").

[176] Much like the conflicting interests of an index fund that currently trouble American scholars, albeit not as a passive investor. See L. A. Bebchuk & S. Hirst, "Index Funds and the Future of Corporate Governance: Theory, Evidence and Policy," *Harvard Law School Forum on Corporate Governance* (Nov. 28, 2018), https://corpgov.law.harvard.edu/2018/11/28/index-funds-and-the-future-of-corporate-governance-theory-evidence-and-policy/.

[177] The theory suggests that when investors have multiple holdings in firms within the same sector, they will adopt an industry-level view and will encourage, explicitly or implicitly, anticompetitive practices at the expense of consumers and the public good more generally. See G. S. Dallas, "Common Ownership: Do Institutional Investors Really Promote Anti-Competitive Behavior?," *Harvard Law School Forum on Corporate Governance* (Dec. 2, 2018), https://corpgov.law.harvard.edu/2018/12/02/common-ownership-do-institutional-investors-really-promote-anti-competitive-behavior/.

[178] The U.S. Department of Justice Antitrust Division and the Federal Trade Commission define common ownership as "the simultaneous ownership of stock in competing companies by a single investor, where none of the stock holdings is large enough to give the owner control of any of those companies." See OECD, *Hearing on Common Ownership by Institutional Investors and its Impact on Competition – Note by the United States* (OECD Publishing, 2017).

[179] This point is different from the "agency costs of state-capitalism," which was raised by Milhaupt and Pargendler based on Gilson and Gordon's "agency cost of agency capitalism." These accounts speak to the conflict of interests between the holding entity and its ultimate beneficiary. In the Chinese case, the state acts on behalf of "all the people." While this comparison is fascinating, I believe that the state, even as a shareholder, does not have a corporate-style "fiduciary obligation" to the Chinese people per se. The Chinese people, as the theoretical ultimate beneficiaries of state ownership, did not electively entrust their economic and governance rights with the state the way that record holders entrust their investment with an institutional intermediary (state-owned pension and social security

It can certainly be the case that state corporate control has overall benefited the Chinese economy, its market development, and Chinese society at large. Rather, the point here is that the state's corporate control in China, under the current organizational and political-economic structure, is particularly alarming for public shareholders. It combines the ills of dispersed ownership with the perils of controlling shareholders and amplifies both. Public shareholders in China are thus open to exploitation from all fronts.

2 *The Party-State's Financial and Capital Market Control*

Considering only the shareholding capacity of the Party-state does not provide a complete picture of China's state capitalism and its implications for the capital market. Apart from its position as a shareholder, the Party-state infuses its interests into the Chinese capital market through its central position in debt financing and human capital. The Party-state implements control over the financial and labor markets through several capacities – its role as the regulator, the enforcer, and the owner of the main players in these fields (thus, the main financier). Along with the Party-state's ownership capacity in industrial firms, these attributes, together, form China's "state capitalism."

This Party-state control over debt financing resources affects the availability of alternatives to equity financing and thus impacts the flow of capital and increases control over the development of the capital market overall. The Party-state controls the flow of capital via bank credit through its ownership of all policy banks and most commercial banks,[180] as well as by fixing financing priorities through its industrial five-year plans (see Part II). The Party-state's hand reaches beyond bank credit and into debt financing as well. A study by Lin and Milhaupt shows the various ways through which the Party-state controls the debt market. In the bond market, for example, bond issuers are primarily organs of the central and the local governments (the government or entities it owns directly such as commercial banks and SOEs), while non-SOEs corporate debt issuance is relatively narrow in scope.[181]

funds are somewhat excepted). Such a relationship thus cannot be addressed by the agency theory alone. A different framework, possibly involving public ownership theories, is required. That concern is outside the scope of this book. See R. Gilson & J. Gordon, "The Agency Costs of Agency Capitalism: Activist Investors and the Revaluation of Governance Rights," *Columbia Law Review* 113 (2013) 863; Milhaupt & Pargendler, *Governance Challenges of SOEs*, note 152. For an additional account of the agency costs of institutional investors, see L. A. Bebchuk et al., "The Agency Problems of Institutional Investors," *Journal of Economic Perspective* 31(3) (2017) 89.

180 Only in 2014, private participants were allowed to establish commercial banks. The banking industry now consists of seventeen private banks only. See G. Sun, "Banking Institutions and Banking Regulations." In M. Amstad, G. Sun & W. Xiong (eds.), *The Handbook of China's Financial System* (Princeton University Press, 2020) 9, at 14.

181 Local Government Financing Vehicles issue 36.8 percent of the total outstanding corporate debt instruments. Central SOEs controlled typically by SASAC issued 28.6 percent, and local SOEs controlled by local SASAC branches issued 21.7 percent of the total. Facially private enterprises issued

The Party-state's dominance in the debt market is felt not only in the identity of bond issuers but also throughout the entire network of market intermediaries. The underwriting industry, despite having a relatively large number of players, which should mean more competition, reveals the absolute dominance of state-owned financial intermediaries. The main banks, securities companies, and other financial institutions conduct the underwriting activity, and the great majority of them are owned by the state. At the time of the study, out of all financial institutions that perform underwriting activity with at least 2 percent of the underwriting market, only one (Minsheng Bank) was not state owned, and even this particular bank maintained a close reciprocal relationship with the government. Similarly, Lin and Milhaupt found that in the credit rating industry, which is also seemingly competitive, the state owns the majority of firms (five out of nine agencies).[182] The potential for conflicts of interest and biased rating is clear. As most bond issuers are politically connected to the Party-state, credit ratings are skewed upwards and thus do not perform well as reputational intermediaries.[183]

Beyond ownership of industrial and financial firms, as a regulator and enforcer, the Chinese Party-state is omnipresent in every step of the way as well: from setting the rules of enterprise organization, capital financing, and trade; to outright suspensions in the capital market as an oversight stability mechanism; a licensing regime that can be exercised to limit the operation of certain market participants; stricter or laxer M&A and antitrust enforcement (at times following geopolitical changes); monetary control over the repatriation of funds, administered by SAFE (the State Administration of Foreign Exchange); and finally, even through protectionist legal and administrative enforcement when violations and/or disputes arise.

Public shareholders – their status and the role they are allowed to play in the capital market – are thus dependent upon the totality of China's state capitalism, on the complete array of Party-state economic controls therein.

The remainder of this chapter addresses the implications of China's state capitalism for the function of traditional corporate governance institutions (both legal and market mechanisms will be addressed).

only 12.7 percent of all outstanding corporate bonds. See L-W. Lin & C. Milhaupt, "Bonded to the State: A Network Perspective on China's Corporate Debt Market," *Journal of Financial Regulation* 3(1) (2017), 1.

[182] Ibid at 21–23, 34–35 (also pointing out that 60 percent of all rated corporate bonds were rated by a state-owned rating agency).

[183] China had recently relaxed some of its limitations on foreign ownership in the financial industry, including with respect to domestic clearing and rating services. These changes may introduce (limited) quality controls. See, for example, Relevant Measures to Further Expand the Opening Up of the Financial Industry [关于进一步扩大金融业对外开放的有关举措], promulgated by Office of the St. Council Fin. Stability and Dev. Comm., July 21, 2019, https://perma.cc/U3EY-A9CD; T. Groswald Ozery, "Illiberal Governance and the Rise of China's Public Firms: An Oxymoron or China's Greatest Triumph?," *University of Pennsylvania Journal of International Law* 42(4) (2021) 921, at 936–937, note 49.

LAW AND POLITICAL ECONOMY CONFIGURATIONS OF CONVENTIONAL GOVERNANCE MECHANISMS

As seen thus far, China's political economic determinants have created a structured predicament in which public shareholders are disempowered and subject to open exploitation by various corporate control parties. Nicholas Howson describes the situation as "a ready invitation to opportunism, 'tunneling', minority shareholder abuse and oppression."[184] In this section, I will examine whether China's embrace of traditional monitoring and disciplining mechanisms helped overcome this structural predicament.

Foundational corporate law theories view the public corporation as a capital-raising vehicle.[185] Corporate governance in public firms (including securities regulation) should be designed to facilitate the development of the capital market as a dynamic and efficient capital allocation mechanism whereby capital is allocated to the most deserving firms. Striving for efficiency, capital markets and corporate governance regimes should minimize the costs of monitoring corporate control parties. These costs emanate from the separation between the owners of the corporation and those who control it, and their potential conflicting interests – which constitute the basic premise of modern public firm theory.[186]

It is asserted that corporate governance should strive to fulfill an economic function. This is to say, since external suppliers of finance expect a return on their investment, corporate governance should focus on assuring and securing investors' rights, through mechanisms that will prevent the exploitation of investors by those who have control over their investment.[187] If investors' expectations for a fair game are met, the theory goes, they will be reassured and encouraged to continue investing. This will keep the cost of financing low and will promote a vibrant capital market with lower monitoring costs. It follows that potential exploitative behavior by corporate control parties (insider management and controlling shareholders) should be minimized through an array of governance mechanisms.

The remainder of this chapter examines traditional mechanisms of corporate governance and their operation in China. By traditional mechanisms, I mean the

[184] Howson, "*Quack Corporate Governance*," note 10, at 692.

[185] H. G. Manne, "Our Two Corporation Systems: Law and Economics," *Virginia Law Review* 53 (1967) 259.

[186] F. H. Easterbrook & D. R. Fischel, "Voting in Corporate Law," *Journal of Law & Economics* 26 (1983) 395, at 403, note 1 (citing A. A. Berle & C. G. Means, *The Modern Corporation and Private Property* 129 (rev. ed. 1967).

[187] See generally M. Jensen & W. Meckling, "Theory of the Firm: Managerial Behavior, Agency Costs, and Ownership Structure," *Journal of Finance Economics* 3.4 (1976) 305; A. Shleifer & R. W. Vishny, "A Survey of Corporate Governance," *Journal of Finance* 52 (1997) 737. For different approaches to corporate governance, see O. E. Williamson, *The Economic Institutions of Capitalism: Firms, Markets, Relational Contracting* (Free Press, 1985) (presenting a broader institutional economics contractarian view). See also S. L. Gillan, "Recent Developments in Corporate Governance: An Overview," *Journal of Corporate Finance* 12 (2006) 381 (2006) (presenting a broad, inclusive approach).

mechanisms that are conventionally assigned a monitoring and disciplining role in corporate governance. Such mechanisms can be divided into two groups: those operating inside the firm or with direct interests in the particular firm (internal governing bodies and constituents of the firm) and those operating outside the specific firm (external markets and legal institutions).

Internal Governance Mechanisms:

- *Shareholders* (institutional investors, other shareholder coalitions)
- *Other Internal Governing Bodies* (board of directors, independent directors, and supervisory board)
- *Other Corporate Constituents* (employees, creditors, consumers, and managers)

External Monitoring Institutions:

- *External Markets* (the market for corporate control, capital market, product market, and managerial labor market)
- *Gatekeepers* (lawyers, accountants and underwriters, and the financial press)
- *The Legal System* (public enforcement – the CSRC, stock exchanges; private enforcement – the People's Courts system)

For each mechanism, I explain its assigned economic function under the conventional understanding in the corporate governance literature and then evaluate how the legal and political configurations in China pre-condition the operation of such mechanisms.

1 *Internal Governance Mechanisms*

Shareholders

The failure of monitoring by the state as a controlling shareholder calls attention to the issue of monitoring by other shareholders, whether public individual shareholders or blockholding shareholder coalitions.

In contrast to controlling shareholders and blockholders, dispersed shareholders have greater information asymmetries, collective action problems, and incentives to free-ride others. These make it difficult and uneconomical for shareholders with few shares to monitor corporate control parties.[188] Individual public shareholders therefore typically take passive holding positions. Yet, dispersed shareholders may form coalitions that increase their ability to monitor and discipline corporate insiders in various ways.[189] Through aggregate action, they are potentially able to collect enough

[188] S. Bainbridge, "The Case for Limited Shareholder Voting Rights," *UCLA Law Review* 53 (2005) 601, 604; Easterbrook & Fischel, *Voting in Corporate Law*, note 186.

[189] B. S. Black, "Agents Watching Agents: The Promise of Institutional Investor Voice," 39 *UCLA Law Review* (1992) 811; M. Kahan & E. B. Rock, "Hedge Funds in Corporate Governance and Corporate Control," *University of Pennsylvania Law Review* 155 (2007) 1021.

votes to make specific corporate governance proposals, challenge the decision-making of incumbent managers, and in some markets even oust underperforming managers and take control of the firm.[190]

In firms with controlling shareholders, public shareholders, even when building coalitions, are generally unable to assemble enough votes to contest control directly. Yet, they can still engage in governance and have some monitoring functions when acting in concert.

Institutional Investors

Over the last few decades, shifts in shareholder composition, particularly in widely held markets, have raised expectations for greater public participation through institutional investments.[191] Although the views on institutional investors' actual engagement in governance and contribution to firm value are far from conclusive,[192] it certainly seems that the recent accumulation of corporate power and potential for activism by institutional investors around the world is transforming the corporate governance landscape.[193]

Certainly, the degree of involvement by institutional investors depends on the country's political economy, including the applicable regulatory framework, the sophistication of the financial industry, and the extent to which such institutional investors have been co-opted. When a controlling shareholder exists, the impact of institutional investors on corporate decision-making and monitoring is limited from the outset. In controlled firms, the presence of institutional investors is more limited,[194] tied to the state,[195] or co-opted within a group of dominant share

[190] See MM Cos. v. Liquid Audio, Inc., 813 A.2d 1118 (Del. 2003) (an example of shareholder participation effort in the context of a contested election battle – "proxy fight"); Blasius Indus., Inc. v. Atlas Corp., 564 A.2d 651 (Del. Ch. 1988) (an example of a shareholder accumulating votes and submitting a precatory proposal to influence company business strategy and board composition).

[191] For the canonical view, see Black, *Agents Watching Agents*, note 189 (depicting traditional institutional investors as promising monitors).

[192] *Cf.* L. A. Bebchuk et al., "The Long-Term Effects of Hedge Fund Activism," *Columbia Law Review* 115 (2015) 1085, and M. Becht et al., "Returns to Hedge Fund Activism: An International Study," *Review of Financial Studies* 30 (2017) 2933; with J. C. Coffee & D. Palia, "The Wolf at the Door: The Impact of Hedge Fund Activism on Corporate Governance," *Annals of Corporate Governance* 1(1) (2016), and S. Gillan & L. T. Starks, "A Survey of Shareholder Activism: Motivation and Empirical Evidence," *Contemporary Finance Digest* (1998), at 10.

[193] J. C. Coates, "The Future of Corporate Governance Part I: The Problem of Twelve" (Harvard Pub. Law, Working Paper No. 19-07, 2018).

[194] Only a small scope of institutional investment, measured by assets under management, was noted for Portugal, Greece, Spain, Turkey, Poland, and other OECD countries. See OECD, *The Role of Institutional Investors in Promoting Good Corporate Governance* (OECD, Corporate Governance Publishing, 2011) at 112; M. A. Ferreira & P. Matos, "The Colors of Investors' Money: The Role of Institutional Investors around the World," *Journal of Financial Economics* 88 (2008) 499, 524–530.

[195] Such as in China (see the discussion that follows), or India, see J. Sarkar & S. Sarkar, "Large Shareholder Activism in Corporate Governance in Developing Countries: Evidence from India," *International Review of Finance* 1 (2000) 161, 166.

holders.[196] Where controlled firms are prevalent (i.e., a concentrated market), institutional investors are often entwined with larger business groups through business or ownership networks. There, while institutional investors are technically able to overcome apathy and collective-action problems that hold back monitoring by dispersed shareholders, they rarely have the incentives to do so. In some cases, institutional investors are even controlled by the listed firm whose public share float they manage. This increases their support for incumbent insiders without accountability to their ultimate beneficiaries. Such a situation has prompted several scholars and policymakers in concentrated markets to propose more mandatory intervention that seek to promote public shareholder engagement through compulsory institutional investor stewardship.[197]

With respect to the PRC, the institutional investment industry experiences the general predicaments that impede the ability of institutional investors to monitor and engage in governance in any concentrated market, and then some. Up until recent years, the young industry was miniscule in scope, a fact that limited its impact. 2014 reports by China's stock exchanges reflect that at that time most retail investors (free float A shares) managed their equity investments individually and not through institutional investor accounts.[198]

The industry saw immense growth over the last several years. Lin and Puchinak note that institutional investors now account for almost half of the free float of A shares, and 18.7 percent of total market capitalization of A shares.[199] And yet, the

[196] Such as in Israel, France, Korea, Singapore, and Brazil. For the Israeli example, see A. Hamdani & Y. Yafeh, "Institutional Investors as Minority Shareholders," *Review of Finance* 17 (2012) 691. For France, see C. Girard, "Success of Shareholder Activism: The French Case," *Bankers, Markets & Investors* Nov.–Dec. (2011), at 26. More Generally, S. Gillan & L. T. Starks, "Corporate Governance, Corporate Ownership, and the Role of Institutional Investors: A Global Perspective" (Weinberg Ctr. for Corp. Governance, Working Paper No. 2003-01, 2003).

[197] Hamdani & Yafeh, ibid., at 711–714 ("it is legal intervention – rather than minority shareholders' voting power – that drives institutional investors to cast a vote" … "Institutional investors tend to be active primarily when legally required to do so."). For recent efforts in the EU, see Directive 2017/828, Amending Directive 2007/36/EC as Regards the Encouragement of Long-Term Shareholder Engagement, 2017 O.J. (L 132) 1, https://publications.europa.eu/en/publication-detail/-/publication/9b871b38-3d20-11e7-a08e-01aa75ed71a1/language-en. See generally, Goshen, *Theory Meets Reality*, note 113 (arguing that corporate laws must incorporate some form of minority protection as a mandatory rule and examining various such forms in different jurisdictions).

[198] See Shanghai Stock Exchange, "Shanghai Stock Exchange Statistics Annual" (2014), at 475–476, www.sse.com.cn/aboutus/publication/yearly/documents/c/tjnj_2014.pdf (in Chinese); and Shenzhen Stock Exchange, "Information Management Department of Shenzhen Stock Exchange, Shenzhen Stock Exchange Market Fact Book" (2013), 269, https://web.archive.org/web/20170722151420/; www.szse.cn/UpFiles/largepdf/20150319145710.pdf (in Chinese), reporting a 0.33 percent and 0.46 percent (respectively) as institutional accounts compared to individual (retail) investors' accounts. These reports, however, might be somewhat misleading as some institutional investors hold individual accounts, see Clarke, *Law without Order*, note 10, at 147, 154 ("official and unofficial investment funds often use [legally or illegally] individual accounts").

[199] L. Lin, & D. W. Puchniak, "Institutional Investors in China: Corporate Governance and Policy Channeling in the Market within the State," *Columbia Journal of Asian Law* 35(1) (2022) 74, at 84–88.

Chinese Party-state is prevalent in the industry through ownership and control of many of the institutional investors.[200] Moreover, the operating scope of institutional investment services in China is still strictly regimented with limited investment choices. For example, pension funds are funded and managed by local-level provincial and city governments and until very recently could only invest in national treasury bonds and deposits.[201] Only in late 2015 did the State Council permit pension funds to invest in equity securities.[202] Similar investment limitations apply to the PRC's National Social Security Fund, which functions as the central government's social security reserve fund.[203] As for mutual funds, in 2012, mutual funds held 7.6 percent of all shares, but at the firm level, their holdings were still marginal, holding a median of 0.067 percent in firms.[204] Here too, there has been a significant growth in recent years, both in terms of the number of registered mutual funds and their total equity holdings. And yet, their ratio out of the total market (market capitalization and share of free float A shares) has actually declined due to the rise of parallel forms of institutional investments.[205]

Scholars note a short-term investment horizon as one factor in institutional investors' firm level small holdings[206] and consequent general lack of influence. Their strategy is to invest speculatively and hold shares for short periods of time. The investment pattern of institutional investors is thus similar to that of individual investors, making them similarly unlikely to monitor. Still, there is no doubt that the institutional investment industry in China is growing in recent years.[207] A growth that was boosted especially after the 2015 and 2016 stock market collapses, when institutional investors were instructed to increase their positions.

[200] For example, the state owns and controls most of the trust companies and securities companies, with more proliferation of private participants in the insurance industry; Lin & Puchniak, ibid., at 102–103.

[201] R. C. Pozen, *Tackling the Chinese Pension System* 3–6, 8 (2013), www.brookings.edu/wp-content/uploads/2016/06/31-reforming-chinese-pension-system-pozen.pdf. Insurance funds and mutual funds have other restrictions. See also C. Xi, "Institutional Shareholder Activism in China: Law and Practice," *International Company & Commercial Law Review* 17 (2006) 287, 251–252.

[202] 2015 regulations allowed pension funds to invest up to 30 percent of their net assets in domestic equities. State Council Administrative Measures for Investment Management of Pension Funds [国务院关于印发基本养老保险基金投资管理办法的通知 (国发 (2015) 48号)], promulgated by the St. Council, Aug. 17, 2015.

[203] 全国社会保障基金理事会 [National Council for Social Security Fund], www.ssf.gov.cn.

[204] Jiang & Kim, note 49, at 197 Table 6, 211.

[205] For the shifting trends in the industry and the relevant regulatory framework, see Lin and Puchinak, *Institutional Investors in China*, note 749.

[206] Jiang & Kim, note 49, at 211 (pointing to an average holding period of less than six months by mutual funds in 2011). Previous research had pointed to even shorter holding periods (one to two months). See Clarke, *Law without Order*, note 10, at 154–155.

[207] See State Council Administrative Measures for Investment Management of Pension Funds, note 202, arts. 36, 37. This move was said to contribute up to RMB 600 billion, managed by the PRC pension fund, into the PRC domestic stock markets. See P. Inman, "China to Allow Pension Funds to Invest in Stock Market for the First Time," *Guardian* (Aug. 23, 2015), www.theguardian.com/world/2015/aug/23/china-to-allow-pension-fund-to-invest-in-stock-market-for-first-time.

Beyond matters of size within individual firms and the duration of holdings shares, an additional impediment that prevented institutional investors from accumulating a meaningful impact on insiders' conduct is related to competency. While the industry is growing, it is still relatively young and inexperienced. Opening the market to Qualified Foreign Institutional Investors (QFII)[208] was expected to aid on that front. QFIIs were expected to bring global experience and professional skills to improve the quality of domestic institutional investors.[209] More than 400 foreign institutions from 31 countries have invested through this scheme since its initiation in 2002.[210] The "market-education" value of QFIIs, however, remained marginal. Confined by operational quotas and informational asymmetries, QFIIs prioritized maintaining a strong relationship with Party-state controlling shareholders. They often entrust the controller's appointees to vote on their behalf, instead of opting for direct action that could maximize value for their unit holders and other public shareholders.[211] It should nevertheless be noted that in recent years, the Chinese government increased the QFII quota allotment several times until finally abolishing the quota regime altogether in 2020,[212] a step that may enhance the impact of foreign institutional investors overtime.

Other recent initiatives outside the QFII system were taken as well. The 2013 Shanghai Free Trade Zone included various experiments with a reduction of barriers to foreign investors' participation in the capital market.[213] The China–Hong Kong Stock Connect initiative and the Mutual Recognition of Publicly Offered

208 The program was introduced in 2002, revised in September 2009, and once again in December 2012. A separate program was approved in 2011 to facilitate the use of Renminbi held outside mainland China for investments in the domestic market – Renminbi Qualified Foreign Institutional Investors. General information on the QFII and RQFII schemes, including summaries of important policy revisions and relevant quotas, is available on the Shanghai Stock Exchange website. *QFII & RQFII*, Shanghai Stock Exchange, https://archive.ph/SV9Ny. For ease of reference, I will refer to these programs together as QFII.

209 See generally T. Khanna & K. Palepu, "Emerging Market Business Groups, Foreign Intermediaries, and Corporate Governance," In R. K. Morck (ed.), *Concentrated Corporate Ownership* (University of Chicago Press, 2000), 265, at 319.

210 "Abolish Restrictions on the Investment Quota of Qualified Foreign Investors (QFII/ RQFII) and Further Expand the Opening up of Financial Markets," *SAFE News* (Sept. 10, 2019), https://perma.cc/2TDC-TUNM.

211 OECD, *Corporate Governance of Listed Companies in China: Self-Assessment by The China Securities Regulatory Commission* (OECD Publishing, 2011), at 39; Lin & Puchniak, *Institutional Investors in China*, note 199, at 115–116 (documenting the scarcity of foreign institutional investors activism). The problem is not unique to China, see C. J. Milhaupt, "Nonprofit Organizations as Investor Protection: Economic Theory and Evidence from East Asia," *Yale Journal of International Law* 29 (2004) 169, at 190.

212 CSRC, PBC, and SAFE Release the Measures for the Administration of Domestic Securities and Futures Investment by Qualified Foreign Institutional Investors and RMB Qualified Foreign Institutional Investors, China Sec. Reg. Comm'n (Sept. 25, 2020), https://perma.cc/SD4L-Z4ZW. For the various paths and scope of foreign investors investments in the Chinese market, see Groswald Ozery, *Illiberal Governance*, note 183.

213 See "Policy Measures for the Capital Market to Support and Promote the Shanghai Free Trade Zone," [資本市場支持促進中國(上海)自由貿易試驗區若幹政策措施] China Sec. Reg. Comm'n (Sept. 29, 2013).

Funds between Hong Kong and the PRC were designed to increase investments by off-shore institutional investors and to introduce a wider range of investment tools into the PRC domestic market. A similar stock-connect initiative was launched with the London stock exchange.[214]

These recent initiatives may enhance the impact of foreign institutional investors over time and thus could, theoretically at least, affect the operating standards in the industry. On the margins, increasing the scope of authorized foreign investors might, with time, bring more engagement by institutional investors that are less embedded in business group affiliations and Party-state control than domestic institutional investment firms.

Given the likelihood that the market share, competency, and sophistication of institutional investors in China will increase in the foreseeable future, the question then arises whether the industry *could* become meaningful in corporate governance and, if so, *how*. Can institutional investors in China become actively involved in the governance of listed firms and might they actively monitor corporate insiders at least to the extent that they do so in other concentrated markets? In my view, other impediments established in China's political economy will continue to stand in the way of a more active and influential institutional investors industry even as the industry grows.

The following factors will likely prevent institutional investors from becoming true stewards of public shareholders' interests in the Chinese capital market. First, institutional investors in China are subject to close regulation, supervision, and enforcement at several administrative levels. Various competing central government ministry-level bodies regulate the industry, mainly: the CSRC, the China Banking and Insurance Regulatory Commission, National Council for Social Security Fund, and the State Administration of Foreign Exchange. This divided regulatory and supervisory system produces multiple, cumbersome, and often overlapping regulations and competing interests that limit institutional investors' initiative and autonomy.[215] It may also hold back policies that the CSRC would have otherwise promoted and that might have encouraged institutional investors to be more engaged. For example, it likely impedes any potential intention to require cumulative voting or to mandate voting by institutional investors on certain matters, as seen in other concentrated markets.[216]

[214] A mutual stock-connect initiative allows off-shore retail and institutional investors mutual stock market access between SSE and the respective partner stock exchange. The Mutual Recognition of Funds opened up an authorization process for off-shore funds to trade in the respective domestic markets. See Groswald Ozery, *Illiberal Governance*, note 183, at 930–931.

[215] For instance, both the CSRC and the State Administration of Foreign Exchange are responsible for the administration of the QFII schemes. See *QFII & RQFII*, note 208. The CSRC and the China Banking & Insurance Regulatory Commission share administrative authority over the operation of pension insurance funds that are also securities investment funds, as well as some authority over mutual funds since financial institutions often operate as securities companies.

[216] The CSRC requires disclosure of the votes of the ten largest public shareholders on certain issues discussed at a shareholders meeting. See Provisions on Strengthening the Protection of the Rights and Interests of the General Public Shareholders [关于加强社会公众股股东权益保护的若干规定],

Most importantly, China's state capitalism attributes are likely to inhibit institutional investor engagement in governance going forward as well. Even compared to other concentrated markets, the conflicts of interest experienced by PRC institutional investors are particularly acute. Firms in the institutional investors industry are closely affiliated with SOE groups, publicly listed firms, and their senior insiders through ownership and contractual arrangements, as well as with key political players at various levels of the Party-state system.[217] Furthermore, as noted before, the Party-state is strongly involved in the capital market not only through its control of many listed companies but also through its control over the financial industry and the major players in the investment sector. Besides the state's direct ownership in financial firms and securities companies, another way the Party-state exercises control over the industry is through the reshuffling of senior executives between firms in the financial and asset management industry and between firms and the relevant administrative state organs.[218]

Thus, in the PRC, central organs of the Party-state have not only both administrative and regulatory control over the financial and investment sectors but also absolute ownership and management control of many of the professional firms operating in these sectors. The PRC Party-state is therefore able to advance its interests through its controlling shareholder position in its subsidiary listed firms, through state regulatory agencies and the legal system, and also through its controlling ownership position in most of China's fund managers, insurance companies and other public investment vehicles, securities companies, and banks.[219]

This control model certainly poses barriers to institutional investors acting autonomously from the larger Party-state apparatus. The solutions applied in other concentrated markets, through which institutional investors are empowered and their conflicts are somewhat mitigated,[220] are simply irrelevant in the Chinese context.

promulgated by China Sec. Reg. Comm'n, Dec. 7, 2004, art. 1.1(5) [CSRC 2004 Provisions]. Yet, there is no affirmative duty of institutional investors to vote (a duty that regulators in other markets, e.g., Israel, require for certain matters). The CSRC could, potentially, push for a corresponding mandatory vote. Without such a requirement and given institutional investors' network affiliation described above, a requirement to disclose the votes is more likely to discourage the vote of these public shareholders altogether.

217 See Firth et al., note 149 (providing an interesting insight into institutional investors' decisions during the split-share structure reform, when mutual funds were pressured politically to accept compensation schemes to rush the implementation of the reform even when not in the best interests of their unit holders); Xi, *Institutional Shareholder Activism in China*, note 201, at 258–263.

218 For example, transfers of executives between the central bank, commercial banks, and branches of the administration such as (then) China Banking Regulatory Commission and the CSRC. Howson, *China's Restructured Commercial Banks*, note 11.

219 Y. Kim et al., *Developing Institutional Investors in People's Republic of China*, (World Bank, Country Study Paper No. 30248, 2003), http://documents.worldbank.org/curated/en/280421468743976037/pdf/302480CHA0deve1titutional0investors.pdf. See also Hong Kong Stock Exchange, *Institutional Investors in Mainland China* (2004), www.hkex.com.hk/eng/stat/research/rpaper/Documents/IIMC.pdf.

220 Such as negative veto rights, supermajority requirements, mandatory participation of minority public shareholders in certain business decisions, minority public shareholder involvement in directors' elections, and their right to submit governance proposals to the board. See, for example, OECD,

For example, the institutional investor industry embedded in the Party-state system will not exercise even a formally granted minority veto *against* Party-state controlling shareholders, such as the one provided for in the CSRC 2004 Provisions.[221] Likewise, an effort like the one recently taken in Israel in which business groups were structurally and actively required to disentangle – separating institutional investors from industrial firms – is not a viable option in the Chinese case.[222] Separating the affiliation of asset management institutions from corporate groups in China will not suffice to eliminate their complex conflicts of interest. Real autonomy and independence of institutional investors from the corporate groups would require their detachment from the Party-state. This scenario is unlikely. Such an overhaul would contradict the reasons for which China's state capitalism was established in the first place and maintained thus far. Hence, even if the market share and proficiency of domestic institutional investors in China grows, that increase will not translate into any reduction in control by corporate insiders or any increase in real stewardship and governance engagement by institutional investors in the cases where it is needed the most.

Coalition-Building Shareholder Monitoring

Nongovernmental organizations, nonprofit organizations, and other social organizations have emerged as significant stakeholders in several concentrated markets.[223] These players are often involved in governance indirectly, by instigating broad public attention that puts pressure on controlling shareholders and directors and by lobbying regulators for public shareholder–friendly corporate governance mechanisms.

Related Party Transactions, note 114, at 30–37. Israel is one example of a highly concentrated market where the state regulator sought to increase institutional investor participation and power by addressing the passivity of institutional investors and their co-option within a larger, dominated group and the potential conflict of interest resulting therefrom. Israel's Company Law requires that an "extraordinary" transaction between the company and its control party (including affiliates) be approved by the shareholders' general meeting, provided that the approving majority votes will include a majority of disinterested (minority) shareholders participating in the meeting (abstentions not counted). The minority approval requirement is in addition to an approval by an audit committee and by the board of directors. See Company Law, 5759–1999, § 275(a), 1 LSI 44 (1999) (Isr.). At the same time, various financial laws and regulations mandate that institutional investors cast a vote in certain matters, thereby leveraging shareholder consent into a regulatory device. Hamdani & Yafeh, *Institutional Investors as Minority Shareholders*, note 196, at 696–700.

221 CSRC 2004 Provisions, note 216, art. 1.1.(5). The ownership-market structure and the network of conflicting interests make it more reasonable to assume that institutional investors, when involved, will take informal private negotiations as their preferred method.

222 In a novel regulatory step, the Israeli legislature adopted "The Law for the Decrease of Concentration and Increase of Competition." It aims to strengthen competition and curtail the excessive clout of a relatively small number of business groups over the Israeli economy by limiting pyramid groups to two holding layers and separating ownership of financial institutions from non-financial corporations.

223 M. Erede, "Governing Corporations with Concentrated Ownership Structure: An Empirical Analysis of Hedge Fund Activism in Italy and Germany, and its Evolution," *European Financial Law Review* 10 (2013) 328, 350–354, and 370; Milhaupt, *Nonprofit Organizations as Investor Protection*, note 211.

In some systems, social organizations may facilitate coalition-building share ownership for public shareholders, especially where institutional investors are less prominent. In this capacity, they may actively participate in governance by exercising their associated governance rights through voting, submitting shareholder proposals, and taking advantage of ex-post legal claims.[224] Their involvement can discipline corporate insiders and control parties, expose problems, and push firms and their management to act in a socially responsible manner.

In the French capital market, for example, *associations d'actionnaires* ([public] shareholders' associations) have become influential institutions able to coordinate minority shareholder action, despite significant ownership concentration in French firms long supported by the government. The French Commercial Code permits public shareholders with at least 5 percent of the voting rights and that have held their shares for more than two years to form *associations d'actionnaires* to act in concert to further public shareholders' collective interests.[225] Scholars have argued that coalition-building efforts enabled by these associations have meaningfully strengthened minority public shareholder engagement in the governance of French firms.[226]

It is unlikely, however, that a role comparable to the one played by the French shareholders' associations is possible for Chinese social organizations in the capital market governed by the PRC's authoritarian, single party regime. The need for social organizations to be able to rely on law and legal institutions to enforce their rights, as well as an ability to publicly critique corporate misconduct through a relatively free financial press, are functions that are not readily available in China. The Chinese People's Courts are not an independent branch of government and are part of the Party-state bureaucracy. This means that the Chinese judiciary is weak and, in many cases, lacks the technical competence, bureaucratic autonomy, or political independence necessary for it to act against far more powerful Party-state actors.[227]

Furthermore, one must understand the current state of civil society in China in order to assess the possibilities for Chinese social organizations, even as shareholders, as corporate governance participants in the PRC. The emergence of civil society, including citizens' access to rights-enforcing institutions, is a matter of some complexity in China, but clearly the Western notion of freedom of association is

[224] E. Sjöström, "Translating Ideologically Based Concerns: How Civil Society Organizations Use the Financial Market to Protect Human Rights," *International Journal of Environment and Sustainable Development* 6 (2007) 153.

[225] See Code de commerce [C. Com.] [Commercial Code] arts. L.225-103, L.225-105, L.225-230-L.225-233, L.225-252 (Fr.).

[226] Girard, *Success of Shareholder Activism*, note 196. Y. Nili, "Missing the Forest from the Trees: A New Approach to Shareholder Activism," *Harvard Business Law Review* 4 (2014) 157, at 197–199, note 229.

[227] Howson, *Corporate Law in the Shanghai People's Courts*, note 93, at 327–356. I discuss the People's Courts more extensively below.

absent. Civil society and social organizations, as well as the financial press, are largely confined to areas that do not threaten central Party-state interests or that can help the center keep local power in control.[228]

In addition to these limitations on the judicial system, the financial press, and civil society at large, there also exists in China remnants of traditional cultural perception that the legal system is a coercive instrument of control and that administration is to be reserved to the state.[229] As Donald Clarke puts it, "The notion that private citizens should be involved in law enforcement for public goals does not find a ready home in… [the] Chinese political culture. The state jealously guards its control over the machinery of coercion…."[230] Thus, law and legal institutions operate so as to restrict any nonstate institutions, especially social organizations, from taking the lead on the enforcement of private rights of any kind. This is certainly the case when they are asked to enforce private shareholders' rights against superior forces of the PRC Party-state.

The exclusion of private rights holders from effective use of the formal legal system, coupled with a strong concern about the maintenance of social and political stability, are evident in the constraints applied on private enforcement through group litigation. These constraints have long denied securities law class actions outright and radically minimize the number of corporate law derivative lawsuits, especially those involving Party-state controlled companies or their management.[231] Thus, while some Chinese social organizations may now operate legally, they are extremely unlikely to be permitted any meaningful role in disciplining and monitoring corporate control parties.[232]

228 The literature on this point is vast. See, for example, D. C. Clarke, "The Private Attorney-General in China: Potential and Pitfalls," *Washington University Global Studies Law Review* 8 (2009) 241; B. L. Liebman, "Changing Media, Changing Courts." In S. L. Shirk (ed.), *Changing Media, Changing China* (Oxford University Press, 2011) 150, 151; B. Van Rooij, "People's Regulation: Citizens and Implementation of Law in China," *Columbia Journal of Asian Law* 25 (2012) 116.

229 D. Bodde, "Basic Concepts of Chinese Law: The Genesis and Evolution of Legal Thought in Traditional China," *Proceedings of the American Philosophical Society* 107 (1963) 375; Z. Liang, "Explicating 'Law': A Comparative Perspective of Chinese and Western Legal Culture," *Journal of Chinese Law* 3 (1989) 55.

230 Clarke, *The Private Attorney-General in China*, note 228, at 242–243 (concerning private litigation, but applicable to other private enforcement channels).

231 Clarke & Howson, *Derivative Actions in the PRC*, note 129, at 254–257. But see H. Huang, "Shareholder Derivative Litigation in China: Empirical Findings and Comparative Analysis," *Banking & Financial Law Review* 27 (2012) 619, at 648–653; W. Xu, *The Enforcement of Securities Law in China: A Law and Economics Assessment* (Springer Nature, 2022), which offer instead economic rationales as explanations for the limited number of securities law private enforcement actions in China, such as collective action problems and cost-benefit analysis. Recent changes in China's class action regime are discussed below under Private Enforcement.

232 A possibility remains that some form of a quasi-public institution will be established with the endorsement of the Party-state, as indeed seems to be the case under the most recent amendment of the securities law. A Party-state-sanctioned institution is vastly more likely to be permitted greater latitude to promote minority public shareholder interests. For my previous exploration of this option, see Groswald Ozery, *Minority Public Shareholders in China*, note 11.

Additional Internal Governing Bodies

Board of Directors

The board of directors plays a central role in corporate governance and is defined as the main internal governance body in many modern corporate laws.[233] The board appoints senior managers, makes major policy decisions and approves others, and generally oversees the operations of the firm. Elected by the firm's shareholders, the directors' oversight replaces a more costly and harder-to-coordinate monitoring by shareholders.

In controlled firms, however, and more generally in concentrated markets, board independence and its commitment to *all* shareholders is challenged on both operational and normative levels. The firm's controlling or dominant shareholders dictate the election of board members in controlled firms. This is clearly the case in China. The Company Law requires listed firms, as well as other CLSs in the PRC, to have at least five directors on their board and no more than nineteen.[234] The shareholders' meeting elects and dismisses the directors and also has the power to decide on matters regarding their salary and other compensation.[235] Majority rule – and thus decisions by the controller or by dominant shareholders – generally determines the results of the shareholders' meetings, including decisions concerning directors.

Most board members, and the board of directors as an organ of internal governance, therefore, lack independence and are largely captured by the controlling shareholders who appointed them. This weakness of oversight by boards of directors in controlled companies is especially significant when corporate malfeasance is done by the controlling shareholders or their affiliates in the firm. To address this concern, some systems have opted to guarantee minority shareholder board representation through different means, such as cumulative voting.[236] China's Company Law, however, includes only an optional cumulative voting provision.[237] The Code of Corporate Governance actually does require listed firms with a dominant shareholder that owns more than 30 percent of the votes to have cumulative voting for the selection of directors and supervisors.[238] However, as mentioned earlier, the Code is rarely enforced and merely offers a standard setting. Surprisingly, a recent study found that a large majority of PRC listed firms have included cumulative voting in their articles of association. Yet, the formal adoption of cumulative voting in these firms had only limited implication

[233] For examples in the United States, see, for example, Delaware General Corporation Law, Del. Code tit. 8 § 141. See also Model Bus. Corp. Act § 8.01 (AM. BAR ASS'N, 2002). Conversely, according to the PRC corporate law, the shareholders' assembly is defined as "the company's organ of power." 2005 Company Law, art. 98.

[234] 2005 Company Law, art. 108, arts. 46–48.

[235] 2005 Company Law, arts. 37, 99.

[236] Non-controlling shareholders' board representation is required in Italy. See Erede, note 223, at 350–354.

[237] 2005 Company Law, art. 105. ("A shareholders' assembly *may adopt* a cumulative voting system to elect the directors or supervisors according to the bylaw or its resolutions.") (emphasis added.)

[238] Code of Corporate Governance, note 95, art. 31.

in practice. Firms either did not exercise their cumulative voting mechanisms or the implementation did not bring more independence to the board through minority shareholder representation for other reasons addressed below.[239]

In sum, board members in China often turn a blind eye or even cooperate with insiders' misconduct when the controlling shareholder herself acquiesce. When board members do monitor management, they do so to protect the interests of controlling shareholders. Their incentives and ability to represent *all* shareholders are undermined. Such weakness emphasizes the importance of having other strong internal monitoring governance bodies, such as independent directors and audit committees, as well as a strong ex-post accountability regime.

Independent Directors

Over the last two decades, particularly following the wave of corporate scandals of the early 2000s, independent directors have become an important element of corporate governance and the focus of corporate legal reform in many countries.[240] While legal systems use different terms and definitions for this internal governance institution, independent directors everywhere are expected to monitor corporate control parties (either generally or with respect to specific transactions).

This development in corporate governance did not skip China. China's Company Law contains a general and obscure provision about independent directors, leaving the matter to secondary regulation.[241] Among the various relevant rules,[242] the most pertinent and comprehensive set of rules is the CSRC-issued 2001

[239] C. Xi & Y. Chen, "Does Cumulative Voting Matter? The Case of China: An Empirical Assessment," *European Business Organization Law Review* 15 (2014) 585.

[240] In the United States, the main relevant governance reforms include the 2002 Sarbanes-Oxley Act, the 2003 revisions in NYSE and Nasdaq listing rules, and the 2010 Dodd-Frank Act. See generally R. W. Masulis et al., "Directors: Older and Wiser, or Too Old to Govern?" (European Corp. Governance Inst., Finance Working Paper No. 584/2018, 2018), https://ssrn.com/abstract=3284874. A greater role for independent directors is reported in the United Kingdom following the release of the Cadbury Report, and similar trends are observed in Japan in the same period. For a review of this trend, see Clarke, *The Independent Director*, note 41, at 150–175.

[241] 2005 Company Law, art. 122. ("A listed company shall have independent directors. The concrete measures shall be formulated by the State Council."). This provision applies specifically to publicly listed firms and not to joint stock companies more generally.

[242] Guiding Opinions for Introducing Independent Directors to the Board of Directors of Listed Companies, [关于在上市公司建立独立董事制度的指导意见], promulgated by the China Sec. Reg. Comm'n., Aug. 16, 2001 [Independent Directors Guidance]; Code of Corporate Governance, note 95, which includes "best practices" guidance with no specific number of independent directors nor specific powers prescribed for conflicted transactions); CRSC 2004 Provisions, *supra* note 769; CSRC Guidelines for the Articles of Association of Listed Companies (2016 Amendment) [上市公司章程指引(2016年修订)], promulgated by China Sec. Reg. Comm'n, Sept. 30, 2016 (which in article 96 limit the number of "inside directors" to no more than 50 percent of all directors but define them as those who concomitantly serve as executives or employee representatives – therefore opting not to refer to their independence from other controlling parties); Guidelines for the Performance of Duties by Independent Directors of Listed Companies [上市公司独立董事履职指引], promulgated by the China Assoc. for Pub. Companies (CAPO), Sept. 12, 2014 (a national self-regulatory nonprofit organization, supervised by the CSRC, that issues recommended best practices to listed firms).

Independent Directors Guidance for Listed Firms (here, Independent Director Guidance, or the Guidance).[243] Per the Guidance, one-third of the total number of directors on the board of any listed company should be independent, with at least one independent director being an "accounting professional." Listed companies are required to establish the mechanism in their articles of association.[244]

The Guidance imposed on independent directors "a duty of good faith and due diligence and care to the firm and all its shareholders." They "shall protect the overall interests of the company and shall be especially concerned with protecting the interests of minority shareholders from being infringed."[245] To that end, the Guidance limits the number of firms in which an independent director can hold a similar concomitant position to five, and emphasizes their independence from the "influence of the company's major shareholders, actual controllers, or other entities or persons who are interested parties of the listed company."[246] From this, it seems clear that the CSRC took the position that an independent director should serve the interests of the company while protecting particularly public shareholders and being free from the influence of any interested party.

Various powers are formally conferred upon independent directors. They are given a role in the auditing, nomination, and compensation board committees, of which they should constitute at least half of the members "when such committees are set

[243] Independent Directors Guidance, note 242. The Guidance was, and still is, the most detailed effort to establish the institution of independent directors in Chinese listed companies, but it was not the first. There had been prior initiatives at various administrative levels – local governments, central ministries, stock exchanges, and the CSRC itself – of various scopes and varying degrees of commitment. For a complete review, see Clarke, *The Independent Director*, note 41, at 175–201. Clarke's review shows how the CSRC in its draft and prior efforts actually aimed to establish a far more rigorous independent director mechanism that would have had broader and more specific powers in the firm than those finally established by the Guidance.

[244] Independent Directors Guidance, note 242, art. I.3.

[245] Ibid., art. I.2.

[246] Ibid. The "Independence Requirement" is further made clear, in article III (emphasis added): "III. Independent directors shall meet the "independence" requirements:
A person may not hold the position of the independent director in any of the following circumstances:

1. a *person who holds a position in the listed company or its affiliated enterprises, their direct relatives and major social relations* (direct relatives refer to their spouse, father, mother and children etc.; major social relations [these are also based on familial ties] refer to their brothers, sisters, father-in-law, mother-in-law, daughter-in-law, son-in-law, spouse of their brothers, sisters, and their spouse's brothers and sisters etc.);
2. a person who *holds more than 1 percent* of the outstanding shares of the listed company *directly or indirectly, or the natural person shareholders of the 10 largest shareholders of the listed company, or such shareholder's direct relative*;
3. a person who *holds a position in a unit which holds more than 5 percent of the outstanding shares of the listed company directly or indirectly, or of the unit which ranks as one of the 5 largest shareholders of the listed company, or such employee's direct relative*;
4. a person meeting any of the three above-mentioned conditions in the immediately preceding year;
5. a *person providing financial, legal or consulting services to the listed company or its subsidiaries*;
6. a person stipulated in the articles of association;
7. a person determined by the CSRC."

up."[247] They are given the power to approve major related-party transactions before such transactions are submitted to board discussion.[248] They can propose engagement with an accounting firm to the board and propose that the board of directors call a special shareholders' meeting or a meeting of the board. Independent directors can appoint outside auditors and consultants, and they can solicit proxies before a shareholders' meeting is held.[249] Nonetheless, none of these powers are binding except perhaps the power to approve major related-party transactions. The binding effect of that approval is also questionable considering that noncompliance requires merely a disclosure.

Independent directors are also required to offer an opinion on certain matters, including decisions on the appointment, dismissal, and remunerations of other directors and senior managers. An opinion is also required on any event that the independent director considers to be detrimental to the interests of minority shareholders.[250] Where the matter is subject to public disclosure by other laws and regulations, their opinion should also be disclosed, and where consensus was not reached, their opinions should be disclosed separately.[251] While these disclosure provisions seem relatively far reaching and might lead independent directors to perform their role in earnest, they might also cause them to suppress their judgment, side with their peers to reach a consensus, or simply default to a no-comment opinion for fear of retaliation by the interested parties.

Existing studies show that most companies have followed the Guidance with respect to the appointment requirements of independent directors and made relevant bylaw amendments.[252] This fact alone, however, does not say much about the directors' performance of the above roles in practice or the benefit to shareholders and corporate governance more generally. Even in the general literature, there is skepticism

[247] Ibid., art. V.4.

[248] Ibid., art. V.1.a (defining "Major related-party transactions" as transactions with related parties in whose "total value exceeds RMB 3 million or 5 percent of the company's net assets audited recently").

[249] Ibid., art. V.4.1.b-f.

[250] Ibid., art. VI.

("1. Apart from carrying out the above-mentioned duties, the independent director shall provide the independent opinion on the following matters to the board of the directors or to the shareholders' meeting:

a. Nomination, appointment or replacement of directors;
b. Appointment or dismissal of senior managers;
c. Remuneration for directors and senior managers;
d. Any existing or new loan borrowed from the listed company by or other funds transfer made by the company's shareholders, actual controllers or affiliated enterprises that exceeds RMB three million or 5 percent of the company's net assets audited recently, and whether the company has taken effective measures to collect the amount due;
e. Events that the independent director considers to be detrimental to the interests of minority shareholders;
f. Other matters stipulated by the articles of association.")

[251] Ibid., arts. VI.2, VI.3. The Guidance does not make clear whether the identity of each independent director should be disclosed along with her opinion.

[252] Clarke, *The Independent Director*, note 41, at 200.

about the ability of independent directors to effectively perform their oversight role, particularly where controlling shareholders exist.[253] The debate around the practical contribution of this institution to corporate governance and firm performance is unsettled.[254] With respect to China, the value brought by independent directors to shareholders and the functional efficacy of this monitoring mechanism are questionable and studies produced vague and even conflicting results. Given that the Guidance has been in effect for two decades, these aspects can now be retested.[255]

Even on a theoretical level, an inspection of the Guidance and related legal framework reveals three major impediments that clearly stand in the way of making independent directors effective monitors in China. First, controlling or dominant shareholders can ultimately elect independent directors. According to the Guidance, the board of directors, supervisory board, and shareholders who independently or jointly hold more than 1 percent of the shares may nominate independent directors.[256] The shareholders' meeting then elects the nominees by majority vote. The very nature of the independence of independent directors is therefore questionable when independent directors might feel that they owe their election to a particular shareholder. The complex network of business, social, and political ties surrounding listed firms in China and the identity of the controlling shareholder,

[253] L. A. Bebchuk & A. Hamdani, "Independent Directors and Controlling Shareholders," *University of Pennsylvania Law Review* 165 (2016) 1271.

[254] See generally R. W. Masulis & E. J. Zhang, "How Valuable Are Independent Directors? Evidence from External Distractions," *Harvard Law School Forum on Corporate Governance* (May 22, 2018), https://corpgov.law.harvard.edu/2018/05/22/how-valuable-are-independent-directors-evidence-from-external-distractions/ ("empirical assessments of the value of independent directors are decidedly mixed, leaving the value of independent directors an important unsettled question in the literature").

[255] Clarke's review includes the limited empirical research that was available at the time, which mainly examined the characteristics of independent directors (educational and professional background and their salary).

More recent studies include: J. Ma & T. Khanna, "Independent Directors' Dissent on Boards: Evidence from Listed Companies in China," *Strategic Management Journal* 37 (2016) 1547 (identifying scarce instances of dissent (only in 119 individual cases within 24,212 independent directors' opinions), finding that dissent is more likely when there is an "end game" situation in the firm); X. Tang et al., "The Effectiveness of the Mandatory Disclosure of Independent Directors' Opinions: Empirical Evidence from China," *Journal of Accounting & Public Policy* 32 (2013) 89 (independent directors' "NO" opinion signals negatively to public shareholders and affect firm value); L. Wang, "Protection or Expropriation: Politically Connected Independent Directors in China," *Journal of Banking & Finance* 55 (2015) 92 (based on 7,487 firm observations between 2003 and 2012, the author suggests that politically connected independent directors enlarge the magnitude of related-party transactions with the controlling party in both listed privately controlled firms and listed local SOEs. Notwithstanding, the author also concludes that a large fraction of politically connected independent directors increases firm value in Chinese-listed privately controlled firms but is detrimental to firm value of listed SOEs, especially those under local-government control); K. Lin et al., "Voice or Exit? Independent Director Decisions in an Emerging Economy" (Oct. 22, 2012) (SSRN paper), https://papers.ssrn.com/sol3/papers.cfm?abstract_id=2166876 (finding that independent directors are more likely to resign than to dissent when they have private information about adverse corporate events.).

[256] Independent Directors Guidance, note 242, art. IV.1. Before elections, proposed nominees should first be approved by the applicable branch of the CSRC. Ibid., art. IV.3.

commonly a state body,[257] make a truly independent director uncommon.[258] For example, despite the procedures set in the Guidance, a recent study found that the chairman of the board in firms, usually the representative of the controlling shareholder, "handpicks" nearly all independent directors from his or her own social network.[259]

Second, under the current legal framework, there seems to be no positive motivation for independent directors to fulfill their intended roles, nor are there any legal consequences for directors or firms that violate the Guidance. This makes the entire intent behind the mechanism dubious. While the general fear of liability under fiduciary duties and procedures established in the 2005 Company Law may motivate independent directors,[260] these general incentives are the same as for inside directors. As Clarke points out, nothing in the legal framework would make independent directors act differently from inside directors.[261] In addition, the binding power of the Guidance is unclear. As a matter of black letter law, the failure to comply with the Independent Directors Guidance (or any other provision pertaining to independent directors under the relevant legal framework) does not seem to constitute illegality or lead to any specific formal enforcement by the CSRC. The CSRC may pressure companies to comply in various soft power-ways, and the general fear of delisting might also encourage compliance, but the Guidance itself does not prescribe any administrative sanctions. This ambiguity concerning enforcement practically renders the implementation of the Guidance selective and leaves it in the hands of firms and their controlling insiders. There is no reason to assume that dominant or controlling shareholders would selectively appoint truly independent supervisors over their heads, particularly given the mixed evidence on the effect of the mechanism on market value.

It is still possible that the pressure of the reputation market would incentivize independent directors, once selected, to monitor on behalf of public shareholders.[262] The market for independent directors is likely much sounder today than it was when the Guidance was established, and reputation can now play a significant role. However, a 2016 study that examined independent directors' dissents found that

[257] The independence criteria are focused on independence from natural persons, not institutions. See ibid., art. III.

[258] A striking example of this was brought by Clarke, quoting a statement of the dean of Changjiang School of Business about his service as an independent director: "I have never thought that the independent director is the protector of medium and small shareholders; never think that. My job is first and foremost to protect the interests of the large shareholder, because the large shareholder is the state." Clarke, *Blowback*, note 35, at 43.

[259] Ma & Khanna, *Dissent on Boards*, note 255, at 1549.

[260] On the firm's right to sue on violations of fiduciary duties, see 2005 Company Law, art. 151. For shareholders' standing with respect to violations of any law, administrative regulation, or bylaws that damaged shareholders' interests, see ibid., art. 152.

[261] Clarke, *The Independent Director*, note 41, at 209–210.

[262] For the effect of the reputation and managerial labor market as external monitoring mechanisms, see discussion below.

dissent rates dropped drastically *after* 2006. Independent directors thereafter generally deferred to top management.[263] While the authors did not offer any causal inferences, it is possible that this was a result of a regulatory change. The inclusion of the independent director mechanism in the 2005 Company Law, or possibly the parallel reform that exposed previously untradeable state shares to market forces for the first time, could have pushed independent directors to be less confrontational, perhaps fearing retaliation by corporate control parties. The evidence of their decreasing dissents might thus reflect that gaining the support of internal corporate control parties substitutes for reputation in the external labor market for future appointments.

Finally, nothing since the Independent Directors Guidance was established has changed the fact that the "requirements" in the Guidance are not mandatory. Firms can still avoid being considered "violators" – and thus avoid repercussions – simply by disclosing their failure to comply with the relevant regulations. A failure to comply with any of the provisions does not automatically invalidate a decision.[264]

Given the above, it seems that despite the adoption of the independent director institution in most listed firms in China today, and regardless of its potential effects on market value on which the evidence is inconclusive, independent directors generally do not function to secure the interests of public investors or monitor against corporate malfeasance by corporate control parties.

Supervisory Board

The PRC's dual board structure combines an Anglo-American style board of directors and a German style supervisory board. In addition to the board of directors, any joint stock company must have a board of supervisors with employee electors. At first glance, it seems that the structure is a transplant of Germany's two-tiered board and co-determination mechanisms.[265] However, the Chinese dual board structure is very different from Germany's mechanism and is widely considered a failure. China's 2005 Company Law does mandate that firm employees elect one-third of the supervisory board members and the general shareholders' meeting elects the rest.[266] The supervisory board is authorized to examine the financial affairs of the company; to propose the removal of directors and senior managers who violated their duties, laws, regulations, company bylaws, or shareholders' resolutions, and under certain conditions initiate a derivative lawsuit following such violation; to demand that the violators rectify their actions; to propose a shareholder meeting or to assemble one where the board of directors fail to

[263] Ma & Khanna, *Dissent on Boards*, note 255, at 1550.

[264] Independent Directors Guidance, note 242, art. V.3.

[265] I discuss the German board structure further below under both the Creditors and Employee Monitoring subsections.

[266] 2005 Company Law, arts. 53, 117, 188. Moreover, article 108 enables the board of directors in CLSs to have employees-elected representatives as well. Ibid., art. 108.

do so; and to put forward proposals at a shareholders meeting. The supervisory board members may also observe the meetings of the board of directors as nonvoters.[267]

However, unlike its German inspiration, not only is there no hierarchical relationship between the PRC's supervisory board and the board of directors, but these two supposedly monitoring bodies also lack independence from the controlling shareholder. The supervisory board has no power whatsoever with respect to appointing members to the board of directors, these are elected by the general shareholders' meeting – which is, again, dominated by the controlling shareholder. Any attempt to empower this institution, which theoretically is supposed to have a supervising function, is entirely missing from both laws and regulations.[268]

Legal reforms and various regulations that have been instituted over the years concerning the governance of PRC listed firms did not even try to correct the sheer irrelevance of the supervisory board. Some options that could have made the supervisory board more relevant to firm governance include granting negative veto rights or requiring the approval of the supervisory board for certain board decisions. Thus, instead of constraining the power of control parties or providing any kind of monitoring mechanism that would benefit employees or public shareholders, the Chinese dual board structure further entrenches the power of those dominating the firm.

Audit Committee and/or other Special Committees

Some legal systems have installed special committees to address intrinsic power imbalances in the ownership structure of firms in their market. These committees are often involved in the approval process for suspicious transactions, in which conflicts of interests are inherent and the independence of traditional governing bodies is compromised. In Israel, for example, the company law mandates the creation of an audit committee with both independent directors and a majority of outside directors, as well as a compensation committee, in every listed firm.[269] The audit committee consists of at least a majority of independent directors. It is entrusted with auditing the conduct of management and with approving certain related-party transactions, while guaranteeing a competitive pricing negotiation process. In certain cases, the audit committee basically receives power to veto the transaction even before it is brought to the board. Israel's compensation committee is tasked with

[267] Especially since cumulative voting is currently not mandatory, note 237 and the accompanying text. See Clarke, *The Independent Director,* note 41, note at 161–162, 173–175 (discussing the supervisory board in Germany and the failure of the supervisory board mechanism in China).

[268] The supervisory board is authorized: to examine the financial affairs of the company; to propose the removal of directors and senior managers who violated their duties, laws, regulations, company bylaws, or shareholders' resolutions, and under certain conditions initiate a derivative lawsuit following such violation; to demand that the violators rectify their actions; to propose a shareholder meeting or to assemble one where the board of directors fail to do so; and to put forward proposals at a shareholders meeting. The supervisory board members may also observe the meetings of the board of directors as non-voters. 2005 Company Law, arts. 52–54, 117–118, 152.

[269] Israel Company Law, 5759–1999, § 114, 115, 117, 118(a), 118(b) 1 LSI 44 (1999).

creating compensation guidelines as well as with approving the compensation of high-ranking company officers every three years.[270] The Israeli regulator designed these mechanisms to handle the inherent conflicts and power imbalances within Israel's capital market, in which firms' ownership reflects strong controlling shareholders and, until recently, concentrated business groups.

In contrast with this regulatory action, China's company and securities laws and regulations do not mandate the creation of similar audit committees or other special committees. As mentioned earlier, independent directors are given a role in the board's auditing, nomination, and compensation committees "if such committees are set up," in which case they should constitute at least half of the members.[271] Thus, internal auditing, including scrutiny of related-party transactions, is left in the hands of the internal governing bodies and is therefore tainted with the problems pertaining to those bodies.[272]

Other Corporate Constituents

In many concentrated markets, corporate governance accommodates a role for stakeholders who do not own any equity interest in the firm. Such nonshareholder constituents have some disciplinary power over corporate insiders. While these constituents monitor in their own interest, their interests sometimes coincide with those of public shareholders.

Creditors

Creditors are perceived to have both the ability, through contractual loan covenants, and the incentives to monitor corporate conduct. Since their earnings are based on interest rates and on the firm's residual assets upon liquidation, which both depend on the firm's financial stability, they would like to see the firm maximize its value. Therefore, conventional wisdom goes, creditors monitor corporate conduct toward this goal. This aligns their interests with those of shareholders to some degree as long as the firm is not facing insolvency. By the same logic, high leverage is known to discipline managers since high levels of debt lead to close monitoring by creditors.[273] In addition, political economies in different systems have created an institutional setting in which creditors own shares in listed firms, thereby aligning the interests of creditors and shareholders more directly.

It is important to distinguish between various types of creditors, which can be roughly classified into external debt providers, such as banks and other loan-providing

[270] For further details on these committees, see I. Fiegenbaum & A. Licht, "Corporate Law of Israel." In C. Walter et al. (eds.), *The Law of Israel* (2019) 10 (noting that, "In addition to these statutorily mandated committees, recent court decisions have facilitated the adoption of ad hoc 'Special Independent Committees'. Purporting to rely on customs and precedents from Delaware courts [...].").

[271] Independent Directors Guidance, note 242, art. V.4.

[272] For scrutiny over related-party transactions and financial audits by external institutions (such as the CSRC and the Stock Exchanges), see below.

[273] M. C. Jensen, "The Eclipse of the Public Corporation," *Harvard Business Review* 67 (1989) 6.

financial institutions, and corporate bond holders. While the interests of these creditors are similar, their characteristics differ in ways that affect their ability to monitor. For example, corporate bond holders' access to information largely depends on the efficacy of information disclosure in a given market. Widely dispersed corporate bond holders' ability to monitor often depends on third-party intermediary institutions, such as trustees, underwriters, and credit rating agencies. In addition, for corporate bond holders to have any disciplinary effect on corporate conduct, they need a well-functioning, liquid debt market through which they can trade their bonds. Finally, since bond issuance agreements are mainly based on boilerplate provisions and rarely provide covenants that involve bond holders in the governance of corporations, corporate bond holders largely depend on ex-post legal enforcement to have their rights protected.

On the other hand, institutional providers of external debt, such as banks, can establish effective information disclosure processes in their loan agreements and are less dependent on other intermediaries. They are better positioned to negotiate for loan covenants that will require their consent for certain corporate acts, thus giving them more direct monitoring capacity. Banks typically also have enough incentive and means to monitor without the need for coalition building. Finally, while banks do sometimes require the help of enforcing institutions (especially for liquidation proceedings), they are less dependent on them and can rely on their financial position and reputation market sanctions in a repeat-transaction environment.

The most-known examples of systems that have encouraged corporate monitoring by financial institutions as external debt providers are those of Japan and Germany. In both systems, this was achieved through parallel equity stakes that large financial intermediaries held in firms. Furthermore, in both systems, the role of financial intermediaries in corporate governance was guided by certain industrial organizational structures and the local political economy that buttressed their preferred monitoring position. In Japan, cross-holding ownership structures within Japanese post-war conglomerates, the horizontal Keiretsu, relied on a main bank to provide each business group with credit, while holding concomitant shares in the borrowing firms. This has historically positioned the main banks at an informational advantage to monitor poor performance in industrial firms.[274]

In Germany, despite some decrease in ownership concentration, there is still a continued emphasis on the interests of third-party stakeholders, including creditors, which are given a path for direct involvement in the affairs of the corporation. This is achieved mainly through the two-tier board system and the mechanism known as

[274] M. Aoki, "Controlling Insider Control: Issues of Corporate Governance in Transition Economies." In M. Aoki & H. K. Kim (eds.), *Corporate Governance in Transitional Economies* (The World Bank, 1995), 3; R. J. Gilson & M. J. Roe, "Understanding the Japanese Keiretsu: Overlaps between Corporate Governance and Industrial Organization," *Yale Law Journal* (1993) 871; C. J. Milhaupt, "On the (Fleeting) Existence of the Main Bank System and Other Japanese Economic Institutions," *Law & Social Inquiry* 27 (2001) 425.

"co-determination."[275] As part of this corporate governance institution, employees and shareholders elect equal numbers of representatives to the supervisory board of large corporations. The supervisory board then appoints the members of the firm's "management board." Since banks in Germany function not only as creditors but also exert influence as direct and indirect shareholders, and in addition act as something like trustees for public investors, banks often de facto exercise the public shareholders' voting power by proxy. This includes the vote on the selection of supervisory board members and, by extension, management board members. Consequently, the banks' monitoring role as creditors is enhanced through a parallel shareholder (and proxy) position, which gives them access to information and positions them to engage, and sometimes even control, the decision-making process.[276]

As one of the richest economies in the world set in a social democratic political system, which has historically strong banks and weak securities markets, Germany offers an interesting model for comparison with China. Indeed, in China too, while shareholding by financial institutions is slowly being more viable, capital financing is still overwhelmingly led by bank lending rather than by equity capital.[277] As opposed to Germany or Japan, however, China's state-owned commercial banks act exclusively as creditors of listed companies because direct equity investment by commercial banks in nonfinancial business enterprises is largely prohibited.[278]

Historically, and to a large degree today, Chinese banks have been conduits of the state and based their lending decisions on political guidance rather than on sound financial considerations. Being connected to the state, therefore, China's main banks lack a "monitoring culture" as well as incentives to monitor. Indeed,

[275] J. W. Cioffi, "Restructuring "Germany Inc.": The Politics of Company and Takeover Law Reform in Germany and the European Union," *Law & Policy* 24 (2002) 355, at 362–368.

[276] The proxy-vote system in Germany provides banks with effective voting powers, as historically the bank that owns shares in the listed firm is also the firm's main creditor Yet, there has been some regression in the scope of monitoring by large banks over recent years M. Goergen et al., "Recent Developments in German Corporate Governance," *International Review of Law and Economics* 28(3) (2008) 175, at 178–186.

[277] Bank debt financing dominates over equity financing which stayed below 5 percent of total bank loans in quantity according to Z. Chen et al., "The Asset Management Industry in China: Its Past Performance and Future Prospects," *The Journal of Portfolio Management* 41(5) (2015), at 12 (measured 1991–2013)). See C. Edelmann et al., "Asset Management in China," Oliver Wyman (Aug. 2014), www.oliverwyman.com/our-expertise/insights/2014/aug/asset-management-in-china.html#.VmTbPa6rRE5 (noting that in 2014, the bulk of China's $145 trillion financial assets were either bank deposits or low risk securities).

[278] Law of the People's Republic of China on Commercial Banks [中华人民共和国商业银行法], promulgated by the Standing Comm. Nat'l People's Cong., May 10, 1995, last amended Aug. 29, 2015, art. 43 [Law on Commercial Banks] (prohibiting such equity investment by commercial banks unless otherwise provided by regulation). Exceptions to the general prohibition were implemented by a debt-for-equity swap scheme during the late 1990s that allowed indirect equity holding through AMCs. A similar scheme intended to handle nonperforming loans and extreme corporate leverage was in the making in more recent years. See L. Wei, "China Is Set to Allow Banks to Swap Bad Loans for Equity in Borrowers," *Wall Street Journal* (Apr. 15, 2016), www.wsj.com/articles/china-plans-debt-for-equity-swap-program-to-help-reduce-corporate-debt-1460649581.

an important critique of the design of China's company law is that it emphasizes creditors' protection against "their own misguided lending decisions" rather than enlisting the help of banks in monitoring corporations.[279] Even more striking is the finding that banks continue to lend to firms even in the face of clear cases of continuous tunneling by controlling shareholders.[280]

One result is the low default rate of distressed companies, which distorts the market to not reflect risk properly. By the late 1990s, the financial system was insolvent due to an extreme level of bank lending to failing SOEs and consequent levels of nonperforming loans. Despite several efforts to rehabilitate and restructure the system, the phenomena of "bad debt" and "soft budget constraints" continue to threaten China's financial strength and resilience (especially from the provincial level down), as seen in the last fallout in China's real estate development sector and its impact on financial and social stability.

Over recent years, it seems that the Party-state is more willing to consider direct equity holding by commercial banks in nonfinancial business enterprises. The Chinese government looks to solve onerous debt burdens seen in many of the PRC's large listed companies, and the central government encourages further rounds of debt-for-equity swaps through various schemes.[281] While China enlisted asset management companies (AMCs) to recapitalize the banks' nonperforming loans in the past,[282] the AMCs were not found to be effective monitors due to the political clout of the debtor's business group and their own government ownership.[283] But in 2016, for the first publicly celebrated time, direct bank equity holdings were implemented through a debt-equity swap in China Huarong Energy Ltd.[284] To note, the Law on

[279] D. C. Clarke, "The Role of Non-Legal Institutions in Chinese Corporate Governance." In H. Kanda et al. (eds.), *Transforming Corporate Governance in East Asia* (Routledge, 2009), at 175–176, note 17.

[280] M. Qian & B. Y. Yeung, "Bank Financing and Corporate Governance," *Journal of Corporate Finance* 32 (2015) 258.

[281] L. Ying, "Li Keqiang: Reform and Improve the Financial System" [李克强：要改革完善金融监管体系], China Network (Mar. 16, 2016), https://archive.ph/oGCVA. See also Opinions on Enhancing the Reform of Financial Investments System [关于深化投融资体制改革的意见], promulgated by the CCP Central Comm. and St. Council, July 5, 2016, art. 10 (pilot projects in which financial institutions will hold equity in enterprises).

[282] Four AMCs were created in 1999, carved out of the big four banks to purchase the respective bank's nonperforming loans. Organized as wholly state-owned corporations held by the Ministry of Finance, these "non-bank financial institutions" issued their own bonds to the banks to fund the purchase of the nonperforming loans, which were then converted to equity. The Ministry of Finance directly guaranteed the AMC bonds. It was intended that AMCs would act to discipline the poorly performing corporations and push for their restructuring when needed.

[283] Clarke, *The Role of Non-Legal Institutions*, note 279, at 177.

[284] The first publicly announced case of a debt-to-equity swap that resulted in direct bank equity holdings in an industrial company was approved in March 2016, whereby a total of RMB 17.1 billion (USD 2.6b) worth of debt in China Huarong Energy Ltd (a shipbuilding company) was converted to shares and distributed among various banks and financial-institution creditors, resulting in the issuance of fourteen percent equity shares to the Bank of China, which became the dominant shareholder in the company after the issuance. See L. Wei, "China Regulators Speed Up Help for Banks on Bad Loans," *Wall Street Journal* (Mar. 13, 2016), www.wsj.com/articles/chinese-regulators-speed-up-bad-loans-1457871782.

Commercial Banks was not yet amended to formally allow direct equity investments by commercial banks.

It will be interesting to see if the set of incentives directing the banks' role will change following the expected increase in their direct equity holdings. If applied on a large scale, this could better align the interests of Chinese banks, as creditor-shareholders, with those of public shareholders. There is a possibility that this would push banks, as equity-investing creditors, toward real financial monitoring, thus leading to more disciplined management of distressed assets and better risk assessment and allocation.

The obvious caveats in this scenario should be noted. Due to the clashing power hierarchy between national firms and leading banks, it is unlikely that the banks will be permitted to have a dominant equity position in firms where a dominant central or local state shareholder already exists. Without a dominant position, marginal bank holding will most likely not create enough incentives for the bank to monitor existing powerful, often politically connected, corporate control parties. Furthermore, and paradoxically, since most banks belong to the state, even if permitted to hold a dominant equity position in firms, there is no reason to believe that the bank will be any different than other state-affiliated controlling shareholders. If at all, they are tied up much more directly to the Party-state's industrial development goals. Thus, theory aside, financial institutions are still instruments of the Party-state and continue to be guided by interests that are different from those of public minority shareholders.

As for the corporate bond market in China and its potential monitoring capacity, there is a similar if not identical political factor. While China's bond market is currently the second largest bond market in the world, trailing behind only the United States, most of the bond market consists of government bonds (central and local) and financial institutions' bonds. Only about a third of the entire bond market are corporate bonds (increased from 10 percent in 2014).[285] While this does not necessarily preclude the monitoring capacity of corporate bond holders, it does suggest that considering the large scope of debt financing versus equity financing and the sheer size of bank loans within it, the market influence of corporate bondholders is relatively small.

In addition, according to data, in 2014, the main corporate bond holders in China were commercial banks with 63 percent of corporate bonds, while individuals represented only 2 percent of corporate bond holders. The composition of holders started changing significantly since 2015, diversified by new entrants mostly wealth management firms. Still, in 2021, foreign institutions, individuals, and nonfinancial firms

[285] In 2002, the corporate bond market represented only 2.8 percent of the total bond market. Kim et al., *Developing Institutional Investors in the PRC*, note 219, at 27–30. *Cf.* H. Xie, *A Changing Bond Landscape in China* (2014), S&P 2014 Report, *with* Seafarer, "The Evolution of China's Bond Market," White Paper July 2021, www.seafarerfunds.com/commentary/the-evolution-of-chinas-bond-market/.

held only 15 percent of the bond market. Most holders of bonds are thus commercial banks and wealth management firms related to the Chinese Party-state (central and the local governments) still today.[286] The common bond holders in China, therefore, are the same credit financiers that provide corporate loans – China's financial institutions, sharing the same characteristics and facing the same impediments to monitoring. Here too firms are shielded through implicit or explicit guarantees by the state.[287] In a cyclical manner, the failure of the general debt market to default distressed firms causes bond holders, as other creditors, to price their risk on the basis of other considerations, such as political connections, rather than on the financial stability of the debtors. This low-risk environment lowers the cost of debt financing and erases creditors' motivation to monitor.

Employees

The embrace of co-determination in China reflects an ambivalent approach toward employee board representation. On the one hand, employee board representation has been an enduring feature of Chinese company law and survived throughout its various legal reforms.[288] China's Company Law still mandates that firm employees elect one-third of the *supervisory* board members of CLSs and the general shareholders meeting elects the rest. Thus, without any share ownership requirement, China's co-determination legal provision could presumably give rise to engagement in governance by employee constituents.[289] While the interests of employees and public shareholders might not always align, both share a general interest in maximizing firm revenue. For employees, it provides job security and can lead to higher salaries; for shareholders, it offers higher profits through dividends or share price increase. Both constituent groups should therefore strive to minimize value-reducing activities through monitoring against management waste, abuse, and corruption.

On the other hand, as mentioned in the context of the supervisory board, the law takes only an enabling approach concerning representation of employees on the board of directors itself. Moreover, absent a hierarchical relationship between the supervisory board and the board of directors, the Chinese dual-board structure is largely failing, and with it, the co-determination mechanism loses its bite. Even within the supervisory board, while employees have a voice in the election of one-third of its members, the remaining two-thirds are appointed by the same body that appoints the regular board members: the shareholders' assembly – de facto, the

[286] *Cf.* S&P 2014 Report, ibid., at 3, with Seafarer, ibid.

[287] The first bond default was recorded in 2014. The number of firms (mainly private) allowed to default has grown since but is still small due to implicit guarantees mostly from local governments. For an analysis of recent default and near-default cases, see L.-W. Lin & Milhaupt, *Bonded to the State*, note 180, at 37–47 (suggesting that the "no-default norm may begin to unravel as the Chinese economy slows").

[288] *Cf.* 1993 Company law, art. 52 leaving the ratio of worker's representatives to be determined in the articles of associations, with art. 51 in the 2005 Company law on its amendments.

[289] 2005 Company Law, arts. 18, 108, 117.

controlling shareholder. Therefore, instead of monitoring the controllers' power, the Chinese dual-board structure, and the employees-constituent's representative within it, further enhances it.[290]

One might expect to see in the PRC, as a communist country, some empowerment of labor as a nonshareholder constituency, even separate from the co-determination role. Labor unions are given a formal participatory role in every PRC firm notwithstanding the lack of any share ownership.[291] However, labor union representatives at PRC firms are actually hired by firm management and are paid by the firm and therefore invariably have a close relationship with incumbent management. Labor unions and their representatives in firms are exceedingly unlikely to advocate an agenda that is supportive of oppressed minority shareholders, much less one that goes against the control parties of the firm. Furthermore, the labor union organization itself is entirely subordinated to the CCP and thus is structurally designed to promote the interests of the PRC Party-state,[292] as do the board of directors, the supervisory board, senior management, the controlling shareholder, and the firm itself.

Consumers

This section puts aside questions of corporate social responsibility or the purpose of the corporation[293] and considers customers as potential monitoring constituents of a firm. The underlying assumption here is that the consumer-base of a firm can potentially monitor corporate behavior. Consumers can push firms to produce more value, for example, reduce costs or improve quality, through consumer behavior and litigation.

Research conducted in Western liberal markets found that an increase in overall market share prices boosts consumer confidence in the economy, leading consumers to spend more. In turn, consumers' behavior in various forms, including quality monitoring and social criticism, affects the profitability of firms and induces further growth. Thus, theoretically, the performance of the stock market and consumers' behavior are mutually related.[294]

[290] Especially since cumulative voting is currently not mandatory. 2005 Company Law, art. 105.

[291] 2005 Company Law, arts. 18, 108, 117 (establishing the grounds for union involvement and presence in every China domiciled company). Art. 18 states the following "…when making a decision on restructuring or any important issue relating to business operations, or to formulate any important bylaw, a company shall solicit the opinions of its labor union, and shall solicit the opinions and proposals of the employees through the assembly of the representatives of the employees or in any other way." Ibid., art. 18.

[292] The unions are members of the "All-China Federation of Trade Unions," which is the official union organization of the Chinese Communist Party. See generally M. E. Gallagher & B. Dong, "Legislating Harmony: Labor Law Reform in Contemporary China." In S. Kuruvilla et al. (eds.), *From Iron Rice Bowl to Informalization: Markets, Workers, and the State in a Changing China* (Cornell University Press, 2011) 36, at 41–45.

[293] For example, recent analysis calls for an alternative "customer capitalism," whereby managers should be first and foremost concerned with increasing customers' satisfaction. See R. L. Martin, "The Age of Customer Capitalism," *Harvard Business Review* 88(1) (2010).

[294] W. J. Jansen & N. J. Nahuis, "The Stock Market and Consumer Confidence: European Evidence," *Economics Letters* 79 (2003) 89; S. Gupta et al., "Valuing Customers," *Journal of Marketing Research* 41(1) (2004) 7.

Throughout the first decades of economic reforms, the consumer market in China was growing but not at the same rate as economic growth. This gap called the attention of China's policymakers as it reflects and contributes to economic imbalances. Particularly with the increase in average wages and the economic shifts from low-income manufacturing industries to higher-earning services and technology-based industries over the past decade, increasing domestic consumption became a priority. The effect was shown in the growth of the consumer market. Chinese consumption is now growing at an annual rate of around 9 percent (pre-COVID), and some have predicted that it will continue growing at this rate even considering an overall economic slowdown of GDP growth to 5.5 percent below official targets.[295] More importantly, the characteristics of China's consumer base has changed to an upper-middle-class household and sophisticated consumers.

Despite growth in China's consumer base, limited research on the relationship between the stock market and consumption in China shows a weak link between capital market performance and consumer behavior.[296] It may partially derive from the small number of investors relative to population. Unofficial estimates show that less than 7 percent of urban Chinese invest in the capital market.[297] Or perhaps the limited scope of available income that retail investors put into the capital market (4 percent of household assets) might explain the attenuated relationship between consumption levels and the capital market in China.[298]

Still, the change in the characteristics of consumers suggests that Chinese consumers will become more sophisticated, demanding more value, and therefore perhaps start being more engaged with firms and their products. Provided that the institutional framework would enable such engagement, consumer activism could be on the rise.[299] A rising volume of consumers' complaints through the media, particularly social media, or through formal judicial proceedings would inflict reputational harm on a company and its managers, reduce profits, and damage the share price and can thus have a disciplinary effect. Therefore, the main impediments that would hold back consumers' activism in ways that effectuate disciplinary mechanisms on firm and managerial performance are intertwined with the

[295] Y. Kuo, "3 Great Forces Changing China's Consumer Market," *World Economic Forum* (Jan. 4, 2016), www.weforum.org/agenda/2016/01/3-great-forces-changing-chinas-consumer-market/.

[296] Ibid.

[297] A. R. Kroeber, "Making Sense of China's Stock Market Mess," Brookings (July 13, 2015), www.brookings.edu/opinions/making-sense-of-chinas-stock-market-mess/ (whereas, according to the same source, in the United States estimates go up to 50 percent of the population).

[298] Only 4 percent of private household asset allocation in China is invested in stocks and mutual funds. See E. Cheng, "Chinese Investors Are Putting Their Money in a Lot of Places: That Rarely Means Stocks," *CNBC News* (Aug. 15, 2018), www.cnbc.com/2018/08/15/chinese-investors-are-picking-other-assets-over-stocks.html.

[299] Mushrooming lawsuits following the introduction of consumer-rights laws even allowed press reports to be submitted as evidence of the merits of a case. C. S. Smith, "Chinese Discover Product-Liability Suits," *Wall Street Journal* (Nov. 13, 1997) (also stating that "In the three years since China's consumer-rights laws took effect, liability lawsuits have risen to more than half a million annually.").

current institutional setting of the press and of group and representative litigation in China.[300]

Managers (ownership and compensation incentives)

Allocating shares to managers and setting performance-based incentives are designed to optimize managers' performance and better align their interest with those of shareholders. These methods were used extensively during various stages of corporate reform in China to incentivize managers to increase firm productivity and profitability, particularly in SOEs.[301]

Nonetheless, a study by Jiang & Kim found that managerial ownership in China is relatively insignificant and therefore plays a limited governance role. Managers' small percentage of ownership in China, it is argued, leaves ample incentives for the insiders to expropriate, as the value from expropriation is greater. Higher levels of managerial ownership exist in situations where the managers are also the dominant or controlling shareholders, which entrench managers and give rise to the tunneling of value through their shareholding capacity.[302]

Concerning performance-based incentives, empirical research shows that until 2007, managers in SOEs were not better compensated than managers of other types of firms, even though SOEs were much larger and continuously growing corporations.[303] This started to change in 2007. One explanation for the change had been that many large SOEs went through IPOs in the mid-2000s, the IPO released their compensation from being tied to salary levels in the government before the offering.[304] In addition, a CSRC document from December 2005 called for SOEs to adopt incentive mechanisms to enhance managers' performance. Despite these changes, performance incentives remained modest when compared to other countries[305] and are limited de facto due to explicit and implicit caps on the compensation of managers in SOEs which affect the market at large. Such caps are in place presumably to avoid social unrest over individual capital accumulation, as well as to reduce the undisciplined use of operational costs that bite into the profitably of SOEs.[306]

[300] The media is discussed below as part of market gatekeepers. The court system, specifically the status of group and representative litigations are discussed below as well.

[301] For empirical research on various methods of managerial incentives in China (such as profit responsibility contracts and profit retention methods), see T. Kato & C. Long, "Executive Compensation, Firm Performance, and Corporate Governance in China: Evidence from Firms Listed in the Shanghai and Shenzhen Stock Exchanges," *Economic Development and Cultural Change* 54(4) (2006) 945, at 948.

[302] Jiang & Kim, note 49, at 197 Table 5, 206 and the references therein.

[303] C.-E. Bai & L. C. Xu, "Incentives for CEOs with Multitasks: Evidence from Chinese State-owned Enterprises," *Journal of Comparative Economics* 33(3) (2005) 517.

[304] Jiang & Kim, note 49, p. 199 Table 8, 203.

[305] Jiang & Kim, note 49, at 203 (in 2012 the median compensation for top managers of SOEs was 470,000 RMB, which was equal roughly to USD 77,000).

[306] X. Mu, "China Ties SOE Employees' Salaries to Profitability," China Daily (June 4, 2015), https://archive.ph/tnqHM.

Other incentives for managers in China are informal pay benefits,[307] such as on-the-job consumption that was found to exceed the average executive pay by *two to fifty* times,[308] hidden payments, and nonpecuniary benefits. The latter includes particularly the prospect of professional advancement to higher ranking positions in the government or the Party.[309]

The evidence of the power of such benefits to incentivize better performing managers is inconclusive. Some studies show that certain nonpecuniary benefits and "hidden payments" with no specific disclosure obligations, such as travel allowances, business entertainment expenses, housing, office expenses, and overseas training, correlate with better firm performance in SOEs.[310] These findings suggest that in Chinese state-controlled listed firms, nonpecuniary benefits and the hope for future promotions in the Party-state system substitute for managerial ownership and compensation in terms of their incentivizing power. Yet, another study found that hidden on-the-job consumption does not positively correlate, and might actually have a significant negative correlation, with company earnings in SOEs.[311]

Either way, while these components influence managerial conduct one way or the other, they do not align the interests of managers with those of public shareholders specifically. Thus, while they may have a disciplinary effect on managers to conform with the goals of the supervising Party-state authority or the controlling state-shareholder, it is not necessarily a goal that increases firm value or otherwise serves the interests of the firm and all its shareholders.

2 *External Monitoring Institutions*

Beyond internal governing bodies and corporate constituents, corporate governance includes market and legal institutions that operate externally to the firm and may discipline corporate managers in ways that enhance firm value and promote the interests of public shareholders.

307 L.-W. Lin, "Behind the Numbers: State Capitalism and Executive Compensation in China," *University of Pennsylvania Asian Law Review* 12 (2016)140.

308 Yang Rong, "Research on Executive Compensation of Listed Companies of Monopolistic Industries: Based on the Job Consumption" [垄断行业企业高管薪酬问题研究:基于在职消费的视角], *Fudan Journal* (Social Sciences ed.) [复旦学报(社会科学版)] 5 (2011) 133.

309 I discuss this elaborately in Chapter 8.

310 P. Adithipyangkul et al., "Executive Perks: Compensation and Corporate Performance in China," *Asia Pacific Journal of Management* 28 (2011) 401; H. Cai et al., "Eat, Drink, Firms, Government: An Investigation of Corruption from the Entertainment and Travel Costs of Chinese Firms," *The Journal of Law & Economics* 54(1) (2011) 55; "Shrouded in Mystery: Chinese Executive Compensation and the Numbers behind the Numbers," Wharton University: Knowledge@Wharton (May 14, 2012), http://knowledge.wharton.upenn.edu/article/shrouded-in-mystery-chinese-executive-compensation-and-the-numbers-behind-the-numbers/.

311 D. Chen et al., Regulation and Non-Pecuniary Compensation in Chinese SOEs [国有企业中的薪酬管制与在职消费], *Economic Research Journal* [经济研究] 2 (2005) 92.

External Markets

The Market for Corporate Control

For widely held firms, the market for corporate control is considered one of the strongest monitoring corporate governance mechanisms.[312] The market for corporate control is generally understood to function as follows: managers who run the corporation poorly or systematically disadvantage equity investors will cause shareholders to sell their shares, with a resulting decline in share price. This will in turn increase the cost of raising new capital and will make the firm a target for takeovers by those who believe they can run it better. These potential insurgents will use the opportunity to acquire shares cheaply, gain control, and oust the existing management.[313] Where there is a market for corporate control, inefficient behavior or self-dealing by incumbent managers thus jeopardizes their own position. The threat of a takeover and market forces, therefore, function as an ongoing discipline and accountability mechanism.

In concentrated markets, however, there is usually no active market for corporate control. In such markets, the controlling shareholder elects its own nominees to the board of directors and is able to direct management absolutely. If the controlling shareholder is unsatisfied with the performance of its appointees, it will simply replace them. It is very difficult for other shareholders to oust the controlling shareholder's strong ownership position in a controlled firm.[314] Changes of corporate control in these markets have to obtain the consent of existing controlling parties. This also implies that when inefficient management stays in place, maximizing performance is presumably not the primary goal of the controlling shareholder. Alternatively, in this scenario, the controller has other means to maximize her returns on investment that are not shared with all shareholders.

As in many other markets evidencing similar concentration, in China as well there is currently almost no hostile takeover activity, and thus no market for corporate control. Nevertheless, there is some evidence that the Chinese market is developing a weak form of a market for corporate control, as limited takeover activity has surfaced in recent years. I hypothesized elsewhere on the possibility that a *partial* market for corporate control is currently underway within China's controlling apparatus – that is, between groups of powerful and politically connected firms.[315]

312 H G. Manne, "Mergers and the Market for Corporate Control," *Journal of Political Economy* 73 (1965) 110, 112–113.

313 The change of control can be affected in various ways: via a direct purchase through a merger or an acquisition or by the purchase of shares in the open market, or by replacing incumbent directors through proxy contests. In any of these ways, control over the firm shifts, and incumbent insiders will be replaced.

314 See J. Armour & B. R. Cheffins, "The Rise and Fall (?) of Shareholder Activism by Hedge Funds," *The Journal of Alternative Investments* 14(3) (2011), at 17–27.

315 Or, in firms in which the Party-state has no interests, mostly within the SME market. I also suggested how the economic disentanglement from the central Party-state may eventually empower public investors through such a budding form of a market for corporate control. See Groswald Ozery, *Minority Public Shareholders in China*, note 11, at 56–62.

Fractures within the political controlling apparatus might set the stage for an *economic disentanglement* in the current structure of firm ownership in the PRC in a way that will have implications for a market for corporate control. In the current Chinese market, business groups are still mainly clustered in specific industries and face a host of impediments regarding investment or business activity outside of their specific industry or sector. Such impediments de facto contain competition, they include strict regulation of permitted "business scopes"; specific franchising grants that create monopoly-like opportunities; path dependency resulting from the corporatization without a privatization process that produced firms tied to specific ministries and thus specific industrial sectors;[316] PRC listed firms' historic dual share structure before 2006 that allowed "state shares" to be transferred only to other state shareholders; the personnel appointment system for senior management with reshuffling of senior managers within the same industry;[317] and finally, Party-state direction and heavy regulation of M&A and takeover activity.[318]

Notwithstanding these constraints and the resulting limited competition between corporatized SOEs across sectoral lines, the Chinese Party-state is not a monolith, and neither are the firms that it has established and controls. In fact, the PRC Party-state has a myriad of internal conflicts, expressed in competition between government agencies at the central and local levels, and between party and state institutions at all levels. Nor does the Party itself lack contradictions, as conflicts exist as well within the various levels of the Party organization and among its individuals. These conflicts reduce the capacity of the PRC Party-state to act in a unified manner with respect to policy generally, or through the firms it dominates. As a result, the system often serves more particularistic interests, whether individual, institutional, local, or across "systems" (*xitong*).[319]

While this of course leads to rampant self-dealing by firm insiders, at the macro level it also gradually leads to economic disentanglement of some firms and business groups from the Party-state. This is especially striking with respect to some local government-controlled firms whose interests have alienated from those of the central Party-state. As was discussed in Chapter 6, China's economic success has

[316] See Chapter 6 on the process of corporatization.

[317] See Howson, *China's Restructured Commercial Banks*, note 11.; C.-S. Liou & C.-M. Tsai, "Between Hierarchy and the Market: Managerial Career Trajectories in China's Energy Sector." In C.-W Kou & X. Zang (eds.), *Choosing China's Leaders* (Routledge, 2014) 124.

[318] Mainly through: (1) required review by the Ministry of Commerce and its approval related to acquisitions and mergers affecting market concentration (equal to an antitrust review); (2) approval by SASAC for mergers and acquisitions involving state assets; (3) approvals by additional ancillary authorities as required according to the industry, business scope, and the involvement of foreign investors (e.g., SAFE, NDRC, and SAIC); and most importantly (4) a review by the CSRC, through its designated "M&A and Restructuring Examination Committee," which has a broad authority to regulate and handle all issues related to mergers and acquisitions of listed companies (including takeovers, and dispute resolutions in cases of hostile takeovers and the use of defensive tactics). See Huang & Chen, *Hostile Takeovers in China*, note 128.

[319] K. Lieberthal & M. Oksenberg, *Policy Making in China: Leaders, Structures, and Processes* (Princeton University Press, 1988) 135, at 141–142 (referring to "*xitong*" as an organizational concept describing vertical functional systems of hierarchy that comprise China's governing bodies).

boosted the power of local governments and local government–promoted firms. Local officials have enormous incentives to maximize economic growth in their jurisdictions, very often at the expense of national Party-state interests.

As local government–controlled firms become ever more invested in profit maximization for their own benefit, the more they try to compete on market share with other PRC firms in their same region and nationally. Mergers and acquisitions activity across industries and regions has been increasing.[320] More market-oriented competitive M&A activity can induce the sales of distressed assets, which in turn can contribute to competition and to firms' efficient operation. The consequence of this form of greater market competition between local government–controlled but listed firms might eventually bring about a partial market for corporate control between dominant blockholders (still mainly among such controlling parties).[321]

A limited number of hostile takeover battles provide examples that this form of a partial market for corporate control is indeed emerging: For instance, in October 2003, the management of ST Meiya (a textile company traded at the time on the Shenzhen stock exchange) applied defensive tactics to push against a change of control in the company,[322] which essentially resulted in the transfer of shares from one state-owned shareholder to another. In this case, the dominant shareholder of ST Meiya – Heshan State Assets Management Bureau, a city-level state asset management office – had signed a share transfer agreement to sell a 27.49 percent stake to the private Wanhe Group. It appears that this move was taken without any involvement of ST Meiya's managers, thus presumably raising alarms for their jobs. Incumbent managers obtained the support of the firm's employees (after finally making delayed payments) and together they opposed the transaction. The main justification for their "anti-takeover" action was that the intended transfer would be harmful to the firm's long-term interests since the acquirer operated in an entirely different industry and was not competent to run the company. Indeed, following these pressures, and despite its contractual obligations, the local government shareholder terminated the share transfer agreement. Instead, it made an agreement with another acquirer that was favored by the management to sell 24.99 percent of its shares. Interestingly, the second acquirer, Guanxin Foreign Trade, one of China's largest import-export enterprises, is a state-owned company.[323] In its public announcement, ST Meiya mentioned that since the new acquirer is state-owned,

[320] See B. Chen, "Chinese Mergers and Acquisitions: What's Next," Manzella Report (July 1, 2015), www.manzellareport.com/index.php/strategies-section/1014-chinese-mergers-and-acquisitions-what-s-next (reporting on a number of 1,536 M&A transactions that were closed in 2014, the majority of which (65 percent) related to SOEs restructuring). See also Dezan Shira & Associates, "Understanding Mergers and Acquisitions in China," *China Briefing*, 166, June–July 2016, www.iberchina.org/files/2016/mergers-acquisitions-in-china.pdf (reviewing latest M&A market trends including proportions and distributions across industries, and reporting an increase of 39 percent in inbound M&A deals from 2010 to 2015).

[321] I elaborate on this possible prospect in Groswald Ozery, *Minority Public Shareholders in China*, note 11, at 56–62.

[322] See Huang & Chen, *Hostile Takeovers in China*, note 128, at 384.

[323] Wanhe Group, the original private acquirer, tacitly consented to the termination of its acquisition agreement, without any disclosed compensation, even though their contractual rights were violated.

its "operational mechanisms are not so different" than those of ST Meiya, which was a major consideration for choosing them as the acquirer.[324]

Other "hostile" efforts and defenses reflecting signs of a partial market for corporate control within China's political economy are reflected in more recent cases. In 2012, locally state-owned Beijing Enterprise Group sharply increased its stake in China Gas Holding Ltd., a Chinese energy company whose shares are listed on the Hong Kong exchange, thereby challenging a prior hostile takeover attempt by another state-owned conglomerate, Sinopec. Sinopec, a state-controlled national champion, had joined with a privately owned, politically connected firm, ENN Energy Holdings Ltd.[325] Similarly, in a more recent bidding war, Baoneng Group, an apparently private Shenzhen-based real estate conglomerate, gradually bought shares in China's largest residential area developer, Vanke Co. Ltd. The gradual acquisition by Baoneng Group overtook state-owned China Resources Co. Ltd. as Vanke's new largest shareholder.[326] Vanke's incumbent managers have applied various anti-takeover measures to fend off a potential takeover by Baoneng, ultimately cooperating with another local-government–owned SOE.[327]

These cases certainly signal an adversarial shift in business conduct and perhaps a more general market-oriented approach by the firms operating in China's capital market. Yet, for a corporate control market to have a disciplinary effect on managers, it must cultivate enough competing control parties. The examples above illustrate how a potential hostile acquirer will find it difficult to acquire control (or a significant block) without the cooperation of an insider, either management or a dominant blockholder.

An attenuated market for corporate control between dominant blockholders is bound to face a challenge from China's legal framework.[328] Current regulations

[324] A. Lu & W. Yao, "The Anti-Takeover Case of Defeating ST Meiya and Wanhe's 'Extremely Fast Match'" [ST美雅的"非常速配"万和兵败反收购案], Xinhuanet (Dec. 9, 2003), http://news.xinhuanet.com/stock/2003-12/09/content_1220874.htm.

[325] A. Guo, "Beijing Enterprises Group Buys More Shares in China Gas," Bloomberg (May 7, 2012), https://archive.ph/azK2c.

[326] X. Li, "Vanke 'Ropes in Govt Help' to Ward Off Biggest Shareholder Baoneng," China Daily Europe (Dec. 22, 2015), https://archive.ph/JTLB9.

[327] The anti-takeover tactics included Vanke's management first initiating a trade suspension on December 18, 2015 and renewing the suspension repeatedly until July 4, 2016, presumably to halt further purchase of shares by the hostile acquirer. See Shenzhen Stock Exchange, "Report on Suspension of Trading due to Major Capital Restructure" (June 15, 2016), http://disclosure.szse.cn/finalpage/2016-06-15/1202368720.PDF. In March 2016, the company applied a "white knight" strategy in which a strategic cooperation with an alternative friendly buyer (in this case a locally owned SOE, Shenzhen Metro group) was sought out to fend off a hostile acquisition. See "Shenzhen Metro Group and Vanke Achieved a Strategic Cooperation," Vanke (Apr. 13, 2016), https://archive.ph/M8sYL. In January 2017, Vanke's dominant state shareholder sold its shares to the same locally owned SOE, Shenzhen Metro Group, which acted as the white knight under the initial management's anti-takeover strategy. See Shenzhen Stock Exchange, "Report on Registration of Transferred Shares" (Jan. 25, 2017), http://disclosure.szse.cn/finalpage/2017-01-25/1203052214.PDF.

[328] For an account of the regulatory and practical impediments for takeovers in China, see H. Huang, "The New Takeover Regulation in China: Evolution an Enhancement," *International Lawyer* 42 (2008) 153.

provide dominant shareholders with the power to block acquisitions in certain circumstances even without equity control. A supermajority (two-thirds) shareholder approval is required for certain corporate decisions, such as the approval of mergers or major asset restructuring.[329] The CSRC 2004 Provisions apply this two-thirds approval requirement to additional issues, including the sale of major assets and share issuance.[330]

Perhaps even more relevant in this context are China's 2005 Securities Law and the CSRC 2006 Takeover Measures that subject takeovers to a mandatory bidding mechanism.[331] Under this regulatory framework, creeping acquisitions are substantially restricted by a disclosure requirement at the 5 and 20 percent thresholds.[332] Furthermore, any acquirer of a listed company (outside investor or inside shareholder) exceeding a 30 percent ownership threshold must undergo a mandatory tender offer to further increase its stock ownership.[333] Another significant provision is Article 33 of the Takeover Measures, which prohibits the use of certain takeover defenses without an approval by the shareholders' meeting.[334] This provision gives dominant stockholders a veto power over the adoption and employment of anti-takeover defenses and turns any possible control battle into a battle between powerful existing blockholders.

Taken together, even if a supply of competing dominant blockholders is developing and can form an attenuated market for corporate control, the existing regulatory framework increases the cost of acquisitions and has a chilling effect on potential acquirers, likely limiting them to China's biggest or most politically connected firms.

329 2005 Company Law, arts. 103, 121.

330 CSRC 2004 Provisions, note 216, arts. 88, 96.

331 2005 Securities law, arts. 88, 96.

The CSRC 2006 Takeover Measures elaborate the bid process. See Measures for the Administration of the Acquisition of Listed Companies [上市公司收购管理办法], China Sec. Reg. Comm'n, July 2006, effective Sept. 1, 2006, amended Aug. 27, 2008, amended Feb. 14, 2012. See also CSRC Decision on Amending Article 62 and Article 63 of the Measures for the Administration of the Acquisition of Listed Companies [中国证券监督管理委员会关于修改《上市公司收购管理办法》第六十二条及第六十三条的决定], China Sec. Reg. Comm'n, Feb. 14, 2012 (amending the CSRC 2006 Takeover Measures).

332 See CRSC 2006 Takeover Measures, ibid., Section II ("Disclosure of Interests"), particularly arts. 12–17.

333 2005 Securities Law, arts. 88, 93, 96. CSRC 2006 Takeover Measures, arts. 22, 23 (stipulating the same). These provisions also distinguish between a "general tender offer" – when a purchaser intends to acquire all of the shares of a company – and a "partial tender offer" – when a purchaser intends to acquire only part of the shares. See also CSRC 2006 Takeover Measures, arts. 26, 35 (stipulating the "equal treatment" and minimum price consideration for all shares of the same class sold). Interestingly, the acquirer can ask the CSRC for an exemption from the bidding process, ibid., arts. 62, 63.

334 Ibid., art. 33 ("During the period between the issuance of the alert by the acquirer and completion of the takeover offer, … the board of directors of the target company may not, without the approval of the shareholders' general meeting, materially affect the company's assets, liabilities, interests, or business results through the disposal of company assets, investment in third parties, adjusting the company's core business, providing security, taking out loans, etc."). What the "etc." at the end of the article stands for is unclear but it opens up the need to approve any material decision in this period at the shareholders' meeting.

Notwithstanding, the development of a partial market for corporate control in China, if it is indeed underway, can have some disciplinary effect against managerial misconduct. It is possible that even a weak and partial market for corporate control will open up greater investment alternatives that are currently completely missing from the PRC capital market, which would in turn empower public shareholders to at least "vote with their feet."

The Capital Market (debt and equity markets)

DEBT MARKET.[335] The theory on the benefits of debt in reducing agency costs suggests that the use of debt in the capital structure of a firm can discipline managers.[336] Creditors, concerned about the firm's financial stability, will require high interest or stringent covenants in their loan agreements. Once debt is granted, failure to pay off the debt will push the firm into bankruptcy quicker. Alternatively, creditors might refuse to give credit to the firm altogether. In that case, the cost of capital for an inefficient, risky, and poorly run firm becomes higher. Debt providers, therefore, keep managers on their toes to ensure enough cash flow exists.

Many Chinese listed firms have high debt financing ratios,[337] and yet debt is not likely to have a strong disciplinary effect on managers. Chinese banks tend to lend to state-owned firms, large firms, and politically connected firms regardless of their financial stability. It is assumed that central and local governments, which rely on employment by large firms for social stability, will come to a firm's aid before it reaches the point of bankruptcy and liquidation. Banks commonly prefer to have nonperforming loans on their statements rather than initiate bankruptcy proceedings. As Donald Clarke summarizes, "because banks are still often required to lend for political reasons, the result is that corporate management has been subject to the discipline neither of the credit market when seeking a loan nor of lender monitoring after obtaining it."[338] Listed firms in China, and especially state-controlled firms, have little fear of bankruptcy. This makes the debt market's penalty for poor management minimal and reduces, if not eliminates, monitoring and the disciplinary effect of debt financing.

EQUITY MARKET. Current indicators of China's capital market growth were brought in the Introduction. The data reflects a continuous growth relative to the domestic economy as well as to other global capital markets. Yet an increase in market capitalization, impressive as it is, does not say much about the role that stock markets play in China's corporate governance system. This is especially so since the share

[335] In my reference to the "debt market," I do not differentiate between credit and bond-based debt. As mentioned, most bond holders in China are typically the common loan providers – China's commercial banks.

[336] M. C. Jensen, "Agency Costs of Free Cash Flow, Corporate Finance, and Takeovers," *The American Economic Review* 76 (1986) 323; Jensen, *Eclipse of the Public Corporation*, note 273.

[337] Estimates suggest a median debt ratio of 50 percent among nonfinancial Chinese listed firms. Jiang & Kim, note 49, at 203–208.

[338] Clarke, *The Role of Non-Legal Institutions*, note 176.

price of Chinese listed companies is not a good signal for real firm value. Indeed, several empirical studies found that while in many markets, there is normally a high correlation and predictive power between various metrics of firm performance (e.g., P/E ratio, ROE, and ROI indicators) and the firm's stock price, this is not the case for China.[339] This suggests that the monitoring effect that a vibrant stock market has on corporate insiders is removed, or at least significantly reduced, when it comes to the Chinese stock markets.

Nevertheless, the Chinese stock market does have an attenuated monitoring capacity, albeit exercised in a very idiosyncratic way. Some theoretical qualifications should first be mentioned on how equity markets are believed to discipline corporate insiders elsewhere: stock market monitoring is carried through the market firm's stock performance as reflected in the firm's public share price. This stock market and firm value indication is influenced by shareholders' exit, colloquially termed "voting with their feet" or "the Wall-Street Walk."[340] This market price mechanism has been shown empirically to have a disciplinary effect on firm management. In fact, even the credible threat of shareholders selling has a disciplinary effect on management. This function of the stock market is believed to provide groups of shareholders some traction in influencing management decisions, thereby amounting to a form of public shareholder monitoring. Of course, this governance leverage is only amplified in situations where there is a functioning market for corporate control, whereby mass selling decreases the price to a level at which a hostile acquirer can purchase control cheaply and then oust incumbent management. Still, in a vibrant stock market, the firm's public share price operates as a disciplinary mechanism even without a threat of a hostile acquirer.

There is no a priori reason why the same principle should not also apply in concentrated markets without a market for corporate control. Without a doubt, a share

339 F. Gul et al., "Ownership Concentration, Foreign Shareholding, Audit Quality, and Stock Price Synchronicity: Evidence from China," *Journal of Financial Economics* 95 (2010) 425 (showing higher synchronicity for firms where the largest shareholder is affiliated with the government, concluding that stock prices are less reflective of firms' specific information for these companies); R. Morck et al., "The Information Content of Stock Markets: Why Do Emerging Markets Have Synchronous Stock Price Movements?," *Journal of Financial Economics* 58(1–2) (2000) 215 (examining country-level synchronicity and finding that stock price movements are more synchronous in emerging markets than in developed markets, attributing the difference to uninformed trade. The authors report that China has the second highest synchronicity among forty sample countries); Z. Chen, "Stock Market in China's Modernization Process – Its Past, Present and Future Prospects" 40–41 (Yale Sch. of Mgmt. Working Paper, 2006) (on file with author) (studying co-movement levels among individual stocks, concluding that Chinese investors treated every stock the same; from the investors' perspective the stocks were indistinguishable from one another). See also Y. Zhao, "The Relationship between Share Price Gains, Corporate Performance and Risk," *IBusiness* 5 (2013) 110; W. T. Allen & H. Shen, "Assessing China's Top-Down Securities Markets," (Nat'l Bureau of Econ. Research., Law and Economics Working Paper No. 16713, 2011).

For recent evidence suggesting contesting views on the level of informational inefficiency in China's capital market, *Cf.* Allen et al. and Carpenter et al., notes 342–343 and the related text.

340 A. R. Admati & P. Pfleiderer, "The "Wall Street Walk" and Shareholder Activism: Exit as a Form of Voice," *Review of Financial Studies* 22 (2009) 2645.

price drop from mass shareholder defections has consequences for firm market value in these markets as well. Similarly, the relative success or failure of a corporation, as measured by firm market value, will almost certainly affect the reputation and/or advancement of corporate insiders in controlled firms too. A controlling shareholder can be similarly affected by a threat of large-scale deflection of public investors and the expected decrease in market value, especially regarding the cost of future capital. Finally, where ownership is concentrated but control is organized through business groups, a reduction in the market value of a given firm in the group and the associated reputational harm caused to the control parties can have negative implications at the group level and on individual firms within the group. Hence, under conditions where there is sufficient liquidity in the public float of a controlled firm[341] – meaning an easy availability of exit for shareholders or the credible threat of it – even firms and their managers in concentrated capital markets can be disciplined by standard capital market mechanisms such as market share price and exit threats.

While the theory makes sense, there are difficulties in this argument when applied to China's capital market. The theory about the disciplining effect of the market price presupposes a certain level of market sophistication and informational efficiency. It also assumes that a certain volume of reliable information is flowing into the market, signaling to investors the relative desirability of a given investment and, at the same time, reflecting investors' assessments of past and future performance of a given firm. The Chinese capital market does not function this way presently, as it is in many ways informationally inefficient. Share prices often seem to be driven not by economic considerations based on information disclosed in the market but instead by factors unrelated to firm fundamentals,[342] suggesting that the market does not allocate capital efficiently.[343]

[341] Most of the research on market liquidity is focused on widely held firms. See P. Bolton & E.-L Von Thadden, "Blocks, Liquidity, and Corporate Control," *Journal of Finance* 53 (1998) 1, 2 (asserting that "the benefits of dispersion are mainly greater market liquidity and better risk-diversification"); A. Rubin, "Ownership Level, Ownership Concentration and Liquidity," *Journal of Financial Markets* 10 (2007) 219 (examining the relationship between liquidity level to ownership concentration measured by insiders' ownership and institutional investors' holdings in US listed firms). Some studies examine liquidity in concentrated markets as well. See M. Becht, "European Corporate Governance: Trading off Liquidity against Control," *European Economic Review* 43 (1999) 1071, at 1077 (asserting that "[f] or the United States, there is extensive empirical evidence … that the number of shareholders is positively related to liquidity" and attempting to provide similar evidence for the German and Belgian markets); D. A. Lesmond, "Liquidity of Emerging Markets," *Journal of Financial Economics* 77 (2005) 411 (examining liquidity of emerging markets on a macro level, cross-country basis).

[342] F. Allen et al., "Dissecting the Long-Term Performance of the Chinese Stock Market" (May 28, 2021) (unpublished manuscript), https://papers.ssrn.com/sol3/papers.cfm?abstract_id=2880021 (positing that China's domestic stock market performs poorly and is disconnected from the overall economic growth, and suggesting several institutional explanations for that, mainly inefficient IPO mechanisms and corporate governance problems).

[343] Importantly, new research suggests that this view of the Chinese capital market is outdated. See J. N. Carpenter et al., "The Real Value of China's Stock Market," *Journal of Financial Economics* 139(3) (2021) 679 (arguing that since the reforms of the mid-2000s, China's stock market became informationally efficient. Stock prices, they argue, reflect future firm profits and are linked to firm fundamentals in ways that are consistent with other large economies).

This does not mean that movements in the share price do not influence managers, but they are simply one factor in the assessment of the firms' success and in the evaluation of managers' performance that are weighted by the relevant bodies of the Party-state. Although incentive-based compensation plays a marginal role in motivating managers of state-controlled firms to perform better, this does not mean that these managers are not penalized for poor performance. The advancement of *nomenklatura* appointees within the management ranks of China's corporatized and listed SOEs is directly influenced by the success of the firms they manage. While in the past empirical research showed a low correlation between managers' turnover and firms' market performance, this has been changing. There is greater consideration today for market price monitoring in the assessment of SOE managers.[344] Of course, the prospect for advancement in the CCP hierarchy motivates successful performance as well. While not much is known about the details of this internal monitoring mechanism, it is known that the public share price of a corporatized SOE is taken into account for Chinese Communist Party personnel system evaluation. A drop in the share price of a PRC issuer, whether or not reflecting actual economic performance, may block firm managers' future advancement within the Party.[345]

Despite this link between public share price and the evaluation of managers and their professional and political advancement, it is important to emphasize that there are also other nonmarket criteria used to measure the firm's success and managers' performance.[346] More importantly, it is not the stock market per se that disciplines managers. Public shareholders in PRC firms in many cases cannot effectively utilize exit, or the threat of exit, as a disciplinary mechanism. The response to the 2015 and 2016 stock crashes by the PRC central government, during which share prices were propped up through massive mandates of purchase orders and blanket suspensions of trade, reflects the limited impact of public shareholders' own assessment of firms compared to the direct influence of government policy on market share prices.[347]

This is one reason why public investors in China tend to invest alongside dominant Party-state shareholders, even if performance is lackluster or a corporate governance violation becomes apparent. Instead of relying on information for performance evaluation and voting with their feet accordingly, many prefer to rely on the inside knowledge and relationships of the Party-state control party.

Hence, the factor of share prices through the capital market creates an attenuated monitoring mechanism, but it functions mainly through the Party personnel

[344] Jiang & Kim, note 49, at 207.

[345] These political–economic incentives will be further discussed in Chapter 8.

[346] Other evaluation criteria include contribution to GDP growth, tax compliance, reduction in environmental footprint, and the amount of social unrest created around corporate conduct (reflected, for example, through shareholder complaints and derivative suits).

[347] By July 8, 2015, 1,300 listed firms, representing 45 percent of the market, suspended trading to hold back share price decrease. See "Almost Half of China's Firms Halt Trading as Market Dives," France 24 (July 8, 2015), www.france24.com/en/20150708-almost-half-chinese-firms-suspend-trading-market-dives.

management system, while the disciplinary effect of massive sales (or threats of a "Lujiazui Walk" as exit) by public shareholders is much more limited.

The Product Market

According to theoretical law-and-economics accounts supported by empirical research in Western developed markets, inefficient firms are eventually eliminated through a natural selection process in the product market. Competitive pressures in the product market, therefore, are considered to restrain tunneling and mismanagement by corporate insiders and compensate for weak corporate governance.[348]

In China, import–export limitations have been gradually reduced, and competition in the product market has increased within state-controlled firms and between state-controlled firms and private firms at least since the early 1990s.[349] This raises the possibility that the product market will become a significant external corporate governance institution in China. Jiang & Kim have indeed suggested that product market competition in China can discipline managers because they do not want to "lose face" when compared to benchmark competitive firms and managers.[350]

Nonetheless, despite the promising disciplinary role of product market competition in China, a few cautionary observations should be noted. First, constant change in China's economic and institutional infrastructure makes it harder for market forces to signal out inefficient firms and eliminate them fast enough. In a rapidly evolving market, it is thus possible that the disciplinary force of the product market actually becomes weaker rather than stronger, at least until institutions are able to adjust.[351] Another possible path for development in the product market views increasing market competition as an opportunity for misconduct, rather than as a disciplinary mechanism. Lacking reliable enforcement institutions, corporate misconduct will be carried out to gain a competitive edge.[352] As is often pointed out, a large number of firms in China operate outside the rules of the market and the legal system, at a time when violations of IP rights, product quality, and safety standards can still be advantageous to them. The turning point in the development trajectory when such violations will become more harmful to firms and their insiders than useful could be rather far away. Finally, even if market competition works as theory predicts and increasingly disciplines insiders' misconduct in the Chinese market, some firms, particularly those affiliated with state entities, remain shielded from

[348] K. M. Schmidt, "Managerial Incentives and Product Market Competition," *Review of Economic Studies* 64 (1997) 191.

[349] J. McMillan & B. Naughton, "How to Reform a Planned Economy: Lessons from China," *Oxford Review of Economic Policy* 8(1) (1992) 130.

[350] Jiang & Kim, note 49, at 213.

[351] Q. Liu, "Corporate Governance in China: Current Practices, Economic Effects and Institutional Determinants," *CESifo Economic Studies* 52 (2006) 415.

[352] H. Cai et al., "Does Competition Encourage Unethical Behavior? The Case of Chinese Corporate Profit Hiding," *Economic Journal* 119(4) (2009) (finding that competition encouraged Chinese firms to hide profits for tax reasons).

competition. In certain industries and regarding specific firms, monopoly power is designed or at least accepted.[353] The potential disciplinary effect of the product market is therefore limited at the outset to certain market segments and firms.

Managerial Reputation and Labor Market

In a widely cited paper, Eugene Fama argued that career prospects induce managers to operate efficiently. Managers' concerns for their reputation and future careers, as well as competition in the managerial labor market, push them to perform better and eliminate unnecessary risky behavior.[354] Similarly, it is argued that sanctions of shaming and moral disapproval by the public bring reputational harm and thus operate as a disciplinary force in corporate governance.[355]

With respect to China, with the development of the financial market and as professional education improves, the supply of professional managerial talent is constantly growing. The labor market for top managers in listed firms is no longer confined to inexperienced bureaucrats and ex-military. True, organs of the Party-state evaluate SOE managers, and the Party's Organization Department dictates the appointments of senior managers in significant firms. Yet, these appointments and career decisions are not merely bureaucratic processes. Market performance is increasingly considered in the appointment, evaluation, and promotion of Party-state managerial appointees. A study conducted during the early managerial reforms in SOEs (1980–90s) found that the allocation of managers in SOEs was already responding to nascent market forces. Managers were subjected to more frequent review, were demoted, or even fired for poor performance.[356] In more recent studies, reputation through relation-based exchanges was found to have an important contribution to China's economic development even outside the SOE and communal settings.[357] Another study reflects the importance of reputation for monitoring and disciplining managers in China, through evidence of public criticism in China's stock exchanges and public shaming funneled by the media.[358] Together, these studies indicate that reputational sanctions, and by extension the labor market for managers, support market governance.

This is true, yet here as well some limitations are worth noting. While growing in size, sophistication, and experience, the managerial labor market for senior positions is still confined to a specific pool of people. Competition is narrow since appointments are limited to candidates with certain backgrounds or to those already fostered within specific business groups or state organs. In state-controlled companies, these are often

[353] W. Zheng, "Transplanting Antitrust in China: Economic Transition, Market Structure, and State Control," *University of Pennsylvania Journal of International Law* 32 (2010) 643, at 660–663.

[354] E. F. Fama, "Agency Problems and the Theory of the Firm," *Journal of Political Economy* 88(2) (1980) 288.

[355] D. A. Skeel, "Shaming in Corporate Law," *University of Pennsylvania Law Review* 149 (2011) 1811.

[356] Groves et al., *China's Evolving Managerial Labor Market*, note 14.

[357] Allen et al., *Law, Finance, and Economic Growth*, note 5.

[358] B. L. Liebman & C. J. Milhaupt, "Reputational Sanctions in China's Securities Market," *Columbia Law Review* 108 (2008) 929, at 973–976.

the fortunate officials and party members who belong to a certain political clique and whose names are listed on the Organization Department personnel lists.[359] Political science research documents how the top of these lists became occupied by the children of the older generation politicians, often called China's "princelings" – *taizi dang*, the princes of the party (or literally, the princes' party).[360] At least the managerial labor market for state-controlled firms is largely confined to this closed knit layer of cronies.

This should not imply that there isn't fierce competition between the members of this class, but it does mean that the demand and supply for managers in many listed firms is not only quantitatively limited but also that the appointments are often motivated by factors outside professional performance assessment. While this has not yet been examined empirically, it appears that the managerial labor market within the Party-state's institutional infrastructure can incentivize managers to perform better and discipline their actions, but not in a way that is guided by efficiency considerations alone. Other political-economy considerations as well guide the appointment, evaluation, and promotion of managers in many listed firms and particularly in state-controlled firms. This affects the efficacy of reputational sanctions and managerial labor market as a corporate governance mechanism in the Chinese market at large.

Gatekeepers

Lawyers, Accountants, and Underwriters

Corporate governance theory prescribes an important monitoring role to third-party gatekeepers. Lawyers, accountants, underwriters, and other third-party market gatekeepers are repeat market participants whose reputation depends on their ability to monitor effectively and expose corporate mismanagement. Because third-party gatekeepers have a legally reserved role in certain corporate activities such as issuances and disclosure systems, they have access to information that gives them the capacity, and often the obligation, to monitor. Moreover, since their future earnings depend on their reputation, they are presumed to also have an incentive to monitor even without the stick of collateral liability. It is commonly believed that incentives for monitoring by third-party gatekeepers (or the sanctions for failing to do so) outweigh the potential gains from cooperating with corporate wrongdoing and mismanagement.[361]

The research on the role of third-party gatekeepers in the enforcement of China's corporate governance and capital market regime is fairly limited. With respect to underwriters, pervasive state ownership and Party-state control over the industry place underwriters in China in a conflicted position and weaken their

[359] Liou & Tsai, *Between Hierarchy and the Market*, note 317.

[360] C. Li, *China's Leaders: The New Generation* (Rowman & Littlefield Publishers, 2001) at 127–175; J. Page, "Children of the Revolution," *Wall Street Journal* (Nov. 26, 2011), www.wsj.com/articles/SB10001424053111904491704576572552793150470.

[361] R. H. Kraakman, "Gatekeepers: The Anatomy of a Third-Party Enforcement Strategy," *Journal of Law, Economics & Organization* 2(1) (1986) 53.

monitoring capacity.[362] There is also doubt as to the gatekeepers' professional capability to monitor. In a 2008 article, Clarke presents the view that the legal and accounting professions in China were not yet equipped to play an effective gatekeeper role.[363] Lawyers and accountants at the industry level still lack the professional capability and the independence needed to expose complex financial fraud. A shortage of qualified accounting firms and the (albeit narrowing) shortage of trained lawyers shrink the potential importance of good reputation in these industries. Ongoing accounting scandals involving Chinese firms suggest that this has not improved much since.[364]

With limited reputational rewards and with little policing against wrongdoing gatekeepers, third-party gatekeepers are less incentivized to monitor corporate control parties. Under the current institutional setting in China, they often have more to gain from cooperating with corporate malfeasance than from monitoring and exposing it.

Financial Press

The financial press is known as a meaningful "watchdog" against corporate malfeasance, taking up an important role as an external corporate governance mechanism in many systems around the world. By exposing corporate wrongdoing and disseminating information, an active financial press also facilitates the monitoring role of other external governance mechanisms, such as the stock market, reputation, and public and private enforcement.[365] Transparency and objectivity are the cornerstone of an effective financial press. These are preconditioned on the financial press' ability to be independent from various interested parties.

Sources of information and media platforms in China are growing constantly, creating increased competition in an industry that until recently was open only to the state. This opens up access to information and potentially leads to competition on the quality and accuracy of the news as well. Liebman points to the rise of the Chinese media as a social influencer in recent decades and to the media's growing role vis-à -vis the Chinese legal system.[366] The commercialization of the media and

[362] See Chapter 7, "The Party-State's Financial and Capital Market Control", discussing the Party-state's control in the financial industry. C. Chen et al., "The IPO Underwriting Market Share in China: Do Ownership and Quality Matter?," *Journal of Banking & Finance* 46 (2014) 177; B. B. Francis et al., "Political Connections and the Process of Going Public: Evidence from China," *Journal of International Money & Finance* 28 (2009) 696.

[363] Clarke, *The Role of Non-Legal Institutions*, note 279, at 181–182.

[364] For example, "SEC Charges China Affiliates of Big Four Accounting Firms with Violating U.S. Securities Laws in Refusing to Produce Documents," U.S. Securities and Exchange Comm. (Dec. 3, 2012), www.sec.gov/news/press-release/2012-2012-249htm.

[365] B. S. Black, "The Legal and Institutional Preconditions for Strong Securities Markets," 48 *UCLA Law Review* (2000) 781, 798–799 (2000).

[366] For the idea that the press has some supervising capacities over citizens in China, see B. Liebman, "The Media and the Courts: Towards Competitive Supervision?," *China Quarterly* 208 (2011) 833, at 847.

expanded editorial discretion has increased critical reporting[367] (at least until the current decade).

Yet, it was also noted how media platforms are still controlled, and in many cases owned, by the Party-state through various means. Formal licensing and content regulation govern the field and impose entry barriers, while libel laws as well as formal and informal Communist Party policy through local propaganda departments direct content management.[368] Most influential among these are informal rules directing editorial decision-making, which are said to control the targets and the subject matter of reports, as well as to limit true investigative journalism to jurisdictions outside the location where the media is operating.[369]

Thus, while the financial press became more autonomous and increasingly influential, it still lacks independence from the most important interested party – the CCP. Media reports are still ultimately subject to Party scrutiny and will therefore continue to be used first and foremost to maintain Party-state legitimacy or advance its other priorities. Examples of this can be viewed in the cherry-picking and timed coverage of officials accused in the anti-corruption campaign[370] and the state-promoted media campaign in the wake of the two recent stock market crashes. In the latter case, state-controlled media covered extensively the arrest of "disloyal" journalists for their contribution to market-price declines, and "foreign forces" were blamed for market volatility.[371] In both examples, it is clear that the press assumes a disciplinary role and can bring light on corruption and other corporate abuse but in a controlled and guided manner that can easily be directed to strengthen the goals of the Party-state.

The Legal System

Public Enforcement – The CSRC

It seems that the CSRC has put the protection of so-called "public" (gongzhong) shareholders at the forefront of its mission. The CSRC has stepped into aspects of internal governance that are traditionally reserved to the Company Law. It has done so not only by issuing recommended best-practices, such as

367 Benjamin Liebman, "Watchdog or Demagogue? The Media in the Chinese Legal System," *Columbia Law Review* 105 (2005) 1.

368 Ibid. See also Liebman, *The Media and the Courts*, note 366, at 845.

369 Liebman, *Watchdog or Demagogue?*, note 367, at 41–56.

370 This was reflected in the scope of anticorruption investigations on which news items were published as opposed to a much higher number of investigations and the vast nation-wide coverage of the case of Bo Xilai, which was presumably to achieve populist legitimacy for the move. See "Anti-Corruption by the Numbers," China Law Translate (Apr. 16, 2014), www.chinalawtranslate.com/corruption-by-the-numbers/?lang=en.

371 "China Is Trying to Blame Its Stock Market Crash on Journalists and Businessmen," *VICE News* (Aug. 31, 2015), https://news.vice.com/article/china-is-trying-to-blame-its-stock-market-crash-on-journalists-and-businessmen.

the 2001 Code for Corporate Governance, but also by enacting a number of mandatory regulations that mandate what is only enabled in the primary statute.[372]

For instance, even before the 2005 amendment of the Company Law, the CSRC issued the Guidance for Independent Directors discussed earlier, which required listed firms to amend their bylaws and appoint independent directors to their boards.[373] Around the same time, it enacted rules that were designed to make the decision-making process with respect to the sale, exchange, or purchase of major assets independent from the controlling shareholders of the firm.[374] Perhaps most reflective of the CSRC's investor protection orientation are the CSRC 2004 Provisions, which promoted minority shareholders participation in governance through a public shareholders' negative veto on certain corporate decisions.

The 2004 Provisions required approval by the shareholders' assembly – with the support of at least 50 percent of the "general public shareholders," understood to mean holders of publicly listed shares not affiliated with the controlling parties – for the following matters: issues that would have a material impact on public shareholders; any new issuance of stock or convertible debt to the public; rights offering; major asset reorganization; repayment of a debt by a shareholder; and any overseas listing by a significant subsidiary of the listed company.[375] This negative veto conferred on noncontrolling shareholders in listed firms outside the statutory law is a meaningful mechanism for minority shareholder protection and provides an opportunity for their participation in governance. The CSRC 2004 Provisions also urge (not require) firms to proactively increase the presence of public shareholders in shareholders' meetings and to enhance their participation by enabling solicitation of voting proxies and cumulative voting.

The rules set forth in the CSRC 2004 Provisions are only one example of how China's capital market's regulator is increasingly intent on responding to broad investors' expectations in order to encourage the flow of capital to the market.[376] However, granting protections and guaranteeing protections are two separate things and the CSRC's enforcement prowess was often questioned.[377] It seems that the CSRC was allowed leeway for regulatory action, yet, until the 18th Party Congress, its power to enforce its policies has been curtailed by design. Many CSRC rules do

[372] Howson, "*Quack Corporate Governance*," note 10.

[373] Independent Directors Guidance, note 242.

[374] Notice of the China Securities Regulatory Commission on Several Issues Concerning Major Purchases, Sales and Exchanges of Assets by Listed Companies [中国证券监督管理委员会关于上市公司重大购买、出售、置换资产若干问题的通知], promulgated by the China Sec. Reg. Comm'n, Oct. 12, 2001, effective Jan. 1, 2002.

[375] CSRC 2004 Provisions, note 216, arts. 1(1)(a)–(d) (referring to the "general public shareholders group" ["*shehui gongzhong gu gudong*"]).

[376] Examples of regulatory activism by the CSRC are numerous. See OECD, "China Country Study: Self-Assessment against the OECD Principles of Corporate Governance" (OECD, DAF/CA/CG(2010)3/REV2, 2011), www.oecd.org/dataoecd/43/52/46931890.pdf.

[377] G. Chen et al., "Is China's Securities Regulatory Agency a Toothless Tiger? Evidence from Enforcement Actions," *Journal of Accounting & Public Policy* 24(6) (2005) 451.

not set forth any enforcing mechanisms and leave remedial measures to be set by primary laws.[378] Without prescribing administrative sanctions or remedies for violations of these rules, CSRC enforcement was largely discretionary. In that endeavor, the CSRC had to navigate the myriad of tensions and power conflicts within the PRC political economy.

Public enforcement by the CSRC, particularly against insiders and other controlling parties in state-controlled firms, is not welcomed by powerful Party-state organs and was often held back. Consequently, publicly listed state-controlled enterprises enjoyed more lenient enforcement of facially uniform legal standards. The CSRC, like other state agencies, was found more likely to enforce laws, regulations, or policies (or enforce them more rigorously) against violators with no connections to the Party-state apparatus than against Party-state affiliates, even in clear cases of oppression or fraud.[379] One example is the fraud case involving Nanjing Textile Import Export Corp., Ltd. The firm was an SSE-listed company with the Nanjing Municipal branch of SASAC as its controlling shareholder (at 35 percent). The company falsified and publicly declared a total of RMB 350 million (approximately USD 54 million) of profits for five consecutive years. The fraud was designed to conceal losses that would have forced the company to de-list. In response, the CSRC merely issued an administrative penalty and minor fines against the company and several of its managers. This was despite broad public calls to apply delisting norms and to enforce more rigorous sanctions, as was the case for other, presumably less-politically connected firms.[380]

Pressures on the CSRC are bound to come from additional interested parties within China's regulatory structure. As mentioned, the CSRC is but one state-organ with a regulatory authority over the capital market. It shares the same hierarchical position as some of the most powerful listed groups and also with other ministry-level state organs that take part in regulating and supervising some of the same firms. Overlapping authorities, as well as regulatory competition, make it difficult for the CSRC to enforce its own prescribed shareholder protections in conflicted cases.[381]

378 While the 1993 Company Law, which was in force when many of the CSRC rules were enacted, only addressed declaratory remedies or cease and desist orders for violations of shareholders rights. See 1993 Company Law, arts. 111, 150.

379 H. Berkman et al., "Political Connections and Minority-Shareholder Protection: Evidence from Securities-Market Regulation in China," *Journal of Finance & Quantitative Analysis* 45(6) (2010) 1391, at 1393.

380 See Administrative Penalty Decision (Nanjing Textile Import & Export Co., Shan Xiaozhong, Ding Jie and 13 Responsible Persons) [中国证监会行政处罚决定书（南京纺织品进出口股份有限公司、单晓钟、丁杰等13名责任人] China Sec. Reg. Comm'n (Apr. 30, 2014). The company was fined RMB 500,000 (approximately USD 76,000), and the individual managers were fined sums between RMB 300,000 and 30,000 (USD 46,000–4,600).

381 See, for examples, the discussion about Institutional Investors *supra* pp. 53–59. Another example is regulatory competition with the Cyberspace Administration of China (CAC), a super ministry that was formed in 2014 to handle, among other things, information security in the market. The CSRC and CAC now compete on certain regulatory authorities concerning approvals for offshore issuances by Chinese firms.

Finally, while the norms and mandatory provisions of the CSRC sometimes result in the empowerment of public shareholders to receive fairer treatment, their overall contribution depends on the relative power of the CSRC within the political apparatus at any given time. The position of the CSRC within China's administrative and political hierarchy has weakened immediately after the 2015–2016 market crash. The market crisis resulted in legal enforcement and Party disciplinary procedures against CSRC leading officials. These developments have discredited the agency and wounded its authority within China's political economy.[382] Since the Third Plenum of the 18th Party Congress, however, when explicit emphasis was made by the Party as to the importance of boosting capital market activity,[383] the CSRC regained momentum. Indeed, there seems to be an ongoing process to increase the effectiveness of the regulatory regime with an emphasis on enforcement prowess. The CSRC has been increasingly active in taking public enforcement actions against securities law violations ex-post.[384] Robin Hui Huang assessed the CSRC's public enforcement of insider trading rules to have now reached a level of insider trading enforcement that is comparable to other countries (incl' the United States, UK, Australia, and Singapore) and in some measures much higher.[385] The CSRC has been particularly active in recent years also in its preventative measures. It had developed innovative market monitoring mechanisms to detect suspicious trading activity in real time and prevent securities market fraud ex ante. These efforts are said to create a "giant network of (market) surveillance" facilitated to protect investors.[386]

The rise in enforcement by the CSRC coincides well with the enhancement of the regulatory state discussed in Part II, Chapter 5, and is thus expected to continue. The March 2020 amendment of the PRC Securities law supports this direction. The amendment added clarity and force to the CSRC's scope of administrative sanctions and remedies, including a pilot scheme in which the CSRC will administer certain alternative enforcement proceedings (i.e., prioritized compensation and alternative settlement mechanisms).[387]

[382] Party disciplinary proceedings took place against Yao Gang, vice chairman of the CSRC, and Zhang Yujun, assistant chairman of the CSRC. See, for example, Investigation of Yao Gang, Member of the Party Committee and Deputy Chairman of CSRC, under Suspicion of Serious Disciplinary Violations [中国证券监督管理委员会党委委员、副主席姚刚涉嫌严重违纪接受组织调查], Central Commission for Discipline Inspection [中央纪委监察部] (Nov. 13, 2015), https://archive.ph/VPFwo. More formal institutional consequences in this direction can be seen in the removal of Xiao Gang, the chairman of the CSRC, from his position following the crises: See "China Removes Xiao as CSRC Head after Stock Market Meltdown," *Bloomberg News* (Feb. 20, 2016), www.bloomberg.com/news/articles/2016-02-19/head-of-china-s-securities-regulator-to-step-down-wsj-reports.

[383] See Part II, Chapter 5.

[384] CSRC Opinions on Further Strengthening Securities Law Inspection and Enforcement [中国证券监督管理委员会关于进一步加强稽查执法工作的意见], promulgated by China Sec. Reg. Comm'n, Aug. 19, 2013.

[385] H. R. Huang, "Enforcement of Chinese Insider Trading Law: An Empirical and Comparative Perspective," *The American Journal of Comparative Law* 68(3) (2020) 517.

[386] Hong & Xie, "*That Calm Chinese Stock Market?*," note 150.

[387] Xu, *The Enforcement of Securities Law in China*, note 231, at 81–85.

At the same time, however, as discussed in Chapter 8, in the last several years direct involvement in market governance by the CCP itself has been on the rise. This political–economic shift in power dynamics within the Party-state could wear away some of the relative regulatory autonomy that the CSRC developed.

Stock Exchanges[388] *– Self-Regulatory Institutions*

As private (or semi-private) institutions that are commonly owned by their own members, stock exchanges have direct incentives to have well-governed firms. Self-regulation by stock exchanges, therefore, commonly constitutes a meaningful mechanism for monitoring and disciplining firms and their control parties.[389] The New York Stock Exchange, for example, promoted rules that ensured investors' protection in the US market at a time when formal laws and institutions were missing.[390] Several concentrated and emerging markets have similarly recognized the potential of stock exchange self-regulation and allowed for the emergence of designated exchanges with higher disclosure and minority protection requirements, alongside their traditional listing arrangement. In Brazil, the "Novo Mercado" segment of the Sao Paulo Stock Exchange was developed to enable companies to voluntarily commit to better minority shareholder protections. The Brazilian arrangement reduced pressures for comprehensive legal reforms and enabled the adoption of governance mechanisms that otherwise would have been thwarted by existing interested parties.[391] Additionally, some systems – including China's – allow firms to cross-list their shares in other markets that presumably offer better corporate governance. Cross-listing in these markets, the argument goes, enables firms to commit themselves voluntarily to higher investor protection standards in exchange for broader capital reach and tapping new markets.[392]

In terms of promoting investor-friendly norms through "private regulation," China's stock exchanges have been relatively active. The two national stock exchanges produced rules for disclosure and voting procedures that preceded regulatory efforts. Furthermore, they were the first to offer comprehensive corporate governance guidelines. Indeed, in October 2000, preempting the CSRC Code for

[388] The analysis looks only at China's main stock exchanges – SSE and SZSE. An additional stock exchange for small and medium enterprises has commenced operations in November 2021 in Beijing.

[389] Mahoney, *The Exchange as Regulator*, note 83.

[390] Coffee, *The Rise of Dispersed Ownership*, note 83.

[391] R. J. Gilson et al., "Regulatory Dualism as a Development Strategy: Corporate Reform in Brazil, the United States, and the European Union," *Stanford Law Review* 63 (2010) 475.

[392] This theory, known as the "legal bonding hypothesis," is mostly based on foreign listings on US markets. See J. Coffee, "The Future as History: The Prospects for Global Convergence in Corporate Governance and Its Implications," *Northwestern University Law Review* 93 (1999) 641; W. A. Reese Jr. & M. S. Weisbach, "Protection of Minority Shareholder Interests, Cross-Listings in the United States, and Subsequent Equity Offerings," *Journal of Financial Economics* 66 (2002) 65.

Yet, some studies suggest that the motivations for cross listing vary: J. Chung et al., "Is Cross-Listing a Commitment Mechanism?: The Choice of Destinations and Family Ownership," *Corporate Governance* 23 (2015) 307; N. C. Howson & V. S. Khanna, "Reverse Cross-Listings – The Coming Race to List in Emerging Markets and an Enhanced Understanding of Classical Bonding," *Cornell International Law Journal* 47 (2014) 607.

Corporate Governance, the Shanghai Stock Exchange released a draft set of corporate governance guidelines for all listed companies.[393] Anglo-American corporate governance norms – primarily US corporate governance principles, the 1999 OECD Principles of Corporate Governance, and the UK Combined Code – heavily influenced these guidelines, which consequently set forth shareholder rights, high disclosure standards, and duties on directors and managers. Perhaps most notably, in 2006, both SSE and SZSE created a detailed chapter in their listing requirements on the approval and disclosure process of related-party transactions in all listed firms,[394] something that the national regulators still fail to do adequately. A year later, the SSE launched its SSE Corporate Governance Board (CG Board). The CG Board is a special listing index with governance rules that seek to prevent public shareholder abuse. Firms included in the index are required to disclose conflicts of interest relating to controlling shareholders, including with respect to dividend distribution, related-party transactions, and board appointments. This resembles the efforts of some stock exchanges in other markets, which enable firms to signal commitment to more stringent investor protection norms within the same capital market.[395]

In terms of the sanctions applied by the stock exchanges for violations of their rules and their overall disciplinary power, the research is limited. The 2005 amendment of the Securities Law broadened the authority of the stock exchanges and granted them powers that until then had been reserved to the CSRC alone: to accept listings, suspend trade, and delist companies.

Despite the amendment's defining them as self-regulatory organizations, the stock exchanges are still in fact conduits of the CSRC who appoints their senior managers and oversees their operations. The traditional view of stock-exchanges as self-regulatory bodies that rely on private, member-run, independent governance is not applicable to China. Nevertheless, commentators evaluate that China's stock exchanges have an important enforcement role through various self-regulatory disciplinary measures. These include the stock exchange issuing oral warnings, letters of oversight and supervision, notices of criticisms, and public criticisms. Other sanctions include deeming individuals to be unsuitable to serve as senior managers or directors in listed companies, and to order companies to remove their secretaries, as well as membership cancellation.[396] Wenming Xu documented a sharp increase in

393 Fu, *Corporate Disclosure and Corporate Governance in China*, note 90, at 11.

394 Rules Governing the Listing of Stocks on the Shanghai Stock Exchange, Shanghai Securities Exchange, May 19, 2006, at Ch. 10 ("Related-Party Transactions") [SSE Listing Rules]. The Shenzhen Securities Exchange installed a similar listing rule at the same time.

More detailed implementation guidelines followed the SSE Listing Rules. Guidelines for the Implementation of Connected Transactions of Listed Companies on the Shanghai Stock Exchange, Shanghai Securities Exchange, May 1, 2011.

395 For example, the Brazilian Novo Mercado and Germany's Neuer Markt. See Gilson et al., *Regulatory Dualism as a Development Strategy*, note 391.

396 Liebman & Milhaupt, *Reputational Sanctions*, note 358, at 945–948.

the utilization of such sanctions since 2014, which he attributed to the rise in competition between the two exchanges.[397]

A self-regulatory sanction functions as a shaming mechanism that brings reputational harm to a sanctioned firm and thus deters the firm itself and other firms from similar conduct. Observing and analyzing a total of 109 cases of public criticism issued by China's stock exchanges against 89 different companies between 2000 and 2006, Liebman and Milhaupt found that public shaming initiated by stock exchange sanctions has significant effects on firms and their insiders (measured by abnormal stock price returns). Interestingly, it was also found that the majority of all sanctioned companies (58 percent) were private listed firms, in contrast to the higher ratio of state ownership of listed firms in the market as a whole at that time. The authors conclude that China's "stock exchanges have carved out a meaningful, if limited, self-regulatory role for themselves despite severe institutional constraints on their independence."[398]

As meaningful as the stock exchanges may be for corporate governance, they are in no way autonomous institutions. They can exercise their regulatory role only within the confines allowed by the CSRC, which in itself is restrained by the various elements within China's political economy as reviewed above. China's stock exchanges, therefore, while no doubt important to market discipline, do not have enough influence on firms and the corporate governance environment on their own.

Private Enforcement – The People's Courts System

The most shareholder-empowering legal standards and even explicitly mandatory provisions can be easily evaded absent reliable enforcement institutions. Compared with administrative enforcement by the CSRC and the latitude of self-regulatory institutions reviewed above, China's People's Court system is considered to be in an even more challenging situation, both politically and in terms of its professional capacity.

The approach to private securities litigation in China has not been particularly welcoming. As in many other systems around the world, an American-style securities law class action was not permitted.[399] Instead, a private right of action based on a securities law claim in China could take the form of either an individual action or a joint action. The latter was available for claims in which the number of plaintiffs was fixed at the time of filing or when the court decides to adjudicate several individual suits together for particular reasons.[400] But recently, the 2020 Securities

397 Xu, *The Enforcement of Securities Law in China*, note 231, at 86–87.

398 Liebman & Milhaupt, *Reputational Sanctions*, note 358, at 964–966 and 983.

399 H. Huang, "Private Enforcement of Securities Law in China: A Ten-Year Retrospective and Empirical Assessment," *The American Journal of Comparative Law* 61 (2013) 757.

400 See Provisions of the Supreme People's Court Concerning the Acceptance and Trial of Civil Compensation Securities Suits Involving Misrepresentation [最高人民法院关于审理证券市场因虚假陈述引发的民事赔偿案件的若干规定], Supreme People's Court (effective Feb. 1, 2003) [2003 SPC Circular] (incorporating article 54 of the PRC Civil Procedure Law and, by implication, rejecting article 55 of the same law which governs class actions).

Law amendment has enacted a provision for an opt-out "representative action" and allows an authorized securities investment service center to bring litigation on behalf of shareholders.[401] Commentators tend to view these developments as paving a new path for shareholders class-action.[402]

Individual actions also do not have a free pass to courts. In the early 2000s, from a complete rejection of private litigation claims based on securities law, courts moved to accept some claims, under substantive and procedural limitations.[403] Primary among these limitations was the narrow scope of underlying claims accepted, which de-facto limited claims to those based on misrepresentation, as well as a requirement that a claim will be heard only following an adverse finding in public enforcement procedures (administrative penalty or a criminal procedure).

This narrow path has been available to injured investors since 2003, under a Supreme People's Court (SPC) internal policy that was issued to guide lower People's Courts on the adjudication of civil securities claims pertaining specifically to misrepresentation claims.[404] Policy statements issued by the SPC as well as its judicial interpretations are nonbinding and are formally considered to be guiding in nature. Still, in practice, these documents have been accepted as authoritative within the judicial system.[405] Practically, this means that without an SPC-issued guidance, lower courts will not hear claims based on other securities law claims.

A formal legal basis for private securities litigation was acknowledged in the 2005 Securities Law revision, but there as well private litigation seems to have been limited to misrepresentation-based claims. In an informal 2007 statement, the vice president of the SPC-guided lower courts to also accept cases based on insider trading and market manipulation claims. This received backing in a 2018 joint SPC

401 2020 Securities Law, art. 95; as well as Provisions of the Supreme People's Court on Several Issues Concerning Representative Actions Arising from Securities Disputes [最高人民法院关于证券纠纷代表人诉讼若干问题的规定], Supreme People's Court (effective July 30, 2020), https://perma.cc/F3J9-JLQZ [the 2020 SPC Provisions]

402 "China Launches Class-Action Lawsuit System for its 167 Million Securities Investors," Clyde & Co., Aug 13, 2020, https://perma.cc/4P3Q-NKYX; S. Shen & A. John, "China Govt-Backed Class Actions Take Aim at Corporate Fraud – with Limits," Reuters, Aug. 18, 2020, https://perma.cc/9GK5-N65R.

403 For more information on the relevant Supreme People's Court circulars and background on private securities litigation in China, see Huang, *Private Enforcement of Securities Law in China*, note 399, at 760–761.

404 For a review of additional procedural and substantive hurdles embedded in the 2003 SPC Circular, see G. Lu, "Private Enforcement of Securities Fraud Law in China: A Critique of the Supreme People's Court 2003 Provisions Concerning Private Securities Litigation," *Pacific Rim Law & Policy Journal* 12 (2003) 781; Xu, *The Enforcement of Securities Law in China*, note 231, at 101–105.

405 Peerenboom, *The Judiciary*, note 21, posits that through this activity the courts perform a "quasi-legislative activity." Taisu Zhang argues that the SPC have been expanding its judicial interpretation capacity through Guiding Cases, a process that gives the SPC a "stare decisis-like authority to select cases." T. Zhang, "The Pragmatic Court: Reinterpreting the Supreme People's Court of China," *Columbia Journal of Asian Law* 25 (2012) 1, at 8.

and CSRC opinion on matters related to disputes in securities.[406] But as Robin Hui Huang pointed out, very few such cases have been brought based on claims other than misrepresentation, and most cases were rejected or withdrawn due to lack of SPC guidance on how to adjudicate them.[407] This is hopefully changing. The 2020 SPC Provisions provide such long-expected guidance.[408] Following the 2020 SPC Provisions, the substantive scope of cases that can be brought to court on the basis of securities law claims is now expanded to include investors harmed not only by misrepresentation but also by insider trading and market manipulation. Certain procedural hurdles have been elevated as well.[409] These changes can prove to be significant over time, in terms of investors' rights protection and perhaps even disciplinary impact.

Nonetheless, it should be noted that the recent regulatory and legal developments also reflect that the People's Courts system is ever more intent on pushing securities claims away from courts into alternative dispute resolution mechanisms.[410] Such an alternative path was also subsequently enshrined in the 2020 revision of the Securities Law.[411]

With respect to a private right of action based on governance claims established in the PRC Company Law, the 2005 Company Law took an important step to protect the rights of shareholders with judicial remedies. These included the enactment of several liability provisions and shareholder access to courts: the accountability of shareholders that abused the interests of the company or other shareholders, with

[406] Opinions of the China Securities Regulatory Commission and the Supreme People's Court on Accelerating the Construction of Diverse Mechanisms for Securities and Futures' Disputes [最高人民法院　中国证券监督管理委员会　关于全面推进证券期货纠纷多元化解机制建设的意见], promulgated by the Supreme People's Court and the China Sec. Reg. Comm'n (Nov. 13, 2018) [SPC & CSRC Joint Opinions], art. 13 ("For civil disputes arising from illegal acts such as false statements, insider trading, and manipulation of the market, the people's courts need to declare legal rules through judicial decisions…").

[407] See Huang, *Private Enforcement of Securities Law in China*, note 399, at 761, note 11.

[408] 2020 SPC Provisions, note 401.

[409] For more information on the relevant 2020 Securities Law amendments and the contribution of the 2020 SPC Provisions, see Xu, *The Enforcement of Securities Law in China*, note 231.

[410] SPC & CSRC Joint Opinions, note 406. The Shanghai Financial Court was apparently the first to formally develop an alternative dispute resolution mechanism for securities law disputes, which received the title "Model Judgment Mechanism." The Beijing Higher People's Court followed with a similar model on a trial basis. Under this mechanism, a securities law dispute (practically limited to misrepresentation claims) may be selected as "a model case" for other "parallel" cases belonging to the same group securities disputes, to be deliberated in principle in mediation, based on the model case's fact-finding process and legal analysis. The first application for approval of a model case was submitted on March 21, 2019. See Regulations of the Shanghai Financial Court on the Model Judgment Mechanism for Securities Disputes [上海金融法院关于证券纠纷示范判决机制的规定], Jan. 16, 2019, https://perma.cc/N3GV-RFHM; Beijing Higher People's Court trial Opinions on the Fair and Efficient Handling of Group Securities Disputes According to Law (for trial implementation) [北京市高级人民法院关于依法公正高效处理群体性证券纠纷的意见（试行）] [No. 243], Apr. 30, 2019, https://perma.cc/6GWG-6QVK.

[411] 2020 Securities Law, arts. 93, 94.

compensation set as a remedy for the company and other shareholders' losses;[412] access to a type of appraisal by the court in certain cases where shareholders are bought out by the company;[413] an option to ask the court to revoke certain decisions for legal and procedural violations;[414] standing rights against directors and managers for violations that have injured shareholders;[415] and finally, the ability to file a derivative suit on behalf of the company.[416]

Shielding the rights of public shareholders with liability provisions and access to courts are of course significant and vital steps in any system that aims to protect investors, but it can hardly ensure implementation. The first impediment to overcome in applying the remedies formally granted to shareholders is the absence of a body that can act on behalf of retail dispersed investors as a group. As reviewed earlier, institutional investors in China are captured within a network of state ownership and control, and other coalition-building efforts that could potentially overcome a collective action problem are restricted. As noted above, the recent revision of the Securities law enabled such coalition-building through a government-backed "investor protection institution,"[417] but it remains to be seen how such an institution would operate and will it be allowed to act independently.

Another serious barrier that limits the formally granted access to courts are institutional impediments within the judicial system itself. Three main impediments are frequently mentioned in the literature: the professional, even if improving, qualifications of judges to adjudicate complex commercial and business law matters;[418] the courts' relative position within the administrative hierarchy, general social distrust in the courts' system, and the limited role historically reserved to courts as a legal institution, all limiting its autonomy; and finally, the court system's capture within the existing political economy, which leads to its complete lack of political independence.[419]

Such impediments are felt particularly when controversial cases arise. These are cases that pose potential threats to the legitimacy of the Party-state system or to social

[412] 2005 Company Law, arts. 20, 21 (determining similar liability and requiring compensation from corporate controllers and insiders who have injured the interests of the company by taking advantage of their affiliations).

[413] Note, however, appraisal through access to court is specified only in the case of limited liability companies, while for listed companies, the law does not specifically mention court proceedings. 2005 Company Law, *Cf.* art. 74, which applies to LLCs, with art. 142(4), which applies to listed companies.

[414] 2005 Company Law, art. 22.

[415] 2005 Company Law, art. 152.

[416] 2005 Company Law, 149, 151.

[417] 2020 Securities Law, arts. 90, 93–95.

[418] W. Gu, "The Judiciary in Economic and Political Transformation: Quo Vadis Chinese Courts?," *Chinese Journal of Comparative Law* 1 (2013) 303.

[419] The Congressional-Executive Commission on China reports "over sixty-eight percent of surveyed judges identified local protectionism as a major cause of unfairness in judicial decisions." Cong.-Exec. Comm'n on China, *Judicial Independence in the PRC*, https://perma.cc/W78H-9LQ3; see also Y. Wang, "Court Funding and Judicial Corruption in China," *China Journal* 69 (2013) 43.

stability, based not only on their substantive matter but also on the identity of the litigants. Cases in which investors' claims are against state-controlled companies and affiliated defendants, claims potentially pertaining to a large number of litigants, or simply those that reflect badly on either the Party or the state (central or local governments) are often pushed away by the courts.

On the other hand, a study by Ang and Jia found that disputes relating to politically connected firms are primarily those that do reach the courts' doorsteps while nonconnected firms prefer alternative dispute resolution paths (the study was conducted on disputes involving private firms).[420] Still this suggests that connected parties rely on their political connections to influence the court to rule in their favor. Either way, this is not good news for public investors.

Both options clearly show that political economy has a determinant effect on the operation of legal institutions and supplants the enforcement of legal rights. A nonindependent court system embedded within the Party-state bureaucracy cannot work to check and balance the power of corporate control parties over public shareholders. Given that the court system is formally and functionally a branch of government enmeshed within the broader hierarchical network, it has even a greater impartiality challenge when the control parties are at an equal or higher position within the Party-state hierarchy – exactly the occasions where checks and balances on abuse of power are most needed.

There have been efforts in the past few years to reform the People's Court system.[421] The institutional structure was changed so as to centralize the management and funding of local courts at the level of the provincial governments (rather than by lower-tier local authorities) and to create cross-jurisdictional courts.[422] Yet, these efforts focus on centralizing control over the judicial system, not reducing it. The reforms focus on increasing professionalism and curbing local protectionism. Most of the changes are aimed to curb courts' dependence on immediate local governments.[423] These efforts may result in more autonomy in some lower-level cases, but nothing in these efforts aims to increase the independence of the court system from the Party-state apparatus more generally, nor to strengthen the autonomy of the court system as an institution.

The institutional setting, legal framework, and academic research overall still portray the People's Court system as a weak legal institution that is unable and unwilling to enforce legal rights against the various elements in China's controlling apparatus, be they the listed units of China's national champions and their corporate control parties, or the local governments as shareholders and their appointees.

420 Y.Y. Ang & N. Jia, "Political Connections and Use of Courts in Dispute Resolution: A Survey Analysis of Chinese Private Firms," *The Journal of Politics* 76 (2014) 318.

421 See "China Issues White Paper on Judicial Reform of Chinese Courts," China Daily (Feb. 27, 2017), https://perma.cc/FZH7-APVV.

422 See C. Minzner, "Legal Reform in the Xi Jinping Era," *Asia Policy* 20 (2015) 4, at 7.

423 See literature in note 419.

The courts' long-standing reluctance to adjudicate in such cases and its emphasis on alternative dispute resolution paths curtails the system's ability to restrain corporate control parties *ex ante* and to hold them accountable *ex post* as well.

***

Political determinants shaped the design of China's corporate governance. This chapter presented the institutional setting within which Chinese listed firms are embedded and examined the range of traditional corporate governance mechanisms that were structured to govern such firms. This chapter showed how such a setting, which was developed along China's continued embrace of state capitalism, resulted in a structured predicament for public shareholders.

The legal and market mechanisms that were embraced facially resembled their counterparts in advanced economies. They too were entrusted with monitoring and disciplinary functions. A close examination of each of the mechanisms, however, reflects that the economic function of most if not all of these mechanisms, perhaps with the exception of administrative enforcement, is structurally weak or altogether missing.

Captured by institutional barriers and conflicts, traditional corporate governance mechanisms in China were not designed to monitor insiders, provide assurances to investors, nor to promote efficient allocation of capital. Instead of fostering private economic activity, they were mainly designed to entrench economic power with the hands of corporate controllers and insiders and boost China's state capitalism.

The process resulted in entrenched and weakly monitored corporate controllers and insiders that can rather easily exploit public shareholders as well as drain out the value of state assets through tunneling, self-dealing, corruption, and theft.

These results at the end of the Legal Modernization Era explain much of the subsequent shifts in China's political economy, and how it translated into the recent developments in the market. To such shifts I turn next.

8

Legally Politicized Corporate Governance

At the turn of the era, side by side with the continuous growth of the capital market, domestic and international threats to the stability of the Party-state system have intensified and destabilized the political–economic equilibrium. Facing rising concerns to its legitimacy, the Party-state has become ever more reliant on its ability to sustain growth. Yet, instead of aligning with global best practices and development assumptions, its response rebuts paradigm predictions once again. China's policy makers have opted to intensify political governance.

As seen in Part II, Chapter 5, a political–economic shift is currently taking place in which political mechanisms are used in the market directly, bolstering and at times replacing the governance capacities of the state. Perhaps most strikingly, this shift is occurring in the guise of the law through the formal legal institutionalization of direct political control. This ongoing shift has substantial implications for governance in China and for the role of law in China's market development particularly.

The current chapter demonstrates this shift toward legalized politicization through the prism of corporate governance. It shows that the Party is exercising an ever more expansive and transparently direct role in corporate activity, constituting what I have elsewhere termed a "politicized corporate governance." Under such evolving framework, conventional internal-governance institutions are undermined by political mechanisms that are deployed in firms, and the disciplinary role of external institutions is being supplanted in a similar fashion.

The institutionalization of political measures under the guise of law reflects a formal retreat from outwardly conventional, facially convergent, corporate governance. It perpetuates the path-dependent political functions of the law in China, even as the market continues to develop. At the same time, it also indicates that the importance of law for governing firms and the market as well as for establishing internal regularity within the Party-state system is rising.

This chapter draws heavily on Tamar Groswald Ozery, The Politicization of Corporate Governance: A Viable Alternative?, *The American Journal of Comparative Law* 70 (2022); https://doi.org/10.1093/ajcl/avac007.

The potential costs and benefits of legalizing politicization and the possible effects on China's ability to sustain capital market growth under these circumstances are explored in Chapter 9.

LEVERS OF CCP POLITICAL GOVERNANCE IN FIRMS

It is commonplace to criticize China's political involvement in firms and the capital market. This dovetails with the common expectation that envisioned (until late) China's future convergence with more market-oriented governance standards. Instead, in recent years, China offers a complete deviation from these orthodox views toward further politicization of corporate governance. Especially since Xi Jinping rose to power, political involvement in corporate governance has been extended far beyond any scope seen since economic reforms began. This political involvement has transcended the overarching shadow control that the Chinese Communist Party (CCP) regularly maintains in the economy, beyond its influence over corporate stakeholders (managers and employees), and even beyond the puppeteering of managerial appointments in large state-controlled firms, which have increased as well.[424] An absorption (at times, a takeover) of internal corporate governing bodies by CCP institutions and a similar replacement of external monitoring institutions and markets by the Party's disciplinary enforcement apparatus is now under way and already reflected in law. In these recent developments, the Party has claimed a mandate over corporate decision-making much more directly and transparently. In this environment, legal instruments such as the corporate form, group structure, and the legal system itself are ever more easily harnessed to advance the Party-state's agendas, be they national industrial policy goals, social and ideological targets, or even sustainable economic growth!

The following sections will discuss the main tools within the CCP's arsenal through which it can impact corporate governance directly. I will explain how utilizing such tools has accelerated and institutionalized into China's corporate governance framework during the current legalized politicization era. Both internal and external governance tools will be discussed, as analogues to the external and internal traditional corporate governance mechanisms analyzed in Chapter 7.

1 *The CCP's Intra-Firm Governance Capacities: Personnel Management and Party Committees*

The Party has ready tools at the firm level to monitor and steer corporate control parties. Its ability to intervene in corporate decision-making is nestled in the Party's institutionalized intra-firm presence, as well as in its control over corporate management. Both routes have recently been formalized and broadened.

[424] Wendy Leutert observes that during Xi Jinping's tenure, using both joint appointments and leadership rotation to place central state-owned enterprise leaders have increased relative to the prior Hu Jintao's administration. Leutert suggests this to be an indication of centralized political authority. W. Leutert, "Firm Control: Governing the State-owned Economy under Xi Jinping," *China Perspectives* (online), 2018/1–2.

CCP Control over Management

Authority over the management of personnel in the Party-state system has always been one of the mechanisms that guarantees the CCP's control over the state apparatus and society at large. This includes authority over the appointment, promotion, transfer, and removal of leaders throughout the Party-state system. The CCP's control over the Party and state apparatus extends from the center through provincial organizations and down to the level of deputy bureau chiefs in the counties. Two of the main facilitators of this management control are the nomenklatura system (*zhiwu mingcheng biao*), conducted and directed by the CCP Central Organization Department and its local branches,[425] and the cadre evaluation system, conducted by the administrative bureaucracy and directed by the party organization.[426] Both of these personnel management mechanisms apply also to leadership positions in state-owned holding companies and their state-controlled subsidiaries, including some of their listed subsidiaries, whether they are traded domestically or off-shore.

The nomenklatura system has roots in Soviet communism. It prescribes a list of Party and state leadership positions and the closed group of elite political members who can be appointed to fill these positions.[427] With respect to state-controlled firms, the list includes not only the potential appointees for the positions of party secretary and deputy secretary at the top of the enterprise's Party committee but also the potential appointees for senior managerial positions in these firms, including the chairman of the board and president, the CEO, and in some firms additional senior positions such as the chief financial officer and chief legal counsel.[428] The appointment of the CEO in (at least) the largest fifty-three corporatized SOEs is vested with Party organs despite the formal provisions in the Company Law and the SOE Assets Law that assign such authority to the firm's internal governance bodies (the board of directors or the SASAC, respectively).[429] This appointment process explains why the general managers of some of the corporatized SOEs enjoy political clout and administrative status that is equivalent to that of a vice minister (or minister in certain cases) or of a provincial vice governor in the state's bureaucracy.

425 J. P. Burns, "Strengthening Central CCP Control of Leadership Selection: The 1990 Nomenklatura," *China Quarterly* 138 (1994) 458.

426 *Ganbu Kaohe Zhidu* (干部考核制度), commonly referred to as the "cadre evaluation system."

427 Brødsgaard, *Politics and Business Group Formation*, note 30, 633.

428 F. Liu & L. Zhang, "Executive Turnover in China's State-Owned Enterprises: Government-Oriented or Market-Oriented?," *China Journal of Accounting Research* 11 (2018) 129. Yet, the reliance on bureaucratic and political appointment is weaker in firms with indirect state ownership, for which open recruitment is a growing trend. See also Burns, *CCP Control of Leadership Selection*, note 426, at 468 and 474–491.

429 An example of the allocation of nomination and appointment authorities of general managers between the SASAC and the board: "The General Manager of the Central Enterprise Was Appointed by the State-Owned Assets Supervision and Administration Commission to Be Nominated to the Board of Directors" [央企总经理由国资委任命改为提名 任命权交董事会], *China Economic Daily* (Jan. 22, 2018), https://perma.cc/U2ZX-38EG.

The cadre evaluation system has a more contemporary origin. It was created in the late 1970s and early 1980s to rebuild China's shattered bureaucracy after Mao's era and was one of the fundamental elements of reforms in China's administrative system. The cadre evaluation system is used to evaluate party leaders and cadres in leading positions at local levels of the government.[430] It is based on performance criteria, which are set by the CCP Organization Department and applied by the immediate superior level of the relevant party or government units. The results of the evaluation guide the decisions about officials' appointment, promotion, transfer, and removal and thus directly affect their career trajectories.[431]

This management control system also impacts the behavior of corporate control parties and other insiders and thus has an effect on the governance of firms. Some of the potential implications of this political governance system extend even to firms without any state ownership.

This operates mainly at two levels:

First, the performance of an enterprise is inspected as part of the assessment of the officials assigned to monitor enterprises and the agents appointed to manage state-controlled firms.[432] Overall economic development and firm performance are measured by revenue growth, total profits, operating profits, investments in technological innovation, environmental protection, legal disputes (for fear of social unrest), and more.[433] Surely, some of these criteria align with better economic results in firms,[434] while others might run counter to classic capitalist corporate aims (e.g., environmental protection expenses or redundantly high employment levels can add inefficiencies).

Second, there is a substantial overlap between China's business elite and its political elite and their career trajectories are highly interconnected.[435] SOE executives who have become local government and party leaders are a sizable and growing

[430] Prior to the introduction of the cadre evaluation system, Party and state officials were appointed and promoted based on loyalty to Party leaders and other political considerations.

[431] See Y.Y. Ang, How China Escaped the Poverty Trap (Cornell University Press, 2016).

[432] See Interim Measures for Remuneration Management for Central State-Owned Enterprise Executives [中央企业负责人薪酬管理暂行办法], promulgated by the State-Owned Assets Supervision & Admin. Comm'n St. Council, May 13, 2003. https://perma.cc/Z3QE-KDPX; Interim Procedures on the Evaluation of the Financial Performance of Central SOE Leaders [中央企业负责人经营考核暂行办法], promulgated by the State-Owned Assets Supervision & Admin. Comm'n of the St. Council, Dec. 28 2009, effective Jan. 1, 2010, https://perma.cc/3GZL-DG3W.

[433] Y. Li et al., "A Survey of Executive Compensation Contracts in China's Listed Companies," *China Journal of Accounting Research* 6 (2013) 211.

[434] Some studies find a correlation between firm productivity (and firm value) and these political incentives. See, for example, J. Cao et al., "Political Promotion, CEO Incentives, and the Relationship between Pay and Performance," *Management Science* 65(7) (2019) 2947 (finding that the likelihood of CEOs in Chinese SOEs to receive political promotion is positively related to firm performance and that CEOs with higher likelihood of political promotion have lower pay levels. Concluding that political career concerns substitute for monetary incentives).

[435] B. J. Dickinson, *Wealth into Power: The Communist Party's Embrace of China's Private Sector* (Cambridge University Press, 2008) (terming this "crony-communism").

group.[436] In turn, experience in provincial government is a primary stepping stone to central party leadership, to which many of these individuals aspire.[437] Thus China's rising crony capitalism as it is embedded in its unique governance structure means that corporate conduct, firm performance, and the political trajectory of its elite are interdependent. This is true even for managers who are not currently subject to the cadre evaluation system but have ambitions to enter the Party-state system. These incentives are therefore relevant to corporate insiders whether or not there is any state ownership in the firm.

The CCP's personnel management system is thus a persistent political institution with monitoring and incentivizing functions that have bearing on corporate governance. It operates outside any mechanisms provided by traditional corporate governance institutions or framework established in law. This Party system is also far more centralized than the formal state system behind which it stands.

Nonetheless, some limitations of this framework should be recognized. First, with respect to incentivizing *officials* tasked with supervising firms, in Chapter 7, I discussed the weaknesses in monitoring by the state in its shareholding capacity due to various organizational impediments.[438] High levels of self-dealing and related-party transactions are evidence to that extent. This suggests that China's personnel management system was not as effective at discouraging corporate wrongdoing as it was at encouraging some other performance measures. For example, the system is largely successful in making local governments pursue research and development opportunities for their region, invest in technology, or bring their GDP figures up, but not as much in promoting investors' rights or enhancing efficiencies. One explanation could be that the personnel management system mobilized officials to monitor firms only within the narrow confines of its defined evaluation criteria. Corporate value maximization or production efficiency were not specifically enumerated but rather implied.

Second, with respect to incentivizing corporate *insiders* tasked with managing; to the extent that the personnel management system is effective in governing the conduct of corporate insiders, it does not necessarily follow that the action taken would be value maximizing. It can instead motivate managers to pursue proxies of success (e.g., growing bigger not better), to avoid risks at all costs, or even to encourage fraudulent reporting. Additionally, other political concerns are tunneled through this system and influence business decisions. The managers, aspiring for careers

[436] Brødsgaard, *Politics and Business Group Formation*, note 30, at 639–641 (noting the representation of industrial business groups in the CCP Central Committee and tracing eighteen corporate leaders who were appointed to high-ranking government positions).

[437] C. Li & L. Xu, "The Rise of State-Owned Enterprise Executives in China's Provincial Leadership," Brookings (Feb. 22, 2017), https://perma.cc/EQ79-2NP4 (noting that provincial governors and Party secretaries that were appointed following their leadership roles in SOEs comprise 16% [10 out of 62] of all provincial-level leaders, a rapid growth during Xi's term). Within the 18th Central Committee, 76% of Politburo members served previously as provincial chiefs.)

[438] Part III, Chapter 7, at "'Chinese-Style' State Capitalism and Its Consequences for Public Shareholders".

in the Party-state system, will opt for business decisions that they believe serve the Party-state's goals in each context whether or not these align with corporate targets or the wealth of all shareholders.[439]

Thus, the Party-state personnel management system functionally substitutes for monitoring by traditional corporate governance to a degree. However, to induce monitoring and incentives that lead specifically to greater operational efficiency or firm value maximization, these goals would have to be expressly adopted as criteria by which officials and corporate control parties are assessed. While these specific goals are certainly *not* at the top of the CCP priority list, there are indications that they are now being given more weight.[440]

Judging by the Party-state leadership's rhetoric, the Party's policy emphasis following the 18th Party Congress seems to be moving in this direction. In October 2016, a meeting of the Politburo Standing Committee with several leading SOE leaders was dedicated to the subject of "building the role of the Party within SOEs." In this meeting, President Xi stressed that the development of SOEs – including specifically, improved corporate profitability, competitiveness, and preserving or increasing the value of state assets – should become a criterion in evaluating the performance of Party organizations. Xi also called to better define the Party's power and responsibilities with respect to SOEs' decision-making and supervision against corruption, embezzlement and other corporate malpractice.[441] The release of the SOE Reform Guiding Opinions[442] and more recently the PRC Supervision Law, both discussed below, operationalize these stated policy aspirations through a legal framework that gives the party-organization specific governance capacities with respect to monitoring conduct in firms.

Formal Stakeholder Capacity: Corporate Party Committees

The Party's presence in firms is exercised through its involvement with various stakeholders in the firm, such as trade unions, the Communist Youth League, and other groups and organizations. The Party also has a distinct corporate stakeholder capacity of its own, which can be used to diffuse its priorities through firms into the market. This capacity is addressed by several articles in the CCP Charter.[443]

Article 30 stipulates that a primary Party organization (also known as the Party unit or committee – *gongsi dangwei*) will be formed in every enterprise, whether

439 I address these "agency costs"-type concerns below in Chapter 9.

440 See Cao et al., *The Relationship between Pay and Performance*, note 434. See further discussion below in Chapter 9, particularly note 518 and accompanying text.

441 "Xi Stresses CPC Leadership of State-Owned Enterprises," China Daily (Oct. 12, 2016), https://archive.ph/vtO6y.

442 CPC Central Committee and State Council Opinions on Deepening the Guidance of State-Owned Enterprise Reform [中共中央、国务院关于深化国有企业改革的指导意见], issued by the CCP Central Comm. and the St. Council, Aug. 24, 2015 [SOE Reform Guiding Opinions].

443 The Charter of the Communist Party of China [中国共产党章程], as amended and promulgated by the Nat'l Cong. Communist Party China, Oct. 28, 2017, https://perma.cc/GKD4-6DBS.

state or privately owned, where there are at least three full members of the Party. Articles 32 (7) & (8) grant this intra-firm political institution a designated monitoring role: to make sure that "Party and non-Party cadres strictly observe the law and administrative discipline and the financial and economic statutes and personnel regulations of the state and that none of them infringe on the interests of the state, the collective or the masses."[444] Article 33 further stipulates the functions of the Party committee, as the political nucleus within firms that carries Party policies. In firms outside the public (utilities) sector, the Party carries out the Party's principles and policies, *provides guidance* to and *oversees* the enterprise in observing the laws and regulations of the state, "exercises leadership over the trade union, the Communist Youth League organization, and other mass organizations, rallies the workers and office staff around it, safeguards the legitimate rights and interests of all quarters, and *stimulates the healthy development* of the enterprise."[445]

At the top of this intra-firm Party organization, the Party appoints a party secretary and deputy secretary as the senior political leaders within the firm. In major corporatized SOEs, the role of the party secretary often conflates with other senior corporate positions, such as the chairman of the board of directors or the firm's general manager.[446]

In addition to these Party Charter provisions, the PRC Company Law as well prescribes a role for a Party committee in any PRC-domiciled company[447] and thus gives a legal basis for Party involvement at the firm level if the Party so chooses. This makes clear that a political presence in firms is not new.[448] A stakeholder capacity was long established by the CCP Charter and has been included in the PRC Company Law at least since its 2005 revision.[449] Under that legal framework, however, the exact functions of the Party committee were not elaborated. Its relation to the formal corporate governance structure was opaque and it was not deployed systematically beyond several meaningful state-controlled firms.

[444] Ibid., art. 32.

[445] Ibid., art. 33 (emphasis added).

[446] See C. Li, "China's Midterm Jockeying: Gearing Up for 2012 (Part 4: Top Leaders of Major State-Owned Enterprises)," *China Leadership Monitor* (Feb. 22, 2011) https://perma.cc/92VF-VGQR (tracking the top leaders of some 130 major companies in China, their demographic background, the fortune of their businesses, and their career path in both business and government).

[447] 2005 Company Law, art. 19 ("The Chinese Communist Party may, according to the Constitution of the Chinese Communist Party, establish its organizations in companies to carry out activities of the Chinese Communist Party. The company shall provide necessary conditions to facilitate the activities of the Party.").

[448] This is the case even with respect to private businesses. It is reported that in 1999, 3% of private businesses had a designated party organization. In 2012, the number reached 13%. At the time, Zhejiang province declared that all private firms with more than eighty employees had established a Party organization. See "How the Communist Party Is Trying to Expand Its Influence in the Private Sector," *The Economist* (Jan. 28, 2012), at 43.

[449] *Cf.* 2005 Company Law, art. 19, *with* 1993 Company Law, art. 17.

Recent Developments

Recently, both levers of CCP intra-firm governance – its stakeholder capacity in firms and its control over management – have been institutionalized and broadened. The requirement to establish an intra-firm Party organization was reaffirmed as statutory (an element in the much broader *dangjian*, "Party building" efforts) by a CCP and State Council joint "guidance" – the SOE Reform Guiding Opinions.[450] This guidance is an obligatory document that applies to all SOEs, regardless of their industry or level of state ownership. Indeed, the Guiding Opinions make clear that establishing a Party organization and carrying out Party work is a requirement for all SOEs, extending to firms with mixed ownership and thus potentially also to enterprises with minority state shares.[451] The corporate governance roles of the Party committee explicated by this document extend far beyond political and social responsibilities that would perhaps be expected for a body of this nature. They encompass a direct and now explicit role in corporate monitoring and decision-making, even while specifically addressing the need to raise operational efficiency (anecdotally, the Guiding Opinions mention operational efficiency fourteen times. Party ideology is mentioned two times, education two times, and corruption five times).

The SOE Reform Guiding Opinions are full of what most Western observers would view as contradictions. The document claims to resolve some of the most acute problems in the management of SOEs and remove "institutional obstacles" and identifies economic development as its central task. Its rhetoric emphasizes corporate autonomy and market-oriented governance in SOEs.[452] Yet it appears that one of the main mechanisms designed to achieve this, according to the Guiding Opinions, is to enhance Party leadership over SOEs.[453] Thus, while the autonomy of internal corporate governance bodies is repeatedly emphasized, it clearly means autonomy from the state's shareholding capacity and excessive regulatory intervention,[454] while at the same time, the dependence on the CCP's intra-firm institution, the Party committee, should increase.

This political dependence is grounded on three, now institutionalized, paths:

(1) An openly declared authority granted to the Party committee with respect to personnel management, including the authority to recommend, assess, and nominate candidates for leading corporate positions (directors and managers);[455]

[450] SOE Reform Guiding Opinions, note 442, art. 1(3) ("[T]he Party building of enterprises shall be comprehensively strengthened ... The Party organizations of SOEs shall enjoy a more solid statutory position in corporate governance, and fully display their core political role ....").

[451] SOE Reform Guiding Opinions, note 442, Section 7, art. 24.

[452] Ibid, Section 1, arts. (2) & (3).

[453] This appears as part of ibid, Section 1, art. (1) ("Guiding Thoughts").

[454] Ibid, art. 8 ("[G]ive full play to the decision-making role of the board of directors ... and effectively resolve the phenomenon where the boards of directors of certain enterprises exist only in name and decisions are solely made by top leaders, so as to achieve standardized corporate governance ... No government department and agency may intervene unless authorized by law."

[455] This authority is scattered along the provisions. Examples include, ibid., art. (9) and art. (25).

(2) Encouraging cross-representation of board members, supervisory committee members and members of the management with members of the firm's Party committee,[456] and setting a formal assimilation of the position of the chairman of the board with that of the Party secretary as the default.[457]

(3) Setting the explicit capacity of the Party committee as one of the firm's internal governing bodies, with the authority to oversee, audit, and assess major corporate decisions.[458]

What is clear from this is the Party's utilization of the corporate structure and the legal system more generally. State-invested firms are viewed not only as a ready venue through which Party dominance can be disseminated[459] but also as a legal vehicle through which the Party legitimizes its involvement in the market. Now that the Party's corporate clout has been openly established, any legal requirement that procedural decision-making must follow the *law* only emphasizes the weakening of traditional corporate governing bodies. Thus, the Party has practically hijacked corporate governance in these firms, and it has done so through the legal system.

Other institutional measures to sidestep traditional corporate governance bodies took place in the past as well, particularly through the SOE Assets Law.[460] But the Guiding Opinions offer something significantly different. The Guiding Opinions import the Party's personnel management system (nomenklatura appointments and cadre evaluations) formally into corporate governance.[461] Moreover, Party-state involvement in internal governance as was carried in the past was formally far narrower than what is now covered under the Guiding Opinions and entrusted to the Party committee.[462] Furthermore, while the SOE Assets Law is focused on enabling

[456] Similar promotion of cross-representation and assimilation of political and corporate roles existed previously only with respect to central enterprises under SASAC. It was internally promoted by the Organization Department and Party Committee within SASAC and thus not part of the SOE Assets Law or a formal SASAC administrative regulation. See Opinions of the Organization Department and Party Committee of the SASAC Concerning Strengthening and Improving the Party Construction Work in the Central Enterprises [关于加强和改进中央企业党建工作的意], promulgated by the Org. Dep't Communist Party China & Party Comm. SASAC, Oct. 31, 2004, Section 2, art. 5. https://perma.cc/8HY9-T9AX.

[457] SOE Reform Guiding Opinions, note 442, Section 7, art. 24.

[458] Ibid, Section 6, art. 23. This alone can naturally lead risk-averse corporate managers to consult with the Party committee before making any corporate decision that might be considered meaningful.

[459] Ibid, Section 1, art. 2 ("Basic Principles").

[460] SOE Assets Law, art. 2. See L-W. Lin & Milhaupt *National Champions*, note 54, at 743–744 (referring to SASAC "super control rights").

[461] It should be noted that the level of intervention as well as the criteria for performance assessment vary according to the industry in which the business operates and not according to the level of state shareholding. In general, "commercial SOEs" are subject to market forces to a greater degree, and thus their managers are subject to business performance indicators more profoundly than managers in commercial SOEs in specifically designated industries or in "public welfare enterprises" where performance indicators are categorically different. SOE Reform Guiding Opinions, note 442, Section 2, arts. 4–6, Section 4, art. 14.

[462] *Cf.* SOE Reform Guiding Opinions, note 442, arts. 21–25, *with* SOE Assets Law, art. 22(3) (whereby the SASAC or similar state shareholding bodies are authorized to "[p]ropos[e] the director and

state involvement in decisions that can have an impact on the value of state assets, the Guiding Opinions advance Party-state priorities more broadly, and can thus encompass industrial policy goals, social and political targets, as well as sustainable economic growth.

Most importantly, the organ authorized to engage in corporate governance is different as well. The SOE Assets Law concerns the state's capacity as a shareholder. Thus, the authority that the law assigns to the state in corporate decision-making is confined to its shareholding capacity and exercised formally through the shareholders' assembly following defined corporate procedures and therefore subject to potential scrutiny.[463] The Guiding Opinions, on the other hand, legalize the omnipresent authority of the Party over firms by granting it a distinct corporate stakeholder capacity that is otherwise not regulated and is not subject to any transparent corporate procedural (or other) checks and balances. The CCP itself, beyond any traditional shareholder role the state may have, becomes a legal corporate constituent with unique interests and a distinct capacity to convey, direct, and monitor the ways in which these interests will be pursued by the firm:

> The core political role of the Party organizations of SOEs shall be fully displayed. It is critical to unify the efforts to strengthen Party leadership with those to improve corporate governance, include the overall requirements on Party building into the articles of association of SOEs, make clear the statutory role of the Party organizations of SOEs in their corporate governance structures, and innovate the channels and means for the Party organizations of SOEs to play their core political role.[464]

As noted above, the opportunity for the CCP to deploy a corporate committee is old news. However, the Guiding Opinions take China's politicized corporate governance to a new level. The Guiding Opinions clarify the functions of this political governance institution in firms and elucidate its organization, operation, and governance relations with other corporate organs. Moreover, SOEs are also required to have this provision inserted in their governing documents, a change that in publicly listed firms entails public disclosure and otherwise would have been at the purview of shareholders' approval under the Company Law.[465] In this way, the operation of a Party committee inside firms is disclosed to foreign and domestic corporate stockholders and to the market at large.

Following such developments, in 2018, the Code of Corporate Governance of Listed Companies was amended to acknowledge the presence of a Party committee in *any listed company* (with more than three Party members, based on the provision

supervisor candidates to the shareholders' meeting"), *and* art. 24 ("assess[ing] the candidates … to be appointed or proposed …"), *and* art. 27 ("determine the standards of remuneration for the managers … appointed by it").

463 Arts. 13, 30, and 33 of the SOE Assets Law make clear that the state in its shareholder capacity will follow shareholder deliberation and voting procedures even with respect to major corporate decisions.

464 SOE Reform Guiding Opinions, note 442, Section 7, art. 24.

465 2005 Company Law, art. 37(10).

of the PRC Company Law and the CCP Charter). Here too, only state-controlled publicly listed firms were required to include provisions about Party building work in their governing documents.[466]

Private firms are currently not required to show the same level of commitment to Party building as SOEs. Still, there is certainly a noticeable push by the CCP to strengthen Party building work and establish Party committees within completely private firms as well. This push dovetails with a broader effort to strengthen the interlinkages between the Party and the private sector, reflected in both rhetoric and Party-state policies in recent years.[467]

While the economic effects are still to be seen, publicly listed firms, and not just national champions, are complying with the requirement. Before the introduction of the Guiding Opinions, the Company Law provision on corporate Party committees was often overlooked, especially among corporatized SOEs that were listed in foreign markets. But recent studies show that the number of firms with a Party organization incorporated in their charters has risen in recent years, including among firms that are listed outside mainland China.[468]

In mainland China, by 2019, of all non-financial *publicly listed* firms, approximately 30.3 percent amended their charters to reflect Party building provisions.[469] Of all non-financial listed SOEs (ca. 1,008–1,078 firms), close to 90 percent amended their governing documents to reflect Party building provisions.[470] Variations were found across studies based on factors such as industry, ownership concentration of state as well as nonstate shareholders, political connectedness, and whether the firm is cross-listed or not. Lauren Lin and Milhaupt found that close to 6 percent of privately owned listed enterprises (143 firms) voluntarily amended their governing documents to reflect the presence of a Party committee.

The number of private firms with a Party committee outside the listed-companies population is only partially available and is based on the Party-state's own survey reporting. Surveys by the All-China Federation of Industry and Commerce

[466] Code of Corporate Governance, note 95, art. 5. To note, the Code is considered to be a standard setting document for "best practices."

[467] While analysts tend to focus on the recent CCP opinions on strengthening the United Front Work, efforts to enhance the Party's influence on the private sector are long standing. For notable recent policies concerning the private sector, see discussion in Part II, Chapter 5, Section 2, note 235. For recent attention in Party rhetoric, see "Xi Jinping: Speech at the Symposium of Private Enterprises," [习近平：在民营企业座谈会上的讲话] China Daily (Nov. 1, 2018), https://archive.ph/I7m6o.

[468] L. Sun, "More than 120 Chinese Stocks Set Up Party Committee Power to Overthrow the Board of Directors" [逾120中資股設立黨委 權力恐凌駕董事會 蘋果新], *Apple Daily* [蘋果新聞] (Sept. 26, 2018), https://perma.cc/3NWL-UPJK.

[469] Y-H. Lin & Milhaupt, *Party Building or Noisy Signaling?*, note 11.

[470] J. Z. Liu and A. H. Zhang, "Ownership and Political Control: Evidence from Charter Amendments," *International Review of Law & Economics* 60 (2019) 1 (finding 84 percent of publicly listed SOEs amended their charter to incorporate Party building provisions by September 2018); Lin & Milhaupt, *Party Building or Noisy Signaling?*, note 11 (throughout 2015–2018, 12.79 percent of central SOEs and 9.19 percent of local SOEs were yet to adopt party building provisions).

(commissioned by organs of the Party-state) reflect a substantial increase in the ratio of private enterprises with Party organizations. By 2018, 48.3 percent of the surveyed private enterprises (3,973 surveyed firms) reported having established a Party organization, up from 35.6 percent in 2012. The survey notes significant variations based on geographic location and industry. These results, of course, do not say much on the absolute number of private enterprises with Party organizations.[471] Another official survey shows that over 92 percent of China's top 500 private enterprises have a Party organization.[472]

With respect to foreign-invested private firms, limited regional surveys suggest a lower presence of Party organizations in foreign-invested enterprises. For example, 12 percent of foreign-invested enterprises in Hangzhou reported in official data to have a Party organization out of a total of 3,248 enterprises surveyed.[473] About 19 percent of Shanghai AmCham member organizations reported having a Party organization, out of a total 434 Shanghai AmCham survey respondent companies.[474]

These developments raise the question of whether this political institution and its members could be held accountable for corporate decisions that they directed but went awry, and by whom? Given that *state* enforcing institutions do not have even a formal authority over Party organizations, the institutionalization and regularization of Party committees substantiates a law-based governance approach but not legal accountability. It is safe to assume that Party committee members will not be subject to any review or enforcement by either the CSRC, the People's Court system, or the Procuratorate. Clearly any accountability measures will be external to both the firm and the legal system and would have to derive from the Party itself.

The obligatory nature of the Guiding Opinions and the absence of internal and external real checks and balances over the Party committee are certainly disconcerting. Yet there is still much that is unknown about how Party committees will function and how they will be accepted by corporate constituents. Investors, for example, might value them negatively but remain invested for the lack of better structured alternatives in the Chinese market. Or, it may well be that investors will be indifferent to this institution, the same way they have been oblivious to governance predicaments

471 China 2019 Statistical Yearbook points to a total of over 16.2 million private companies by the end of 2017.

472 Note that the reports analyze the scope of private companies in their broad sense, that is, "people-run" (or civil-run) enterprises (*minying qiye*), which encompasses enterprises that are not state owned or controlled, including but not limited to the narrower array of firms normally termed "private," that is, are ultimately owned by a private individual (*siying qiye*). ACFIC reports on its surveys' results are available here: "An Analysis Report about the Status of Building Party Organizations in Civilian-run Enterprises," [我国民营企业党组织建设现状分析报告], May 23, 2019, https://archive.ph/H4mys, "All-China Federation of Industry and Commerce Research & Analysis Report: '2020 Top-500 Chinese Civilian-run Enterprises'," [全国工商联发布《2020中国民营企业500强调研分析报告], Sep. 10, 2020, https://archive.ph/UhzCq.

473 N. Thomas, "Party Committees in the Private Sector: Rising Presence, Moderate Prevalence," *Macro Polo* (Dec. 16, 2020).

474 *2018 China Business Report* (American Chamber of Commerce in Shanghai, 2018), at 19.

in Chinese firms many times before, even when they have faced disclosures of corporate malpractice and sheer fraud. On the other hand, there is also a possibility that Party committees might be added to the list of unconventional substitutions, locally developed institutions that provide reliable assurances, secure investors' confidence, and support further growth. These possibilities will be discussed in Chapter 9.

2 *The CCP's External Corporate Governance Capacity: Monitoring and Accountability through Disciplinary and Enforcement Functions*

The recent politicization of corporate governance in China can be seen also through the partial substitution of external market discipline and legal enforcement by another external system – the disciplinary and accountability institutions of the CCP.

Political and social discipline is one of the cornerstones of the CCP's control over its 90 million members and 4.5 million grassroots organizations. In the last decade, and especially since Xi rose to power, the Party's disciplinary inspection and enforcement efforts have been intensified,[475] not only toward social control in general but also specifically with respect to firms and their insiders. It seems that the Party is utilizing the corporate organization and the business group structure to gain access to information and to detect, punish, and prevent corruption.[476] Corporatized SOEs are being harnessed to facilitate the Party's disciplinary efforts. At the same time, the process fulfills some of the corporate governance functions otherwise not achieved by traditional legal and market institutions.

The Party's focus on enforcement against corporate corruption is achieved through two main paths. The first provides for discipline and inspection responsibilities as part of the Party committee's role within a firm. The second is by intensifying the CCP's enforcement drive against corporate corruption externally.

Enforcement against Corruption: Relevant Institutions

Corruption is one of several conducts by officials that are forbidden by different PRC laws *and* CCP rules. Yet the fine lines that define corruption and distinguish it from other forms of economic malfeasance by officials are unclear.[477] It is often interpreted broadly to capture many different forms of "improper" behavior by state

[475] See S. Yuen, "Disciplining the Party – Xi Jinping's Anti-Corruption Campaign and Its Limits," *China Perspective* 3 (2014) 41. ChinaFile provides general year over year data: "Visualizing China's Anti-Corruption Campaign," ChinaFile (Aug. 15, 2018), https://perma.cc/U5QJ-LBAM.

[476] The causality here is hard to determine and requires empirical research. Is it that the CCP tries to detect corruption and happens to find it in corporatized SOEs due to, perhaps, their group structure, the high-level suspects involved, or the prevalence of crony capitalism? Or is it that the Party targets corporatized SOEs, perhaps due to the reasons I emphasize next? I take the latter view and offer the rationale behind it but cannot support it empirically.

[477] The relevant legal and policy framework against corruption is specified in Tamar Groswald Ozery, The Politicization of Corporate Governance: A Viable Alternative?, *The American Journal of Comparative Law* 70 (2022), in footnote 115.

officials and Party members.[478] In the context of corporatized SOEs, I treat corruption as the illicit use of public authority by either Party members or state officials, or their employees and assignees, for private gain, in the course of their formal or informal affiliation with corporatized SOEs.

Until recently, corruption cases involving corporatized SOEs were typically pursued through the state's administrative and criminal enforcement proceedings (involving the People's Procuratorate, the SASAC, and the CSRC in certain embezzlement cases in publicly listed firms), and by a parallel "extra-legal" Party disciplinary process in cases applicable to Party members. The latter were directed by the Central Commission for Disciplinary Inspection (CCDI), whose oversight and enforcement roles were established in various Party norms and disciplinary codes of conduct.[479] The CCDI's methods (generically known as *Shuanggui*) do not comply with transparency and predictability standards nor with due process required under the law, and are widely criticized for being opaque and brutal.

Recently, both state and Party corruption enforcement capacities went through a fundamental structural reform and were centralized under a new central commission, the National Supervision Commission. The operations of the new Commission were established under a new law, the PRC Supervision Law, and further enshrined in a Constitutional Amendment.[480] The new Commission is a Party-led state organ, following the principle of one body two names "一套人马，两块牌子" (*yi tao renma, liang kuai paizi,* literary "one centaur two brands"). It is situated directly under the National People's Congress and incorporates the CCDI as its main operating body. Notably, the CCDI's chief is a member of the CCP Politburo Standing Committee. Thus, de facto, the state supervisory organs have been absorbed under a now legalized form of the CCDI, rather than the other way around, since the top leader of the CCDI has the upper political rank. The scope of authority in the new Commission is in line with Party investigative powers and methods (albeit with a new and now "legalized" name, *liuzhi* "detention in custody"[481]).

478 A. Wederman, "The Intensification of Corruption in China," *The China Quarterly* 180 (2004) 895, at 897, 901–903.

479 President Hu Jintao gave the message on the release of the primary normative framework on January 12, 2004. See, "The Central Committee of the Chinese Communist Party of China Promulgated Inner-Party Supervision and Disciplinary Regulation" [中共中央颁布党内监督条例和纪律处分条例], People's Daily Online [人民网], https://perma.cc/2LW3-YM5E. Earlier versions of inner Party supervision regulations are documented as well. See D. Xu, "Regulations on Inner Party Supervision Came before and After" [权威人士透露《党内监督条例》出台前前后后], *People's Daily Online* [人民网] (Jan. 4, 2004), https://perma.cc/ZP7H-4V3L.

Following the 18th Party Congress, the CCP Central Committee issued new disciplinary regulations that are considered much stricter and more comprehensive, see note 492.

480 Amendment to the Constitution of the People's Republic of China [中华人民共和国宪法修正案], promulgated & effective by the First Session Thirteenth Nat'l People's Cong., Mar. 11, 2018, Sec. 7, https://perma.cc/SE6A-4338.

481 See the various threads of interpretation and discussion on this term on the *ChinaLaw* listserv: "Lianggui versus Shuanggui," Chinalaw, https://hermes.gwu.edu/cgi-bin/wa?A2=CHINALAW;e753c272.1711 (last entry, Nov. 13, 2017).

Within the new Commission, the CCDI is assigned an all-encompassing authority to monitor, investigate, and sanction misconduct by both Party and state agents.[482] The reform thus expands the scope of Party anti-corruption and disciplinary authority and methods over additional millions of public sector organizations and individuals, many of whom are not party members. Corporatized SOEs and their state-appointed managers and other functionaries are now formally included as well.[483] This change also potentially subjects all employees of SOEs who could be viewed as civil servants or as performing public roles to CCP disciplinary enforcement.[484] Note that the term "SOE" is interpreted broadly and may include firms in which the state has only a minority equity stake, thus potentially further broadening the scope of individuals under CCP disciplinary supervision.[485]

Corporatized SOEs and Corruption

Since economic reforms began, China has developed a reputation for widespread corruption.[486] Corruption is widely considered an unfavorable condition for development,[487] which can thus impede China's growth plans. This has been the common understanding despite inconclusive evidence about a causal link.[488] Public criticism against corruption is on the rise and alienates the people from public officials.[489]

[482] PRC Supervision Law, arts. 15–18, 41, 43. Note that at least formally, following a CCDI investigation and in addition to any disciplinary sanction applied by the CCDI, corruption cases involving criminal offenses must be transferred to the People's Procuratorate and the People's Courts and be pursued according to the criminal law. See generally, J. Daum, "Unsupervised – Initial Thoughts on the Supervisory Law," China Law Translate (Nov. 9, 2017), www.chinalawtranslate.com/en/unsupervised.

[483] PRC Supervision Law art. 15.

[484] Ibid (especially art. 15(3) & (6)).

[485] While the Supervision Law itself does not define the term SOEs, this broad interpretation is reflected in the SOE Reform Guiding Opinions, note 442 (in commercial SOEs the state "may be the absolute or relative controlling shareholder, or be merely a shareholder"). Moreover, the SOE Assets Law refers to state *invested* enterprises. SOEs in many other instances are viewed by Chinese authorities in the broader sense to include enterprises with state invested capital.

[486] The Corruption Perception Index, published by Transparency International, ranked China 66 out of 180 country spots in 2021 (the lower the points, the more corrupt is the country). For the Index, see *Measuring Corruption*, Transparency Int'l UK, www.transparency.org/en/cpi/2020.

[487] P. Mauro, "Corruption and Growth," *The Quarterly Journal of Economics* 110 (1995) 681.

[488] This perception is deeply rooted even though the Chinese economy has performed remarkably well since reforms ensued. For an exception to this view revealing empirical evidence to the contrary, see C.-J Huang, "Is Corruption Bad for Economic Growth? Evidence from Asia-Pacific Countries," *The North American Journal of Economics & Finance* 35 (2016) 247. At the other end of the spectrum, there is also a view that it is the fight against corruption that contributes to the economic slow-down in China: J. Yang, "Is Anti-Graft Anti-Growth? Weighing the Economic Impact of the Anti-Corruption Campaign," *The Economist* (Aug. 2, 2014), https://perma.cc/U4D4-57NE. For a more comprehensive overview on the complex relationship between corruption levels and economic growth, see A. Wedeman, *Double Paradox: Rapid Growth and Rising Corruption in China* (Cornell University Press, 2012); and between different types of corruption and economic growth, see Y.Y. Ang, *China's Gilded Age: The Paradox of Economic Boom and Vast Corruption* (Cambridge University Press, 2020).

[489] "China Focus: Income, Corruption Top Concerns for Two Sessions: Polls," Xinhua (Mar. 4, 2015), https://perma.cc/LRR6-GZ6A (reporting public polls that show corruption as the second most concerning issue in China, following income distribution).

The Party itself views corruption as an imminent threat to the regime's stability, Party unity, and legitimacy, and President Xi stated that corruption, if not treated, "will inevitably lead to the fall of the party and the state" (*wangdang wangguo*).[490] Indeed, the need to combat corruption is repeatedly emphasized by Party leadership and was even incorporated into the Charter of the CCP.

China's crony capitalism, the overlap between its business and political elites amplifies opportunities for corruption and increases the number of cases in which corrupt conduct is exercised through, or simply involves, firms and corporatized SOEs,[491] thus making corporatized SOEs key venues for corruption but also key avenues for battling corruption. Indeed, corporatized SOEs and their group structure are being harnessed in this process, a development that is producing important externalities on corporate governance.

Harnessing Business Groups and the Effect on Corporate Insiders

Several signals suggest that the CCP intensified its anti-corruption enforcement efforts with respect to firms and corporatized SOEs specifically. The first is a change in the normative framework – the norms that guide the conduct of Party members and the operation of its enforcing institutions. The Central Committee of the CCP revised its inner-party disciplinary norms twice in the last few years.[492] The revisions included specific provisions that deal with various misconducts by Party members and state employees in the course of their business involvement and positions within

[490] "China's Xi Amassing Most Power since Deng Raises Reform Risk," *Bloomberg News* (Dec. 30, 2013), https://perma.cc/2NJH-TL6S.

[491] Statistical data shows that throughout 2016 there were 1458 cases of criminal violations in business enterprises with 1827 individual offenders involved. Out of these cases, 203 cases involved state-owned enterprises and 1255 cases involved private enterprises (13.9% and 86.1%, respectively). The most common crimes committed in SOEs are corruption and bribery crimes, 229 cases, accounting for 78.2% of the cases (a decline from 90.3% in 2015); while with respect to private enterprises, corruption and bribery crimes accounted for 170 of the cases, only 9.9% (a decline from 15.3% in 2015). For the full report, see Y. Zhang, "2016 Chinese Enterprises Criminal Risk Analysis Report" [2016 中国企业刑事风险分析报告], *Journal of Henan Police College* [河南警察学院学报] Vol. 26 no. 4 (2017), at 17.

[492] The former document was in place since 2004. See note 480. A new comprehensive framework was revised twice since the 18th Party Congress. For the revisions, see "Interpretation of the Revised Regulations on Disciplinary Actions of the Communist Party of China: Where Is 'Strictness'?" [中国共产党纪律处分条例修订解读："严"在哪儿？], Xinhuanet [新华网] (Oct. 21, 2015), https://perma.cc/84PW-XJDR.

See also Regulation of the Communist Party of China on Disciplinary Measures [中共中央印发，中国共产党纪律处分条例], promulgated by the Cent. Comm. Communist Party China, Oct. 21, 2015, effective Jan. 1, 2016. This was recently replaced by another normative document of the same title, effective Oct. 1, 2018. See "The Central Committee of the Communist Party of China Issued the "Regulations on Disciplinary Measures of the Communist Party of China" [中共中央印发，中国共产党纪律处分条例], Xinhuanet [新华网] (Aug. 26, 2018), https://perma.cc/N7CK-VFNG.

SOEs.[493] The CCDI as well formally dedicates a specific section of its "investigative work plan" to central SOEs and financial institutions.[494]

Another signal for this recent focus is the change in practices that reflect an increase in the number of corruption investigations related to corporatized SOEs. Immediately after President Xi's anti-corruption campaign began in 2012 and over a short period of eighteen months, a large number of SOE executives (124) were investigated for corruption through the Party disciplinary system in one sector.[495] Media reports also indicated that SOEs and their insiders have been "targeted" in waves.[496]

Until recently, anti-corruption work and other disciplinary inspections within central SOEs were in the hands of internal disciplinary teams (*qiye jiwei jijian zu*).[497] These teams were either formally dispatched by the SASAC or were self-organized by firms under the SASAC's encouragement and guidance. Either way, the SASAC trained and supervised them with CCDI guidance. The Party criticized this intra-firm disciplinary mechanism for lacking real powers within the corporate and administrative hierarchy.[498] To rectify this, in 2015 the SOEs Reform Guiding Opinions assigned the lead authority over disciplinary inspection to the firm's internal Party committee. This has shifted supervision and investigative authorities from SASAC-organized intra-firm supervisory teams to the firm's Party committee. This recent move opens a more direct route for CCDI oversight and investigative capacities with respect to firms.

The role of the intra-firm Party committee with respect to discipline inspection was reinforced as one of its main responsibilities.[499] Meaning, aside from its

[493] See ibid., at Ch. VIII arts. 88–101 ("Acts Violating the Rules of Integrity and Self-Discipline"), Ch. X arts. 121–127 ("Disciplinary Actions for Violations of Work Discipline").

[494] See CCDI website, section reporting on "Supervision Exposure: 'Central and national bodies,' 'units of state-owned enterprises,' 'state-owned financial institutions'" [中共中央纪律检查委员会, 监督曝光: 中央和国家机关 国有企事业单位 国有金融机构)] CCDI, https://perma.cc/EYY2-FMCB.

[495] A. Meng, "A Quarter of Chinese SOEs Executives Investigated for Corruption Work in Energy Sector," *South China Morning Post* (Apr. 28, 2015), https://perma.cc/C57Z-EAVZ.

[496] Ibid. See also F. Fang, "Anti-Corruption Campaign Targets China's State-Owned Enterprises," *Epoch Times* (Feb. 20, 2015), https://perma.cc/8HZN-5NDP (reporting that the CCDI had marked twenty-six central SOEs as targets for next round of investigations); L. Hornby, "China Anti-Corruption Drive Targets Sinopec – Oil Group among Several State-Owned Enterprises to Face Probe," *Financial Times* (Dec. 4, 2014), https://perma.cc/96LS-QDPE.

[497] On the work and training of such inspection teams, see The State-Owned Assets Supervision and Administration Commission Held the Opening Ceremony of the Central Enterprise Disciplinary Committee Secretary and the Discipline Inspection Team Leader Training Class [国资委举行中央企业纪委书记、纪检组长培训班开班式], SASAC (Apr. 1, 2012), https://perma.cc/6HPC-CGR7. The State-Owned Assets Supervision and Administration Commission Held a Training Course for the Secretary of the Central Enterprise Disciplinary Committee (the Leader of the Discipline Inspection Team) [国资委举办中央企业纪委书记(纪检组组长)培训班], SASAC (Mar. 21, 2013), https://perma.cc/D62G-883N.

[498] See X. Meng, "State-Owned Enterprises Disciplinary Inspection System Should Serve as 'a Good Woodpecker'" [国企纪检机构要当好"啄木鸟"], *People's Daily* (Chinese) [人民日报] (June 26, 2018), https://perma.cc/Z4HH-CC44.

[499] SOE Reform Guiding Opinions, note 442, art. 1(3).

expanded roles in corporate decision-making discussed earlier, the Party committee is also the leading organ within the firm assigned to promote party line education, conduct disciplinary inspection work, investigate the conduct of enterprise leaders, strengthen tour inspections in SOEs, form an intra-firm accountability system, and facilitate the work of external anti-corruption institutions (i.e., the CCDI).[500] In the context of corporate corruption, therefore, the Party committee functions as a whistleblower for the Party.

A particularly interesting method taken by the CCDI to expose corrupt corporate insiders and Party-state leaders is its use of the business-group organization and its access to intra-firm governance. It appears that the CCDI has applied targeted inspection tours, in which the corporate group is utilized to facilitate work against corruption. The CCDI starts its probe with a "disciplinary inspection tour," during which it dispatches investigators into a specific state-controlled group and activates the Party committees within firms in a systematic search for corruption ("crackdown" in the media). The primary targets are often high-level political figures with parallel positions at the corporate group organization. The inspection teams spread across various lower-level enterprises within a business group, collect information, and build an "evidence" line while climbing up the group ladder and across its network of affiliates (including private firms) until the CCDI reaches the top leadership in the group and sometimes beyond to a related political leader. To facilitate this tactic, the CCDI steers the group's internal governance, which often means enlisting the help of Party institutions at the group or firm level. The investigation includes interrogations of corporate employees, individual business affiliates, and corporate insiders.

Thus, the use of the corporate form and of the SOE group organization makes the CCDI's work in monitoring and enforcing against corporate corruption a highly collaborative network.[501] The consequences inside firms are clear. Once the Party's disciplinary inspection apparatus has signaled that an individual is suspected of a disciplinary violation, whether this has been disclosed to the public or not, the individual will likely be removed or forced to step down from his corporate positions. This happens in many cases before any legal accusation has been made and regardless of any proof of damage to the corporation or its stakeholders. Disciplinary punishment by the Party (e.g., admonition, a downgrade in rank, revoking Party

500 Although the CCDI is not mentioned formally. See SOE Reform Guiding Opinions, note 442, art. 7(26) ("The Party organizations of SOEs shall earnestly perform their duties as the primary players responsible, while their disciplinary inspection agencies shall effectively perform supervisory responsibilities." It includes a fanfare instruction to "keep using the thinking and methods of the rule of law to fight corruption, fine-tune anti-corruption institutions and systems, strictly enforce the provisions against formalism, bureaucracy, hedonism and extravagance, and strive to build effective mechanisms where enterprise leaders dare not to, are not able to, and do not want to, engage in corrupt practices.").

501 Recent discipline and inspection work reports in both SASAC and specific SOEs also reflect this. See News of the Discipline Inspection and Inspection Team [驻委纪检监察组要闻], SASAC, https://perma.cc/TW7L-MGRF; "Business Work" [业务工作], SASAC, https://perma.cc/ZP7T-NV5Y.

positions, and finally expulsion from the Party altogether) will also often precede criminal charges.[502]

Recent probe targets include firms in the healthcare sector, commercial and investments vehicles operating off-shore (state-controlled as well as private), and the financial sector.[503] Some cases against ostensibly private firms, such as Dalian Wanda, Fosun International, HNA Group, and Anbang Insurance, emphasize how Party-led disciplinary enforcement influences and determines the operations of state enforcement actions in the private sector as well. Some scholars posit that these purges serve multiple purposes, including cleaning and improving the financial system, enforcing against dubious business practices, and "getting rid of tycoons with dubious political loyalties" at the same time.[504]

Illustrative Example

Examples of how the above mobilization of the corporate form and group structure work can be seen in the targeted probes in one of China's most valuable sectors – energy. By targeting two of its most important corporate groups, the CCDI opened a hornet's nest that led to the exposure and punishment (both disciplinary and legal enforcement) of several corrupt Party members and state officials at the national and local levels, as well as senior business executives.[505] The well-known fall of Jiang Jiemin can be used as a good illustration to the above. Jiang rose through the ranks of the oil industry to head China's biggest oil business, China National Petroleum Corporation (CNPC),[506] and was eventually appointed as the

[502] B. Spegele & W. Ma, "Wison Engineering Says Chinese Police Arrested Chairman," *Wall Street Journal* (Mar. 10, 2014), www.wsj.com/articles/wison-engineering-chairman-hua-bangsong-was-arrested-by-chinese-authorities-1394425858 ("Neither Mr. Jiang nor several other oil executives removed from their posts in recent months have been formally charged.").

[503] One example of an investigation of a state-owned commercial firm is the case of Song Lin, the former chairman of China Resources, a Hong Kong based trading company and one of China's largest state-owned enterprises, who was accused of power abuse in corporate dealings and was arrested in April 2014. The Party removed Lin from his positions in the firm and the Party. Two years later, he was charged under criminal law. J. T. Areddy & L. Burkitt, "China Communist Party Ousts Chairman of Major State-Owned Firm," *Wall Street Journal* (Apr. 22, 2014), www.wsj.com/articles/SB10001424052702304049904579517513621726 46; C-y. Choi, "Song Lin, Former Chairman of China Resources, is Formally Charged with Corruption," *South China Morning Post* (Dec. 8, 2016), https://archive.ph/kQu95.

For other examples of SOE executives investigated for corruption and released from their corporate role, see "9 Chinese SOEs Slammed for Discipline Violations," Xinhua (June 17, 2015), https://archive.ph/AsaAv. Examples of investigations against private firms that seem to also entail Party disciplinary investigative work include Dalian Wanda, Fosun International, HNA Group, and Anbang Insurance. See L. Hornby et al., "Big China Companies Targeted over 'Systemic Risk'," *Financial Times* (June 23, 2017), www.ft.com/content/23c8ba54-5710-11e7-9fed-c19e2700005f.

[504] M. Pei, "Xi Jinping's War on Financial Crocodiles Gathers Pace," *Financial Times* (June 25, 2017), www.ft.com/content/19810ea2-5814-11e7-80b6-9bfa4c1f83d2.

[505] Meng, *Chinese SOEs Executives Investigated*, note 496; "Former China Energy Chief Jiang Jiemin Jailed for Corruption," *BBC News* (Oct. 12, 2015), www.bbc.com/news/world-asia-china-34503469.

[506] J. Page et al., "China Probes Former Oil Company Head," *Wall Street Journal* (Sept. 1, 2013), www.wsj.com/articles/china-probes-former-oil-company-head-1378018593.

head of SASAC. Some point to a connection between the pursuit after Jiang and the final ousting and criminal conviction of Zhou Yongkang who was regarded as a political rival of Xi.[507] The entire process involved the detention, investigation, and punishment of dozens of senior managers in the parent holding company CNPC, its listed subsidiary PetroChina, and even in private affiliated firms.[508] Figure 8.1 below illustrates how the corporate group structure can aid in pursuing CCDI inspections (the complete list of people probed and indicted as a result of the CCDI inspection tours into the oil industry is of course much wider than illustrated).

A similar inspection was taken thereafter into another of China's centrally controlled energy champions, Petroleum & Chemicals Corporation (Sinopec Group) and its main listed subsidiary, Sinopec Corp Ltd. The inspection into Sinopec Group led to the detention of managers in several subsidiary firms,[509] finally reaching the president of the group, Wang Tianpu. Wang, who chaired the Group's board at the time and was also the general manager of its listed subsidiary, was put under Party disciplinary proceedings for taking bribes and abuse of power. Wang was removed from his corporate positions, expelled from the Communist Party, and eventually prosecuted under criminal law.[510]

507 W. Lam, "With Zhou's Circle Down, Xi's Purge May Turn to Hu," *Jamestown Brief*, vol. 14 no. 13 (3 July 2014), https://jamestown.org/program/with-zhous-circle-down-xis-purge-may-turn-to-hu/.

508 The proceedings against private affiliated firms are worth noting since they instigated from, and likely rely on, evidence obtained during the political disciplinary enforcement process, thus reflecting the high collaboration between the Party and state enforcing institutions. D. Kwok & C. Zhu, "PetroChina Supplier Wison Says Record Seized, Can't Contact Chairman," *Reuters* (Sept. 18, 2013), www.reuters.com/article/uk-wison-cfo-idUKBRE98I01120130919 (in which the chairman and subsidiary executives of HK listed private firm Wison Engineering Services Co Ltd., a major supplier of PetroChina, were investigated as part of the Chinese corruption investigation in PetroChina and its parent company CNPC). In March 2014, Wison's founder, primary shareholder, and chairman of the board was formally arrested. He was accused of conspiracy to commit a "tender-offer fraud," as well as for offering bribes for state officials. In August, 2015, he was found guilty for offering bribes and acquitted from tender offer fraud. He was sentenced to 36 months in prison.

Spegele & Ma, note 503; "PetroChina Supplier Wison Says Found Guilty of Bribery in China," *Reuters* (Aug. 5, 2015), www.reuters.com/article/wison-petrochina-idUSL3N10H08120150806.

509 Such as the case of Xue Wandong, the vice chairman and CEO of Sinopec Oilfield Services Corp who was detained and investigated by the CCDI and dismissed from his role in Sinopec immediately. See Hornby, *Anti-Corruption Drive Targets Sinopec*, note 497.

510 Circular of the Chinese Communist Party on the Inspection and Ratification in China Petroleum Chemical Corporations [中共中国石化党组关于巡视整改情况的通报], promulgated by the CCDI, Apr. 30. 2015, https://archive.ph/ZwiA8.

Notice by the CCDI on the Disciplinary Investigation of Wang Tianpu [中国石油化工集团公司总经理王天普涉嫌严重违纪违法接受组织调查], promulgated by the CCDI, Apr. 28, 2015, https://archive.ph/bJvE6; Notice by the CCDI on Wang Tianpu's Expulsion from the Party [中国石油化工集团公司原董事、总经理、党组成员王天普严重违纪被开除党籍], promulgated by the CCDI, Sept. 18, 2015, https://archive.ph/hZtJg.

On the consequent legal criminal prosecution, see "China to Prosecute Former Top Executives for Alleged Graft," *Reuters* (Sept. 29, 2016), www.reuters.com/article/us-china-corruption-sinopecidUSKCN11W0VX.

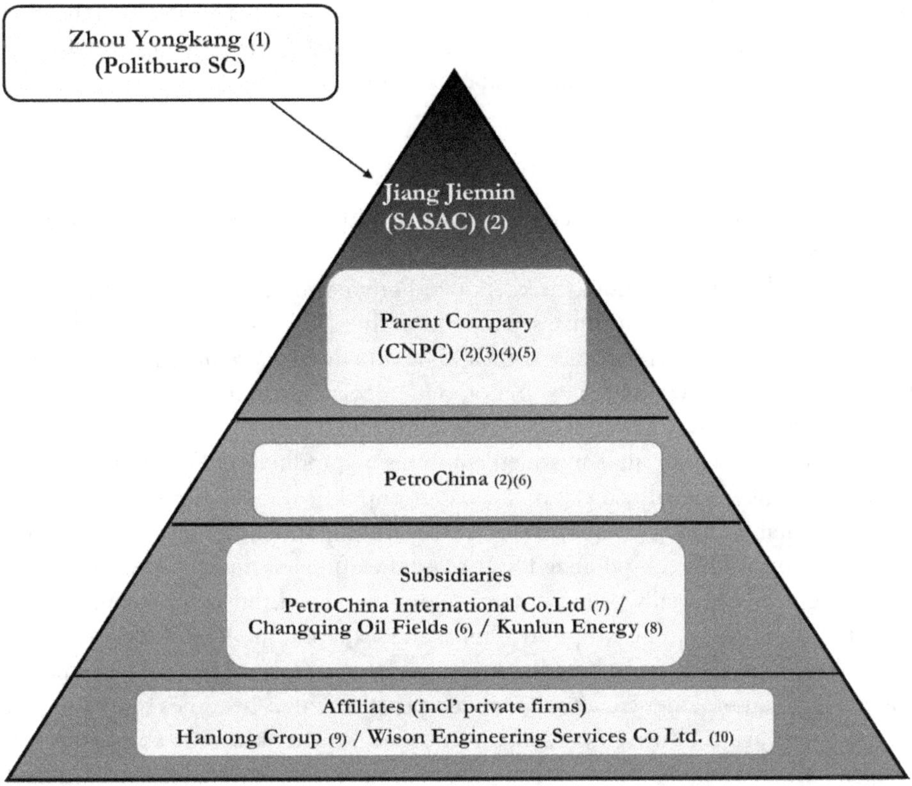

Data assembled from WSJ, BBC reporting as well as from CCDI website

(1) Politburo Standing Committee Member; CCP Secretary of Central Politics and Law Commission. Former CEO and Vice-president of CNPC. Convicted and sentenced to life in prison.
(2) Chairman of SASAC when investigated and indicted; Chairman and President of PetroChina and Vice-chairman at CNPC during the offenses. Convicted and sentenced to 16 years in prison.
(3) Wang Yongchun, VP at CNPC. Expelled from CCP. Convicted, sentenced to 20 years in prison.
(4) Li Hualin, Deputy GM at CNPC, investigated, resigned, received disciplinary exemption from duties.
(5) Wang Daofu, Chief Geologist. Investigated. Resigned from duties.
(6) Ran Xinquan, VP at PetroChina & GM Changqing Oil Fields. Investigated. Received Disciplinary exemptions from political roles.
(7) Shen Dingcheng, Vice-president, Party-secretary at PetroChina Int'l. Investigated.
(8) Tao Yuqun, Executive of Kunlun Energy subsidiary. Investigated.
(9) Liu Han, Board Chairman of Hanlong Group. Executed (for crimes not necessarily related to the corruption investigation).
(10) Hua Bangsong, Chairman of the Board and primary shareholder at Wison Engineering. Convicted, sentenced to 36 months in prison. Additional executives were investigated.

FIGURE 8.1 Corporate group corruption pyramid

These cases reflect that a CCDI investigation has ripple effects throughout the investigated group and its web of affiliates. They also reflect that Party-led enforcement receives a high-level of collaboration from state institutions. For example, SASAC, CSRC, and the China Banking Regulatory Commission assisted in confiscating documents, freezing bank accounts, stopping the trade in shares of firms under investigation, and other measures.[511] This assistance is given often even

[511] Ibid. Wison Engineering Services Co Ltd. bank accounts were frozen, and the trade in its shares was suspended.

before formal legal proceedings are initiated for the case. It can be assumed that this interagency cooperation will further increase following the recent consolidation of authority under the National Supervision Commission.

SUMMARY REFLECTIONS

Given the analysis above, the recent legal politicization of corporate governance has brought the following:

First, a political institution, the corporate Party committee, is established as an internal stakeholder within firms, separate from the state's capacities in the firm. In its corporate stakeholder capacity, the CCP has obtained a *formalized* and *disclosed* role in overseeing law obedience; in corporate decision-making; and in personnel management and evaluation, with assessment criteria being increasingly attentive to firm value mainly through an added emphasis on production efficiency in SOEs.

Second, a newly legalized external capacity of political institutions for discipline and accountability, now operating specifically through the corporate structure and group network. While corporatized SOEs and the affiliated businesses surrounding them might be especially prone to corruption, the use of the same organizational structure facilitates anti-corruption efforts and expands the Party's enforcement reach into the market more broadly. In this process, the separation between political and legal enforcement against certain corporate offenses becomes blurry, so that enforcement against corruption spills over to enforcement against corporate misconduct more generally. The vast authority of these institutions has blurred the lines between political enforcement against corruption and legal enforcement against corporate wrongdoing. The Party thus performs many of the monitoring, accountability, and deterrence functions otherwise provided by China's weakly functioning external markets and legal institutions.The potential implications for firms and investors are addressed next.

9

Legally Politicized Corporate Governance as a Functional Alternative

Corporate governance addresses two main concerns: opportunistic behavior and mismanagement (bad decision-making). While these concerns are shared across all systems, the optimal machinery to mitigate them is different in each system and is contingent on the particular organizational structure in the market and the given political–economic environment.

The first concern – opportunistic behavior – is essentially the same across all systems even though it manifests differently in systems with different ownership structures (e.g., self-dealing by corporate insiders in markets with widely dispersed ownership basis, extraction of private benefits of control by controlling shareholders in concentrated markets, rents and corruption by government affiliates in state-led markets). The resulting effects of opportunistic behavior on firm value are negative across all systems. Thus, in all corporate governance systems, less opportunistic behavior benefits firms and their public shareholders.

The second concern, however, mismanagement (i.e., bad decision-making), is a more open concept whose normative value depends upon each system's priorities and economic ideals. Different markets have different approaches to the purpose of the corporation. These approaches determine how mismanagement is interpreted (or, what is good performance) and what are the optimal mechanisms to control bad managers. Anglo-American corporate capitalism sanctifies value maximization, and corporate governance in these systems is designed to reduce inefficiencies and to incentivize managers to increase firm (or, by some, shareholders-) value. In several other systems, corporate governance is designed to promote a more inclusive vision that considers the interests of additional stakeholders and assesses mismanagement accordingly (e.g., through the codetermination mechanism in Germany), even at the price of lesser market efficiency.

China's approach is somewhat similar to the latter set of systems but it adopts an even broader societal vision. Corporations are expected to serve the "national development

The discussion in this chapter is drawn from my article, Groswald Ozery, *The Politicization of Corporate Governance*, note 477.

process" (wealth creation as a macroeconomic goal) and to contribute to social stability.[512] This explains why even while production efficiency is increasingly emphasized as a measure of good managerial performance, it is nevertheless accompanied by other practices and goals that do violence to the functions of the corporation as commonly perceived under notions of corporate capitalism. While good performance in the Chinese context includes contributions to firm value and better production efficiency, these are but elements in a broader growth and social development targets to which firms are expected to contribute. Thus, reduced mismanagement (or improved performance) in the Chinese context does not necessarily translate to an increase in firm value or other benefit to the specific firm. It could even disfavor the firm, as the interests of an individual firm and its shareholders may be discounted for other broad-market or national priorities.

By the same token, corporate governance in China cannot be expected to advance efficiencies at all costs. It is on this basis that convergence theorists and development scholars envision a glass ceiling to China's development prospect. Facing the pressures of global competition, the theory goes, less efficient institutions and models will have to adjust or else perish.[513] But instead, we witness in China a prolonged development process that exceeds the expected limits of systems that lack well-functioning "good" corporate governance institutions.[514] Nor has this continued development led to convergence with corporate capitalists norms and practices. Instead, as this book shows, we witness persistent attributes that have now been enshrined further through a formal reversal from an outwardly convergent corporate governance system.

As seen above throughout Part III, China's facially convergent framework does little to restrict opportunism by corporate control parties. Quite the contrary. Traditional governance mechanisms have been deployed in ways that favor the interests of incumbent managers and Party-state functionaries, who have captured the regulatory and enforcement capacities of the state and held back effective reforms.

From a public investor perspective, this poses both traditional agency challenges of imperfect monitoring against opportunistic behavior by insiders, as well as the extraction of private benefits of control by controlling shareholders. As discussed above, both types of agency costs are exacerbated in the Chinese context due to the complex ownership structures deployed under state capitalism which bring about

[512] 2005 Company Law, art. 5.

[513] "Perish" in that local alternatives will be neglected or will not be able to support further growth. Coffee, *The Future as History*, note 392, 642–653 (describing the views for convergence as corporate "evolutionary survival" and its competing theories); H. Hansmann & R. Kraakman, "The End of History for Corporate Law," *The Georgetown Law Journal* (2001) 439 (arguing that around the world corporate systems are converging toward a single, shareholder-oriented model).

[514] Conventionally understood as the legal and market institutions that protect investors against opportunistic behavior and promote efficient allocation of capital. Capital markets without effective "good corporate governance" are found to be smaller and narrower. See Chapter 1, and the references to La Porta et al., notes 38–40.

goal setting, coordination, and rent-seeking challenges that breed corruption and opportunistic behavior. These structures inhibit the capacities of the central state to monitor, regulate, and enforce against corporate wrongdoing. Given these realities, it is not surprising that traditional corporate governance institutions largely fail to curb opportunistic behavior and to incentivize good management.

Bearing this political–economic environment in mind, the Party's new emphasis on integrating private and public capital through mixed-ownership and adding market-based criteria to officials' and managerial assessments, while *at the same time* deepening the pathways for a politicized corporate control, become more understandable. The Party organization has become the most interested and, more arguably, capable "organ" within China's controlling apparatus to curb opportunistic behavior and, as a consequence, develop assurances for investors. It does so by instituting its own functional substitutes for conventional monitoring, incentives, and accountability.

The question to ask then is whether the Party will be able to overcome the self-capture that has so far inhibited the state.

To be sure, the CCP's commitment to growth and its incentives to take a more direct role with respect to firms does not necessarily mean that it now has an interest in promoting changes that prioritize efficiency or benefit investors specifically, but it is a possibility.[515]

This idea is certainly counterintuitive. First, it may seem to suggest that individuals within the Party suddenly prioritize the "greater good" of the market and will forgo opportunities to enrich themselves for the sake of developing more efficient, deeper capital markets. Second, it suggests that the Party is able to better mobilize its agents and can overcome the capture that has thus far inhibited the state from doing the same.

Surely, many individuals within the political apparatus have enjoyed private benefits from their clout or their direct control of publicly listed firms through rent extraction, asset tunneling, self-dealing, and other corporate malfeasance. Incumbent controllers (corporate insiders and the agents assigned by the state *quo* controlling shareholders to supervise them) have both the incentive and the power to reject true reforms that could reduce their opportunities to extract rents and/or private benefits of control.[516] This almost compels us to assume that the same controlling apparatus would continue capturing the Party-state from promoting effective reforms that could reduce its ability to extract value – a phenomenon shared in many systems.[517] As seen, this assumption held true throughout most of China's

515 V. Nee & P. Lian, "Sleeping with the Enemy: A Dynamic Model of Declining Political Commitment in State Socialism," *Theory & Society* 23 (1994) 253, at 273 ("[A]nalysts need to pay attention to the organizational health of the communist party"; attempting to explain why communist rule initiates reforms).

516 J. Wu, "China's Economic Reform: Past, Present and Future," *Perspectives* 1 (2000) 5.

517 M. Olson, *The Rise and Decline of Nations: Economic Growth, Stagflation, and Social Rigidities* (Yale University Press, 1982) (suggesting a theory on the resistance of the established economic and political elite to growth-promoting reforms); R. Rajan & L. Zingales, "The Great Reversal: The Politics

Modern Reform era, with respect to the real implementation of conventional corporate governance mechanisms embraced formally.

Nonetheless, while these individuals might not be motivated nor deterred by state institutions, they are certainly concerned about their political future. As noted, incentives matter for the behavior of economic actors, and here economic incentives may be trumped by, or are at least merged with, political ones. It is the Party organization, rather than the state, that controls the incentives system through its control of the appointment and promotion of individuals in the Party-state system. Through its Organization Department, the Party organization at each level of the state's hierarchy, including in corporatized SOEs, directs the careers of individuals in the system, controlling their reputation and their chances for prosperity. As explained in Chapter 8, this set of incentives impacts corporate insiders even in private, connected, firms. Added to that are the coercive methods of the Party that can induce compliance through discipline and fear governance across the market.

At the individual level, this translates to a growing linkage between firm success (through reduction of opportunistic behavior and mismanagement) and one's career prospects.[518] The compliance of corporate insiders with the goals projected through the politicized corporate governance system is therefore simply a way to protect her own vested interests. All these factors together make the Party organization stand out from state institutions, and enable it to mobilize firms and their insiders to submit more readily to goals that are advanced by the Party organization directly.

POTENTIAL IMPLICATIONS: FIRM AND MARKET LEVELS

As seen above, the recent politicization of corporate governance in China solidifies the CCP's mandate in the realm of corporate governance and strengthens the Party's overall market control. It can be said to have formally shifted an unrestrained power from corporate insiders to corporate Party committee members. As I argued elsewhere,[519] a political–economic analysis of China's market realities suggests

of Financial Development in the Twentieth Century," *Journal of Financial Economics* 69 (2003) 5; L. A. Bebchuk, "A Rent-Protection Theory of Corporate Ownership and Control" (Nat'l Bureau Econ. Rsch., Working Paper No. 7203, 1999).

518 See C. Mutlu et al., "Corporate Governance in China: A Meta-Analysis," *Journal of Management Studies* 55(6) (2018) 943 (arguing that the quality of monitoring in state-owned corporations became more strongly related to firm performance); A. Bryson et al., "How Much Influence Does the Chinese State Have over CEOs and Their Compensation?." In J. Ortega (ed.), *International Perspectives on Participation* (Emerald Group Publishing, 2014) 1 (finding that the state's influence extends beyond SOEs into many privately owned firms and that incentive schemes are typical in these firms and include contracts linking CEO pay directly to firm performance); Cao et al., *The Relationship Between Pay and Performance*, note 434 (finding that the likelihood of CEOs in Chinese SOEs to receive political promotion is positively related to firm performance).

519 Groswald Ozery, *The Politicization of Corporate Governance*, note 477.

that Party-state functionaries as well as corporate managers can overall be better incentivized to curb opportunistic behavior and to improve performance under a politicized system than under the traditional framework alone. Nonetheless, the broader implications of these developments on firms and their constituents depend greatly on how party committee members will implement their new mandate on the ground.

There are, of course, tradeoffs in the recent politicization drive. There are several efficiency gains as well as potential costs. It is important to note that the various aspects in the recent politicization have been introduced gradually and their consequences are still unfolding. The discussion here, therefore, does not aim to offset various implications normatively nor to quantify their relative costs and benefits, but simply to bring them to the fore for the benefit of future studies.

A politicized corporate governance in China potentially brings better monitoring, greater enforcement, performance-based political incentives, and signaling.[520] Currently, available empirical evidence suggests the following main benefits[521]:

(i) greater controls on the power of corporate insiders and their Party-state affiliates, reducing agency costs of monitoring with consequent gains to firms and their shareholders.
(ii) greater enforcement against opportunistic behaviors. This produces gains from: the removal of bad managers and corrupt officials; greater availability of capital (through the repatriation of misappropriated funds and access to new capital); and future gains from added deterrence.
(iii) formally established Party presence can add clarity to growth priorities and reduce coordination costs as well as resolve conflicts of interests between the various levels of the state. This brings direct gains for the Party-state's governance system and potential gains for firms.
(iv) tightening the link between performance efficiency and career prospects encourages an increase in firm-value and thus offers direct efficiency gains for shareholders (relative to the former system).
(v) importantly, the functions above also provide important signals to investors on the regime's commitment to growth. This commitment-signaling effect is even more crucial under the current market conditions where information is still lacking.

A word on the latter point, since the capital market in China is informationally inefficient, suppliers of capital look for alternative sources of information about

[520] One ought to remember that the relevant point for comparison is the former situation in which conflicting goals were advanced by the state, self-dealing, unmonitored related party transactions, and corruption were rampant; rather than some idealized situation of a centralized firm-value oriented decision maker.

[521] For a review of relevant studies that indicate costs and benefits of politicization, see Groswald Ozery, *The Politicization of Corporate Governance*, note 477, at 46–50.

managerial performance instead of stock price and accounting measures.[522] In this sense, political institutions fill a crucial "intermediary" signaling role in an environment where information is scarce and unreliable.[523] A politicized corporate governance system thus can contribute to investors' confidence by providing some level of assurances that are needed for external finance in an environment of limited transparency.

Notwithstanding these benefits and even efficiency gains, it cannot be ruled out that Party individuals operating therein might misuse their newly institutionalized powers. In which case, opportunism, favoritism, arbitrariness, and misguided decisions would continue. Similarly, when national policy dictates so, Party functionaries, like state functionaries before them, will continue to prioritize national and political goals, some of which will naturally run counter to the economic interests of the firm. These firm-level concerns are not substantially different from those that materialized under the corporate system that preceded the recent overt politicization.

But some concerns are newly introduced through the recent politicization and might offset or even override the benefits it offers. Tightening control over the business environment and the *awareness* of insiders to a closer Party presence also have costs.

Fear governance is created and will likely have consequences for managerial discretion that were less present when Party control was exercised in the shadows. Fear governance could lead to risk-averse management. Concerned about political surveillance and retribution, managers could become paralyzed. If this occurs, not only would it prevent some value-increasing transactions, but it could also have a chilling effect on developing market forces, such as the managerial labor market, product market competition and innovation, and perhaps deter investors (foreign, particularly) and cool off available new capital, thus making equity capital financing more costly. These effects would create further inefficiencies, could ultimately harm capital market development, and perhaps even slow general growth. Some might say that the indications for that are accumulating.[524] The above risks of political intervention

522 Chen, *Stock Market in China's Modernization Process*, note 339 ("[T]he Chinese stock market as a whole has acted to determine stock prices in a way totally detached from the economic growth process."). Generally, on the "inefficiencies" in the Chinese stock markets, see G. Li, "China's Stock Market: Inefficiencies and Institutional Implications," *China & World Economy* 16(6) (2008) 81.

523 This could possibly be inferred based on market reaction: H. Ding et al., "Equilibrium Consequences of Corruption on Firms: Evidence from China's Anti-Corruption Campaign" (Nat'l Bureau of Econ. Rsch., Working Paper No. 26656, 2020), https://cpb-us-w2.wpmucdn.com/web.sas.upenn.edu/dist/3/517/files/2020/01/w26656.pdf (overall stock market responses to announcements on CCDI inspections were significantly positive); C. Lin et al., "Anti-Corruption Reforms and Shareholder Valuations: Event Study Evidence from China" (Nat'l Bureau of Econ. Rsch., Working Paper No., 22001, 2016, rev' 2018, www.nber.org/papers/w22001 (concluding that the expectation of reduced corruption adds value to Chinese firms listed in China and Hong Kong).

524 Though it is likely impossible to discern whether any current rise in negative investors' sentiment derive from the impact of politicization. It could be affected from other variables such as greater regulatory presence of the state (discussed earlier); the current geopolitical climate and U.S. restrictions

are straightforward. These types of risks were the ones that motivated the drive to depoliticize corporate governance in many transitional economies to begin with.[525]

China's policymakers, however, seem to believe in the opposite end of the tradeoff. When considering China's recent approach toward the Party-state's direct role in the market and the functions of law within it (Part II, Chapter 5), it becomes clear that the leaders of the CCP, at least according to rhetoric and formal promulgations, believe that establishing a politicized corporate governance would add value and can improve the situation for firms and their stockholders. Here too, the political and economic functions of law align.

If this is indeed the case (as opposed to market politicization for the sake of increased political control alone), when considering the complex interests of the Party in promoting strong and attractive financial markets, a certain alignment of interests between the political apparatus and capital market constituents becomes more plausible. To be sure, while political institutions do not replace all functions of legal and market institutions (e.g., party discipline does little to address individual stakeholders' grievances), still, in many respects the interests of firms and the Party-state could be mutually served through growth-committed, albeit political, institutions.

on American capital market investments in certain Chinese firms; consequences of China's "inward turn", COVID-19 and generally a global and domestic economic slowdown.

[525] See Chapter 1; Black et al., *Russian Privatization*, note 12; M. Boycko et al., *Privatizing Russia* (MIT Press, 1997).

Conclusions

With modern, successful firms that operate globally and a capital market that is the second largest in the world, corporate governance in China has long passed the point of an "adjust or perish" prognostic. Yet, its firm governance and capital market functions maintain strong idiosyncrasies that go against many fundamentals in economics and legal thought. These idiosyncrasies are products of the underlying configurations of China's political economy and the shifts within it. Political economy in China has a determining effect on the ways in which corporate ownership is organized, firms operate, and the capital market functions. It is responsible for many of the infirmities in the Chinese market but at the same time also holds the key to understanding its development and growth.

Unpacking China's market development trajectory points to an iterative process, a mutual interaction between politics, law, and economic outcomes. In this process, the corporate governance framework that applies in the market is advanced in ways and for reasons that are fundamentally different from those offered by corporate capitalism. This suggests that economic development and the growth of public firms are not conditioned on one specific menu of rules, legal or otherwise. Public firms can prosper even under heavy state ownership and political control. Capital markets can develop and thrive with concentrated ownership and even while bearing functions that diverge from efficient allocation of capital. External finance will flow to where the opportunities are, provided that effective assurances exist – no matter their form or motives – to fend off exploitative behaviors.

Different systems of market governance are thus possible, but the system applied must be able to adjust to change. A responsive corporate governance system that aligns itself with shifts in a dynamic political economy can enjoy greater legitimacy from market participants and be sustained. Such a system can survive even if its configurations are strikingly unfamiliar and patently political. China's capital market development is a potent example of this.

One of the main facilitators of the adaptive, yet authoritarian, nature of China's political–economic system is its use of law. China's political–legal governance system allows just enough flexibility to enable shifts from lax approach to and fro centralized responses, according to the changing interests and demands from within. This enables the system to provide both the space and stability needed for growth while deflecting political and economic incursions as they accumulate, and to survive even at the price of lesser efficiency.

—

In this book, I have examined the dual functions of law (economic and political) and their relation to economic development, to shed light on China's growth puzzle and the role of law within it. The political–economic dynamics that motivated, *yet were also secured by*, legal change suggest that the law plays a meaningful role in China's reform and market development project and has been undervalued.

Certainly, China's socialist market economy and the nation's economic rise cannot be viewed as a "juridical project," i.e. a project brought about primarily through the realm of law. But as Ben Liebman notes, "the legal system has not been a passive participant in the reform process."[526] While the laws largely reflect the interests of the Party-state rather than the rights and interests of market participants (as most China law scholars acknowledge), this book has shown that such narrow instrumentalist interpretation would be too simplistic. As the analysis throughout the book demonstrates, legal reforms have also been used to allocate economic authorities and to impose limitations on political and economic powers within the Party-state system itself. This indicates that law, as a particular form of social and political interaction, has been central to China's development project in ways that transcend the conventional neoliberal view about what the role of law in economic development *should be* (law in the service of economic rights), while it also complicates the path-dependent notion of what the role of law in China *is* (an empty politicized instrument).

It is of course possible that an eventual exhaustion of substitutions, along with China's need to surpass the middle-income trap, will ultimately lead to a shift to a law-based governance of the rights-securing type that will utilize the law's economic functions in more efficient, traditional, ways. If so, the growing place for the law would align with the conventional premise about the role of law in financial market development, simply with much delay.

Clearly, the space for law in China's economic reforms is evolving. Yet the recent politicization of market governance mechanisms and the legalization of political instruments indicate that the Party-state's embrace of the law in governing markets aims at the opposite direction. The recent emphasis on using the law to deepen the reforms has been accompanied by massive legalization of "Party building" efforts,

[526] B. Liebman, "A Return to Populist Legality? Historical Legacies and Legal Reform." In Heilmann, S. & Perry, E. (eds.) *Mao's Invisible Hand: The Political Foundations of Adaptive Governance in China* (Harvard University Asia Center, 2011), at 167.

which have progressively infiltrated even the "private" spheres of the economy. These ongoing efforts show that the increasingly modern and sophisticated economic laws are everything but neutral, rights-oriented, economic devices. The level and breadth of market legal reforms have developed over time, but the economic utility of the laws *to private market participants* remain of secondary importance. This suggests that we must overcome an obsession with the normative economic functions of law and look for its additional utilities in the market if we want to evaluate the real contribution of law to China's development.

The analytical framework taken in this book indicates that the contribution of law to market development (and by implication to growth) can exist not only through the rights-securing economic functions of law but also through its political functions. The legal configurations of shifts within China's political-economic equilibrium presented in Part II reflect that the Party-state uses the law as a medium through which internal economic power hierarchies are allocated, maintained, and contained. Put differently, the law functions as a mediating institution that translates and gives shape to the relations between politics and economics. The micro-level analysis of corporate governance and the Chinese capital market, pursued in Part III, shows that such power allocation, through law, have implications on the ground. By allocating and reallocating market-governance authorities and mobilizing market participants, both private and public, to push growth forward within the confines of a socialist market economy, the law in China facilitates political–economic regularity in the market. This has meaningful effects on market participants, at times impeding, yet at times supporting, economic activity, development, and growth. This process also increases the efficacy of the regime in pursuing its economic and social development goals. The law has supported China's growth process through these political-economic functions, which conventional analytical frameworks often miss.

Appendix – Methodology and Data Selection

The book draws mostly on textual legal analysis and time-series data visualizations of an extensive body of publicly available formal governing documents issued by the three central-level pillars of governance in the Party-state organization: The Chinese Communist Party, the National People's Congress, and the State Council on its commissions, agencies, and departments. The documents collected and analyzed for the purposes of this book are economic laws and regulations and policy documents that were identified as specifically related to the Chinese market.

FORMAL LAWS

The legal dataset was collected from Chinese language legal databases, namely PKUlaw.com (*Beida Fabao*) also known as "lawinfoChina," as well as "China Law & Reference." I examined documents that were issued by organs of the central Party-state only. I looked at PRC constitutional revisions throughout the period for their market related aspects. I followed Keller's taxonomy,[1] with some expansions, when collecting the body of primary national laws (*falü*) by the NPC; secondary administrative regulations by the State Council (*xingzheng fagui*) including additional regulatory documents that are commonly treated as secondary regulations, that is, regulations, provisions, decisions, measures, implementation rules, and guiding opinions (*guiding, tiaoli, jueding, banfa, shishi xize, and zhidao yijian*, respectively); as well as tertiary administrative regulations, meaning departmental rules (*bumen guizhang*) issued by relevant organizations under the State Council, that is, national-level ministries and commissions, including their notices (*tongzhi*) and joint notices (*lianhe tongzhi*). To clarify, while opinions and guiding opinions (*zhidao yijian*) are not a source of authoritative formal law under the PRC

[1] P. Keller, "Sources of Order in Chinese Law," *The American Journal of Comparative Law* 42(4) (1994) 711, at 724–729.

Legislation Law, they are normative documents with a binding regulatory effect in practice and thus were included in my data and analyzed accordingly. The entire data collected and analyzed included both effective and expired norms, as well as their interim provisional form.

POLICY

The inspected dataset includes all PRC National Economic and Social Development Plans (China's "five-year plans") issued since reform and opening began; CCP Charter revisions; publicly available Communiques of the CCP Central Committee Plenary Sessions, Central Committee decisions, circulars, opinions, and joint guiding opinions collected from various formal websites of the CCP as well as from PKUlaw.com. These were complemented by media coverage about CCP interactions and speeches to the business community, including news and reports by designated CCP media outlets (primarily the CCP's Journal *Qiushi* and *People's Daily*).

ADDITIONAL SOURCES

In constructing the theoretical framework in Part II, beyond analyzing the data, I additionally drew on secondary sources and particularly the works of political scientists whose studies identify political power shifts within China's Party-state organization. These cover mostly the Early Development Era and the Legal Modernization Era. At the time of writing this book, studies documenting political power shifts during the Legalized Politicization Era were scarce. I thus relied solely on textual legal analysis and market observations for identifying political power shifts during that era.

In Part III, where the analytical framework is applied to observe changes with respect to corporate reforms and the capital market specifically, I complemented the textual analysis with occasional case observations based on public firms' disclosures (drawn from the SSE and SZSE disclosure platforms and from cninfo.com.cn), and media reports. Also in Part III, where I discussed the CCP's disciplinary functions in SOEs, beyond formal laws and policy, I relied on disciplinary enforcement cases that I collected from the online roster of the Central Commission for Disciplinary Inspection, and media reports.

Data Selection

The databases used in this book were surveyed chronologically (starting from 1978 and ending in 2021). The results supported my initial assumption that China's development trajectory can be classified and analyzed chronologically and divided to three eras. See the "Classification of China's Development Trajectory" (Part II).

Since relevant terms, as well as the names of the enacting regulatory bodies, changed over time, selecting documents based on unified search criteria would have been challenging and even misleading. This challenge is particularly acute for the Early Reform Era when laws and regulations about economic activity were scattered across different fields and used different terms. For example, there was no point to try and sift through the data by the search term "company" for the period prior to the establishment of the modern corporate form in 1993. Similarly, applying the thematic categorical search criteria that are offered by the commercial databases such as "business administration," "individual economy," and "companies" would have, for example, missed the Economic Contract Law of 1981. This is because the law governed economic agreements between domestic "legal persons" which at that time included only state sector entities and collectives (i.e., non-incorporated). Since that particular law was the only national-level legal document at that time to govern economic relations, it was vital for the research. To overcome the challenge, for the Early Reform Era, I did not rely on keyword search nor on the thematic classifications offered by the commercial databases but rather screened *all* central-level documents issued during that period and looked for those that seemed even marginally relevant to economic activity in the budding market.

For example, based on the above data selection method, close to 700 legal documents came up in the initial screening for the Early Reform Era alone. The results produced a substantial number of duplicates which I filtered manually. To make the legal analysis manageable, I excluded from the results documents that regulate firms' engagement in the land market, intellectual property, trade, and industry-specific regulations. After an initial screening, I identified 185 documents on which to conduct textual legal analysis (23 issued by the NPC and NPC standing committee, 147 issued by the state council, and 15 issued by the CCP Central Committee). Additional 296 tertiary market-related regulations were issued at that period by relevant departments and institutions of the state council.

As reforms progressed, the PRC moved to establish a "modern legal system," for which a more recognizable legal taxonomy was applicable and made identifying relevant documents easier. While this also meant that the number of laws and regulations relevant to the market increased significantly for the period (57 NPC laws, 115 state council administrative regulations, 1325 tertiary administrative regulations, and 84 CCP promulgations), I was able to shift to a more efficient and "thematic" identification of laws and regulations from the second reform era onward. My initially screening process thus turned to rely on the categories provided by the legal databases along with relevant keyword search to cross-check the results.

The final dataset for the entire period included a total of 735 market governance documents as the basis for textual legal analysis. Out of these, 120 were issued by the NPC and NPC standing committee, 386 by the State Council, and 229 by the CCP (Table A.1).

Additionally, a large number of relevant tertiary administrative regulations was assembled and documented for the process of assessing shifts in the allocation of economic governance powers throughout the eras (Table A.2). These were quantified and included throughout the book mainly in data illustrations. Textual legal analysis of tertiary regulations was performed only when I identified that the regulations were directly and primarily about governing SOEs, corporations, and the capital market as was needed for the micro layer of the book – corporate governance and capital market analysis in Part III.

TABLE A.1 *Total market rules (excl' tertiary), per era*

Years	*CCP	State Council	NPC	Total per era
1979–1991	23	147	15	185
1992–2009	84	115	57	256
2010–2021	122	124	48	294

* CCP values in Table A.1 exclude five-year plans, Plenum Communiques, and Charter amendments. These were analyzed qualitatively but not included in the quantitative data and visual illustrations in the book.

TABLE A.2 *Total tertiary market rules, per era*

Years	Tertiary regulations
1979–1991	296
1992–2009	1325
2010–2021	647

Index

Footnotes are indicated by n. after the page number, and figures by fig. For the titles of the figures, see the List of Figures in the book's preliminary pages. The index uses the abbreviations CCP for Chinese Community Party and SOEs for state-owned enterprises.

www.ingramcontent.com/pod-product-compliance
Lightning Source LLC
LaVergne TN
LVHW011811200926
848484LV00005B/1141

* 9 7 8 1 0 0 9 1 5 8 2 4 4 *